A
RESPECTABLE
SPELL

LEMANN CENTER FOR
BRAZILIAN STUDIES SERIES

*A list of books in the series appears
at the end of this book.*

A RESPECTABLE SPELL

TRANSFORMATIONS OF SAMBA IN RIO DE JANEIRO

CARLOS
SANDRONI

TRANSLATED BY
MICHAEL IYANAGA

**UNIVERSITY OF
ILLINOIS PRESS**
Urbana, Chicago, and Springfield

Library of Congress Cataloging-in-Publication Data
Names: Sandroni, Carlos, 1958– author. | Iyanaga, Michael,
     translator.
Title: A respectable spell: transformations of samba in Rio de
     Janeiro / Carlos Sandroni; translated by Michael Iyanaga.
Other titles: Feitiço decente. English
Description: Second, expanded edition. | Urbana: University
     of Illinois Press, 2021. | Series: Lemann center for
     Brazilian studies series | "Originally published as Feitiço
     decente: Transformações do samba no Rio de Janeiro
     (1917–1933)"—Title page verso. | Includes bibliographical
     references and index.
Identifiers: LCCN 2021037434 (print) | LCCN 2021037435
     (ebook) | ISBN 9780252044021 (cloth) | ISBN
     9780252086083 (paperback) | ISBN 9780252052965
     (ebook)
Subjects: LCSH: Sambas—Brazil—Rio de Janeiro—20th
     century—History and criticism. | Popular music—Brazil—
     Rio de Janeiro—20th century—History and criticism.
Classification: LCC ML3465 .S29513 2021 (print) | LCC
     ML3465 (ebook) | DDC 781.640981—dc23
LC record available at https://lccn.loc.gov/2021037434
LC ebook record available at https://lccn.loc.gov/2021037435

To Elisa, Nonai, and Walter Santos Pinto

Contents

Translator's Foreword:
  The Decolonial Spark of a Translated Spell   ix

Acknowledgments   xxvii

Introduction to the English Translation   xxix

Original Introduction   xxxv

Musical Premises   1

PART ONE. FROM *LUNDU* TO SAMBA

CHAPTER 1. "Sweet *Lundus*, for Massa to Dream"   21

CHAPTER 2. *Maxixe* and Its Antecedents   42

CHAPTER 3. From Bahia to Rio   63

CHAPTER 4. From the Dining Room to the Drawing Room   78

CHAPTER 5. "Pelo telefone"   95

PART TWO. FROM ONE SAMBA TO THE OTHER

CHAPTER 6. When Did Samba Become Samba?   111

CHAPTER 7. Of Birds and Commodities   122

CHAPTER 8. From *Malandro* to Composer 135

CHAPTER 9. A Respectable Spell 148

CHAPTER 10. On the Gramophone 166

Conclusion 197

Glossary 203

Notes 209

Works Cited 251

Index 263

The Decolonial Spark
of a Translated Spell

MICHAEL IYANAGA

Translating is a bit like blazing a trail through an untrodden forest whose flora and fauna comprise clusters of words, intimations, and feelings. While competent translators can always eventually make their way through the rhetoric, it is never entirely possible to shake the nagging sensation that they took a number of wrong turns and missed a lot of the beauty along the way. After all, other paths may have been easier, more picturesque, or simply more direct. Were they in too much of a hurry—too busy searching for a quick path through the trees—to notice the grandeur of the canopy or the lyrical humming of the rustling leaves? Or, conversely, did they obfuscate the path by stopping for too long to admire the forest's poetry, distracted by the sunlight splashed across the understory or the enmeshed branches curving wondrously around each other?

And there you have it, dear reader: your first chance to say, Was that really necessary? Wasn't that flowery paragraph you just read—or skipped, perhaps—entirely dispensable? Too many silly metaphors . . . oh goodness, you might be thinking. Is this what we're in for? No, luck is in our favor, for Carlos Sandroni doesn't write like that; nor do I (usually), for that matter. But this is precisely the point. Translating is, as Jiří Levý famously emphasized, "a decision process."[1] In translating we are (or we're?) faced with an infinite number of decisions about what to include and what to exclude, what to rephrase and what to rearrange, which target-language word should serve as an "equivalent" to a given source-language word. But a translation is not simply a sequence of arbitrary choices; the whole process is governed by our own a priori assumptions about what matters and what a given word communicates. As such, to understand a bit about my assumptions and the values that guided my approach to Sandroni's writing, allow me to begin with the book's title.

The book's original Portuguese-language title, *Feitiço decente*, tripped me up almost before I even stepped foot into our metaphorical forest. As Sandroni will later show us, this is a phrase taken from the lyrics of a song by famed *sambista* Noel Rosa. This ostensibly paradoxical expression serves to represent one of the book's main points about the way in which samba, samba practitioners, and the popular music industry more generally were reconceptualized, reshaped, and redefined around 1930. But how can this phrase—and its cluster of connotations—be brought to life in English? It was the first fork in my road: would I go down the road of cognates, given that both *decente* and *feitiço* have entirely legitimate cognates in English (decent and fetish, respectively), or would I choose a different path? As the reader will already have noted, I chose a different path: "respectable" (*decente*) and "spell" (*feitiço*). But why? Would a title like "Decent Fetish" have been more correct, more appropriate, or simply better? Or are we dealing here with what the French call *faux amis*? (Incidentally, do we translate this French phrase as "false cognates," "false friends," or the cutest option, "phony friends"?)

I will spend some time on the process by which I arrived at this particular translation for two important reasons. First, it is not an accident that Sandroni chose this phrase as the title of the book: these highly charged words encapsulate the major themes dealt with in the pages that follow. And second, the thought process behind my translation of these two terms reveals something about my approach to translating the whole book.

A "Decent Fetish": Thinking Translation

If we play the dictionary game, we discover that according to one definition or another, "decent fetish" would indeed be *a* translation of *feitiço decente*. "Decent," according to Merriam-Webster's online dictionary, has a range of meanings, from "marked by moral integrity" and "free from obscenity" to "fairly good" or "adequate." And indeed, these definitions carry with them connotations that could intersect with the Portuguese word *decente*, the adjective form of *decência*, which, for its part, is defined by the authoritative *Houaiss* dictionary as "conformidade com padrões morais" (that is, conformity to moral standards), "respeitabilidade" (respectability), and "recato" (modesty).[2] As for "fetish," the English-language term has diverse definitions, ranging from a thing ("object . . . believed to have magical power" or "an object or bodily part whose real or fantasied presence is psychologically necessary for sexual gratification"), to a behavior ("fixation"), to a group/activity ("rite or cult of fetish worshippers"). The *Houaiss* dictionary, on the other hand, understands the Portuguese-language cognate *feitiço* more simply: "bruxaria" (witchcraft or sorcery) or "encantamento" (enchantment or spell).[3] Here, finding the overlap between *feitiço* and "fetish" appears to require a bit more creativity, unless we play the etymology game, which shows us that the terms are much closer to each other than these dictionary definitions suggest.

"Fetish" in English is in fact derived—by way of the pidgin word *fetisso*—from the Portuguese *feitiço*.[4] Although in the Middle Ages the Portuguese term *feitiço* generically referred to "sorcery or magical arts,"[5] it took on a new specificity in its use on the African coast, in Portuguese Guinea, starting in the fifteenth century. There the Portuguese used the term *feitiço* (as opposed to *ídolo*, or idol) to refer "to an object worn about the body which itself embodied an actual power resulting from the correct ritual combination of materials."[6] *Feitiço* then developed into the pidgin *fetisso*, which by the eighteenth century had already come to refer to something that was simultaneously a quasi-personal power and a material object "capable of being influenced both through acts of worship . . . and through manipulations of material substances."[7] And it is this *fetisso* that becomes the word we know today (in English) as "fetish." As for *feitiço* in the context of Afro-Brazilian religions in Brazil—which, it's worth noting, is generally viewed by practitioners as a pejorative term—it refers to a spell, hex, or curse that is mediated by the assembly of a material concoction made up of spiritually charged objects.

This summary glance at the term's etymology has two important implications for how we might understand the "fetish." The first concerns its materiality. As William Pietz notes, "essential to the notion of the fetish is that of the fetish object's irreducible materiality. . . . Marxism's commodity fetish, psychoanalysis's sexual fetish, and modernism's fetish as art object all in an essential way involve the object's untranscended materiality."[8] And although in Brazil *feitiço* can signify its medieval Portuguese meaning of magical arts generally (for instance, in the spells and incantations central to so many European-derived fairy tales), the term tends to be understood—particularly in the Afro-Brazilian context of which Noel Rosa's lyrics are a part—as something with an irreducible materiality, albeit always linked to people's beliefs and to a spiritual world teeming with different energies. It is not just any spiritual world of energies, however; it is a specifically African-derived world of energies. And this is the second important quality of the meaning of "fetish." In Pietz's words, "[as] a novel object not proper to any prior discrete society, [fetish] originated in the cross-cultural spaces of the coast of West Africa during the sixteenth and seventeenth centuries."[9] In other words, the concept of "fetish" is intrinsically linked to Africa and to the Atlantic world within which it was born. It is not by chance, therefore, that Africa and Africans served as foils even in later European theorizations of the "fetish" (especially by Marx and Freud).[10] In fact, anthropologist J. Lorand Matory goes as far as to argue that with the "skin-tight black leather, . . . the centrality of master-slave role play, . . . and the common use of whips," even sexual understandings of the word "fetish" "invite interpretation as a subliminal reenactment of circum-Atlantic racial history."[11]

There thus seems no more apposite English-language translation for *feitiço* than its own progeny, "fetish." So why did I choose "spell" over "fetish" in this case? To me, translating is not an etymology game, however fascinating that game might be. Rather, it is an investment in meanings and in trying to find the words that are most successful in evoking in target-language readers something close to that which the "original" authors aimed (or appear to have aimed) to evoke in their source-language readers. In many ways, then, it is to me less a "meaning" game than one of feelings and sensations. And here, as the reader may already have surmised, "fetish" does not evoke (to speakers of English) what *feitiço* does (to speakers of Portuguese). We find a great anecdotal example of this when Matory relates his exchange with Queen Alethia, a shopkeeper at a so-called "fetish store" in Ohio: "When I asked Queen Aletheia what a 'fetish' is . . . she simply defined a fetish as 'an obsession' and 'anything that makes you happy.'"[12] Incidentally, this understanding of "fetish" is, in Portuguese, not *feitiço* but rather *fetiche*. In other words, while "fetish" might mean *feitiço*, it does not (to the English speaker) mean it in the same way. Put simply, it does not *feel the same*. And as I see it, the job of the translator—the "intimate reader,"[13] in Gayatri Spivak's words—is to try to *feel* the original and render those feelings accessible in the target language.

Not by chance, this is precisely what is at the heart of Sandroni's investigation: how could samba mean different things—how could it *feel* different—to given groups of people depending on their eras and places in society? The book is about recognizing that "samba" in 1917 was different from "samba" in, say, 1933. We learn that the meanings surrounding the word "samba" changed; the things it evoked—compositional structures, rhythms, musical instruments, rights to authorship, and so forth—changed. This is indeed a study of the shift in what the word "samba" felt like in Rio de Janeiro around 1930; the masterfully executed analysis shows that how a word *feels, and how it is meant to feel*, correlates directly to people's expectations.

Translating words strikes me as a similar endeavor. It is an attempt to read intimately two languages—in my case, Portuguese and English—in order to interpret the signified worlds that particular words and phrases might evoke. This is why the fluidity of a translation will often attest to how closely it hits the mark. In this particular case, I will leave it up to the reader to judge how well the language of this translation approximates a book that, in its original Portuguese, was described by Ernesto Donas as "'catchy' and easy to read."[14]

But for now, back to the title. If not "decent fetish," what should Sandroni's book be called? Here I had to consider not just where Sandroni got the title and what it meant in that original context but also *why* Sandroni chose this as the book's title.

I have already touched on the first two questions (and Sandroni will go into great detail in his own analysis), but what of the last? I briefly mentioned one reason earlier, which is that the title effectively encapsulates the text's central issues: the transition of "samba" (again, as a word referring to a specific set of expectations) from Brazilian society's Black margins to a place of broad, racially diverse appeal, not by shedding its Blackness but rather by embracing a redefined understanding of such Blackness and making it an integral part of the nascent music industry. But there is more. None of this was agentless, as no *feitiço* can be; none of it just happened. (In this sense, it seems not entirely irrelevant that the term *feitiço* "derives linguistically from the Latin *facticius* or *factitius*, an adjective formed from . . . the verb *facere*, 'to make,'"[15] meaning thus something made.) "Samba" was defined and redefined by people with names, experiences, birthplaces, and desires; and all of it mattered. As such, samba's newly discovered *decência*, or "respectability," had little to do with any internal changes. Rather, samba's transformations resulted from—while also being an active force in—broader social changes regarding people's expectations, biases, and understandings toward Afro-Brazilian cultural practices generally.

It thus seemed clear to me that *decente* would best be understood as "respectable," for the term carries with it an implication of presentability (that is, presentable publicly to Brazilian society). My solution for *feitiço* was less intuitive and, frankly, less satisfying. After all, the term that would ostensibly be the most accurate, "fetish," seemed to me incapable of translating the symbolic power of *feitiço*. One could argue that English has terms that approximate *feitiço*: charm, hand, or conjure bag (also called gris-gris, mojo/mojo hand, toby, root bag, juju, and the like),[16] in addition to more explicitly pejorative terms derived from the "voodoo" imaginary, such as "hex" or simply "voodoo" (as in "doing voodoo"). However, most of these terms struck me as too object specific, too antiquated or obscure, too ambiguous, or too regional to resonate with the broad comprehensibility of the word *feitiço*. And the only term that seemed to be in the ballpark (at least to my mind's ear) was "voodoo." In fact, a "respectable voodoo" *feels* just about right, but only if we can abstract it from its particular geopolitical context without also losing the implied anti-Black racism (I'm thinking, for instance, of the infamous "voodoo economics" of George H. W. Bush). The problem, of course, is that the term "voodoo" carries far too much historical/geopolitical weight—immediately indexing Haiti and Louisiana's mystical role in the popular imaginary, as in Hollywood's "voodoo doll" or "voodoo witchdoctor"—to make it symbolically effective or appropriate in the Brazilian context, where the Afro-Brazilian religion Candomblé is Brazil's "Voodoo," so to speak, and where the cognate *vodum* can designate, in certain Candomblé temples in Brazil (particularly those of the Jeje nation), a specific pantheon of deities.

In the end, then, I found a middle ground in the term "spell." Indeed, "spell" seems to me to evoke the ambiguous space between Europe and Africa that *feitiço* does. *Feitiço* is, like "spell," a fairy-tale word as much as it is a reference to non-fairy-tale witchcraft and sorcery. That is, in both English and Portuguese, the term "spell"/*feitiço* is as appropriate in the context of Snow White/Branca de Neve as it is in the context of African and Afro-Diasporic religions (children in the United States are indoctrinated early on to fear "voodoo spells," for instance; though I recognize that here, too, we need "voodoo" to modify "spell" for us to see it as necessarily African derived). And although "spell" seems to lack the materiality so central to *feitiço* in the Afro-Brazilian context, it only takes remembering the "eye of newt and toe of frog" from Shakespeare's *Macbeth*, for example, to be reminded of a spell's potential materiality. Finally, if we note that Noel Rosa used *feitiço* in his song lyric as a metaphor for samba, and if we remember that a spell must be *cast*—in other words, it is necessarily both a verbal and a corporeal act—it seems hardly a stretch to suggest that samba (which is above all else a song-dance expression) could be reimagined as a spell indeed.

All of this is simply a glimpse into what I intended to do with my translation of the whole book, *Feitiço decente*. I will not take you, dear reader, through my translation process in each instance; that would be intolerable for us both. But I will take a moment to review a few general issues. While I tried my very best to translate the poetry of Sandroni's prose into English without deforming the flow or the feeling, I did not do the same with the song lyrics he cites. And except perhaps for the song titles and for a verse here or there, I prioritized clarity and meaning above all else. While I recognize that this is a transgression against the original composers, to whom, as Vladimir Nabokov notes, "it comes as a shock to discover that a work of art can present itself to the would-be translator as split into form and content,"[17] it is a pragmatic choice designed to serve Sandroni's interpretations and arguments. I felt that trying to cook up translations that could fit into the original rhyme schemes, for instance, would too easily risk obfuscating meanings, thus inhibiting the reader's understanding of Sandroni's analysis. However, I included the original titles and song lyrics in Portuguese together with the English as part of the text so that readers somewhat familiar with Portuguese (or another Romance language) could stop to appreciate the songs' poetry (or check my translations) whenever they felt so inclined.

As for citations, I treated them a bit more literally than in my approach to Sandroni's own words, and I was much more deliberate in translating in accordance with the sociohistorical contexts in which they were originally written. This differed a bit from my approach to Sandroni's writing, which was updated in a few minor spots in order to avoid the risk of the prose feeling dated. (It is surprising how much can change in twenty years!) As for citations of works that exist in translation, whenever possible I cited the published English-language versions of sources. Although I did not necessarily agree with all of the decisions made by the translators of these published works—and in a few cases, duly observed with notes, I went ahead and altered a word or two in their translations to render them more accurate—I nevertheless went with this approach because it allows readers easier access to material already available in English, should they wish to confer or conduct further research.

While *A Respectable Spell* is not necessarily designed to read like an "overt" translation (to use Juliane House's terminology), there is also nothing "covert" about the text.[18] In other words, evident from the profusion of translator's notes alone, this translation does not seek to fool the reader into thinking it was originally written in English. And this is further reinforced by the repeated appearance of words in Portuguese. For cases in which the Portuguese-language terms are not explained by Sandroni within the text itself, utilitarian definitions or short explications are offered between parentheses or in the notes. There is also a glossary at the book's end that will hopefully clear up any confusion the reader might still have along the way. Now, when translators leave words or phrases in the "source language" (untranslated), they are always making an implicit statement of some sort. And while I will not go into any detail here about the politics of language, suffice it to say that the words I left in Portuguese were ones I felt would be meaningless in translation (what some might call "untranslatable"), were so specific to the Brazilian context that they should indeed be left in Portuguese, or were repeated so many times that they seemed worthy of becoming part of the reader's vocabulary.

Finally, it is worth mentioning my fidelity to Sandroni's use of names throughout the text. He refers to many people by their first names, nicknames, and other terms of endearment: Noel, Mário, Ismael, Tia Ciata, Cartola, Caetano, among many others. My translation maintains the designations employed by Sandroni. And while some readers of English, accustomed to seeing only full names or surnames in scholarly texts, may be surprised by what appears to be an informal treatment of historical figures, I see it as Brazilian convention. For instance, there is nothing odd about seeing former president Luís Inácio Lula da Silva referred to as "Lula"; in fact, it would be odd to see him referred to as "da Silva." Sandroni's use of intimate names is part of bringing readers into a world in which the name "Cartola," for example, means far more than would "Oliveira," the *sambista*'s legal surname. As such, this translation tries to transmit some of the evocative power of the names readers will encounter in the text.

The Dialogic Process of Assembling *A Respectable Spell*

My name alone is listed as translator of *A Respectable Spell*. This means I take full responsibility for any of the translation's successes and failures. And not without good reason: I spent a tremendous amount of time researching, even more time thinking, and I was the one who typed up the manuscript. To take the credit/ responsibility for the translation, however, is not to suggest that it is mine alone; I received help here and there from the internet, colleagues, and my wife (not to mention a reviewer and the copy editor).[19] My most important interlocutor, however, was someone who was fully invested in my getting it right: Carlos Sandroni. He was my main collaborator and an integral part of the translation even before it began. What this means is that *A Respectable Spell* is a decidedly dialogic translation, the product of Sandroni's and my joint efforts to render *his* rhetoric—and consequently his ideas, analyses, and eloquence—meaningful and expressive in what is almost entirely *my* English. In other words, our collaboration was not limited to me bringing him questions about his text. (Which is, incidentally, a common practice among translators when translating works written by living authors.) Indeed, our dialogue was not a question-and-answer session but rather a series of in-depth conversations that lasted months. What's more, we painstakingly went through the translated text line by line (including "my" translator's notes), discussing words I chose, removing or changing terms, adding phrases and explanations, correcting errors, and so forth.

While this approach could be a burden to some—the translator is giving up autonomy and the author is doing "extra" work—it seemed entirely routine to us both. It was akin to so much of the collaborative ethnomusicology we had both done throughout our careers, particularly in the Brazilian context. For this reason, it seems to me hardly coincidental that our dialogic approach to this translation was quite in step with what Angela Lühning has noted as the distinctively "participatory" nature of much of Brazil's ethnomusicology,[20] an ethnomusicology characterized by—in the words of Lühning, Carvalho, Diniz, and Lopes—"the steady replacement of participant observation with dialogic, shared, and collaborative processes."[21] And despite being a historical study, *Feitiço decente/A Respectable Spell* offers a glimpse of this Brazilian approach to ethnomusicology—a discipline whose solidification in Brazil over the past two decades is in fact deeply indebted to Sandroni (as I'll discuss to follow)—in the horizontal way it treats the differing perspectives of positionally distinct cultural agents.

More than just resonating with Brazilian ethnomusicology, however, our dialogic approach to translation overlaps with some of the more recent attempts to decolonize research methodologies generally. For instance, if we substitute the word "translator" for "ethnographer" in the following outline for a decolonial ethnography, we get a general sense of what a "decolonial translation" might mean: "anti-objectivist—or, in another sense, anti-objectificationist—in that it asks ethnographers [translators] to regard their study populations [that is, authors and their words] not as objects, but as fully equal subjects capable of becoming their own ethnographers [translators]."[22] But what's the point in finding a decolonial method to translating if we are still translating into English, a language that has been the hegemonic language of the social and hard sciences par excellence for the better part of a century (especially in more recent decades)?[23] First off, it is worth recognizing that English is, as Lawrence Venuti notes, "the most translated [language] . . . worldwide, but one of the least translated into."[24] As such, there is arguably something decolonial about translating into English, as it fights the common current of knowledge imposition. At the same time, however, if we were to translate *everything* into English, we would do little more than feed the hegemonic notion that English is (and should continue to be) the academic "lingua franca."

The decolonial quandary seems obvious. Nevertheless, if we want to give peripheralized and excluded voices a chance to be heard/read in what is still the most widely spoken second language in the world, translating into English might be a necessary evil or, as Sherry Simon puts it, "a practical necessity."[25] Ultimately, it is precisely the accessibility of English that leads Spivak to insist that women who write in Arabic or Vietnamese "must be made to speak English."[26] Thus even if these "foreign" ideas, epistemologies, approaches, perspectives, histories, and terminologies can be made available outside of their original language only by making them speak in a different language (an inevitable "distortion," in the most literal sense), this process nevertheless allows them—albeit in altered form—to reach another (presumably larger) audience. With this in mind, translation can *always* potentially be a tool in decoloniality—that is, a tool in helping to undo the "logical structure of colonial domination."[27]

While this may seem to place an excessive amount of power in the hands of the translator, translators have always wielded such power. Although they may sometimes be conceived as neutral vessels that ferry the author's voice from one linguistic shore to another, Bassnett and Trivedi rightly remind us that "translation is not an innocent, transparent activity."[28] In fact, the agency of translators is ever present; they use *their own* words to present the ideas and narrative style of the author, which is always an effective silencing of the author as a speaking subject. This is precisely why Rolando Vázquez, in discussing a broader "epistemic translation" that nevertheless includes language, describes translation as a process of erasure, "an exercise of . . . appropriation, incorporation."[29] And whether we choose to call it "appropriation" or not, this is indeed what is expected of translators; good ones, in other words, are expected to assimilate the author's words in order to make them intelligible to a different community of readers. Translations could thus be said to be little more than elaborate paraphrases. Put otherwise, translators imperceptibly interject themselves in between readers and authors, thus dispossessing the latter of their voice; translated authors can *only be heard* through the voice of their translator(s).

Ideally, then, my/our dialogic approach to this translation—facilitated by Sandroni's command of the English language and the close relationship we already had—has helped assuage some of the dangers of allowing my voice to overpower his. Nevertheless, the end result of this translation should look no different from any other "good" translation. (Incidentally, many translations we read are far more dialogic than we could ever tell.) All of this is therefore much less about the end result than about the process of getting there. And the extensive explanation I am offering here is simply an effort to bring the reader into the spirit of the text—both the one we created and the one that was translated—in which authority belongs not to a single person's voice alone but rather to the dialogue that emerges from the multiplicity of voices. Indeed, for dialogic translations, "official" translators relinquish total control; the translation is *never* entirely theirs.

As for the nuts and bolts: I began the translation process by doing research (mainly consulting written sources) and going through several analyses and interpretations of *Feitiço decente* prior to giving my questions to Sandroni. His answers sometimes moved me to rethink my translations of whole sections of the book; at other times his answers made it necessary for me to consult secondary sources, and all of this often resulted in additional questions. After the first few rounds of questions, we got into the nitty-gritty of the translation itself. As we fine-tuned the translation, a constant question was, Will this work in English? Indeed, we shared the common goal of effectively communicating Sandroni's quite Brazilian prose (filled with idiomatic expressions and local cultural/musical references), though we each exercised different roles. I was the first and last "barrier"; I was the one who put together the first complete draft of the translation; and I, the native English speaker, was also the final judge of the effectiveness of a term or sentence. Sandroni, by contrast, was the main consultant and font of information, as well as the ideal editor. We went back and forth, sometimes revisiting the same line—even the same term—multiple times until we could get it as close as possible to just right. I lost count of how many e-mail, WhatsApp, and phone exchanges we had over the course of translating the book. It was a dynamic and vibrant dialogue; it was, I think, a true collaboration.

The dialogue was not unidirectional, however. In other words, it was not just Sandroni participating in my translation of his book; I was also involved in the evolution of this book as it now appears (in translation). My questions sometimes moved him to adjust a phrase. And I also suggested alterations that he always entertained whether or not he decided to accept or reject them in the end. This means that *A Respectable Spell* is not just an English-language version of *Feitiço decente* that has been retooled by us to ensure that it resonates effectively with an English-reading audience. It is also a newer version—the newest, in fact (for now, at least)—of *Feitiço decente*, whose limits have now been expanded and pulled in new directions. With this translation, then, *Feitiço decente* "attains," as Walter Benjamin put it, "its latest, continually renewed, and most complete unfolding."[30]

A Respectable Spell is simultaneously a new and an old book. It is a previously published book that, by passing through this dialogic translation process, becomes a new publication altogether. Indeed, our dialogue has resulted in another version—a variation—of the original, existing as its own isolatable "original" but never truly isolated from the original. In this way, the translation becomes an extension of the old work while at the same time being new (but also neither!); we might thus think of it as a "becoming-(its own) book," in a Deleuzean/Guattarian sense, constituting "a zone of proximity and indiscernibility, a no-man's-land, a nonlocalizable relation sweeping up the two distant or contiguous points, carrying one into the proximity of the other."[31] It is novel in its form, content, rhetoric, and process of construction while still never being entirely distinct from the original.

An Evolving Dialogue:
Contextualizing Carlos Sandroni's Work

The dialogic process that produced this translation did not begin with it in mind. Rather, this text is part of a much larger dialogue on samba and ethnomusicology that Carlos Sandroni and I have been engaged in for well over a decade. My first ever interaction with him took place by e-mail in 2007, and it was indeed a dialogue about samba. In that instance, however, the topic was not the Carioca samba that is at the heart of *A Respectable Spell*; instead, it was the Bahian *samba de roda* that had, in 2005, been proclaimed a UNESCO Masterpiece of the Oral and Intangible Cultural Heritage of Humanity thanks to the dossier Sandroni had organized for Brazil's Ministry of Culture. When I cold e-mailed him in 2007, he was quick to respond. At the time, I was a young student just beginning to take graduate courses in ethnomusicology at the Universidade Federal da Bahia and was, moreover, a complete stranger to him. Consequently, I remember being surprised and grateful that he took the time to respond to me. After all, Sandroni was already one of the leading voices in Brazilian ethnomusicology. And this renown was in no small part thanks to the book that is translated in the pages ahead.

Feitiço decente had been published six years earlier (in 2001), making waves right off the bat. The book was celebrated first and foremost as a scholarly milestone in samba and Brazilian popular music research. We can see this enthusiastic reception, for instance, in popular music historian Marcos Napolitano's 2002 book review: "Sandroni's work is obligatory not only for those who study samba from the first three decades of the twentieth century, but also for all popular music scholars."[32] The work was, moreover, viewed as a watershed publication for Brazilian ethnomusicology. In 2003 it was one of the three books[33] singled out by the late Brazilian ethnomusicologist Elizabeth Travassos, a luminary and pioneer in her own right, as exemplary of one of the "directions of Brazilian ethnomusicology . . . attest[ing] to the growth of the discipline in Brazil."[34] But the book reverberated outside of Brazil, too, as Uruguayan music scholar Ernesto Donas makes clear in his laudatory 2006 review: "In all, *Feitiço decente* impels Brazilian (and I venture to say Latin American) ethnomusicology from its merely descriptive stage to a more analytic phase."[35]

Yet by the time I first corresponded with Sandroni in 2007, his reputation within the ethnomusicology community was not based solely on this important book. Indeed, he had already racked up quite a few accomplishments. After defending his PhD dissertation in musicology at the Université de Tours in 1997, Sandroni returned from Paris to take a visiting position—which later became the permanent position he still holds today—in the Department of Music of the Universidade Federal de Pernambuco (UFPE), located in Recife, the capital of the state of Pernambuco. Although Sandroni was certainly not the first Brazilian to get a PhD and teach ethnomusicology courses in Brazil,[36] he has been a steadfast advocate for Brazilian ethnomusicology, even serving as the first president (2001–2004) of Brazil's main professional ethnomusicology organization, the Associação Brasileira de Etnomusicologia. Over the next few years, in addition to his institutional work at the national level, he played a crucial role in helping to create the graduate program in music at the Universidade Federal da Paraíba (in the nearby city of João Pessoa). Suffice it to say, he was—and continues to be—a leading figure in shaping Brazilian ethnomusicology (as a named, institutionalized, and national discipline) from its earliest stages. But more was to come.

Not long after arriving in Recife, Sandroni began work on what would be his next big ethnomusicological splash: a restudy of a seminal fieldwork project by famed proto-ethnomusicologist Mário de Andrade (1893–1945). In 1938 Andrade, then head of São Paulo's Department of Culture, created the Missão de Pesquisas Folclóricas (that is, the Folk Research Mission), sending a group of researchers to document—via sound recordings, film, and photography—musical traditions in the states of Pernambuco, Paraíba, Maranhão, and Pará. Sandroni decided to return to several of the cities originally visited by the Missão and seek out the original performers or their descendants, sharing with them the Missão's recordings and also making new recordings,[37] which were released in 2004 as a two-CD set (with detailed liner notes) titled *Responde a roda outra vez: Música tradicional de Pernambuco e da Paraíba no trajeto da Missão de Pesquisas Folclóricas de 1938.*[38] It was an exciting and well-conceived (and well-received) project, resulting in a beautiful collection of field recordings. What's more, it seemed to offer a clear lesson in thinking beyond the ivory tower (something not uncommon in Sandroni's work generally) not only in the deliberate attempt to repatriate the Missão's recordings but also in the idea of producing a CD rather than, say, an academic book. Finally, if we consider this CD project as having been ethno-musicological (as I believe most, including Sandroni, feel is the case), it appears to make a clear—albeit implicit—statement about the important place of Mário de Andrade in the history of Brazilian ethnomusicology, despite the fact that he died before the term "ethnomusicology" came into existence.

We also find in *Responde a roda outra vez*, when viewed within the context of Sandroni's oeuvre, the continuation of a career-long exploration of the multifac-eted legacy of Mário de Andrade. In *A Respectable Spell*, for instance, readers will note the ease with which Sandroni navigates Andrade's voluminous writings on music and Brazilian culture, mining them for hidden gems and unexpected in-spiration, demonstrating an enviable familiarity with the modernist writer's work (though this is not to say Sandroni is not equally familiar with the work of many of the other authors he cites; Andrade just casts a much longer shadow). But his interest in Andrade predates *Feitiço decente*; Sandroni's first book, in fact, which was published in 1988, was also a study of Mário de Andrade's life/work. In *Mário contra Macunaíma* (*Mário against Macunaíma*),[39] a revised version of his master's thesis in political science, Sandroni focuses on the political side of Andrade (who, it is worth repeating, ran São Paulo's Department of Culture from 1935 to 1937). In some ways, then, we might even interpret Sandroni's own more "activist" work as following in Andrade's heavy footsteps. In 2000 Sandroni founded the Asso-ciação Respeita Januário, a nonprofit organization that still today supports local musicians and traditional music of northeastern Brazil through various research projects and activities. Thus, Sandroni's involvement with intangible cultural heritage clearly began well before heading the project that led to UNESCO's 2005 decision to inscribe *samba de roda* on its III Proclamation of Masterpieces of the Oral and Intangible Heritage of Humanity.

I have just presented all of this information not only to give readers a sense of Sandroni's incredible versatility and experience. The biographical sketch was also designed to substantiate the fact that by 2007, when I first contacted Carlos Sandroni, he was a well-established samba scholar and professor of ethnomusi-cology, and also one of the most prominent and respected voices on intangible heritage in Brazil. (He has since embarked on countless other important projects, with a continued devotion to strengthening Brazilian ethnomusicology through his work, publications, vision, and teaching.) Two years later, Sandroni and I met in person, again to talk about *samba de roda*. And a few years after that, we con-ducted a two-day fieldwork trip together in Bahia. Consequently, what started out as a cordial dialogue between a young student and a welcoming senior scholar developed into a far more robust dialogue focused no longer only on samba, but also on ethnomusicology, research, writing, language, and life experiences.

In terms of a working relationship regarding Carioca samba, however, our dialogue began in earnest when I moved to Recife in 2013. By chance, my wife decided to get her master's degree in the theory of literature at UFPE, the university at which Sandroni had begun teaching a decade and a half earlier. When my wife and I first arrived in town, Sandroni, showing his usual generosity, not only took a night to show us around Recife but also put me in touch with UFPE faculty members in music and anthropology and people connected with his nonprofit. In the meantime, he also asked me to revise something he had written in English, and then later to translate a couple of short *sambista* biographies, which led to other larger projects. I was of course quite familiar with his work and had a sense of him as a person, but this was the first time I had really begun thinking of the sound of Sandroni's scholarly voice. His scholarly writing is not a far cry from how he comports himself: poetic but clear, erudite without being pedantic, deliberate but not tedious, confident without the customary arrogance, deeply knowledgeable but unafraid not to know something.

Here is the point of this slightly autobiographical tangent: the dialogic translation we employed in *A Respectable Spell* was only possible because of our prior dialogues, as they facilitated our communication and ability to interact in a rigorous, honest, and unhesitant way. Furthermore, after so many years of different types of dialogue, I have gradually developed a sense of what Sandroni's academic voice might sound like in English. And it's different, I think, from Sandroni's actual voice in English, a language in which he expresses himself well. (He has lived in the United States for short periods, having spent semesters teaching at Indiana University and the University of Texas, Austin.) So, when I was contacted by the University of Illinois Press, at his request, to translate *Feitiço decente*, I felt quite ready to take on the challenge. And this was especially the case as I knew that Sandroni would help ensure that my translation—my "intimate" reading—would be as close to accurate as possible.

A Final Thought on Translation and Its Decolonial Spark

I hope you are ready, dear reader, to be submerged into roughly 150 years of Brazilian popular music history. As you turn the book's pages, you will learn about *lundu, modinha, maxixe,* and countless other musical genres. And soon enough, you will find yourself before the book's central focus: the samba(s) practiced in Rio's private homes, public festivities, and recording studios. Along the way, you will learn about people—performers, composers, journalists, matriarchs, poets, scholars—and the social contexts in which they lived and exercised their roles.

Moreover, although the Brazilian context is always the focus, there are neverthe-less more abstract "theoretical" lessons we might extract: sounds (and rhythms in particular) can be coded racially and ideologically; words can aggregate and shed meanings depending on social and historical context; and methodological eclecticism can produce tremendous fruits.

A Respectable Spell offers a glimpse of an approach to music, ethnomusicology, and Brazilian culture that is difficult to find in English. Here I do not *just* mean Sandroni's approach. I am also alluding to the approaches of towering figures like Mário de Andrade, Oneyda Alvarenga, and Edison Carneiro (among many others), from whom we have only to gain by moving their tremendous contributions from the academic periphery (in Brazil) to the academic center (in the English-reading world), even if we only get their ideas in fragments via Sandroni's citations or in-terpretations. In this way, *A Respectable Spell* gives those who are unfamiliar with Brazilian music scholarship a point of entry, so to speak, from which to begin ex-ploring its rich history, including a possibility for some engagement with Brazilian ethnomusicology (though doing so will require continued efforts from publishers like the University of Illinois Press).[40] After all, although scholars from Brazil (and the Global South generally) tend to keep up with the scholarship coming from the United States and Europe, the inverse is rarely true. But of course, this has noth-ing to do with the quality or relevance of the scholarship produced in the Global South, in these cosmopolitan peripheries. Rather, it is yet another consequence of coloniality and the hierarchical position of the United States and Europe (and the resulting linguistic, cultural, epistemological, and racial superiority complex).

A Respectable Spell also gives us a chance to "hear"—albeit in the "wrong" language—some of the thoughts and perspectives of those who are most mar-ginalized within Brazil itself (for the South American nation, like everywhere in the Western Hemisphere, suffers from its own internal coloniality). Of particular importance in this regard are the voices of *sambistas*, nearly all of African descent, whose ideas and perspectives are meticulously sought out by Sandroni; the author ends up finding them primarily in published interviews, song lyrics, and musical recordings. More importantly, he takes seriously what these cultural agents say, not merely exposing their perspectives and analyses but giving their subjectivities weight, validity, and authority, generally following *their* lead in what is perhaps a decolonial approach to understanding a foundational historical moment in Carioca samba (and in Brazil generally).

Herein lies a broader lesson concerning the need to invest our time and our money into translating works such as this. I am referring not to the patent impor-tance of *Feitiço decente* itself but rather to its decolonial spark. That is, dormant in this or any translation of a work from the Global South is a more profound decolonial potential, for it makes ideas, perspectives, and knowledge from the geopolitical peripheries available in the geopolitical center. Translations, as I see them, help peripheralized works penetrate the linguistic bubble from which the center exerts its power. In the most effective cases, then, translation would harbor the potential to ignite a decolonial fire. Thus, like samba in the first decades of the twentieth century, the value of translating a work from the Global South may primarily be in constructing a vehicle that helps the marginalized and oppressed receive some sort of acknowledgment from those in power. With any luck, then, our *feitiço*—the English-language "spell" that Sandroni and I have assembled here—will not only take hold of readers and carry them through the formative period of Brazilian popular music and the development of a "national" samba. Hopefully, it will also serve as an enchanted reminder of the brilliance, ingenuity, and agency that are relegated to the margins by the noxious spell of coloniality.

Notes

1. Jiří Levý, "Translation as a Decision Process," in *The Translation Studies Reader*, ed. Lawrence Venuti (London: Routledge, 2000), 148. In the original, the phrase is written in all caps. I have chosen to reproduce it here without such emphasis, as the formatting decision would appear out of place and be unnecessarily confusing.

2. Antônio Houaiss and Mauro de Salles Villar, *Minidicionário Houaiss da língua portuguesa* (Rio de Janeiro: Objetiva, 2003), 145.

3. Houaiss and Villar, *Minidicionário*, 238.

4. William Pietz, "The Problem of the Fetish, I," *RES: Anthropology and Aesthetics* 9, no. 1 (1985), 5; Pietz, "The Problem of the Fetish, II: The Origin of the Fetish," *RES: Anthropology and Aesthetics* 13, no. 1 (1987), 40. The term "fetishism," for its part, appears to come from the French *fétichisme*, coined by Charles de Brosses in 1757 "by way of contrast to the term 'polytheism.'"

5. Anne McClintock, *Imperial Leather: Race, Gender, and Sexuality in the Colonial Contest* (New York: Routledge, 1995), 185.

6. Pietz, "Problem of the Fetish, II," 36.

7. Pietz, "Problem of the Fetish, II," 40.

8. Pietz, "Problem of the Fetish, I," 7.

9. Pietz, "Problem of the Fetish, I," 5.

10. J. Lorand Matory, *The Fetish Revisited: Marx, Freud, and the Gods Black People Make* (Durham, NC: Duke University Press, 2018).

11. Matory, *The Fetish Revisited*, xiii.

12. Matory, *The Fetish Revisited*, xii–xiii.

13. Gayatri Chakravorty Spivak, "The Politics of Translation," in *Outside in the Teaching Machine* (New York: Routledge, 1993), 183.

14. Ernesto Donas, review of "Feitiço decente: Transformações do samba no Rio de Janeiro (1917–1933) [Decent Enchantment: Transformations of Samba in Rio de Janeiro (1917–1933)] by Carlos Sandroni," *The World of Music* 48, no. 1 (2006), 139.

15. Pietz, "Problem of the Fetish, II," 24.

16. Jason R. Young, *Rituals of Resistance: African Atlantic Religion in Kongo and the Low-country South in the Era of Slavery* (Baton Rouge: Louisiana State University Press, 2007), 119; Cheré Dastugue Coen and Jude Bradley, *Magic's in the Bag: Creating Spellbinding Gris Gris Bags & Sachets* (Woodbury, MN: Llewellyn, 2010), 7.

17. Vladimir Nabokov, "Problems of Translation: 'Onegin' in English," in *The Translation Studies Reader*, ed. Lawrence Venuti (London: Routledge, 2000), 77.

18. Juliane House, "Overt and Covert Translation," in *Handbook of Translation Studies*, vol. 1, ed. Yves Gambier and Luc van Doorslaer, 245–246 (Amsterdam: John Benjamins Publishing, 2010).

19. Without the input of my wife, Fabiana Campos, this would be a far poorer translation. She was an important interlocutor from the beginning to the end, and was especially essential to helping me pull apart the more idiomatic and complex phrases. I also want to thank Marc Hertzman, whose comments after a meticulous reading of the manuscript made the translation immeasurably better. I am moreover grateful to Jennie Gubner, Ananya Jahanara Kabir, Francesca Negro, and Dan Sharp, whose help with particular words/phrases was crucial. Finally, Carlos Sandroni gave me access to three chapters of *Feitiço decente* that had been translated years ago by Susanna Sharpe; her work was a helpful resource for me as I mulled over translation decisions.

20. Angela Lühning, "Brazilian Ethnomusicology as Participatory Ethnomusicology: Anxieties Regarding Brazilian Musics," in *A Latin American Music Reader: Views from the South*, ed. Javier F. León and Helena Simonett, 379–392 (Urbana: University of Illinois Press, 2016); "Temas emergentes da etnomusicologia brasileira e seus compromissos sociais," *Música em perspectiva* 7, no. 2 (2014), 18–21.

21. Angela Lühning, Tiago Carvalho, Flávia Diniz, and Aaron Lopes, "Ethnomusicological Goals and Challenges in Brazil," *The World of Music* 5, no. 1 (2016), 40.

22. Carolina Alonso Bejarano, Lucia López Juárez, Mirian A. Mijangos García, and Daniel M. Goldstein, *Decolonizing Ethnography: Undocumented Immigrants and New Directions in Social Science* (Durham, NC: Duke University Press, 2019), 8.

23. Renato Ortiz, *La supremacía del Inglés: En las ciencias sociales* (Buenos Aires: Siglo Veintiuno Editores, 2009), 95–140.

24. Lawrence Venuti, *The Scandals of Translation: Towards an Ethics of Difference* (London: Routledge, 1998), 10; on the north-south relationship of translation, see also Richard Jacquemond, "Translation and Cultural Hegemony: The Case of French-Arabic Translation," in *Rethinking Translation: Discourse, Subjectivity, Ideology*, ed. Lawrence Venuti (London: Routledge, 1992), 139–140.

25. Sherry Simon, "Translation, Postcolonialism and Cultural Studies," *Meta* 42, no. 2 (1997), 468.

26. Spivak, "Politics of Translation," 182.

27. Walter Mignolo, *The Idea of Latin America* (Malden, MA: Blackwell, 2005), 7.

28. Susan Bassnett and Harish Trivedi, "Introduction: Of Colonies, Cannibals, and Vernaculars," in *Post-Colonial Translation: Theory and Practice*, ed. Susan Bassnett and Harish Trivedi (London: Routledge, 1999), 2.

29. Rolando Vázquez, "Translation as Erasure: Thoughts on Modernity's Epistemic Vio-

lence," *Journal of Historical Sociology* 24, no. 1 (2011), 32; see also Mignolo, *Idea of Latin America*, 144.

30. Walter Benjamin, "The Task of the Translator," in *Walter Benjamin: Selected Writings Volume 1, 1913–1926*, ed. Marcus Bullock and Michael W. Jennings (Cambridge, MA: The Belknap Press of Harvard University Press, 1996), 255.

31. Gilles Deleuze and Félix Guattari, *A Thousand Plateaus: Capitalism and Schizophrenia*, translated by Brian Massumi (Minneapolis: University of Minnesota Press, 1987), 293.

32. Marcos Napolitano, "Feitiço decente," *História: Questões & debates* 36 (2002), 332.

33. The other two works mentioned by Travassos were Glaura Lucas's *Os sons do Rosário: O congado mineiro dos Arturos e Jatobá* (Minas Gerais: Editora da UFMG, 2002) and Suzel Reily's *Voices of the Magi: Enchanted Journeys in Southeast Brazil* (Chicago: University of Chicago Press, 2002).

34. Elizabeth Travassos, "Esboço de balanço da etnomusicologia no Brasil," *Opus 9* (2003), 76.

35. Donas, review of "Feitiço decente," 139.

36. See the list of ethnomusicologists, including the dates they obtained their PhDs and when they began teaching in Brazil, in Lühning, Carvalho, Diniz, and Lopes, "Ethnomusicological Goals and Challenges," 32–33.

37. Carlos Sandroni, "O acervo da Missão de Pesquisas Folclóricas, 1938–2012," *Debates* 12 (2014), 55–62.

38. *Responde a roda outra vez: Música tradicional de Pernambuco e da Paraíba no trajeto da Missão de Pesquisas Folclóricas de 1938.* Audio collection edited by Carlos Sandroni, Maria Ignez Ayala, and Marcos Ayala. Recife and João Pessoa: Associação Respeita Januário/Coletivo Meio do Mundo, 2004, compact disc. The translated title is *The Ring Responds Again: Traditional Music of Pernambuco and Paraíba along the Path of the Folk Research Mission.*

39. Carlos Sandroni, *Mário contra Macunaíma* (São Paulo: Vértice, 1988).

40. The University of Illinois Press is also responsible for the important essay collection *A Latin American Music Reader: Views from the South*, edited by Javier F. León and Helena Simonett (2016). Also worth acknowledging are important efforts such as the Society for Ethnomusicology's "Ethnomusicology Translations."

Acknowledgments

CARLOS SANDRONI

The first version of this book was conceived as a PhD dissertation in music, defended at the University of Tours, France, in January 1997. A great number of people helped me during my time in France (1991–1997) and during the research periods I spent in Brazil (mainly in 1994). I owe many thanks to all of them. Here I would like to mention, in particular, Jairo Severiano and the late Ary Vasconcelos, important researchers who, in Rio de Janeiro, made their precious collections of old recordings available to me (at a time when I could never have dreamt that such recordings would one day be available on the internet).

I am also grateful to my parents, Laura and Cícero, who supported me in every way possible during the years I lived outside of Brazil (not to mention at other times); to my Franco-Brazilian "family," the late Lúcia and Albert Laborde, my adopted parents, and the late Violeta Corrêa de Azevedo, my adopted grandmother; to my dear friend Chiara Ruffinengo, who translated the dissertation from Portuguese, the language in which it was originally written, into French, the language in which it was defended, in addition to offering me crucial assistance; to Stéphanie Morvant and Philipe Lesage, who revised the French and also supported me in important ways; to the late professor Jean-Michel Vaccaro for his trust and support from the time I first arrived in Paris in 1991; to my adviser and friend Jean-Michel Beaudet for his interest, suggestions, critiques . . . and for introducing me to ethnomusicology; to Dominique Dreyfus, Patrick Régnier, Ralph C. Waddey, Marco Antônio Lavigne, Guy Farelle, João Máximo, Jean-Pierre Estival, and Ricardo Canzio for the books, the cassette tapes, the suggestions; and to all of the Carioca guitarists I interviewed for my research in 1994: Luiz

Otávio Braga, Maurício Carrilho, Paulão Sete Cordas, Betinho Maciel, Alfredo Machado, Luiz Cláudio Ramos, Guinga, and the *mestres* of the group Época de Ouro, the late Carlinhos, César Faria, and Dino.

Among the people with whom I made friends and who supported me in different ways during the writing of the dissertation, I would like to thank Teca Calazans, Yves Pérreal, Brigitte Moreau, Bertrand and Nathalie Loiseau, Didier Biven, Guillermo Carbo, Elena de Renzio, Pauline Ridel, and Manoel Nunes.

In transforming the dissertation into the book in Brazil, the interest and suggestions of Cristina Zahar, André Telles, Ana Paula Tavares, and Juliana Freire were invaluable, and to them I owe my gratitude. The great literary critic Walnice Nogueira Galvão honored me by writing the preface to the Brazilian edition, for which I am very grateful. I am also thankful to my mother, Laura Sandroni, for the thorough revision of the manuscript in Portuguese. I am moreover grateful to Clarinha Teixeira, a longtime friend, for the crucial support in inserting the musical examples into the text of the Brazilian edition—and now, again, also in the present edition!

For this edition in English, I am immensely grateful to Michael Iyanaga for his tireless and insightful dedication to the translation. For me it was a pleasure and a privilege to be able to discuss different aspects of the book with Michael over the course of many months, following the text as it moved to a third language, after the Portuguese and the French. I learned a lot about my own book through the process, and I am sure that a new edition in Portuguese will benefit immensely from Michael's contributions and from the ideas that emerged from our conversations.

I am also grateful to Marc Hertzman for the support that, from the outset, led to the publication of the book by UIP, and for reading and commenting on the translated manuscript.

Finally, I thank Danny Nasset for his interest and dedication to the project.

The dissertation that led to the book was originally dedicated to my wife, Elisa Toledo. I met Elisa when I first began conducting my research, and I married her a week after submitting the dissertation to the university. In every way this work is linked to our story and to our love.

When the book was published in 2001, I maintained the first dedication and added another person, my grandmother Alzira Sandroni, beloved "Nonai." At the time she was already ninety-one years old, and she passed away just months after receiving her exemplar.

The present edition in English is also dedicated to Elisa and now, to the memory of Nonai. But I would like to add one more dedication, in memoriam. It is to Walter Santos Pinto, my dear guitar teacher who taught me, among other things, how to play the samba rhythm. In some ways, everything began in those guitar lessons, back in 1974 and 1975. *Obrigado*, Walter!

Introduction to the English Translation

CARLOS SANDRONI

A Respectable Spell: Transformations of Samba in Rio de Janeiro was, in its first iteration, a PhD dissertation in music defended in 1997 at the University of Tours, France. I originally wrote the dissertation in Portuguese, which means that the version in French submitted to the university, "Transformations de la samba à Rio de Janeiro, 1917–1933," was a translation. With several edits and a few additions, the original Portuguese text was published in Brazil in 2001 as *Feitiço decente: Transformações do samba no Rio de Janeiro, 1917–1933*, with a second edition published in 2012.

The present version, in English, is based on the text of the second edition of the book. It is being published in English now, more than twenty years after it was originally written, with only a few changes. These changes are mainly found in the first chapter, where I discuss *lundu*, a genre considered to be a distant predecessor of samba, and *modinha*, a type of song historically linked to *lundu*. I felt these changes were necessary because in the last twenty years, the historiographical discussion about *lundu* and *modinha* has given us data that undermine assertions I made in previous editions of the book.

As for the samba from Rio de Janeiro between 1917 and 1933, the primary focus of the book, I do not feel the relevant bibliography that has emerged in the last twenty or twenty-five years affects the information, analyses, or conclusions I present. This absolves me from having to write the book all over again. Without a doubt, the most important work on this topic to have been published in English since my book first came out is Marc Hertzman's *Making Samba: A New History of Race and Music in Brazil* (2013). I also recommend, for those who are interested, Bryan McCann's *Hello, Hello, Brazil: Popular Music and the Making of Modern Brazil* (2005), as its first two chapters deal with topics directly related to my book.

Something that would no doubt be different were I to write another book on the same topic today is the section dealing with African rhythm, and with the way in which theories about African rhythm apply to the study of samba's rhythm. I began to develop this part of my work when I discovered Simha Arom's book, *Polyphonies et polyrythmies d'Afrique Centrale*. Published in French in 1985 and translated into English in 1991 (as *African Polyphony and Polyrhythm*), it became one of the most influential books on African music of the last quarter of the twentieth century. My reading of it in 1993 was decisive for the direction my research ended up taking. Upon noting that the rhythmic processes described in Arom's book shared important similarities with rhythmic elements of Rio de Janeiro's samba, I felt I had found a key to constructing an interesting argument about the genre's history and its transformations. I attended Arom's seminars in Paris from 1994 to 1995, and his approach to musical rhythm made a profound impact on my work.

"African rhythm," though, is a broad topic that has led to rivers of spilled ink, as noted by Kofi Agawu, among others. Although I am still interested in the topic, my work has not continued to deal with the relationship between African and Afro-Brazilian rhythms. And in the end, because the topic of this book is Brazilian samba and not African music, I decided not to update the parts of my book that address African music. I hope that any of the African and/or Africanist ethnomusicologists who read the book will forgive me for this.

A Reflection on "Popular Brazilian Music"

A recurring issue in this book's argumentation concerns a distinction between "folk samba" and "popular samba," and I often discuss "popular music" as a nascent field of production during the early twentieth century. As such, it is important to clarify the way in which "popular music" is thought of and experienced in Brazil.[1]

At first glance, the idea of "popular music" in Brazil is not entirely different from the one adopted in the United States. In both cases, "popular music" is situated within a tripartite division in which it is distinguished, on the one hand, from "folk music," and on the other, from "erudite" or "art music." But hidden behind this apparent similarity is a significant difference in conceptualization. Allow me to discuss these differences by way of a few examples.

Choro is a type of instrumental music that began to emerge in Rio de Janeiro around 1870. According to its scholars (and as we will see in the book), *choro* arose from some of the looser performances of musical scores by Brazilian musicians who played polkas, waltzes, mazurkas, and other European dance genres.

Gradually, *choro* became disassociated from dance, becoming a music of virtuosos, instrumentalists, and composers, all highly sophisticated and, to a certain extent, elite. Not by chance, many people compared it to jazz. But *choro* is considered by most critics (whether academic or journalistic) to be part of Brazilian popular music. Thus, I was more than surprised to learn that jazz, with which *choro* has so much in common, is not generally considered (today) to be "popular music" in the United States. Nevertheless, it wasn't difficult to understand the point: neither jazz nor *choro* is popular in the sense that Madonna or the Brazilian romantic singer Roberto Carlos is. Neither genre—and in this Brazilians and U.S. Americans certainly agree—is part of "pop music." But in Brazil, "pop" is not treated as an abbreviation of "popular"; to the contrary, the two designations are, to a certain extent, seen by many to be opposites. In the United States, the expression "popular music"—or "pop music," for the sake of abbreviation—always seems to refer to music that sells hundreds of thousands of records, plays to huge radio audiences, and is associated in some way with what the philosopher Theodor Adorno called the "culture industry." (Both jazz and *choro* are, to be sure, also related to the culture industry, but that relationship cannot be said to best characterize them.) In Brazil "popular music" is also, in part, defined by these same features, but not by them alone, and certainly not in the same manner as it is defined in the United States.

Choro, like jazz, largely exists in a cultural sphere independent of big record companies and the entertainment industry. Its inclusion in our idea of "Brazilian popular music" is tied to the fact that this category is seen not only, and perhaps not even principally, as show business or entertainment but also as an artistic expression of national identity. In the United States, to the contrary, it seems that the concept of "popular music" is not especially tied either to the idea of artistic elevation or to national identity. Therein lies the difficulty in translating one idea to the other.

Another confusing aspect of the subject relates to a phrase that is not just musical. The term *cultura popular*, in Brazil, is used to mean almost the opposite of "popular culture" in the United States. Studies of media idols, radio and television programs, comic books, or advertising are more recent and fewer in number in Brazil than are studies of folklore. Perhaps for this reason, academics and Brazilian cultural institutions tend to use the expression *cultura popular* as an up-to-date synonym of folklore.

In Brazil, "popular music" is the opposite of "folk music," but "popular culture" is synonymous with "folklore." The paradox can perhaps be explained in part by looking at the way in which the cultural influences of France and North America converged in Brazil. The connotations associated with the Portuguese word *povo* are different in the two languages. In France, *le peuple* always has a political connotation, which cannot be said for the English "the people," or "people." The French equivalent of "people" would be *les gens*. In Brazilian Portuguese, the French *le peuple* is translated as *povo*, and the English "people," like the French *les gens*, is translated as *as pessoas* (persons). The former is politically charged; the latter is merely descriptive. In the land of Rousseau, the word is always used along with the definite article (*le peuple*), as if to accentuate their indivisibility. Of course, in the language of Rousseau, "the people" can also carry a political meaning, but the term is regularly used without the article to designate any more or less heterogeneous group of persons.

In Brazil, the word *povo* tends to be used more in the French sense. But the corresponding adjective, "popular," is ambiguous, appearing with two different meanings. There is a "quantitative popular," that which refers to the number of people reached, or records sold; this is the "statistical popular," so to speak, or even the "popular by induction." And there is a popular that refers to the *povo* as political entity: the "qualitative popular," or "popular by deduction."

In Brazil, when we speak of "popular music," these different concepts of popular are at play. Definitions of the "Brazilian people" (*povo brasileiro*) have been debated since the end of the nineteenth century—the period of slavery's abolition (1888) and the proclamation of the Republic (1889)—until the beginning of the twenty-first century, when Luiz Inácio Lula da Silva, a former labor leader and representative of the Workers' Party, took office as president of the Republic. Intellectuals like Sílvio Romero, Mário de Andrade, Gilberto Freyre, Florestan Fernandes, Roberto DaMatta, and many others helped to make these definitions explicit. And, as Bryan McCann points out in *Hello, Hello Brazil*, even Brazilian musicians and lyricists have made their songs a laboratory for ideas regarding the *povo* and Brazilianness.

Thus, books as diverse as *Cantos populares do Brasil* (Sílvio Romero, 1883), *Música popular brasileira* (Oneyda Alvarenga, 1946), *Pequena história da música popular* (José Ramos Tinhorão, 1974), and songs as diverse as "História do Brasil" (Lamartine Babo, 1931), "Aquarela do Brasil" (Ary Barroso, 1939), and "Que país é este?" (Renato Russo, 1987) attest to the conceptual changes regarding the Brazilian *povo* and its musical expressions.

Through this process, the most expressive musical personalities—like Noel Rosa in the 1930s and João Gilberto in the 1960s—and proponents of the most dramatic artistic trends—like the tropicalist explosion of the 1960s—always associated the national-popular vein with the cosmopolitanism and consumerist orientation of the masses, typical of modern popular music, whose paradigm is, without a doubt, North American. Add to this the fact that Brazilian folk music is not revivalist and not even very rural; its performers maintain in many cases a dynamic aesthetic dialogue with the recording industry. The result is that the opposition between the ideas of "popular" and "folk" is, in Brazil, much subtler than it seems to be in other countries, including perhaps the United States. In Brazil, at least according to musicians, if "popular" is different from "folk," it is far from being its opposite; and they would conceive of "popular music" as different, to at least the same extent, from "pop music," the latter perceived as having the least critical relationship with the market and cosmopolitanism.

This difficult mediation between quantitative notions of popular, politicized notions of popular, nationalism, and cosmopolitanism contributes a great deal to the contradictions and paradoxes, but also to the richness and the fecundity, of Brazilian popular music.

Analyzing Commercial 78s

A final word. I have the satisfaction of being able to connect the research I present in this book with ethnomusicological tendencies signaled by Philip Yampolsky in his 2015 essay "Commercial 78s: A Rediscovered Resource for Ethnomusicologists."[2] Allow me to explain what I mean.

When I was originally writing the dissertation (that would spawn this book) in the context of French ethnomusicology during the 1990s, and despite the steadfast encouragement of my academic adviser, Jean-Michel Beaudet, I could not shake the feeling that I was doing something that did not fit into the field of ethnomusicology. I wrote about people whom I had never met personally, some of whom had died well before I had even been born; I presented neither interviews conducted by me nor ethnographic observations, and worst of all, perhaps, I was doing musical transcriptions of commercial recordings! For Brazilian researchers of popular music history, my topic's importance was self-evident, but for card-carrying ethnomusicologists at the time, nothing could seem less self-evident. With the unrelenting support of Beaudet, and perhaps the not-so-unrelenting support of one or another of the members of my committee, my dissertation was approved.

Upon returning to Brazil and securing a permanent teaching position in the 2000s, I sought to delve deeper into English-language ethnomusicology, a literature that, as one can tell, is not extensively represented in the bibliography of this book or the dissertation. While these new references allowed me to feel less eccentric in my decision to study urban popular music, it still seemed a bit eccentric to have chosen a repertoire of the past and, in particular—once again—to have attributed so much analytical value to commercial recordings.

Only in reading Yampolsky's essay did I learn that, even back in the 1990s, I was not alone. Taking as a pioneering example A. J. Racy's PhD dissertation on Egyptian commercial music in the first half of the twentieth century, Yampolsky calls attention to a number of works from the 1990s and 2000s that took full advantage of commercial recordings to support their studies. Citing, among many others, the work of Danielson on Umm Kulthum (1997), Moore on Cuban music (1997), and Maliangkay on Korean music (2007), Yampolsky encourages twenty-first-century ethnomusicologists to turn to the "gold mine"[3] that is historical commercial recordings: "These studies devote attention to illuminating the character or tracing the development of a genre or musical sphere through relevant commercial recordings."[4] This was precisely what I intended to do in my work, for the case of samba. It is now up to readers to decide for themselves if I was successful in my undertaking.

Original Introduction

In samba lyrics, the guitar is commonly treated as the composer's confidant. In "Cordas de aço" ("Steel Strings"), for example, the great *sambista* Cartola sang:

Só você, violão	Only you, guitar
Compreende porque	Can understand why
Perdi toda a alegria.	I've lost all joy.

With this, the lovesick composer humanizes the instrument, turning it into an understanding listener who allows him to share his woes.

The guitar, however, is an indiscreet confidant. In the first place, of course, it does not keep to itself the secrets with which it has been entrusted. Much to the contrary, it is literally a resonant box that amplifies and transfigures the composer's secrets, allowing them to be echoed on the lips and in the hearts of millions of listeners. However, the guitar is perhaps even more indiscreet than is suggested by its role in carrying lovers' woes; composers might very well also entrust it with some of the secrets of their trade.

Allow me to explain. During the Carnival season in Rio de Janeiro, a given samba can be performed by three hundred percussionists and countless more singers; while at any other time of year the same song can be performed in chamber versions, by a lone singer with a guitar. If such an intimate rendition is indeed possible, the instrument must surely take on an extraordinary power of synthesis. And if so, the guitar's indiscretion—which is useful to composers, who can thus condense a collectivity—would be useful to musicologists, too, for it allows them to find, in a compacted version, certain key characteristics of the multifaceted phenomenon that is samba.

Indeed, this book began with an observation regarding a difference in samba guitar styles. Like so many other Brazilian guitarists, I learned, as a teenager, to play what we call the samba "rhythm": an accompaniment pattern, prone to a certain degree of variation, which is employed when the song to be accompanied pertains to the genre of "samba." Yet when my interest in popular music led me to 78 rpm samba recordings from Rio de Janeiro dating back to as far as 1917, I was quite surprised to hear the guitarists using an accompaniment pattern different from the one that was so familiar to my contemporaries and me. If this other pattern were judged according to the Brazilian musical criteria prevalent today, it would be considered entirely inappropriate for samba.

Yet a rhythmic accompaniment is not a neutral backdrop against which a song can saunter with indifference. Rather, the former tells us quite a bit about the content of the latter. In fact, within the context of Brazilian popular music, the accompaniment pattern is one of the primary elements by which listeners recognize musical genres. In Brazil, and certainly in other countries as well, when we hear a song, it is the melody, lyrics, singer's style, and context of the performance that allow us to classify it as pertaining to a given genre. But even before all of this is perceived by us, we will already have done such classifying thanks to the accompaniment pattern that, preceding the singing, has plunged us into the song's meaning, literally *giving it its tone.*

This is why the existence of a different rhythmic pattern in the older sambas immediately struck me as a matter worthy of interest, and it became the knot around which this project was built. I felt that the existence of two styles of accompaniment, which my sensibilities as a guitarist suggested to me were clearly incompatible, could not but indicate profound divergences in the meaning of samba. Furthermore, it was clear to me that these divergences, as I hope to show, spoke not only to the rhythms, instruments, and sung verses but also to types of people, economic exchanges, festivities, Black-white race relations, and conceptions about what it is to be Brazilian.

The main focus of this book is samba's transformations in the early 1930s in the city of Rio de Janeiro. Other scholars have already observed these transformations, but to date there has not yet been any systematic analysis of them. There are many types of transformations—social, choreographic, musical, political-cultural; inasmuch as I am able, I will refer to all of these transformations. My analysis, however, will revolve around a particular aspect of the music, the rhythmic accompaniment patterns, from which I believe I have extracted new insights for understanding the larger changes.

The study begins with the "Musical Premises" (in technical terms) on which the project is based. Any reader who is not at least somewhat familiar with so-called classical "music theory" will likely find this part a bit challenging. Such a reader is hereby formally authorized to skip it without a second thought. Although the technical musical arguments represent a significant part of what I have to say, I do not believe they are indispensable to enjoying the rest of the book. Nonetheless, allow me to offer here a discreet suggestion: even readers who are complete musical laypeople (if such things even exist) might consider arming themselves with the patience necessary to venture out among the syncopations and sixteenth notes. In preparing the final edit of the book, I set out to make this task a bit easier by using technical terms only when necessary.[1]

Part 1, "From *Lundu* to Samba," opens with a study of aspects of the Brazilian salon music genres from the nineteenth century (and even a bit earlier) that are associated with the origins of samba: *modinha, lundu, maxixe,* and their close relatives, *polca-lundu* and *tango brasileiro,* among others. This incursion into the past will help us understand a musical and ideological universe of which samba, in its initial phase, was still a part.

From there, I move on to the first references to samba, still in the nineteenth century, and then to the pioneering phase of the genre's creation, which took place in early twentieth-century Rio de Janeiro. Some of the most important pioneers were a group of immigrants from the state of Bahia who had relocated to Rio de Janeiro. The most illustrious representative of these Bahians was Hilária Batista de Almeida (1854–1924), known to this day among samba aficionados as "Tia Ciata" (Aunt Ciata). This pioneering phase reached its apex in 1917 with the release of the song "Pelo telefone" ("On the Telephone"), whose authorship was attributed to both Ernesto dos Santos (1890–1974), known as "Donga," the Afro-Brazilian son of a Bahian woman, and the white journalist Mauro de Almeida. "Pelo telefone" was the most successful song of Rio's Carnival that year, and it was decisive in ushering the word "samba" into the vocabulary of popular commercial music. Over the course of the twentieth century, the historiography of samba came to embrace "Pelo telefone" as the genre's starting point. Indeed, the "centenary of samba" was widely celebrated in Brazil in 2017, precisely one hundred years after the song's release.

Part 2, "From One Samba to the Other," looks at the difference between two types, or "styles," of samba. The sambas recorded between 1917 and the late 1920s were eventually considered to be too close to *maxixes,* and thus "fraudulent" sambas; whereas the style of samba born in the late 1920s and recorded with increasing regularity over the course of the 1930s was widely considered to be the Carioca[2] samba (that is, the samba from Rio de Janeiro) par excellence.

This difference will initially be shown in the discourse on samba—the discourse of *sambistas,* of their biographers, of journalists who were interested in the topic, of musicologists. Then we will turn to the social spaces in which samba was performed: the homes of Bahian migrants to Rio, such as Tia Ciata; establishments for drinking, eating, and gathering, known in Brazil as *botequins*; and the city's neighborhoods, such as Cidade Nova and Estácio de Sá. We will also look at differences in the types of economic relations that were created by the circulation of samba, from house parties to commercial recording studios, whether as "harvested" sambas (seen as "natural," public domain objects) or as "stolen" or "purchased" sambas (when, for the first time, performers, composers, audiences, and record companies worked together to attribute monetary value to the songs). The differences are audible in the replacement of improvised lyrics and melodies by fixed "second parts" (*segundas partes*), as they were called, replacements that, as we will see, go hand in hand with the transformation of sambas into objects that could be documented via graphic, phonographic, and legal avenues.

Also relevant to these differences are the appearance and rise in popularity, in late 1920s Rio de Janeiro, of a paradoxical character, the *malandro* (hustler), who has already been the focus of important studies in Brazilian sociology and literary criticism. I say paradoxical because while the *malandro* is, one could say, the personification of the new style of samba, the fact that this style is ultimately victorious suggests the possibility of the *malandro*'s transcendence by becoming a composer.

Chapter 10, "On the Gramophone," is, just as is "Musical Premises" (at the beginning of the book), a bit more demanding as far as a technical line of argumentation goes, and thus the reader is welcome to skip it too, or take the modest suggestion made earlier. In this section, I analyze a significant group of recordings from the period under examination. The goal of the analysis is to retrace, via the recordings, the aural steps by which the new version of the genre was constituted, and by which it assumed, little by little, its definitive characteristics.

In speaking of "definitive characteristics," I am not suggesting that samba has remained frozen since 1940. Rather, despite countless subsequent changes, the fundamental characteristics that defined it up until at least the 1990s—characteristics that perhaps still define it for a significant portion of the population today—were created around 1930. As such, although a Carioca samba recording made after this era would be recognized as Carioca samba (even absent other information) by a contemporary aficionado of the genre, the same would not be true of an earlier recording. I am not denying that "Pelo telefone" and its immediate successors are "samba," as has been done by some of the researchers I will cite. We must not forget that these compositions were recognized as sambas by both their authors and the public. Rather, it has been left up to us to explain the circumstances responsible for the fact that the sambas of 1917 sound so different from the sambas of 1930.[3]

* * *

This book might be defined as a work of "historical ethnomusicology." Indeed, we will speak here of popular music, a subject that, at least in departments of music in Brazilian universities, has been studied mainly by ethnomusicologists. If, however, we consider ethnomusicology as being characterized by formalized fieldwork conducted in a culture to which the researcher figures as a "foreigner," this book cannot be classified as such. The fact that it studies music of the past and dedicates considerable space to the analysis of written music would equally contribute—according to ideas not yet entirely extinct in the 1990s (when the text was originally written)—to placing it instead within the field of musicology.

But such a discussion is only of interest inasmuch as it contributes to attenuating the rigidity of methodological borders. I think it is more important to recognize my debt to an important tradition of Brazilian music studies. The two great pioneers of such studies, Mário de Andrade (1893–1945) and Luiz Heitor Corrêa de Azevedo (1905–1992), wrote about both popular and classical music, about music of the present and music of the past, about written and orally transmitted music. The same can be said of some of their most talented successors, researchers such as Mozart de Araújo (1904–1988), the priest Jaime Diniz (1924–1989), Gérard Béhague (1937–2005), or José Miguel Wisnik (b. 1948). In Brazil, the divisions between musical categories appear to be more fluid than in other countries. It thus seems reasonable, and in my opinion beneficial, for Brazilian music studies to follow the same path.

Musical Premises

Brazilian Syncopation

The 1st Congresso Nacional do Samba (National Conference on Samba) took place in Rio de Janeiro between November 28 and December 2, 1962. Among those at the meeting were "composers, performers, sambistas [samba performers],[1] scholars, and friends of samba in general."[2] As a concluding act after the work of the conference, the participants approved a "Carta do samba" (Letter on Samba), drafted by anthropologist and folklorist Edison Carneiro (1912–1972). According to Carneiro himself, the document "represent[ed] an effort to coordinate practical measures . . . to preserve the traditional characteristics of samba."[3] After a brief preamble, the substantive part of the "Carta" begins as follows:

> Music: Samba is characterized by the constant use of syncopation.
>
> Therefore, to preserve the traditional characteristics of samba means, in short, to value syncopation.[4]

This reference to syncopation is the only instance in the entire "Carta" where an attempt is made to define, via a "technical" term, the traditional musical characteristics of samba the participants were seeking to preserve. In fact, some musicologists viewed syncopation as a defining characteristic not only of samba, but also of Brazilian popular music more generally in the twentieth century. Mário de Andrade (1893–1945),[5] an important writer and musicologist I will cite many times in this book, asserts that "syncopation . . . on the first beat of 2/4" is the "most significant characteristic of Brazilian rhythm."[6] Likewise, writer and music critic José Cândido de Andrade Muricy (1895–1984) laments the "fine artists [whose] . . . rhythmic sense is addicted to regular rhythms, and [are] unable to reproduce with confidence and precision a characteristic Brazilian rhythm, the syncopated rhythm."[7]

The fact that both samba and Brazilian music are characterized by the presence of syncopations is hardly out of place for a cultural context in which the former has been taken as the preeminent expression of the latter. In any event, it became commonplace to consider syncopations to be indices of a particular Brazilian "musical specificity." This was true for scholars of Brazilian music, such as the two cited above; for academic composers seeking to add a "local flavor" to their works; and even for practitioners and connoisseurs of popular music (which is precisely what many of those in attendance at the Congresso Nacional do Samba would likely have been), who without ever having opened a music theory book, commonly used expressions such as "syncopated sambas." Appealing to the idea of "syncopation" grants both musicological validity (seen as "universalistic") and a seal of authenticity (seen as "particularistic"), thus explaining the impact syncopation has had on Brazilian musical thought in the twentieth century. Brazilian musicologists and *sambistas* began to find a shared vocabulary.

But the word "syncopation," in music, designates a concept created by European theorists, and it may therefore be worth examining how it has been conceptualized by them. Let's look, for example, at what the entry on *syncope* in the *Dictionnaire de la musique,* by Marc Honneger, has to say: "Effect of *rupture* that is produced in musical discourse when *the regularity* of accentuation *is broken* by the *displacement of the expected rhythmic accent*" (emphasis added).[8] This definition suggests that syncopation is viewed as a deviation from the normal order of musical discourse. It would break the regularity and counter listeners' expectations; for them, a syncopated articulation would thus be out of place, implying that its proper place would be as a nonsyncopated articulation.

Likewise, the entry on *sincope* in the *Dizionario della musica* by Alberto Basso says, "change in the normal metric accentuation."[9] Finally, the definition in the *Harvard Dictionary of Music,* by Willi Apel:

> Syncopation is, generally speaking, any deliberate disturbance of the normal pulse of meter, accent and rhythm. The principal system of rhythm in Western music is based on the grouping of equal beats into two's and three's with a regularly recurrent accent on the first beat of each group. Any deviation from this scheme is perceived as a disturbance or contradiction between the underlying (*normal*) pulse and the actual (*abnormal*) rhythm. (emphasis added)[10]

With these definitions in mind, we can understand the Andrade Muricy passage cited above, in which "syncopated rhythm" is contrasted with "regular rhythm." The author applies the traditional definition strictly, viewing syncopation as an irregularity, an exception to the rule. But this does not resolve what thus becomes a paradox in the Brazilian case: the "irregular" ends up being the "characteristic," the most common. Syncopation is, in a word, the rule.

This paradox can only be undone by recognizing that syncopation is *not* a universal musical concept, but rather a notion generated as a practical necessity in Western classical music, and as such, has limited validity. Furthermore, the great strength of Apel's definition, cited above, is that it openly acknowledges this limitation; syncopation is a phenomenon specific to Western classical music.

As far as I am aware, ethnomusicologist Mieczyslaw Kolinski was the first to call attention to the cultural specificity of the concept of syncopation, in a 1960 review of A. M. Jones's book *Studies in African Music*. Kolinski postulates, as do other authors, that musical rhythm has two structural levels: that of meter and that of the rhythm itself.[11] Meter would be the permanent infrastructure upon which the rhythmic superstructure weaves its variations. As such, in a waltz, for example, the meter would be the 3/4 that constitutes the constant foundation, and the rhythm, the different temporal articulations of the actual music. In the European polyphony of the late Middle Ages and early Renaissance, the meter would be the *tactus*, the neutral beats that allow for the synchronization of voices; the rhythm, the different temporal segmentations of each of the voices. In African polyrhythms, the meter would be the isochronous pulsations that, allowing for the coordination of the ensemble, are sometimes manifested in participants' handclaps or in their dance steps; the rhythm, the varied durations that constitute each of the complementary parts of the musical performance.[12] In all of these cases, the varied character of the rhythm can *confirm* or *contradict* the given metric expectation. Kolinski coined the terms "commetricity" and "contrametricity" to express these two possibilities. The "metricity" of a rhythm would be the degree to which it approximates or diverges from the underlying meter.

The first advantage of Kolinski's terms is their neutral character: neither co- nor contrametricity would be a priori more "normal" or "regular" than the other. In Western classical theory, however, words such as "syncopation" and "off-beat" express cases of contrametricity while comparable technical terms were never created for cases of commetricity. This once again demonstrates that, in this context, commetricity is considered the norm, the default, needing no explanation, while contrametricity would be the exception.

But this is not merely a terminological issue. Evident in the definitions of syncopation I cited is that they understand musical rhythm as being structured according to the periodic recurrence of accentuations. This periodic recurrence, which the above-cited authors also called "normal," "expected," and so forth, finds its formalized expression in the idea of "measure." But measures, not unlike syncopations, are culturally specific musical concepts and practices. And they are also historically specific, for within Western music itself, they have been widely used only since the seventeenth century.

It is not by chance that Kolinski first elaborates his ideas about metricity in his review of a book on music from sub-Saharan Africa. The idea of a necessary recurrence of strong beats is foreign to this music. One source of its infinite rhythmic wealth is its freedom of articulations and accents, without needing to fit within structures that "measures" would adequately represent. Therefore, ethnomusicologists began to recognize that to transcribe African polyrhythms using measures was equivalent to forcing them into Procrustean beds.

What's more, in many forms of African music, contrametricity is not the exception, being instead as common as commetricity.

> We may say that the most striking property of rhythm [in Central African music] is a very strong tendency towards contrametricity, which gives rise to a permanently conflictual relationship between the *metric structure* of the period and the *rhythmic events* which take place within it. (emphasis in original)[13]

This systematic, regular, normal aspect of contrametricity in African music led scholars such as Simha Arom and Gerhard Kubik to eschew not only measures but also the very concept of syncopation as a tool in analyzing the music.[14]

The Brazilian researchers who have written about the importance of syncopation have tended to view it as having been inherited from the music of enslaved Africans.[15] Mário de Andrade dealt with the issue on a number of occasions without ever arriving at a satisfactory conclusion. A good summary of his misgivings appears in an unfinished text of his, which was published by his disciple Oneyda Alvarenga:

> Most of the affirmations made to date regarding the African elements of American popular music . . . are peremptory affirmations consistently lacking the documentary evidence on which to base them. . . . However what seems to me the trickiest part of the problem is the issue of syncopation. And it is primarily with this in mind that my charge of imprudence matters. The syncopation that runs through all American music with such formidable constancy is generally held to be derived from Africa. . . . This is possible and I am not here to deny it. What I recognize is that such an affirmation requires a reexamination based on more solid foundations and abundant evidence. . . . Given certain musical coincidences among the primitive musics of the Portuguese, Spanish, Africans, and Amerindians, the way these affirmations are going is imprudent and they are in need of a thorough reexamination. . . . Who did the influencing? Who was influenced? Or was it merely a coincidence of white, black, and

4

red elements that contaminated one another, strengthened one another, and spawned novel expressions that by being born under the auspices of America, we can call American?[16]

The richness of this citation justifies its length. Andrade, first of all, notes that syncopation is commonly held to be of African origin; second, he notes that this common notion is not based on solidly documented evidence, something that, if it is true today, was even more so the case when he wrote this.[17] Finally, he suggests that the issue of origins would be difficult to resolve and perhaps even irrelevant, as the fusion created on American soil was something novel, and equally novel were the social conditions that made way for it.

I agree with the idea that the novelty of American music is irreducible to any of its constituent elements; I also think that the search for the origins of specific rhythmic patterns, melodic contours, or specific songs is of little interest unless it is linked to an understanding of the newly created musics. Margaret Kartomi writes the following, using an example close to ours:

> African drum rhythms may be at the base of many syncopated rhythms idiom-atic of jazz. But their musical and extramusical meanings have all been changed in their very essence in the new context. An investigation into jazz that simply involved the mechanical invoicing of its African, European, and other musical traits would be missing the point of the whole process that brought this music into being.[18]

On the other hand, it would be absurd to entirely dismiss the validity of an inquiry regarding the origins of certain musical traits. Such an inquiry can be considered pertinent as long as it meets two conditions: first, that the ascription of origin can be convincingly argued from a historical, philological, organologi-cal, or other such point of view; second, that this ascription tells us something about what the music in question means in the present.

As for the case of syncopation, if we wish to meet the first of these criteria, we need to spend a bit more time on what scholars of African music have to say. From early on these scholars noted the strong presence of certain rhythmic phrases in African music that were unprecedented according to Western classical music norms. The chief aspect of these phrases was the mixture of binary and ternary units (which in technical terms could be represented by quarter notes and dotted quarter notes).

A. M. Jones, author of the aforementioned book reviewed by Kolinski, for-mulated the issue in the following way: Western rhythm is *divisive*, for it is based on the division of a given duration into equal parts. Thus, as every music theory textbook teaches us, the subdivision of a whole note is two half notes, the subdivi-sion of each of these is two quarter notes, and so forth. Whereas African rhythm

Western classical music theory understands two types of meter: simple and compound. In simple meters, the units of time are binary. For example, in 2/4, 3/4, and 4/4, the units of time are quarter notes, whose subdivisions, which are always based on twos, are equivalent to *two* eighth notes or *four* sixteenth notes, and so forth. (The cases in which quarter notes are divided in a ternary way constitute exceptions to the rule; these are called "triplets" and require specific indications.) On the other hand, in compound meters, such as 6/8 or 12/8, the units of time are ternary and are represented by dotted quarter notes (subdivided thus into *three* eighth notes). But the fact is, there are no meters that systematically mix groupings of two and three pulsations, such as quarter notes and dotted quarter notes. It is precisely this mixture that plays such an important role in the musics of sub-Saharan Africa.[1]

1. Any of the conventional rhythmic figures can be used to illustrate the difference between binary and ternary values. Here I used quarter notes and dotted quarter notes, as they are used in the most common meters, such as in the given examples. However, in this book's transcriptions and analyses, I will generally use eighth notes and dotted eighth notes to represent ternary and binary values, respectively. This is in following common conventions for the notation of sambas, in which the meter is typically 2/4.

is *additive*, for it arrives at a given duration via the sum of smaller units that are grouped to form new units, which need not share a common denominator (as is the case with two and three).[19]

Simha Arom later revisited the issue. He recognized in African music an important group of rhythmic patterns that mixed binary and ternary groupings (our quarter notes and dotted quarter notes) to produce *even* rhythmic periods. For example, the sequence 3+3+2 (that is, two dotted quarter notes + a quarter note) constitutes a period of eight units; the sequence 3+2+3+2+2 constitutes a period of twelve units, and so forth. But any attempt to split these even periods in two, respecting their internal structuring, would invariably lead to two unequal *odd* parts. As such, in this type of rhythmic logic, a period of eight cannot be divided into 4+4, but only 3+5 (or 3+[3+2]); a period of twelve cannot be divided into equal parts (6+6), but only into near-equal parts (5+7, or [3+2]+[3+2+2]). Arom called this phenomenon "rhythmic oddity."[20]

How do these rhythmic patterns appear in African music? How do they behave within the repertoires? We cannot examine these issues at length without deviating too much from the topic of this book. But two observations will be useful. The first concerns what J. H. Kwabena Nketia called "time lines."[21] In many musical repertoires of sub-Saharan Africa, "time lines" articulated in handclaps, or on percussion instruments with high-pitched and penetrating timbres (like metallic idiophones such as the *agogô* [or bell] of Brazilian samba schools), function as a type of metronome, an aural guide that allows for a general coordinating amid astonishingly complex polyrhythms. The fact is that "time lines" have a special predilection for the types of asymmetrical patterns mentioned earlier, and these patterns are repeated as *ostinati*, from the beginning to the end of particular pieces.

The second important observation speaks to the fact that in many such cases, the repetition is not strict but rather constitutes what Arom baptized as "ostinato with variations."[22] Consequently, the asymmetrical rhythmic pattern is repeated or varied in an improvised fashion by the musician responsible for the "time line."

These variations in many cases obey the principle of subdivision. That is, they are broken down into smaller values, always in accordance with the main groupings of the rhythmic pattern. For example, 3+3+2 can be subdivided into (2+1)+(2+1)+(2) or into (1+2)+(1+2)+(2), and so forth.

Although these types of rhythmic figures can occur in Western classical music—especially in so-called "contemporary music"—they are not the common practice and are considered to be difficult to perform. In sub-Saharan Africa, on the other hand, these figures are widespread in the region's music, even being found in children's songs.

But of more direct interest to us is that on this point Brazil is much closer to Africa than to Europe. Indeed, Brazilian music is brimming with cases that could be described much more adequately using concepts such as those presented above than by way of the theory of measures. In Maranhão's *Tambor de mina*, in Pernambuco's *Xangô* and its *maracatu*, in Bahia's Candomblé and its *capoeira*, in Rio's *Macumba* and its samba,[23] among others, patterns such as 3+3+2, 3+2+3+2+2, and 3+2+2+3+2+2+2 are part of musicians' daily lives.[24] These patterns in many cases act precisely as "time lines," appearing in the form of handclaps or the rhythm of the *agogô* or *tamborim* (small frame drum), in strict or varied *ostinati*, often serving to coordinate polyrhythms that are nearly as complex as those of Africa.[25] It therefore seems reasonable to suppose that they are part of a musical heritage brought from the continent of Africa, even if the context and the meaning of this heritage have been greatly transfigured.

It is important to note that I am not proposing here the attribution of a specific origin to a given rhythmic pattern. As Fernando Ortiz wrote concerning a topic close to ours, that of Afro-Cuban music, "a rhythmic pattern, as with a simple geometric figure (a triangle, zigzag, circle, spiral, etc.), can be found in a number of cultures at the same time, without it being necessary nor probable that they communicated amongst each other."[26] But the same cannot be said of a rhythmic *system*, of a general logic of organizing durations (a case of what John Blacking would call "deep structure"[27]). This shift in the level of generality, as I see it, allows us to establish a more solid foundation for inquiries regarding the parentage of Brazilian rhythmic patterns.

In the nineteenth century, when academically trained composers began trying, for different reasons, to reproduce in their written music something of the rhythmic vivacity they sensed in the music of Africans and Afro-Brazilians, they did so, of course, by relying on the resources that were offered to them by the system in which they were educated. As noted above, this system does not foresee the interpolation of binary and ternary groupings (among other aspects of African music). The result is that these types of rhythms appeared in the sheet music as displaced, abnormal, irregular (requiring, for their proper performance, the graphic tool of the tie and the analytical tool of counting)—they appeared as, in a word, syncopations. As such, even if the notion of syncopation does not exist in African rhythm, it is through syncopations that, in Brazil, aspects of it came to be expressed in written music; or, if we prefer, it is through syncopations that written music makes reference to that which is African in the orally transmitted music of Brazil. It is in this sense, and this sense alone, that those who insisted that the origin of Brazilian syncopation was in Africa were correct.

But what is interesting in the Brazilian case is that it was by way of its contact with Afro-Brazilian musical practices that the classical European system of rhythm—of which written music in Brazil (including written popular music) is a part—began to be questioned. That which was permitted in the European case as merely a deviation from the norm—a tolerated deviation to be sure, a deviation even sought out as a type of variation, but always a deviation—began to be practiced as a quasi norm, even by musicians whose academic training had been limited to classical parameters. But the repetition and normalization of syncopation changed its meaning, constituting a different system that was no longer African or purely European, a system in which the academic notion of syncopation loses its *raison d'être*. (A line of reasoning similar to the one developed in the last two paragraphs might also be applicable to "syncopations" in jazz and in Cuban music, among others.)

Still, the use of the word "syncopation" to designate contrametric articulations was so constant in Brazil that it became, if you'll forgive the expression, a veritable "imported native category," not unlike coffee and mangoes. As such, today it is not only theorists and conservatory-trained musicians who speak of Brazilian "syncopations"; the word has entered the vocabulary of lay musicians and those who play popular music, whether they read music or not.

It is for this reason that, in contrast to Arom, Kubik, and other scholars of African music, who expunged the word "syncopation" from their vocabulary, I am going to allow myself to employ it occasionally in accordance with its local meaning, where "syncopation," unlike what European dictionaries and Greek

A rhythmic articulation will be said to be commetric when it occurs on the first, third, fifth, or seventh sixteenth note in 2/4; and will be said to be contrametric when it occurs at any of the other positions, as long as it is not followed by a new articulation in the subsequent position.

Commetric:

Contrametric:

In cases where the articulation occurs at the subsequent position, an articulation in the even positions can still be contrametric if there is some type of accent mark.

Commetric:

Contrametric:

etymology tell us, refers neither to a fracture nor a break, but rather to a perfectly regular, continuous, and common rhythmic tool.

As for the expressions commetricity and contrametricity, which I will adopt here, I think they need further elaboration, for Arom uses them with meanings different from those of Kolinski, and in both authors' uses there are internal contradictions, which I will not be able to discuss here without distancing myself considerably from the objectives of this book. I will employ these expressions in the limited sense described below, which I hope will suffice for the purposes of the book's argument.

The 3–3–2 Paradigm

One of the asymmetrical rhythms mentioned previously has been identified by Cuban musicologists as having played a significant role in their nation's music. It is a rhythm built on a cycle of eight pulses, or 3+3+2—two durations that are slightly longer than the third duration (to be exact, each of the two first durations is one and a half times longer than the third). Using conventional Western musical notation, this rhythm can be represented as follows:

Given that this rhythm is made up of three articulations, the Cubans call it *tresillo*, a term I have used in a number of publications.[28] But in an e-mail I received from the great Uruguayan composer and musicologist Coriún Aharónian (1940–2017), in which he was commenting on the first edition of *Feitiço decente* (the Portuguese version of the present book), he explained to me that to a non-Cuban Spanish speaker, it would be inappropriate to use the word *tresillo* in this way. Indeed, the most widespread meaning of the Spanish word *tresillo* is, in English, "triplet"— that is, three durations of *equal* value occupying the time normally attributed to two equal durations, which obviously does not apply here. He suggested that instead of *tresillo*, I use "3–3–2 pattern," an expression I have adopted for this book.[29]

The use of the 3–3–2 rhythmic pattern is one of many points of overlap between the popular music of Cuba and that of Brazil. The pattern can be found today in orally transmitted Brazilian music. We find it, for example, in the handclaps that accompany the *samba de roda* from Bahia, the *coco* of the northeast, and the *partido-alto* from Rio; and also in the *gongués* of the *maracatus* of Pernambuco,[30] as well as in various types of rhythms for Afro-Brazilian divinities, and so forth.

The 3–3–2 pattern also shows up in Brazil's printed music at least as early as 1856, when it figures in the intro to the *lundu* "Os beijos de frade" ("Friar's Kisses"), by Henrique Alves de Mesquita.[31] Subsequently, it shows up as the rhythmic accompaniment pattern in a vast number of printed popular music pieces, such as those of Ernesto Nazareth and his lesser known contemporaries, as well as in many pieces written by art music composers of the so-called *nacionalista* (nationalist) generation during the first half of the twentieth century, such as Heitor Villa-Lobos (1887–1959), Francisco Mignone (1897–1986), and Mozart Camargo Guarnieri (1907–1993).

In the printed Brazilian music of the nineteenth and early twentieth centuries, moreover, specific variations or subdivisions of the 3–3–2 pattern were particularly prominent. This is the most important of them:

The remarkable presence of this rhythmic figure in the era's music led Mário de Andrade to coin the expression "characteristic syncopation" as a reference to it. It is a debatable term, as we have seen, albeit legitimized through its usage, and will be adopted here for the sake of convenience.

I have noted that the "characteristic syncopation" could be considered a variation of the 3–3–2 pattern. Yet the grouping of the rhythmic values proposed in the conventional written version does not make it a subdivision of the 3–3–2 pattern but of the Western 2/4 meter, with its characteristic symmetry:

But in fact the same rhythm can be read within an asymmetric frame:

As such, what to Mário de Andrade was a "syncopation" (albeit "characteristic") can be viewed as a 3–3–2 pattern in which each ternary group is subdivided into (1+2).

Moreover, if we approach it from the other direction—that is, if we subdivide the ternary groups into (2+1)—the result is a rhythmic figure that also shows up frequently in Brazilian popular music (for example, in *cavaquinho* [small four-stringed guitar] accompaniment patterns of early twentieth-century *choros*). Furthermore, since it is constituted by five articulations, Cuban musicologists have dubbed this figure (which is also common in Cuba) a *cinquillo*[32]:

If, finally, we subdivide the second ternary group, but not the first, we get another rhythmic figure that is widespread in the Brazilian music of the second half of the nineteenth century and early twentieth century:

This is the internationally known "habanera rhythm." The name is misleading, as it suggests the rhythm was introduced into Brazilian music (indeed, into Latin American music generally) by way of the *habanera* musical genre. Yet as we will see, the *habanera* is but one of the ways in which this rhythm is articulated in these musics. In particular, this accompaniment pattern was also associated with the tango until the early twentieth century and was known, too, as the "tango rhythm." But, once again for the sake of convenience, "habanera rhythm" is the phrase that will be used in this book.

I propose calling this set of variations the "3–3–2 Paradigm." Its most notable characteristic is the recurring contrametric emphasis on the fourth pulsation (or, in conventional notation, on the fourth sixteenth note) of a group of eight, which subdivides it into two unequal near-halves (3+5). This emphasis distinguishes it from rhythmic patterns common in Western classical music practices, in which the equivalent emphasis would not be on the fourth, but rather on the fifth, pulsation (that is, at the beginning of the second beat of a conventional, "divisive," and symmetrical 2/4).

We therefore have here the logic of rhythmic oddity being applied to rhythmic figures typically treated according to the binary logic of "regular" meters. In this way, I am in step with the intuition of the few twentieth-century musicologists who sought to overcome their own biases regarding the rhythmic organization they encountered in their studies of Latin American music. Argeliers León, for example, says of the *tresillo* that "the accentuations have not been misplaced; what happened was that the music freed itself from regular and constant accentuations, and in their place a new rhythmic meaning took root... Not a misplacement, but a new rhythmic articulation."[33] And Eurico Nogueira França: "In Afro-Brazilian music, the polyrhythm derives from smaller metric units than those utilized in European meters. Our typical formula: sixteenth note, eighth note, sixteenth note, has nothing to do, of course, with the unit constituted by quarter notes."[34]

But it is necessary to clarify that it is not solely by way of formal criteria that I understand the "characteristic syncopation" as a variation of the 3–3–2 pattern. The matter, so well put by Argeliers León, is above all about "rhythmic feeling." From the "purely formal" point of view—if such a thing exists—there is no reason to consider the sequence 12122 to be segmented as 12/12/2 instead of as 121/22; both readings are possible. Nevertheless, as an ethnomusicologist, my task is to understand the relevant readings from the point of view of a given historical and cultural context, or, more broadly, how the different "readings" align. Ultimately, I am concerned with comprehending the meanings and contents that organize the rhythmic material (and are organized by it), for without such meanings and contents, the rhythm remains *indeterminate*.[35] Only thenceforth will we be ready to move from music's surface structure to its deep structure (to take up the somewhat outmoded Chomskian terms employed by John Blacking in *How Musical Is Man?*).

Indeed—and speaking at quite a broad level of generality—I think a significant parcel of Brazilian musical culture "reads" the "characteristic syncopation," just as with the "habanera rhythm," as variations of the 3–3–2 pattern; and that my contribution here does little more than give this reading an explicit formulation.

At least as far as the printed Brazilian music from the second half of the nineteenth century and the first decades of the twentieth century is concerned, the three rhythmic patterns I mentioned above seem to meet certain cultural criteria of equivalence. They are accepted as interchangeable by composers, publishers, and the public. Their reversibility is demonstrated in a number of ways: they turn up—sometimes one, sometimes another—as the underlying accompaniment to different pieces of the same genre, in different parts of the same piece, and even in different sections of the same part of the same piece (as an example, and as the apotheosis of this practice, listen to "Batuque"[36] for piano, by Ernesto Nazareth). From the point of view of the musical content, what allows for this relative indifference concerning the use of one rhythm or another is, as we have seen, the fact that all of the rhythms share the syntactic mark on the fourth sixteenth note of the cycle of eight. But, from the point of view of the language (found in lyrics, titles, dedications, announcements, and so forth) that is associated with these rhythmic patterns, the interchangeability results from the link that—as Nazareth's "Batuque" once again demonstrates—had been constructed between these rhythms and certain representations of Afro-Brazilians (as viewed, of course, from the perspective of the portion of society that participated in sheet music commerce).[37]

These representations are also expressed in the names of certain musical genres, which were as interchangeable as the accompaniment patterns. Consequently, we will see that *lundu, polca-lundu, cateretê, fado, chula, tango, habanera, maxixe*, and various other combinations of these names, which were stamped onto the covers of nineteenth-century Brazilian sheet music, basically told us that the music was "syncopated," "typically Brazilian," and conducive to the "requebrados mestiços" (*mestiço*[38] hip shakes).[39]

The argument that there is a link between the 3–3–2 Paradigm's contrametricity (or a conception of what "syncopated" music might be) and a particular conception of the "Afro-Brazilian" and the "typically Brazilian" will be developed in part 1 of the book. In part 2 we will see that around 1930, these musical conceptions and their extra-musical associations transition toward a new rhythmic paradigm and toward new ideas about what it is "to be Brazilian," and samba replaces the entangled genres that preceded it as Brazilian popular music par excellence.

The Estácio Paradigm

This new rhythmic paradigm, which becomes prominent in the 1930s, includes rhythmic patterns that, in contrast to the rhythms discussed in the previous section, went nearly unnoticed in the Brazilian musicological literature of the twentieth century. The first person to draw my attention to these other rhythms was the musician and researcher Carlos Didier. In 1984 he published a small note in the magazine *O Catacumba*:

> The sambas of Ismael Silva, Bide, and Nilton Bastos [*sambistas* of the Estácio neighborhood, who became prominent in the 1930s], among others, differentiated themselves from those enshrined by Sinhô [a *sambista* of the Cidade Nova

neighborhood who rose to prominence in the 1920s], at least in the greater complexity of their rhythmic pulsation. While these retained vestiges of old *maxixes*, the sambas that came from Estácio [were characterized] by the aggregation of another rhythmic pattern to the beat. Or else, let's listen: tap the subdivision described below on the top of a table, on a bottle, or on a guitar. At the same time, whistle the introduction to the samba "Jura" ["Swear"], a composition by Sinhô [1928]:

Now, try it with the following subdivision, and change the repertoire. This time hum the samba "Se você jurar" ["If You Swear"], by Ismael Silva and Nilton Bastos [1931]:

It's a whole different thing, right? And that was just one of the tricks of those *bambas [sambistas]*[40] who spent their time up there in Estácio![41]

The composers and sambas cited by Didier will be looked at in great detail in part 2 of the book. For now, what I would like to use from this citation is the second musical example, which introduces us to a rhythmic pattern that is entirely different from those that have heretofore been examined.[42]

In terms of academic works, I have found references to such patterns only in the work of Kazadi wa Mukuna, Samuel Araújo, and Gerhard Kubik.[43] These references, however, are concerned with samba from the period between the 1970s and the 1990s, rather than, as in Didier's case, with the transition from the 1920s to the 1930s.

In his work on Bantu elements in Brazilian popular music, Mukuna notes a particular rhythmic cycle (to which he does not give a specific name) found in samba and that "has not been discussed by scholars."[44] He contrasts this rhythmic cycle with the "characteristic syncopation," also present in samba, but only by way of *lundu*.[45] Here it is:[46]

Mukuna offers a variation of this rhythm, shown below:

Not only the "characteristic syncopation" but also the cycle we just cited and its variation are, according to Mukuna, found in the music of certain regions of the Democratic Republic of Congo.[47]

The author subdivides this rhythmic cycle into sixteen eighth notes, segmented into two groups, one of seven and another of nine. Going further still, however, it is also possible to conceive of it—at a second level of segmentation—as being composed of $(2+2+3)+(2+2+2+3)$ eighth notes, which, as we have seen, constitutes a case of rhythmic oddity. Mukuna then affirms the following: "Of these two samba rhythms, that is, the one inherited from lundu and the [new] cycle, the latter can be considered to be the most representative samba rhythm, especially in its popular form."[48] And later he speaks of "Rio de Janeiro, where the timeline of 16 pulsations [that is, the rhythmic figure in question] would have been introduced into samba, thus characterizing so-called 'Carioca samba.'"[49]

As such, we see a series of variables being associated with the two rhythmic figures Mukuna counterposes. The new cycle is associated with both samba's "popular" form (as opposed implicitly to its "folk" form) and its "Carioca" form (as opposed implicitly to the "Bahian" form, which we will see later). On the other hand, the "characteristic syncopation" is associated with *lundu*, a genre of music and dance that was popular in Brazil roughly one hundred years before samba. This suggests that the new cycle, precisely because it is new (at least in the context of samba), would be "more representative"—that is, capable of representing samba in all its most original aspects and independent of older Brazilian genres.

Finally, Mukuna affirms that the new cycle "is often played by the *tamborim* in the percussion orchestration."[50] The *tamborim*'s association with the rhythm is reinforced by Samuel Araújo, who offers an example similar to Mukuna's, calling it the "*tamborim* cycle" or "*tamborim* pattern" (albeit notating it using the sixteenth note as the smallest unit rather than the eighth note):[51]

From the outset, I want to note that in my own transcriptions of this rhythmic figure and its variations, I will use the graphic convention that has been customary in samba sheet music since "Pelo telefone" ("On the Telephone"), and which is used by Didier and Araújo (but not by Mukuna): I will take the sixteenth note as the smallest unit. Moreover, and also in accordance with the customary use in Brazilian popular music over the course of the twentieth century, I will write these rhythms using a 2/4 meter, which means the complete cycle (sixteen sixteenth notes) constitutes two measures.

For his part, Kubik writes the following:

Anyone familiar with Brazilian street *samba,* as it can be seen at Carnival time in Rio de Janeiro . . . might be conscious of a characteristic percussive pattern which permeates this music as a most persistent trait. It can be played on various instruments, for instance on a high-pitched drum . . . or even on a guitar. It is a focal element in which all the other instrumentalists, the singers and dancers find a pivot point for their orientation.[52]

Kubik echoes Mukuna in emphasizing the significance of the rhythmic figure underscored here. It is, he insists, a focal element, a pivot point around which the other elements revolve. The Austrian ethnomusicologist subsequently transcribes—using a method he created—two versions of this rhythmic figure (which he claims, moreover, is characteristic of certain parts of Angola and the Democratic Republic of Congo). These are quite similar to what was notated by Mukuna and Araújo, with only one difference: they invert the positions of the "7" and the "9." In other words, whereas Kubik writes (2+2+2+3)+(2+2+3), they write (2+2+3)+(2+2+2+3).

Figures such as those notated by the above-cited authors can commonly be heard on Carioca samba recordings from the 1960s onward, if not earlier. I will offer just a few examples to illustrate this. Given that the authors attribute such importance to the *tamborim* in introducing the figures, it is with this instrument that I begin.

The following rhythmic pattern can be heard played by the *tamborim* on the recording "Sobrado dourado" ("Golden House") (public domain, LP *Rosa de ouro,* 1965) and on that of "Leva, meu samba" ("Tell [Her], Samba of Mine"), by the samba's author Ataulfo Alves (LP *Ataulfo Alves e suas pastoras,* 1958), among others:

But it is not only the *tamborim* that performs these patterns. These rhythms can also be found in the *cuíca* (friction drum) part. And in fact, it is the *cuíca,* together with the *surdo* (bass drum) and indeed the *tamborim,* that will make up, as we will see, the trio of instruments emblematic of the new samba style that emerges in the 1930s. The following rhythmic patterns can be heard, performed by *cuícas,* on the recordings of "O bem e o mal" ("Good and Evil") (Nelson Cavaquinho-Guilherme de Brito) as recorded by Nelson Cavaquinho (LP *Quando eu me chamar saudade,* rereleased on CD by EMI, 1991) and "Sei lá, Mangueira" ("Whatever, Mangueira") (Paulinho da Viola-Hermínio Bello de Carvalho), as recorded by Elizeth Cardoso (LP *A bossa eterna de Elizeth e Ciro,* vol. 2, Copacabana, 1969), among many others:[53]

Interestingly, Mukuna mentions only one variation in the passage I cited at the beginning of this section, and I could not find it in either the *tamborim* part or the *cuíca* part on the recordings I consulted. Where I did find it, though, was in the rhythm with which a bottle is struck on Paulinho da Viola's recording of "Duas horas da manhã" ("Two O'Clock in the Morning") (Nelson Cavaquinho-A. Monteiro) (from the LP *Quando eu me chamar saudade*, rereleased on CD by EMI, 1991).

Any resident of Rio de Janeiro who has had some contact with *rodas de samba* (samba rings or, less literally, samba gatherings) will have no problem aurally recognizing these figures, or even tapping out the rhythms on a table.[54] But we do not yet know what their formal properties are, what makes it possible to recognize them. In other words, we do not know what is common to all the variations cited by Didier, Mukuna, Araújo, and Kubik, heard on recordings by Paulinho da Viola, Nelson Cavaquinho, and so many others, played on *tamborins*, *cuícas*, and bottles—not to mention the other instruments of which I have given no examples. Nor do we know what allows us, in all these cases, to clearly recognize that this rhythm belongs to Carioca samba in its most well-known version, a version that was incredibly widespread from the mid-1930s to the late 1980s.

The reader will surely have noted that defining this commonality is easier if we turn to what we have already learned about African rhythm. The rhythmic patterns we are discussing here, just like those of the 3–3–2 Paradigm, correspond to the definition of Jones's "additive rhythms," of Nketia's "time lines," and of Arom's "rhythmic oddity." As such, the 3–3–2 Paradigm corresponds to the rhythmic oddity in a cycle of eight pulses (3+3+2, and its variations); meanwhile, the new paradigm, which is prevalent in more recent Carioca samba, corresponds to the rhythmic oddity in a cycle of sixteen pulsations (2+2+3+2+2+2+3, and its variations).

We could go into more depth describing these two paradigms, but for the purposes of this book, I believe that what has heretofore been said is sufficient.[55] I would like only to add that in the case of the Estácio Paradigm, the existence of a larger number of binary groupings (five) allows for the existence of two basic versions. The first, introduced above, is predominant in more recent samba (at least until around 1990). It corresponds to the rhythmic oddity of the version Arom presents, where the values can be grouped in 7+9 or 9+7; the five binary groupings end up being two on one side, three on the other.

But in part 2 of the book, we will encounter another version, predominant in the 1928–1933 period, which is that of the birth and consolidation of the style. This version was not one of those described by Arom and it consists of moving one of the binary groupings to the other side, leaving only one on one side and four on the other: (2+3)+(2+2+2+2+3), or 5+11. It shares with the previously mentioned version the asymmetry and the interpolation of ternary and binary values, which is what distinguishes both from "regular" meters. But this other version permits the realization of more commetric variations than the first. This leads me to think it can be treated as a "transitional version," more easily assimilable by performers and the audience at a time when the new samba style was first taking root. This point will be discussed in the book's final chapters.

PART ONE

FROM *LUNDU* TO SAMBA

"Sweet *Lundus*, for Massa to Dream"

The word *lundu*, also sometimes written as *londu, lundum, landum*, and other variations, has designated different things at different times, but all of them are generally considered to be interconnected. It was the name of some of the Black and *mestiço* dances at the turn of the nineteenth century, of a nineteenth-century genre of salon music for piano and voice, and of an early twentieth-century repertoire of commercially recorded songs. I will deal primarily with the salon *lundu* to which we have access via the sheet music published in Brazil during the second half of the nineteenth century; other aspects of *lundu* will be addressed more briefly over the course of the exposition. As I will later explain, this chapter also dedicates space to *modinha*, a Luso-Brazilian genre of romantic song historically associated with *lundu*.

The oldest known reference to a dance called *lundu* comes from 1780, in a letter written by the count of Povolide,[1] a Portuguese aristocrat who had been governor of Pernambuco. In the letter the count defended some of the enslaved Black celebrants' dances against accusations made by the Tribunal of the Inquisition:

The blacks . . . dance and spin like harlequins, and others dance with diverse body movements, which even if not the most innocent, are like the *fandangos* of Castile, and *fofas* of Portugal, and the lundus of whites and *pardos* [people of mixed race] of that country [Portugal].[2]

Lundu is also mentioned around 1780 in verses penned by the Portuguese poet Nicolau Tolentino.[3] In two popular Portuguese *entremeses*[4] from 1784 and 1787, which included Black characters, José Ramos Tinhorão has found mentions of a *baile* (dance) called *lundu*.[5] In Brazil, also in the late eighteenth century, the poet Tomás Antônio Gonzaga mentions this dance in his *Cartas chilenas* (*Chilean Letters*).[6]

The African origin of the *lundu* dance was accepted as fact by researchers in the twentieth century. According to the *Dicionário musical brasileiro* (*DMB, Brazilian Musical Dictionary*), it is a "dance of black-African origin, brought by Bantu slaves from the regions of Angola and the Congo."[7] Mário de Andrade speaks of *lundu* as "a characteristic form of Negro folklore, perhaps the most characteristic of the time [that is, the late eighteenth century], and certainly the most widespread."[8] And Araújo writes that "the lundu ..., a direct descendent of the African *batuque*, was the valve of emotional balance utilized by slaves to temper the hardships of exile and the pains of slavery."[9]

Put in this way, however, these statements are debatable, for the eighteenth and early nineteenth-century documentation does not mention *lundu* as either an African dance or as a dance characteristic of enslaved Africans. The letter from the count of Povolide, cited above, speaks of *lundu* as being "of whites and *pardos* of that country [Portugal]." In the aforementioned *Cartas chilenas*, the person who dances *lundu* is a "*mulata*" (mixed-race woman).[10] And in the *entremeses* cited by Tinhorão, which were sung popular theater plays, Black *characters* are the ones who dance "*lundum*" during scenes set in the homes of the white masters, who also participate. However, these characters were portrayed by white actors for an audience that was also white and frequented the theaters of Lisbon and other Portuguese cities. Furthermore, the descriptions of the *lundu* choreography we have from the beginning of the nineteenth century inhibit us from attributing it exclusively to Black people, for in the *lundu* dance, notwithstanding the bodily movements attributed to Africans (such as the *umbigada* [belly bounce], which we will discuss later), we also see a strong Iberian influence, as Tinhorão and others have noted.[11]

In sum, *lundu* dancing was, as Tinhorão affirms for the turn of the nineteenth century, "more cultivated by whites and *mestiços* than by blacks."[12] The "*mestiço*" *lundu* was, however, proposed as a representation, direct or veiled—and as we will see, nearly always humorous—of aspects of the era's Afro-Brazilian context.

From the 1830s on, when the printing of music began in Brazil, the word *lundu* also starts to be used to designate a genre of music independent of any dance: a genre of printed music for piano and voice. *Lundu* as a genre of song, however, is indissolubly linked to *modinha*, a word whose musical usage began in Lisbon also during the late eighteenth century. In his important study of *modinha*, Mário de Andrade writes the following: "the fact is that *modinha* and *lundum* were completely entangled."[13] And Bruno Kiefer: "In the previous century [the nineteenth,] confusing *modinha* and *lundu* was not uncommon."[14] The classic book on the topic, by Mozart de Araújo, is in fact titled *A modinha e o lundu no século XVIII* (*Modinha and Lundu in the Eighteenth Century*); later musicologists, such as Edilson Lima and Paulo Castagna, have also connected the two genres in the titles of their texts. The conjoined scholarly treatment of the genres reflects what Araújo calls their "historical connections."[15] Because of such connections, despite the fact that my main point of interest here is *lundu*, I will also discuss *modinha*.

Modinha is, first of all, the diminutive of *moda*, a word that in the eighteenth century, in both Portugal and Brazil, was widely used to designate popular songs. We see, for example, in a traveler's account published in the early eighteenth century, a reference to the existence, in Bahia, of a "famous musician and performer of these profane *modas*" (in which *modas* means "songs" or "tunes"), without further elaboration.[16]

As Luiz Heitor Corrêa de Azevedo notes in his entry on *modinha* for the *Dicionário do folclore brasileiro* (*DFB, Dictionary of Brazilian Folklore*), "it is in the nature of the [Portuguese] language and in the tradition of the composers such use of the diminutive; the same thing happens with *fado* and *fadinho*, *polca* and *polquinha*, tango and *tanguinho*, *choro* and *chorinho*, etc."[17] In this case, however, the use of the diminutive spread at precisely the moment during which its meaning was changing. While the word *moda* continued to be used as a generic term for "song,"[18] *modinha* began to be used, in Lisbon, during the 1780s, no longer as a diminutive but rather as a designation for a specific type of song.[19] These were urban songs, *novamente compostas* (newly composed), as they would say. That is, these songs were presented as "novelties" and in many cases signed by their authors, who signed and published them commercially as sheet music with their respective lyrics in print. *Modinha* was, starting in the late eighteenth century, the Portuguese name for these songs, which were produced and consumed in an urban context, anticipating in part what came to be called, in the twentieth century, a "popular" or "pop" song, in contrast to a "traditional" or "folk" song.

We see this new use of the word *modinha* in the *Jornal de Modinhas*, published in Lisbon between 1792 and 1796 by French publishers Milcent and Maréchal. This was the first Portuguese musical periodical, routinely publishing two *modinhas* per month, one on the first of the month, another on the fifteenth.[20] As Marcos Magalhães notes, one of the most striking aspects of the way in which the periodical presented the *modinhas* is the "emphasis given to the issue of novelty."[21] Of the 104 *modinhas* published by the periodical, no fewer than twenty-nine had the word "new" or the expression "newly composed" (meaning recently composed) in their very titles.[22]

Some late eighteenth-century documents associate these new *modinhas* with a musical influence arriving in the Portuguese metropolis from what was then an immense overseas colony, Brazil. While never mentioning *modinhas*, the German botanist Heinrich Friedrich Link, who spent some time in Portugal during his youth (1797–1799), bears witness to these musical influences in his book of travels. The scene takes place at the mansion of a wealthy family in a small city near Serra da Estrela, in northeastern Portugal:

> We were daily in company with the principal people of this little town, where the young but half speechless girls, and the young but cheerful married women, passed their time in a pleasant manner without play. . . . General conversation prevailed, and they joined in a general chorus. We heard a number of soft plaintive Portuguese songs, generally on the pains of love, and frequently on some charming shepherdess (*linda pastora*). Among these the Brasileros [*sic*], or brasil [*sic*] songs, were distinguished by their great variety, gaiety and wit, like the nation from which they spring.[23]

But the most well-known account of the era, which does explicitly mention *modinhas* of Brazilian origin, is that of the English writer William Beckford, who was in Portugal a number of times between 1787 and 1798. Although well known by those who are familiar with the history of *modinhas*, the text is perhaps worth citing in full:

> Those who never heard modinhas must and will remain ignorant of the most voluptuous and bewitching music that ever existed since the days of the Sybarites. They consist of languid interrupted measures, as if the breath was gone with excess of rapture, and the soul panting to fly out of you and incorporate itself with the beloved object. With a childish carelessness they steal into the heart before it has time to arm itself against their enervating influences. You fancy you are swallowing milk and you are swallowing poison. As to myself, I must confess I am a slave to modinhas, and when I think of them cannot endure the idea of quitting Portugal. Could I indulge the least hopes of surviving a two month's voyage, nothing should prevent me setting off for Brazil, the native land of Modinhas, and living in tents . . . , and swinging in hammocks and gliding over smooth mats with youths crowned with jasmine and girls diffusing at every motion the perfumes of roses.[24]

Literary evidence such as this was cited by Brazilian researchers throughout the nineteenth and twentieth centuries to assert *modinha*'s Brazilian origin. However, this assertion runs up against two problems. The first is that there is not a single document from the eighteenth century that attests explicitly to the existence of *modinhas* in Portuguese America. The second is that, although some *modinhas* published in late eighteenth-century Lisbon have titles such as "Moda brazileira" ("Brazilian Moda"), "Moda nova brazileira" ("New Brazilian Moda"), and "Xula carioca" ("Carioca Xula"), these represent but a tiny fraction of the repertoire in question. Moreover, in neither these few *modas brasileiras* (Brazilian *modas*) nor the rest of the published repertoire is there any indication of anything in the music that is specifically "Brazilian."

Also central to the argument about the Brazilian origins of *modinha* is Domingos Caldas Barbosa, a *mestiço* Brazilian poet—perhaps even a guitar player—who found fame while living in Lisbon from the mid-1770s to his death in 1800. Born around 1740 in Rio de Janeiro to a Portuguese father and an African mother who was enslaved and later freed, Caldas Barbosa studied with the Jesuits in his city of birth, leaving in 1763 for the University of Coimbra, in Portugal, to pursue the study of law.[25] Prior to 1775 he established himself in Lisbon under the patronage of aristocrats, becoming well known in the court and in circles of what was known as *poesia árcade* (Arcadian poetry).[26] Quite a bit of literary evidence attests to the activities and success of Caldas Barbosa in Lisbon at the end of the century as a poet, even as an improviser of verses. Some of his poetic work was collected at the end of his life in a book called *Viola de Lereno* (*Lereno's Viola*).

Caldas Barbosa has been viewed by Brazilian researchers as the person who introduced *modinhas* (and sung *lundus,* as we will subsequently see) into Portugal. The problem is that although his poems appear in a number of *modinha* collections of the era, there are no cases in which the music's authorship is ascribed to him. Instead, the authorship of the music is generally anonymous, with some exceptions of pieces by Portuguese musicians, such as Marcos Portugal, António Leal Moreira, and António José do Rêgo. The musical style of the anonymous *modinhas* is in no way different from the style of the *modinhas* signed by Portuguese composers.[27]

The first volume of *Viola de Lereno* appeared in 1798, thus it was while the author was still alive. But the second volume was not published until 1826, well after Caldas Barbosa's death. In the first volume—the only one the author himself could be said to have put together—the word *modinha* appears only twice (but in the same stanza), and the word *lundu* (or any cognate) not a single time. Here Caldas Barbosa calls his compositions *cantigas.* In the second volume, however, six poems are called *lundum.* (The word *modinha* appears just once in the second volume; it is the only time, in the work's two volumes, that it appears as a designation of a poem's genre.)

Two closely related aspects distinguish the latter of these from the other poems: the "lyric speaker" assumed by the poet, and his vocabulary. Here it is necessary to clarify that Caldas Barbosa used a literary *persona,* as was common among the so-called "Arcadian poets."[28] The title of the book itself references this: "Lereno" Selinuntino was Caldas Barbosa in the figure of an Arcadian shepherd, whose muses were also shepherdesses, answering to Latin names such as Nerina, Márcia, Lília, and Ulina.

But in the six *lundus* of the second volume, and there alone, Lereno the shepherd disappears without a trace and in his place appears another character, who designates himself as *o teu moleque* (your boy) (the word *moleque* being defined by the *DFB* as a "young black boy, a black male adolescent"[29]); whose muses are *iaiá* and *nhanhazinha* (terms defined also by the *DFB* as "a version of 'senhora' [miss] ... used by slaves in reference to the girls of the master's house"[30]); and who uses in his vocabulary terms such as *xarapim, arenga, moenga, angu,* and *quingombô,* which Andrade called a true "compendium of terminological Brazilianisms."[31]

What's more, in some cases the link between the lyric speaker and his muse takes on features of what Tinhorão called the "psychological position of the *moleque* [boy] in love [with his white ma'am]."[32] As such, we even find references to physical punishment, highlighting more explicitly the context of slavery and lending a masochistic tone to the amorous situation:

Chegar aos pés de iaiá	Come to the feet of *iaiá*
Ouvir chamar preguiçoso	Get called lazy
Levar um bofetãozinho	Get a little slap
É bem bom, é bem gostoso.[33]	It's quite good, it's quite delectable.

Only one of the six *lundu* poems does not display these characteristics, "Gentes de bem pegou nele" ("Good People Grabbed Him").[34] On the other hand, there is only one poem in the volume that displays these characteristics without being called a *lundu,* "Doçura de amor" ("The Sweetness of Love").[35] As such, we see that whoever organized the second volume of *Viola de Lereno* made some important decisions. First, the decision was made to include a type of poem that Caldas Barbosa himself had not included in the volume for which he was responsible, a type of poem in which the poet identifies himself not as the shepherd Lereno, but rather as an Afro-Brazilian. Second, these poems adhered nearly perfectly to the set of criteria used to categorize *lundus* more generally, criteria that, as we will see, correspond to those used by Brazilian *lundu* publishers starting in 1830, but which cannot, without anachronism, be attributed to Caldas Barbosa himself.

The poetic use of Brazilianisms, Afro-Brazilianisms, and words associated with the context of slavery also turns up in another Portuguese litero-musical corpus from the turn of the nineteenth century: Mss. 1595 and 1596 of the Biblioteca da Ajuda in Lisbon, introduced to the public in a 1968 article by Gerard Béhague.[36] These two manuscripts are rather aptly called *Modinhas* and *Modinhas do Brazil.*

Ms. 1596, *Modinhas do Brazil,* an anonymous document from the late eighteenth century, presents a number of pieces containing the terminological characteristics already noted for the *lundus* of the second volume of *Viola de Lereno*. In the case of *Modinhas do Brazil*, however, in contrast to *Viola de Lereno*, we also have access to the corresponding music, which allows us to analyze the subject more completely.

Appearing here once again are the terms *iaiá* and *nhanhazinha*, as well as *nhonhô* (*massa*)[37] and *sinhá*, which is not only a "gentle word for girl," as Béhague writes in the aforementioned article, but also "a version of 'senhora' [miss] . . . used by slaves in reference to the girls of the master's house."[38] The term *moleque* does not appear, but in one of the *modinhas* the author brazenly labels himself *nigrinho* (Black boy); and we see additional Brazilianisms, such as *mugangueirinha* and *fadar*.

On the other hand, in Ms. 1596 the poet never presents himself as "Lereno," and the only name with an Arcadian flavor is the "Nerina" from *Modinha 14*. As such, the contrast between the two literary *personae* found in *Viola de Lereno* is practically nonexistent in *Modinhas do Brazil*. This contrast, though, reappears in full force when these latter pieces are compared with the other manuscript of the Biblioteca da Ajuda that Béhague brought to light in the same article: Ms. 1595, titled simply *Modinhas*. The text of this other collection, as Béhague affirms, "corresponds exactly to the idyllic type of 18th century Portuguese popular poetry, dominated by the favorite subject of love and its resulting sufferings."[39] The manuscript employs Arcadian references (shepherd, Anarda, Márcia, and so on) in eight of its eleven pieces in Portuguese. And its solid European pedigree is reaffirmed (as if it were still necessary) by the interpolation of a piece in Italian, the aria "Nel cor più non mi sento," from the opera *L'Amor contrastato*, by Paisiello. In the world of Ms. 1595, however, there are only shepherds and shepherdesses; there are neither slaves nor *iaiás*. None of the Brazilianisms mentioned above finds a place here.

As for the musical aspects of the collection, here is what Béhague says: "the distinctive feature of this collection of Modinhas do Brasil [in opposition to the Ms. 1595, of Portuguese *modinhas*] . . . results, in fact, from the systematization of syncopations."[40] The insistent syncopations are not seen as merely a formal characteristic; they are understood as semantically charged. They are associated with "Brazil," with "Blackness," and with "the popular," three things that, in turn, seem to be associated with each other: "systematic syncopated vocal lines . . . can be associated with the 'vulgar' style of Brazilian modinhas"; "the syncopated figure [sixteenth note–eighth note–sixteenth note] is indeed identified with New World negro tradition"; the syncopations are "characteristic rhythmic traits of folk and popular music." Béhague also speaks of the "national qualities of the modinhas of the Ajuda collection," which would offer "a genuine Brazilian character, textually and musically."[41]

Béhague explicitly refers to the accompaniment patterns used throughout *Modinhas* 8, 17, and 18:

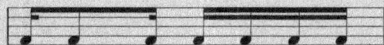

And in *Modinha* 16, measure 41:

The musicologist makes a distinction between the syncopations found in the accompaniments and the particular characteristics of the melodic syncopations:

> The vocal line of modinha no. 5 typically systematizes a rhythmic procedure much closer to the Brazilian musical vernacular than the above-mentioned syncopation. This procedure is a simple suspension (by ties over the bar line) used at cadential points provoking feminine endings of the phrase.[1]

The same type of syncopation was treasured by Mário de Andrade in his analysis of the 1834 *lundu* "Lá no Largo da Sé" ("There in Sé Plaza"):

> [Something] that only living national composers, interested in the work of Brazilian musical matter, had to specify: the syncopated anticipation, *going from one bar to another*, in cadential movements. . . . In an extremely rare case of which I only know [one other example] from the second half of the century . . . , Cândido Inácio da Silva already firmly systematizes the eighth-note syncopation in the first beat of a 2/4 [meter], just as [the *lundu* composers of the second half of the nineteenth century], and, *more than these*, with an attuned ear, the rhythmic anticipations of our popular song; it is extraordinary. (emphasis added)[2]

Both Béhague and Andrade implicitly establish a hierarchy between two types of syncopation: the syncopation within the measure—and even within a single beat—and that which goes from one measure to another. The latter is considered closest to popular music practices in Brazil.

Here are the corresponding musical examples:

Os   me   dei - xas   que   tú   dás____   etc....

da   al - gi - bei - ra   ti - ra'a   pa - ta - ca

In the following paragraphs, I will try to establish a typology of the contrametricity of Ms. 1596, aiming to go beyond the initial steps taken by Béhague and Andrade to classify the syncopations they encountered.[3] After all, Andrade speaks, as we have seen, of the "characteristic syncopation," while Béhague states that certain syncopations are "much closer to the Brazilian musical vernacular."[4] These statements establish a differentiation between types of syncopations, thus contrasting the vague manner in which "African American syncopations" are typically treated. I would like to go a bit further in this differentiating, specifying characteristics of the melodic contrametricity we encounter here.

The first type of contrametricity found in abundance in Ms. 1596 is what I will call, together with Mário de Andrade, the "characteristic syncopation." It appears, for example, in *Modinha* 1, measure 2, among various others:

One of the possible variations of the characteristic syncopation consists of omitting its first sixteenth note, as is done repeatedly in *Modinha* 17. Another variation includes substituting two eighth notes in the second beat for a new syncopation that mimics the first, as in *Modinhas* 4, 6, 16, and 17. In some cases, these two identical syncopations are joined by a tie, generating a first instance of syncopations across beats rather than an isolated syncopation within single beats.

Another case is that of anacrustic phrases beginning with eighth-note syncopations, such as in *Modinha* 6, measure 5 (and throughout the whole refrain of this *modinha*):

A third type of contrametricity, different from the preceding one, appears at the end rather than at the beginning of the musical phrases. This has already been mentioned, and is seen in phrases with weak endings, which Béhague considered to be "much closer to the Brazilian musical vernacular."[5]

To conclude this summary presentation of the different types of contrametricity that come into play in Ms. 1596, I will give two examples—albeit occurring much less frequently—in which the types of syncopation we have examined come together, giving rise to heavily contrametric phrases. These come from *Modinha* 6, measures 3 to 5, and *Modinha* 17, measures 18 and 19:

Examining the music in Ms. 1596 allows us to see the occurrence of three types of contrametric rhythmic figures: phrases based on the "characteristic syncopation" and its variations; contrametric anacruses; and contrametric weak endings. Generally speaking, it shows a preference for syncopations within beats, and above all on the first beat (in 2/4). Syncopations across beats and across bar lines also appear, but to a lesser degree. These characteristics will be compared later with the types of contrametricity found in other contexts.

1. Béhague, "Biblioteca da Ajuda," 62.

2. Andrade, "Candido Inácio da Silva," 220.

3. My source here is Béhague, "Biblioteca da Ajuda," which provides in facsimile the music of twelve of the thirty *modinhas* from Ms. 1596: that of numbers 1, 2, 3, 4, 5, 6, 7, 8, 16, 17, 18, and 26. The last of these is in 6/8, and the others are in 2/4, a meter, as Béhague says, "so common in the whole of Brazilian urban popular music which emerged in the late XIXth century" (p. 59). All of the *modinhas* in 2/4 presented by the musicologist present a strong contrametric character, with the exception of number 3.

4. Béhague, "Biblioteca da Ajuda," 62.

5. Béhague, "Biblioteca da Ajuda," 62.

Ms. 1596's association with the Afro-Brazilian context is reinforced considerably by the written indications that precede two of the pieces: "Este acompanhamento devese tocar pela Bahia" (this accompaniment must be played in Bahia), as it says for number 8, and "*rasgado*" (literally, "torn," also referring to the accompaniment), for number 17.

Béhague interprets the first phrase as an attribution of origin ("pela Bahia" = "around Bahia," in Béhague's translation),[42] while Tinhorão interprets it as a stylistic indication ("pela Bahia" = "as it is done in Bahia").[43] Either of the two interpretations would suggest a link between the accompaniment style and Black Brazilians, for, according to Béhague, the "New World negro tradition [is] best represented in Brazil by the state of Bahia."[44]

As for *rasgado*, Béhague sees it as "a very specific colloquialism of slangy character, meaning 'with enthusiasm, or impetuosity.'"[45] That is, as an indication of
musical expression. The word also appears in nineteenth-century sources with
the same meaning, such as in the comedy *O juiz de paz na roça* (*The Judge in the
Countryside*), by Martins Pena.[46] What is interesting about this word, however,
is that it was originally an indication not of expression but of instrumental technique, a technique employed by the right hand when playing the guitar. *Rasgado*
is the Portuguese-language version of the Spanish *rasgueado*, in which the right
hand strikes all of the strings at the same time with all of the fingers instead of
plucking each string as in *punteado* (in Portuguese, *ponteado*).[47]

The shift from *rasgado* as a type of technique to a term indicating expression can
be found in an article published around 1880, in a description of a performance
by a *viola* player who, after demonstrating the possibilities of the instrument for
concert music (played in the plucked style), moves on to a popular repertoire
(the writer mentions *fado*, *cateretê*, and samba): "spreading the right hand over
the bout of the instrument, while the left traversed the strings, he excited all of
his surroundings with one of these *rasgados*, which has been the ruin of many a
serious person."[48] The description of the *rasgado* from the point of view of technique is flawless. "The ruin of many a serious person," however, derives not from
the technique itself but rather from the affective expression to which it gives
way. The origin of this affective expression is the semantic charge conferred to
the *rasgado* by its particular repertoire (in Brazil). The word *rasgado* in the cited
article designates both things, and perhaps this is also the case in Ms. 1596.[49] It is
because of its association with a repertoire that is already in itself associated with
Black genres (*fado*, *cateretê*, and samba) that the word appearing at the beginning
of *Modinha* 17 may be so significant.[50]

We can thus conclude this exploration of the general characteristics of the contrasts between the two manuscripts with a small chart, which takes us from the
contradistinction between *modinhas* (which are not explicitly called Portuguese,
but are understood as such) and Brazilian *modinhas* to one between *modinhas*
and *lundus*, discussed in the paragraphs to follow.

Modinhas:	[Portuguese]	Brazilian
Poetic persona:	Shepherd	Nigrinho
Muse:	Anarda, etc.	Sinhá
Geographical Reference:	Italy (Aria by Paisiello)	"In Bahia"
Rhythm:	"Regular"	"Syncopated"
And starting in 1830:	Modinhas	Lundus

* * *

Printed music in Brazil begins in 1834, with Frenchman Pierre Laforge's move to Rio de Janeiro. But a collection of *modinhas* by the Carioca J. Francisco Leal, which included two *lundus*, "Menina vossé" ("You Girl") and "Esta Noite" ("Tonight"), had already been published by 1830.[51] As for the lyrics, the first of these could easily be attributed to Caldas Barbosa:

Menina, você que tem	Girl, you who have
Que comigo se enfadou	Who became distressed with me
Será porque seu Negrinho	Might it be because your Black guy
A seus pés não se curvou?	Did not bow down to your feet?

The second song raises an important issue regarding the characterization of *lundu* texts. Its categorization as a *lundu* is not due to any Afro-Brazilian references, for it contains none (or contains them only indirectly, as we will see), but rather because of another characteristic: it is "devoid of the sentimental sadness of the subject matter of *modinhas*," as Andrade writes. Or, to put it positively, it deals with love in a way that is cheerful and sexual rather than romantic. Instead of sentimentalism, we find the humor of the double entendre:

Esta noite, oh céus, que dita,	Tonight, oh heavens, what luck,
Com meu benzinho sonhei . . .	Of my love I did dream . . .
Eu passava pela rua,	I was out in the street
Ela chamou-me, eu entrei . . .	She called to me, I entered . . .
Deu-me um certo guisadinho	She gave me that stew
Que comi muito e gostei	Of which I ate much and did enjoy
Do ardor das pimentinhas	The heat of those little peppers
Nunca mais me esquecerei.	I will never forget it.

This *lundu* is the oldest example, as far as I know, of the all-too-common trope found in popular Brazilian music (and probably elsewhere), which consists of using food as a metaphor for sex. A brief list of *lundus* and sambas in which we find this trope includes "Muqueca sinhá" ("Moqueca Stew Ma'am") (1889), "O mugunzá" ("The Porridge") (1892), "Canjiquinha quente" ("Hot Little Canjica")[52] (Sinhô, 1930), "Vatapá"[53] (Dorival Caymmi, 1942), and "Os quindins de iaiá" ("Ma'am's Quindins") (Ary Barroso, 1941).[54] While it is not my intention—though it is not coincidental, either—all of the examples on this short list point to Bahia, either directly by way of the chosen delicacy, or somewhere within the lyrics themselves. This suggests that the sexualization of food would in itself be an allusion to the Afro-Brazilian. The *mulata*, after all, being the preferred object of masculine desires in *lundus* and in many sambas, was also the person responsible, in the kitchen, for the slave master's meals.

But whether the interpretation is accurate or not, it is nevertheless a fact that "Esta noite" is hardly an isolated case and that countless *lundus,* from the point of view of the lyrics, were considered *lundus* solely on the basis of their humor and not their Afro-Brazilian references, whether these were direct or veiled. Let's see why.

Here is Mário de Andrade's analysis of the *lundu* "Lá no Largo da Sé," an 1834 satire of progress that contains no hints of Afro-Brazilianisms:

> This [*lundu*] has ... an antilunduism. Its subject matter differs from the ideological textual conception with which the [salon] lundu would be established. The true and legitimate textual "style" of the lundus [implies a] sexual but comical text, or more generally graceful, humorous, devoid of the sentimental sadness of *modinhas.* The lundu of Cândido Inácio da Silva is not amorous in the least, let alone does it make any references to sexual Negro women or *mulatas,* as would the best and most characteristic "style" of the traditional bourgeois lundu. As for the character of its text, "Lá no Largo da Sé" is only a lundu for dealing cheerfully with ... the subject matter.[55]

Andrade establishes here the textual characteristics of what he calls a "traditional bourgeois lundu." First, cheerfulness; second, a sexual subject matter; third, references to *mulatas* and Black women. A typical *lundu* ("true and legitimate," "best and most characteristic") meets the three criteria. The *lundu* "Esta noite," mentioned above, meets only the first two; "Lá no Largo da Sé," for its part, meets only the first. But Cândido Inácio da Silva's *lundu* is not an exception either. It anticipates, in this regard, a great many of the *lundus* printed in the second half of the nineteenth century, which deal with a wide range of topics but nevertheless all fit under the umbrella of cheerfulness.

In fact, in the argumentation that begins in the paragraph following the one cited above, and which continues through the last third of his article, Andrade turns his attention precisely toward the role cheerfulness plays in characterizing *lundu.* The first point the author seeks to establish is Brazilian society's resistance—from its colonial formation to the mid-nineteenth century—to Black artistic expressions. Andrade recognizes that such expressions existed, were tolerated, and at times were even encouraged. But he insists that they never fused with white expressions, each continuing as "impenetrable," "hermetic chambers." As the author put it, "even Negro African words, designators of choreographic or musical things, samba, *urucungo,* marimba, etc., exclusively designated *things of Negroes* rather than of Brazilians in general"[56] (emphasis in original).

For Andrade, *lundu* would have been precisely the first of these "things of Negroes" to overcome the impermeability of white society:

lundu . . . is the first Negro African musical form to be disseminated amongst all the Brazilian classes and to become "national" music. It is the door opening for the characteristic syncopation. . . . It is the door cracked open for the texts that sing sexually of unchaste loves [between masters and slaves], the *mésalliances*, and becomes specialized in the extolment of the *mulata* above all else.[57]

But the opening of this "door" between the two hermetic chambers would have been helped along by a tactical resource:

The comicalness, the tease, the smile, was the psycho-social disguise that permitted the diffusion [of *lundu*] into the dominant classes. . . . The *mulata* initiated [it], and the Negro woman and Negro man, being literarily admitted into the classes of the haute and petite bourgeoisie. . . . But . . . the lundu freed them from any pain or any drama whatsoever. . . . It is a phenomenon identical to the Italian appearance of *opera buffa*, in which a figure from the masses was admitted within the aristocracy of opera . . . , but admitted by way of his comicalness.[58]

As such, the comicalness is explained, in the end, as a reference to the Blackness found at the origins of *lundu*. A *lundu* would, in essence, be any song that highlights a Black context; subsequently, by way of a type of distortion resulting from social pressures, it would be a cheerful song—portraying not the arduous realities of slave labor, but rather the Black man who dances and who, above all, makes his white masters laugh. Finally, *lundu* is treated as a genre of cheerful song *tout court*, detaching itself from any references to what is said to be its hidden source, and, one might say, autonomizing itself from it, as in the case of "Lá no Largo da Sé." Andrade sees in the humor of *lundus* what psychoanalysis would call a "symptom," a display that distortedly expresses a repressed conflict, in this case the latent social conflict between masters and slaves.

But the autonomy gained by *lundus* that were solely cheerful, such as Cândido Inácio da Silva's, was relative, for although Black references are absent from the literary text, Mário de Andrade identifies them in the musical text. Just as in Béhague's study of Ms. 1596, the syncopations serve as references. And as with that study, the syncopations are said not only to be Black, but also to be both popular and Brazilian:

Here the very Brazilian syncopation is heavily systematized. . . . I am clearly not insisting that these are exclusively Brazilian processes of syncopation, but no one would contest, I think, that they are characteristically national rhythms, and even particular to us, amongst the Negroed syncopations of all Atlantic America, from the United States to Argentina. As such, there is no doubt that certain very characteristically Brazilian consistencies of popular syncopation already existed in Candido Inácio da Silva's time.[59]

34

The last phrase here deserves our attention. From the syncopations found in the sheet music of Silva's *lundu*, Andrade deduces that such rhythms were also a part of the music the people performed. Such a deduction also appears in the writer's affirmation that certain Brazilian syncopations in this *lundu* were "dictionaried" for the first time.[60] Yet a word is dictionaried only when its quotidian use has become so widespread that it begins to be recognized in the world of official lexicography. But presumably it is already in existence, used commonly by the masses or by a given segment of society; it was lacking only stability, recognition, or sufficient importance to overcome the barrier separating it from academic culture.

The comparison thus established between music and language continues when Mário de Andrade employs the expression "Brazilianisms" in reference to the syncopations of "Lá no Largo da Sé."[61] A "Brazilianism" (*brasileirismo*), according to the *Aurélio* dictionary, is a "word or locution unique to Brazilians, a fad unique to the speech of Brazilians."[62] For Andrade, then, Cândido Inácio da Silva's syncopations reflected, on the sheet music, practices already common in Brazilian popular music.

Such use of these rhythmic procedures, which are supposedly present in popular music, moves Mário de Andrade to say the composer is of mixed race. The number and variety of syncopations in this piece was so much greater than in the rest of the nineteenth-century documentation known to the musicologist that it was only explicable by way of the "spontaneity of blood and social milieu and not only [by the] ear . . . of the observer."[63] The musicologist infers the "blood and social milieu"—that is, the *mestiço* condition of the composer—from his (relatively) more abundant use of syncopations. It would be difficult to find a better illustration of the way in which, in Brazil, certain rhythmic figures are linked to Black culture by way of the meanings tied to them.

Andrade thus deduces that Silva is *mestiço* from the surprising (to Andrade) variety and subtlety of the syncopations employed by the composer at such an early date as 1834. What might he have said about the pieces from Ms. 1596, which predate Silva by fifty years and whose "syncopations" are even more varied and subtle? Moreover, it is an entire collection with such characteristics, while the Silva case is of only one piece, the *lundu* "Lá no Largo da Sé."

If, as Béhague supposes, the music from Ms. 1596 had been written by Caldas Barbosa, who was of mixed race,[64] Andrade's supposition in relation to the "spontaneity of blood" would in this case be justified. But I prefer to take this reference to blood as a figure of speech, stemming from a role Mário de Andrade also played, that of poet. Ethnomusicology has already convincingly taught us that as far as musical style is concerned, it is social milieu that matters, not blood; or rather, blood matters only inasmuch as it indexes a social milieu (which allows us to understand the meaning of Andrade's expression). Among professional *lundu* composers of the second half of the nineteenth century who "syncopated" much less than Cândido Inácio da Silva, it is clear that some of the most celebrated were Portuguese, such as Francisco de Sá Noronha and Rafael Coelho Machado; but it is likely that some were as racially mixed as Silva may have been, and at least two definitely were: Januário da Silva Arvellos Filho and Dr. Nunes Garcia.[65]

As for Caldas Barbosa, his "social milieu" was no doubt quite different from that of his nineteenth-century successors. He was not a professional composer, but rather a palace troubadour and priest by convenience, supported by aristocrats for whom he ended up writing poems of flattery. If he sang the *modinhas* from Ms. 1596 (which is uncertain), it was surely not he who put them down on paper—for according to his biography, he did not write music. The task would instead have been carried out by a faithful scribe with a refined ear.

Meanwhile, the *lundus* we have from the era of the Empire of Brazil (1822–1889) and from the first years of the Republic (which started in 1889) are perfectly bourgeois music—that is, composed by professionals (who received a music education in a European mold, and whose function is distinct from that of lyricists), financially supported by way of sheet music sales, and performed in the homes of families that owned pianos and in variety theaters for paid admission. These composers employed syncopations in the manner of white actors who wore blackface: the musical dialect of the bourgeois *lundu* is "marked" by a bumpkin accent. In their compositions for orchestra or choir, in their polkas or *modinhas*, composers such as Januário da Silva Arvellos Filho, Sá Noronha, and Coelho Machado all employed the internationally dominant "classical romantic" style, in which the syncopations, if any appear at all, are used with complete discretion. Yet in composing *lundus*, they employed syncopations in a tawdry way. They were ingredients used as a characterization; they were designed as imitations of what would be, to white ears of the era, musical "Blackness" (it is not by chance that Mário de Andrade and others call the sixteenth note–eighth note–sixteenth note figure the "characteristic syncopation").[66]

On the other hand, if we examine Ms. 1596 in detail, we see that the syncopations are not there as a characterization of anything. In the texts that, according to nineteenth-century criteria, would be considered "*modinha* texts" (such as those of *Modinhas* 1, 2, 4, and others), as well as in the "*lundu* texts" (such as those of *Modinhas* 5, 7, and 16), the music is of a type that, by these same criteria, would be considered *lundu* music. Romantic or comical, with or without Africanisms, the composer syncopates. This suggests that for the author of the pieces from Ms. 1596, the syncopation was not a characterization but rather part of a general style. He would not have syncopated to imitate Black music making, but rather because it was his own style.

* * *

The most complete collection of printed *lundus* is probably that of the Biblioteca Nacional do Rio de Janeiro (BNRJ, National Library of Rio de Janeiro), which holds forty *lundus* published in Rio de Janeiro between 1837 and 1900.[67] The general characteristics of the collection's *lundus* are the same as those that have heretofore been detected: syncopations, humor, references to an Afro-Brazilian context. As for the Afro-Brazilian references, some are indirect, as in the atypical *lundu* "Marília, meu doce bem" ("Marília, My Sweet Love") (anonymous, 1855–1862), with its *modinha* lyrics (even including references to the most fortunate muse[68] of the Brazilian lyric tradition), which, in taking up that oft-visited figure of "eyes to kill," glosses, in the last stanza:

Porém se teus olhos matam	However if your eyes kill
Sabem dar vida também	They also know how to give life
Por um certo requebrado	By a sure hip shake
Que tudo pode, meu bem.	That makes everything possible, my love.

It is a common place to turn "eyes" into the area of the body directly linked to sex, in what psychoanalysis calls "displacement"; but this stanza places this mechanism in plain sight, so to speak, by way of its mention of the *requebrado* (hip shake), which designates the hip movement typical of Afro-Brazilian choreographies.

But there are also many *lundus* of the classic case as described by Mário de Andrade: humorous and alluding to sexual intercourse between masters and slaves. In the *lundus* of the BNRJ collection examined here, the most frequent type in this category is that which describes an attempt by the *sinhozinho* (little massa) to seduce the Black or mixed-race woman. "Gentis, você já vio já?" ("Peoples, Have You Seen It?") ("composed by the curious B.B. and put to music by professor Dorison," 1850) says, imitating the way in which enslaved people were caricatured to speak:

Gentis, gentis, você já vio já	Peoples, peoples, have you seen it
Iôiô mais sidotô [*sic*, "sedutor"]?	Iôiô and seductor?

In the same vein, "Lundu das beatas" ("*Lundu* of the Pious") (Januário da Silva Ramos, 1862–1863) sings:

Yôyôsinho, vá-se embora	Little massa, go away
Qu'eu não gosto de brincar	'Cause I don't like to play
Não venha com seus carinhos	Don't come along with your touch
Minha reza atrapalhar.	Messing up my prayer.

Finally, "Sinhô Juca" ("Massa Juca") (M. J. Coelho, prior to 1869), says:

Sinhô Juca é forte teima	Massa Juca is mighty stubborn
Não bula comigo não	Don't mess with me, please
. . . Sinhô Juca arrede lá	. . . Massa Juca get movin'
Senão leva bofetão	Or else you'll get a slap
. . . Ah meu Deus, Sinhô Juquinha	. . . Oh my God, my Massa Juca
Você é os meus pecados	You're my sins
Vá-se embora, já lhe disse	Go away, I already told you
Não me queira dar cuidados	Stop wanting to give me your touch
. . . As artes de Sinhô Moço	. . . The arts of young Massa
São mesmo artes do demônio	Are just like the devil's
Não me posso livrar delas	I can't get away from them
Nem rezando a Santo Antônio.	Not even praying to Saint Anthony.

Ioiô, *sinhô*, and *nhonhô* (massa) are the grammatical masculine forms enslaved people used in speaking to their masters.

These *lundus* have an ancestor in "Xula carioca" ("Carioca Xula"), published in *Jornal de Modinhas* by Milcent and Marchal, which, as early as the late eighteenth century, already sang:

Onde vais, linda negrinha?	Where are you going, beautiful little Negress?
. . . Não fujas com tanta pressa	. . . Don't run off in such a hurry
Não te faças tão ingrata	Don't be so ungrateful
Sou sinhorzinho do Reino	I'm the little massa of the Kingdom
Não sou nenhum patarata.[69]	I'm no fool.

And "Xula carioca" continued to have successors well into the twentieth century, demonstrating a thematic constancy in Brazilian society—such as in the song that animated Rio's Carnival in 1905, "Vem cá, mulata" ("Come Here, *Mulata*"):

—Vem cá, mulata!	—Come here, *mulata*!
—Não vou lá não!	—No way I'm going there
—Sou Democrata	—I'm a Democrata
De coração.[70]	With sincerity.

As the reader will have noted, these *lundus* present a shift in discursive position in relation to the equivalent pieces by Caldas Barbosa. In those, it was the *negrinho* (Black guy or Black boy) who spoke, in love with his *sinhá* (ma'am); here, it is about the *negrinha* (Black girl) pursued by her *nhonhô* (massa). The latter case is what Andrade defines as being the classic one; as for the other one, in fact, I found not a single example in the BNRJ collection.

And how do the *lundus* examined here behave in terms of music and metricity? The first thing to note is that they differ from Ms. 1596 in what is an even greater preference for syncopations within beats. Rare in the *lundus* of the BNRJ are cases in which syncopations cross bar lines, or even cross from the first to the second beat in 2/4, whereas such cases were frequent, albeit still a minority, in Ms. 1596.

But what is even more interesting is the accompaniment patterns. These include three variants of the 3–3–2 Paradigm, studied in "Musical Premises." (We will later see that this fundamental trait is what, from the perspective of rhythm, makes *lundu* and its equivalents different from post-1930 Carioca samba.)

This trait is not, however, equally present in all of the collection's *lundus*. In fact, over the course of the nineteenth century, there is a progressive solidification of the accompaniment patterns in both the *lundus* and the other printed music considered to be "typically Brazilian" (*polcas brasileiras*, *tangos brasileiros*, and so forth). In the oldest *lundus*, these patterns are limited to just a few measures and coexist with completely commetric accompaniment patterns (sixteenth-note arpeggios, Alberti bass, and so forth). In the late nineteenth-century *lundus*, the 3–3–2 Paradigm, especially in its version as a "characteristic syncopation," is found throughout.

At any rate, *all* of the *lundus* I examined have either contrametric accompaniment patterns or syncopated melodies, or both. The melodic syncopation seems to be the most common characteristic. It can happen with an entirely commetric accompaniment, as in "Marília, meu doce bem" ("Marília, My Sweet Love") (anonymous, 1855–1862), measures 9, 11, and 19, among others. Or in "Querem ver esta menina" ("You Want to See This Girl"), by Father Telles (ca. 1850), which has syncopations across bar lines practically every two measures. But I found no case in which this was flipped—a contrametric accompaniment with a commetric melody.

We will now see what takes place with the music of the three *lundus* whose lyrics were cited above. "Gentis, você já vio já?" is a *lundu* whose introduction and first part are in 2/4, while the second part is in 3/4. The first part is almost entirely commetric. The "characteristic syncopation" appears once in the introduction (measure 8) and once in the accompaniment (measures 16 and 17), while a phrase with three syncopations comprises the melody.

"Gentis, você já vio já?," measures 16–18

Meanwhile, "Lundu das beatas" is built almost entirely on the "characteristic syncopation," in both its melody and its accompaniment. The eight-measure introduction has three syncopated measures. When the singing begins (measure 9), the accompaniment is syncopated and continues in this way until measure 29, where a commetric arpeggio reappears and lasts until the end. As for the melody, it is composed of twelve phrases, of which four are totally commetric and eight use the "characteristic syncopation."

não ve - nha com seus ca - ri - nhos mi - nha re - za 'a - tra - pa - lhar

"Lundu das beatas," measures 17–20

As for the *lundu* "Sinhô Juca," whose lyrics were also cited above, the various rhythmic figures are especially interesting. In measures 11 and 15, the pianist's right hand plays the non-subdivided version of the 3–3–2 Paradigm; in measures 42 and 47, the voice and the pianist's right hand perform the "habanera rhythm," and they both perform the "characteristic syncopation" in measures 44 and 48; the voice alone employs the "characteristic syncopation" in measures 34, 36, 38, and 40. The rest of the piece, in contrast, consists of commetric rhythmic figures in both the accompaniment (arpeggiated chords, Alberti bass) and the voice.

Fa - zei com que si - nho - zi - nho não me fa - ça ten - tar

"Sinhô Juca," measures 45–48

Our study of *lundu* has taken us from the *lundu* dance (the first traces of which come from the eighteenth century) to Caldas Barbosa and the *modinhas brasileiras* of Ms. 1596 (which we can call "proto-*lundus*"), until finally arriving at the *lundu* song (*lundu-canção*), whose earliest printed sheet music dates to 1830, and which by the end of the century had become a type of comical vaudevillian revue song. This study showed us the significant presence of references to Afro-Brazilian contexts. This was clear not just in the texts but also in the music, where the particular types of contrametricity can be viewed as musical references to such contexts.

Next, we will see what happens with other genres practiced in Brazil in the late nineteenth century. This allows us to complete the panorama of the "musical family" that fits what I call the 3–3–2 Paradigm.

Maxixe and
Its Antecedents

Maxixe is a popular urban dance that was created in Rio de Janeiro during the second half of the nineteenth century. The 1974 book *Maxixe, a dança excomungada* (*Maxixe, the Excommunicated Dance*), by Jota Efegê, which will be cited repeatedly, is the most important study on the topic and tells us that the first printed mention of *maxixe* dates to 1880.

The book also shows us that the dance has always been considered vulgar and low class. Raul Pederneiras, in an article from 1906, attributes its invention to the inhabitants of "Cidade Nova." The neighborhood emerged in Rio de Janeiro around 1860 on the banks of the swampy region near the Mangue Canal.[1] By 1872 it had already become the city's most populous neighborhood and infamous for its musical activities. As Pederneiras explained it in 1906:

> Characteristic dances of Cidade Nova, the *assustados* or *sambas*, belonged, then, to a resolute, audacious group that held in modest anonymity the glory of this invention. . . . It was because of these crude groups that the maxixe first appeared, an obligatory dance in the old amusements. . . . And all of you, circumspect men of today, who traveled along the youthful path of Carioca amusements, upon hearing today one of these fast-paced musical pieces, will feel in your legs the nostalgic tingle of the good old days when, in the still of the night, you would partake clandestinely in the sambas of Cidade Nova.[2]

The word "samba" appears here meaning a party or popular dance, a meaning that, as we will see in the next chapter, was the preeminent one at the turn of the twentieth century.

Maxixe was therefore associated with crude groups, and practiced clandestinely, in the still of the night, and in a disreputable neighborhood. Not being thus in good taste, it is reasonable to presume that in order to appear in the newspapers in 1880, it must already have been practiced anonymously prior to this. Mário de Andrade points to the preceding decade as the period during which *maxixe* probably emerged.[3] If the "circumspect men" to whom Pederneiras refers were in their fifties in 1906, it would indeed have been in the mid-1870s that they had their fun in Cidade Nova. Yet whatever was happening there left no written traces. The only places in which official society recognized these suspicious musical activities were in variety theaters and Carnival clubs. Consequently, Jota Efegê's research in the aforementioned book focused "on newspapers, on the satirical publicity that they [theaters and Carnival clubs] put together for their shows, for their dances."[4]

Indeed, we have an announcement from the Clube dos Celibatários (Club of the Celibates) published in February 1876 that presents, in its characteristically flashy language, another printed mention of the word "samba," one of the first in an urban context: "Attencion! Beaucoup of Samba! Attencion!"[5] This was imitated the following year by the Sociedade Carnavalesca Estudantes de Heidelberg (Students of Heidelberg Carnivalesque Society), which, on January 27, announced a dance as follows: "It's today, look guys, Heidelbergs, the day of the second *samba*!"[6]

During the second half of the nineteenth century, Rio's Carnival was very different from what it is today. The main Carnival organizations did not comprise the working class, as do today's samba schools. The Estudantes de Heidelberg, which, as the name suggests, brought together youths who were taken with German culture, gathered "lads who study medicine, some public servants, and a few, but of high standing, in commerce."[7] In other words, they are the future circumspect men mentioned by Raul Pederneiras, the same men who were already familiar with *maxixe* from their nocturnal incursions into Cidade Nova. The carnivalesque dances of the "Heidelbergs," extrapolating from what is mentioned in the announcements, sought to somewhat re-create the atmosphere felt during those incursions.

The writer Lima Barreto also offers us a hint that the Carnival clubs, due to their pronounced permissibility, were the first to present bourgeois society with dance styles that were considered vulgar. In his short story "Cló," from the collection *Histórias e sonhos* (*Stories and Dreams*), he describes a late nineteenth-century, middle-class Carioca family during the Carnival period. At the end of the day, the father comes home, "where they were playing [music] and dancing. . . . It was his wife who played [a tango[8]]. . . . When he entered, the piano ceased and, on the couch, his daughter rested her fatigue from the sensual dance she had been practicing with her brother. The old man even indulgently heard his son say: this is how they dance in the Democráticos."[9]

The Clube dos Democráticos (Club of the Democrats) was one of the main Carnival groups of the era. It was similar to the Estudantes de Heidelberg, but a much larger and more important group. The brother is characterized as a "knower of carnivalesque things," as he is a regular at the club, where he learns the sensual dance that he teaches his sister, the young candidate for *demimondaine* and the character who gives the short story its title.

The idea that *maxixe* came from Cidade Nova by way of Carnival clubs is significantly reinforced by "a version promulgated by [composer Heitor] Villa-Lobos, who is said to have collected it from an octogenarian," according to whom "maxixe took its name from a person nicknamed 'Maxixe' who during Carnival, at the society 'Os Estudantes de Heidelberg,' danced *lundu* in a new way."[10] The new way of dancing *lundu*, as so noted by Villa-Lobos, would thus probably have been learned, or copied, from Cidade Nova dances and introduced into larger social circles by way of Carnival clubs.[11]

Consequently, we see our first correlation between *maxixe* and *lundu* dancing. But what did this new manner of dancing look like, a manner that simultaneously demonstrated both difference and an essence common to both dances? Let's compare them. The following discussion is based on descriptions of *lundu* dancing given by, among others, Sant'Anna Néry,[12] Gonzaga, Lindley, and Tollenare;[13] regarding *maxixe*, the best source is once again Jota Efegê's aforementioned book.

We can already find significant differences just by looking at the general organization of the dances. In *lundu* all of the participants, including the musicians, form a *roda* (ring) and actively accompany, with handclaps and singing, the dancing itself, which is executed by alternating pairs. In *maxixe*, on the other hand, all of the pairs dance at the same time, and the music is "external" to the dance. That is, the musicians are not part of the *roda*—for it is dissolved, replaced by the space of the so-called *salão de baile* (ballroom)—nor do the dancers sing, given that the music is exclusively instrumental. *Maxixe* was a modern, urban, and international dance (it arrived in Europe together with the Argentine tango[14]); *lundu* put its roots down in the rural world and in Brazil's colonial past.

But the most important difference concerned the way in which the dancing couples were arranged: *maxixe* is a dance of intertwined couples (partner dancing or closed-hold couples), *lundu* of separated couples (partners who do not physically embrace each other during the dance, or open-hold couples).[15] We will take a moment to understand how the dances fit into these two basic types, as these categories will reveal themselves to be quite useful throughout this work.

The enormous cultural difference between dances of separated couples and those of intertwined couples was studied by Carlos Vega.[16] Dances of intertwined couples appeared in Brazil in the 1840s, with the waltz and the polka. As modern innovations, they were adopted enthusiastically by the wealthiest families in the big cities along the coast, but it took some time for them to be accepted in the interior, in small cities, and by the masses in general. There are many accounts of this in late nineteenth-century novels. One of them says, with a reference to the city of Maceió, the capital of the state of Alagoas, "dance gatherings in Maceió were very rare in 1845, and except for nobility no one else danced quadrilles and polkas."[17] We find another account in *D. Guidinha do Poço* (*Mrs. Guidinha do Poço*), by Manoel de Oliveira Paiva (written in 1891), which takes place in the interior of the state of Ceará, a place that, not unlike Maceió, "trailed behind" Rio de Janeiro as far as customs were concerned:

> The *matutos* [yokels] were not really accustomed to *figuradas*, about which they were willing to go at it. They say that during last year's party one of them approached a gentleman with whom his daughter was executing a polka as best she could, and said to him formally:—Pull yourself away, young man!—and since there was such shock, there was great approval of the moralizing and isolating act.[18]

The name *figuradas* is generally applied to dances with group choreographies similar to quadrilles,[19] but here they encompass everything danced at the most au courant affairs, and this thus included polka. The *matutos*—that is, the inhabitants of the interior, in contrast to those from the coast, who are more open to innovation—were accustomed to different types of dances, ones in which the couples have much less physical contact. Oliveira Paiva offers a description of the latter at another point in his novel, and the name he employs for it: "samba."

Machado de Assis, too, in the novel *Quincas Borba* (*Philosopher or Dog?*), contrasts Sofia, a married woman from the capital who "waltzed and polkaed with vivacity,"[20] with her cousin Maria Benedita, who had come from the countryside, had not studied piano and "had not studied French either, and this was another lacuna that Sofia found ... hard to excuse,"[21] and topping off her backwardness, she had different dance customs. "[Maria Benedita] had danced a great deal, everything but polkas and waltzes. And why had she not polkaed and waltzed too? Her cousin shot her a resentful glance: —I don't like those dances. —What do you mean, you don't like them? You're afraid of them. —Afraid? —Not used to them, explained Sofia."[22]

Even in 1950, a practitioner of *batuque* (the name of a specific dance performed in separated couples[23]) from the interior of São Paulo affirmed: "*Batuque* is not immoral. 'To dance *baile*,' now that's immoral. The gentleman is there pushed up against the lady, with their bellies up against each other the whole time. In *batuque* there isn't the time that there is in the *baile* to whisper in the lady's ear."[24]

This informant employs the word *baile* to designate intertwined couples dancing, in contrast to *batuque*. Indeed, as can be gleaned from the novels cited above, *baile* was the term used to designate the nineteenth-century dance parties of the wealthy, where waltzes and polkas occupied a place of prestige.

Consequently, from the preceding discussion we are going to take the differentiation of *baile* (designating intertwined couples dances, mainly the waltz and polka) from separated couples dances, called either *batuque* or samba, both of which, as we will see in the following chapter, are *umbigada* (belly bounce) dances.

Now, popular *lundu* belongs to the latter category, as descriptions of it attest, while *maxixe* pertains to the former. Indeed, what is interesting about this is precisely the fact that *maxixe* is the first intertwined couples dance in Brazil to become popular among the masses. It is the result of the masses adopting ways of dancing contrary to their old practices. But it was not a mechanical adoption, for it incorporated choreographic elements that were not found in either the elite's polka or its waltz. Moreover, the elites were unable to see themselves in the imitation, and part of the horror *maxixe* caused elites—as Jota Efegê so effectively demonstrates in his book—may well have been in seeing the unsanctioned appropriation of what had once been a mark of distinction.

In fact, as far as the dancing couple is concerned, the only "new manner" that could transform *lundu* into *maxixe* is the adoption of the intertwined position of the dancers. And this is implicitly admitted by Villa-Lobos himself elsewhere, when he writes, "the maxixe . . . is derived from the lundu. . . . The celebrants [adopted the *lundu*], dancing it but with much greater liberty in the movements, so that the couples, completely joined together, could expand their sensuality further."[25]

Still, in order for it to make sense to define *maxixe* as a transformation of *lundu*, something of *lundu* must have endured. First, it is important to note that at the turn of the twentieth century, *maxixe* took the place of *lundu* in the Brazilian imaginary as the "national" dance par excellence. In 1803 Lindley described *lundu* (without mentioning it by name) thusly: "this is the national dance, and all classes are happy when throwing aside punctilio and reserve, and, I may add, decency, they can indulge in the interest and raptures it excites."[26] In 1875 the Teatro São Pedro de Alcântara (São Pedro de Alcântara Theater) announced the performance of a variety show with the presentation of "grand *kan-kan* [can-can] and national lundu."[27] We also saw that Andrade, in "Cândido Inácio da Silva e o lundu," speaks of *lundu* as "the first musical form to acquire marks of nationhood."[28]

Yet at the beginning of the twentieth century, it is *maxixe* that assumes this position. The following appears in a 1907 newspaper article opposing the repression of *maxixe*: "The maxixe is banished! It, which is in music the *vatapá* [traditional dish] of the national menu!"[29] In a 1909 Carnival club announcement, the dance is called a "marvelous invention of the *mulata*! . . . Genuine product of the always remembered Pedro Álvares Cabral."[30] As we can see, at least some segment of the population did not need to wait for Gilberto Freyre to praise the *mulata* as the Brazilian "racial type" par excellence. In another Carnival announcement, from 1913: "It's all dances in a Portuguese way, an English way, a French way, and, especially the Brazilian maxixe!"[31] Lastly, in the caption of an editorial cartoon from 1914: "—Does your mommy consent to you dancing the tango?—God forbid! Mommy is very patriotic—she'd rather I danced the maxixe."[32]

Evidence suggests that the choreographic gesture *maxixe* shared with *lundu*, which allowed them both to be seen as national and mutually interchangeable, was the hip movement known as *requebrar* or *quebrar* (that is, to shake or sway the hips).[33] In 1853 the "Lundu da Marrequinha" ("Mallard's Lundu"[34]) (by Francisco Manuel da Silva, who would also later compose the music to the Brazilian national anthem) went:

Dançando à brasileira	Dancing in a Brazilian way
Quebra o corpo iaiazinha.[35]	Shake your body little *iaiá*.

Similarly, "Cateretê,"[36] composed by Manoel Joaquim Maria for the parody *Orfeu na roça* (*Orpheus in the Countryside*), debuting in October 1868, went like this:

Quebra quebra bem quebrado	Shake shake a good hip shake
O fadinho brasileiro	The little Brazilian *fado*
Numa roda deste fado	In one of these *fado* rings
Tudo fica prisioneiro . . .	Everyone is caught . . .
Tomara achar quem me diga	Hopefully finding someone to tell me
Quem é que pode aguentar	Who can take
A mocinha brasileira	The young Brazilian woman
No fadinho a requebrar.	Shaking her hips in the little *fado*.

Note that the word *fado*, today associated with Portuguese national song, was used in nineteenth-century Brazil to designate a popular dance similar to *lundu*, and like it, was understood as characteristically Brazilian.[37]

Tinhorão addresses the choreographic implications of the verb *quebrar* but appears to assume it is associated with *maxixe and with it alone* (though this is easily belied by its mention in "Lundu da Marrequinha").[38] The entry for *lundu* in Morais and Silva's *Dicionário* had also already noted it as "a crass dance from Brazil, in which the dancers indecently shake their hips"; that is, "they requebram."[39] And already by 1817, Tollenare had observed the following in regard to a Black dance in Recife:

The pantomime of the three dancers would have little value were it not for a very spicy movement, which never ceased to accompany it. It was a very lively tremor and very extraordinary of all the body's chief muscles, and a very indecent movement of the hips and the thighs. This tremor and this movement, products of considerable muscular force, require much art and much training.[40]

It is worth appreciating Tollenare's perspective in conceding, even in 1817, that the movement of the hips (albeit regarded as "indecent") is the product of art and training. What is important here is that the choreographic element that most attracts his attention in this excerpt is the same as that which is mentioned so many times by poets and *cronistas*,[41] and common not only to the exclusively Black dances such as the one he describes, but also to *mestiço* dances like *lundu*, to a modern dance like *maxixe*, and to the choreography of our contemporary samba (which, as we will see, will eventually take its turn as Brazil's national dance). Lastly, Corrêa de Azevedo has said of the choreographic gesture, "such hip shakes [*requebros*], direct descendants of the *crioulo*[42] way of dancing, are what would have characterized maxixe."[43]

Returning to the other side of the issue, let's look at where *maxixe* got the characteristics that differentiated it from *lundu*. As we have seen, *maxixe* was not the first intertwined couples dance to animate Brazilian salons. Prior to it were the waltz and the polka, which introduced new choreographic practices from Europe. And *maxixe* inherited its general structure from these: intertwined couples, exclusively instrumental "external" music, and the simultaneous participation of all the couples.

In França Júnior's *Folhetins*—the publication of which began in 1876—there is an excellent account of the way in which polka was adopted by the masses in Rio de Janeiro.[44] Here we see that this was an adoption that also had the virtue of being a *transformation*, in a process identical to that which is described by Alejo Carpentier in speaking of the adoption of the contradance by Santo Domingo's Black population:

> This collective dance, so action-filled, took greater license as it grew more popular. Hence the black musicians of Santo Domingo adopted it with enthusiasm, imbuing it with a rhythmic vivacity overlooked by the original model. The contradanzas . . . acquired a unique trepidation, filling the bars with dots . . . and sixteenth notes. The so-called tango rhythm was featured in the bass. . . . Once more there was a process of transubstantiation at work, due to what Carlos Vega so aptly calls "a way of doing things."[45]

Such "transubstantiation" is an example of what poet Oswald de Andrade, in 1928, called "anthropophagy"—Cariocas "devoured" polka, incorporating the aspects of it that pleased them while making it something that was intrinsically theirs. As França Júnior writes:

> There are first, second, and third class dances, just as with funerals. . . . We now look at second class dances. Imagine, readers, a loft with windows that have sills at Prainha, Valongo, Livramento street, or in any spot of Cidade Nova. Let's enter through the poorly-lit hallway and go directly to the living room, where an orchestra, composed of an ophicleide, a trumpet, a fiddle, and a wily clarinet, executes the polka "Zizinha." . . . A half-dozen black women . . . comment on what's happening:—Are you seeing how talkative seu Chico is today?, says one.—Everyone! Look at how he shakes his hips [*requebra*] in the polka, says another. . . . The dancing done there is different from first-class dances. . . . As for the polkas, they consist in shuffling the feet and giving the hips a certain fado movement, which nevertheless has its originality. The musical repertoire for this dance genre comprises—"Zizinha," "Que é dela as chaves" ["Where Are the Keys"], "Só para moer" ["Just to Grind"], "Sai cinza" ["Shoo, Ashes"], "Capenga não forma" ["The Lame Don't Stand Up Straight"], "Quebra tudo" ["Everyone Shakes"], and so forth. . . . [In the third-class dances,] the music, which is composed of flute, guitar, and fiddle, is performed by amateurs.[46]

The topic is polka, but countless references bring to mind *lundu* and *maxixe*. For instance, the whole scene takes place in Cidade Nova, and there is mention of the term *requebra*, both of which are references we have already addressed. And there is also the description of the dance itself, the originality of which appears to consist of a *fado* hip movement. Here, Villa-Lobo's point of view finds a contemporary confirmation, for *fado* is considered by some researchers to be a variation of *lundu*.[47] As such, polka is danced by the people of Rio de Janeiro in an original way (and becomes, in the end, a new dance: *maxixe*) by way of the incorporation of a typical *lundu* gesture. The best illustration of this is the emergence of the musical genre known as *polca-lundu* (*lundu* polka), which starts appearing on published piano sheet music in 1865.

This is moreover suggested in França Júnior's description of the orchestras, for it corresponds nearly perfectly to the groups called *choros* that, together with military bands and *pianeiros*,[48] were among the primary groups to perform the music used for dancing *maxixe* until the early twentieth century. The only discrepancy in relation to other accounts is the fiddle, which is mentioned twice; this leads us to believe that França Júnior, fooled by their similar sizes, may have mistaken for fiddles what were in fact *cavaquinhos*, which were obligatory in *choros*, as we know from both firsthand accounts and early twentieth-century *choro* recordings.

And lastly, we must consider the repertoire, for in the BNRJ there are copies of a number of the pieces mentioned by França Júnior. Consulting this collection revealed that much of the repertoire indeed included *lundus* or *polcas-lundu*.[49] "Capenga não forma" is a *lundu* by R. Pagani, published by José Maria Alves da Rocha in the 1860s. "Que é dela, as chaves" is rather "O que é da chave?" ("Where Is the Key?"), a "celebrated polka" by José Soares Barbosa, as Vicenzo Cernicchiaro wrote, adding that it was "sung and danced with extraordinary success among the masses in Rio and in Paris."[50] The genre indicated on the copy at the BNRJ, published by Narciso and Artur Napoleão, is *polka-lundu*. The Narciso and Artur Napoleão publishing group existed from 1869 to 1875, which coincides with the 1872 date mentioned by Cernicchiaro as well as with the date of França Júnior's article. And it is in this article, furthermore, that we get a reason for such a strange title; the author tells us that some of the hosts of the second-class dances "go so far as to close the door to the street and hide the key, so that daybreak catches them dancing."[51]

"Quebra tudo" was likely a *lundu* or *polca-lundu*, given the connotation of the verbs *requebrar* and *quebrar*, as has already been discussed. Incidentally, in the catalogs and announcements of the sheet music covers I consulted, I found three titled "Quebradinha" ("Little Hip Shake"), one of which was a *polca-lundu*; a song called "Quebra quebra, minha gente" ("Shake Shake, My People"), a *polca-cateretê*; and "Tudo quebra" ("Everyone Shakes"), a *polca*.

And while I did not find "Sai, cinza," I did find "Sai, poeira!" ("Shoo, Dust!"), again at the BNRJ; it is a *polca-lundu* by J. O. Maia, published by Canongia between 1866 and 1872, and it includes the following note: "in response to the polka 'Sai, cinza!'" Indeed, it was common for polka composers to use titles that "responded" in one way or another to the titles of other pieces. The aforementioned "O que é da chave?" spawned "Que é da tranca?" ("Where Is the Lock?"), also a *polca-lundu* and also housed in the BNRJ, as well as "Não sei da chave" ("I Don't Know about the Key") and lastly, "Achou-se a chave" ("The Key Has Been Found"). "Capenga não forma" is part of a series that also includes "Gago não faz discurso" ("Stutterers Don't Make Speeches") and "Vesgo não namora" ("The Cross-Eyed Don't Date"), among others of the same tenor. Perhaps "Sai, cinza!" was, as with its cousin "Sai, poeira!," a *polca-lundu*.[52] The fact is that in the jokes and mutual taunts communicated via titles, the humor that we have already learned is a characteristic of *lundus* contaminates the polkas, even if the *polca-lundu* genre is not explicitly indicated on the sheet music.

"Zizinha" is a polka by João Elias Cunha, published by Alves da Rocha in the late 1860s, whose title makes no reference to a *lundu*, unless we consider relevant the fact that a revue entitled *Zizinha Maxixe* premiered in 1897.[53] This polka led to "Fifina"—whose subtitle is "response to 'Zizinha'"—and to "Irmã da Zizinha" ("Zizinha's Sister").

Lastly, "Só para moer" is a polka by Viriato Figueira da Silva, still played by *choro* musicians today.

As far as the music is concerned, what makes these (Brazilian) polkas different from European polkas? In the words of Mário de Andrade:

> Note that the [Brazilian] polkas from the Second Empire [that is, from the second half of the nineteenth century] are readily distinguishable from each other,[1] some polkas are based on

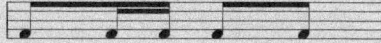

> while others present a tendentious and sustained

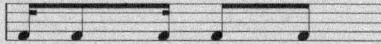

> It is in these that the melodic syncopation appears frequently. In the others it is quite rare. Subject this observation to careful review. The fact is that there is an essential difference in character, even in the melodic [character], between the polkas that have in the accompaniment the two rhythmic types determined earlier.[2]

My view after having combed through the enormous collection of piano polkas at the BNRJ, while not exhaustive, generally confirms Mário's observation. There are indeed two types of polka, and one of the primary criteria by which to differentiate them is their rhythmic accompaniment patterns. But this is not always the case, as we can find exceptions: the melody of the first part of the polka "Zizinha," in which the left hand follows the traditional accompaniment pattern of European polka, has repeated instances of the "characteristic syncopation."

I need to add the caveat that we can judge these polkas only by way of their representation in piano sheet music, the only musical record we have of them. When, however, França Júnior tells us that "Zizinha" was performed by a *choro* and danced at a social dance in Cidade Nova, by Black women who shook their hips in a *fado* movement, he leads us to suppose that in the actual performance, in this case, the syncopations were not limited to the melody.[3]

But what I wish to add to Andrade's characterization of the two polka types is that in addition to the pattern he mentions as being distinct from European polka, we also find the two other variants of the 3–3–2 Paradigm already mentioned. As such, although the polka "Vesgo não namora" (1865–1875) employs the 3–3–2 pattern, the rhythm is substituted by a measure of the "habanera rhythm" at the end of each part:

"Vesgo não namora," measures 6–8

The *polca-lundu* "O que é da tranca?" (1873) also alternates between these two rhythms, employing one in the first part, and the other in the second:

"O que é da tranca?," measures 1–3

"O que é da tranca?," measures 17–18

The sheet music of the polkas that contain this type of accompaniment is different from European polkas not only because of the more frequent melodic syncopations, as noted by Andrade, but also because of other aspects, such as the language associated with them. First, we see this in the titles, as has already become clear.[4] They are characterized by humorous titles, titles that respond to each other, but often also titles that could be titles of *lundus*, with their references to an Afro-Brazilian context: "Yayá, por isso mesmo" ("Yayá, That's Exactly Why"), "Socega, nhonhô!" ("Stop It, Massa!"), and "A bahiana" ("The Typical [Black] Bahian Woman"), for example.

Indeed, the first measures of "Socega, nhonhô!":

"Socega, nhonhô!," measures 1–3

Another aspect of the language is the dedications, such as that of "O senhor Padrevigário" ("Sir Father-Vicar") (José Soares Barbosa, 1876; he is also the author of the aforementioned "O que é da chave"), which is "dedicated to Carnival societies," or that of "Yayá, por isso mesmo" (A. Freza, 1888), which is dedicated "to the young ladies of Cidade Nova." Both of these dedications suggest that these polkas were danced in Carnival clubs and in Cidade Nova, places where, as we have seen, *maxixe* was taking shape, precisely because choreographic aspects of polka were being mixed with *lundu*.

As for "Yayá, por isso mesmo," this shows that over the course of the 1880s the "characteristic syncopation" became increasingly common in printed music. The obsession with it as a "characterization," however, inhibits its rhythmic variety. In fact, we do not find in it even a single case of a syncopation extending from one measure to the next, a type of syncopation whose popular qualities were celebrated by Andrade and Béhague.

Lastly, the link between the language and the musical characteristics we are seeking to establish was also reflected in the name for a new genre, emerging for the first time in the late 1860s, which we have already mentioned: *polca-lundu*. This designation appears often, chiefly in the sheet music published during the 1870s. But it is not the only genre that denounces the presence of a "syncopated" polka. We also find *polca-chula* (*chula* polka), *polca-cateretê* (*cateretê* polka), *polca brasileira* (Brazilian polka), and *polca de estilo brasileiro* (Brazilian-style polka).

The first one listed here, a carnivalesque *polca-chula* titled "Se eu pedir você me dá?" ("If I Ask Will You Give It to Me?"), is by Januário da Silva Arvellos Filho (1865), who has already been mentioned as a *lundu* composer. The tune points us yet again toward Carnival and, within the staffs, the accompaniment in "habanera rhythm," from measure 20 to 43.

As for the *polca-cateretê*, in addition to the already briefly mentioned "Quebra, quebra minha gente," whose sheet music I could not find, there is "A bahiana," whose title was chosen by Henrique Alves de Mesquita in the early 1870s. The omnipresent accompaniment pattern in the composition's three parts is the 3–3–2 pattern.

So as not to take too long with the examples, I offer only one more, which is the "Polca de estilo brasileiro" ("Brazilian-Style Polka") by Calixto X. da Cruz, which was impossible to date with precision, but likely comes from the last quarter of the nineteenth century. It intersperses, in a remarkably even way, the "characteristic syncopation" (primarily in the melody), the "habanera rhythm," and the 3–3–2 pattern; and it also shows an aversion to syncopation between measures, which we are coming to see as typical of the era's popular music.

"Polca de estilo brasileiro," measures 43–46

---

1. Andrade's words refer specifically to the two groups of Brazilian polkas of the era, which are distinguished by the accompaniment patterns outlined by him (and reproduced by Sandroni). —Trans.

2. *DMB*, "maxixe," 323.

3. Obviously, moreover, this would not be the only difference between what was documented via sheet music and what happened during live performances.

4. Carpentier offers comments that closely approximate my approach here, though he does not develop it further: "From 1850 on, titles alluding to blacks and black concerns come out of their *guaracha* enclaves and pass over into the *contradanza*: 'Los ñáñigos,' 'Tu madre es conga,' 'La negrita,' 'Quindembo,' 'Mandinga no va,' 'El mulato en el cabildo.' Here black themes are expressed principally by certain rhythmic elements." Alejo Carpentier, *Music in Cuba*, trans. Alan West-Durán (Minneapolis: University of Minnesota Press, 2001), 220–221. *Guaracha* and *contradanza* are Cuban musical genres that play, in Carpentier's logic, the same roles as, in our case, those played by *lundu* and polka.

We find another account of polka's popularity in 1870s Rio de Janeiro in the short story "Um homem célebre" ("A Famous Man"), by Machado de Assis, which is set in this period, despite having been published in 1896 (in the collection *Várias histórias*). Its main character is a polka composer, Pestana. His first polka was said to have been published in 1871; in November 1875, when he starts to get popular, he is said to have already composed "about thirty." In 1878 the publisher offers him a new contract, according to which he would be obliged to compose "twenty polkas in twelve months."[54]

The first scene of the story takes place at a party, a small birthday get-together, with twenty attendees. After dinner, the person for whom the party is being held asks the composer to sit at the piano and play one of his polkas:

> As soon as the first measures sounded, a new, different happiness spread through the room, the gentlemen hurried over to the ladies, and they began to shake their hips in time to the latest polka. The latest: it had been published three weeks ago, and there was no corner of the city where it was unknown. It had reached the point where it was being whistled and hummed in the streets at night.[55]

Machado de Assis tells us the title of the polka: "Nhonhô, não bula comigo" ("Massa, Don't Mess with Me"). This title suggests it is a *polca-lundu;* we saw in chapter 1 that the sexual assault of enslaved women by their masters was a classic theme of imperial[56] *lundus. Nhonhô,* we have already learned, is one of the many ways by which enslaved people would address their masters; and *bulir* (or *bula*) with someone[57] means to approach someone lovingly or sexually. We saw this in the aforementioned *lundu* "Sinhô Juca": "Massa Juca is mighty stubborn / Don't mess [*bula*] with me, please." The title chosen by Machado de Assis synthesizes the theme perfectly and leaves no doubts as to what type of polka it was. In fact, this title is perfectly equivalent to that of the polka "Socega, nhonhô!," whose "syncopated" music we saw an example of earlier.

Still, it is Machado de Assis himself who warns us against presuming that the titles of the polkas have anything to do with their content:

> Pestana, when he'd composed his first polka, in 1871, wanted to give it a poetic title, and chose this: "Sun-Drops." The publisher shook his head, and said that the titles ought themselves to appeal to the popular mind, either by alluding to some event of the day—or by the charm of the words themselves. He suggested two: "The Law of 28 September" ["A lei de 28 de Setembro"] or "You'll Not Get Your Way with Me" ["Candongas não fazem festa"].
>
> "But what's the point of 'You'll Not Get Your Way with Me'?"
>
> "There isn't one, but it'll spread like wildfire." . . .
>
> Now, when Pestana handed over his new polka and they came to the title, the publisher said that for the few days he'd had one in his head for the first work that came along, a really terrific title, long and with a swing to it. Here it was: "Hey lady, Hang on to That Basket" ["Senhora dona, guarde o seu balaio"[58]]:
>
> "And for the next time," he added, "I've got another in mind."[59]

"Candongas . . ." and "Senhora dona . . ." are in fact titles that have a markedly popular flavor.[60] In the novel *Til*, from 1872, José de Alencar has an enslaved person sing the following, in the middle of a dance that is called "samba":

Candonga, deixe de partes	Darling, leave it be
É melhor desenganar	It is better to think again
Que este negro da carepa	'Cause this unbeatable Negro
Não há fogo pra queimar.[61]	No fire can burn.

Meanwhile, "Balaio" ("Basket") is the title of a famous popular song that had first been a Bahian *lundu*.[62] As for the popularity of the title "A lei de 28 de setembro," the reasoning is quite clear: this is the "Law of the Free Womb," promulgated on September 28, 1871, according to which any child of an enslaved person born thenceforth would be free. Sometimes people would even say, "the little *crioulo* is September 28th," meaning that he was free because he was born after that date.[63]

Of course, we should not take this short story as a faithful portrayal of reality. Would publishers really have given polkas their titles? It is doubtful we will ever know. On the other hand, we do know that these titles—considered by Mário de Andrade to be "a true treasure of astuteness, pretention, affection, and humor"[64]—were not necessarily reserved only for their respective musical pieces. As we saw above, there was a "back-and-forth among titles," in which they independently responded to each other, parodied each other, and so forth, without this entailing "responses" or "parodies" at the level of the musical content. Still, just because the relationship a title had with a piece's musical content was not unique, we should not infer that there was no relationship at all. The "popularity" of the titles, defended by Pestana's publisher, is but part of what made a musical piece popular. "Nhonhô, não bula comigo" could be called "Eu sou bahianinha" ("I Am a Little Bahian Woman") or "Ó xente, sinhá" ("Oh Gosh, Ma'am"), but these sorts of titles would not be given to waltzes, nor would they be given to European-style polkas.

Indeed, when polka composers entered into this back-and-forth dialogue of titles, they were implicitly postulating an affinity for the musical genre of the corresponding pieces—in the same way that classical composers, in calling their works "sonatas" or "symphonies," implicitly postulate a musical dialogue with these specific genres. Others stayed out of the game, choosing instead titles that pulled from other realities, such as the polka "Passagem do Humaitá" ("Passage of Humaitá"), which references an operation from the Paraguayan War (1864–1870) and brings with it the following subtitle: "offered to the valiant official of the Brazilian Armada." In this case, the musical material wholly corresponds to the hardly choreographic stiffness of its verbal references.

* * *

We have so far discussed two of the genres from which *maxixe* is said to have come: *lundu* and polka. But there are others, among which we should mention so-called *tango brasileiro*. Today, talking about tango tends to conjure the idea of modern Argentine tango, of the dance that invaded European runways in the 1920s, of songs such as "Mano a mano" ("Fair and Square") and "El día que me quieras" ("The Day You Love Me"), by performers such as Aníbal Troilo, Carlos Gardel, and Astor Piazzola. It is difficult to forget these references when the topic is tango; however, in studying what tango meant in the nineteenth century, we need to forget them, for this is a different notion, a "different tango."

Carlos Vega writes, "What is notable in the use of the word tango is its tendency to refer primarily to things of the popular American sphere. . . . The word 'tango' applies to things of Afro-Americans."[65] Vega, in the cited article, and Vicente Gesualdo[66] give various examples of the use of the word in the early nineteenth century in the Río de la Plata region, in Cuba, and in Mexico, meaning Black dances, the place where these dances took place, and the music to which they were danced. For example, in 1816 the Council of Montevideo decided the following: "prohibited in the city are the dances known by the name of Tangos, and will only be permitted outside the city walls in the afternoons on festival days."[67]

Jota Efegê provides various examples of "tango" being used in Brazil as a reference to Black and *mestiço* South Americans. He cites the following satirical poem published in Rio de Janeiro in 1881:

Não viste alguma vez em tua vida	Have you never in your life seen
Uma dança africana e que se	An African dance called tango?
chama tango?	
Se tal bambolear os teus quadris	If such a swing invites your hips
convida	
Repara que a lição te ensina o	Notice that the lesson teaches you
orangotango.	the orangutan.[68]

Other references with this meaning are found in some of the tangos from the second half of the nineteenth century in the BNRJ collection, such as in the operetta *A pera de Satanás* ("Satan's Pear"), by Henrique de Mesquita, the title page of which says "tango dos pretos" (tango of the Blacks). Or in the "tango dos capoeiras" (tango of the *capoeiras*), which was part of the repertoire of the periodical *D. Sebastiana*, from 1889, for at the time the word *capoeira* denominated the practitioners of the well-known "athletic game[69] of black origin, brought to Brazil by Bantu slaves from Angola."[70] Tinhorão mentions a "Bahian tango" from the revue *O Bendengó* (which debuted in Rio in January 1889), which was called "Muqueca, sinhá" ("Moqueca Stew, Ma'am") and had the following lyrics: "Eu sou da terra do vatapá / Muqueca, sinhô / Muqueca, sinhá" (I'm from the land of *vatapá* / *Muqueca*, massa / *Muqueca*, ma'am).[71] *Muqueca* and *vatapá*, like with *sinhô* and *sinhá*, as we have already noted, are words understood as typical of a particular Afro-Brazilian vocabulary.

In this sense, yet another testament to tango's Afro-Brazilian association is its connection to *batuque*,[72] for the latter genre alludes quite explicitly to the Afro-Brazilian musical context. Two of Brazil's most famous *batuques* for piano, that of Ernesto Nazareth (from 1906) and that of Henrique de Mesquita (from the 1870s), were called tangos by their authors. It is also worth mentioning Chiquinha Gonzaga's famous 1897 composition "Gaúcho (Corta Jaca)."[73] The genre noted in the sheet music is "tango"; the subtitle, "Corta-jaca," designates "one of the samba steps existing in Bahia";[74] and the first section is indicated as *batuque*.

The first composition by Ernesto Nazareth (1863–1933) to be labeled explicitly as a "tango" is his 1893 piece "Brejeiro" ("Chipper"). But as early as 1877, he had already composed pieces with similar characteristics; the genre attributed to these, however, was not tango, but rather *polca-lundu*. But in this, Nazareth is not exceptional. Indeed, in my careful—albeit not exhaustive—examination of the tangos and *polcas-lundu* in the BNRJ collection (ca. 1870–1900), I found that all of the pieces shared similar accompaniment patterns. On this, I cite Brasílio Itiberê:

> On one occasion my friend Oscar Rocha, music lover and folklorist and one of the men who best knows the life and work of Nazareth, asked him how he had come to compose his tangos, with such a varied rhythmic character. . . .

Nazareth responded simply that he spent a lot of time listening to the polkas and the lundus of Viriato, Calado, Paulino Sacramento and felt the urge to transpose the rhythm of these *polcas-lundu* to the piano.[75]

Ernesto Nazareth is a special case as far as Brazilian tango is concerned. Indeed, he has been overwhelmingly accused by critics as having pulled some sort of scam in calling his piano pieces tangos, when in fact they would actually have been *maxixes*. At the inception of this topic is Mário de Andrade, who in a 1926 article notes Nazareth's own "repugnance regarding the confusion by which his tangos are called maxixes. He has told me that tangos 'are not as vulgar' as maxixes."[76]

It thenceforth has become commonplace in the literature on Brazilian music to insist that, as Renato de Almeida put it, "Ernesto Nazareth, *arbitrarily*, called all of his maxixes tangos, because he thought that the word maxixe was too vulgar for his compositions" (emphasis added).[77] Echoing Almeida, Luiz Heitor Corrêa de Azevedo wrote, "[Nazareth composed] a special, very Brazilian, tango that *disguised* under this more polished name the *true* nature of the plebeian and questionable maxixe that inspired it" (emphasis added).[78] And as Eurico Nogueira França put it, "[Nazareth] called his maxixes tangos . . . encouraged by a desire to ennoble himself . . . but I believe he would never have confessed, or even have recognized, the Afro-Brazilian meaning of his maxixes, called tangos as if to repudiate [the music's] Negro origins."[79]

There is no doubt that the word *maxixe*, at the turn of the century, carried a much more vulgar connotation than did "tango," which had even been employed by classical music composers such as Isaac Albéniz and, in Brazil, Alexandre Levy. Efegê shows that by 1879, tango could be played in a context as aristocratic as that of the Imperial Theater D. Pedro II[80] and gives countless examples of the unedifying connotations attributed to *maxixe*. It is hardly surprising that Nazareth did not like seeing his compositions called by this name, given that around 1886, the term served, among other purposes, "to designate anything bad, of poor quality."[81] But how can we propose that "he would not have ever recognized the Afro-Brazilian meaning" of his works given that the genre of the first piece he composed is *polca-lundu*, and that one of his masterpieces is called "Batuque"? Thus, the true enigma surrounding the genres indicated on Nazareth's compositions is, rather, the unanimity with which critics deny their accuracy.

Nazareth was not an exception, nor was he acting arbitrarily in using the term "tango" to label his piano pieces, the accompaniments for which were based on variations of the 3–3–2 pattern—the practice was common. Baptista Siqueira (one of the only researchers to explicitly defend Nazareth's nomenclature) provides a list of composers who did the same, focusing only on the two-year period between 1881 and 1882. In addition to Chiquinha Gonzaga, he cites Cinira Polônio, Arthur F. da Rocha, and a half dozen others.[82]

To demonstrate just how common the word "tango" was in popular music and dance in early twentieth-century Rio de Janeiro, we can read this excerpt from an article condemning the repressive measures taken against it, published in the newspaper *Jornal do Commercio* in 1914: "In this land of the Holy Cross, the Tango is not the unexpected invader, it is the old and familiar resident; it is not a foreigner, it is a compatriot; . . . the Tango, our Tango, which has always enjoyed the freedom to shake, more useful than freedom of thought, will be taken aback by the strictness of the day."[83]

Yet starting in the 1920s, Argentine tango, following important rhythmic changes (abandoning the accompaniment pattern thenceforth known as "the habanera rhythm"), becomes an international fad and begins to impose itself everywhere as the very definition of "tango." Most writers saw the use of the name "tango" by Nazareth and other composers as having been influenced by the international fad, despite having become popular well after Nazareth had already composed his "tangos." From Maria Tereza Mello Soares, for example, we find a reference to the "success of porteña music" (that is, music from Buenos Aires) as an explanation of the use of the name "tango" in early twentieth-century Rio.[84] Oneyda Alvarenga also speaks of the influence of the "platino Tango" (or tango from the Río de La Plata region)[85] during this same period. However, this later tango had nothing to do with Nazareth's compositions, nor did it have anything to do with any of the tangos of the nineteenth century.

Contributing to the confusion is the fact that people only really began writing about Nazareth after his death, for his music had no official recognition until 1920; in fact, the first time there was an attempt made to add his music to the program of a concert at the Escola Nacional de Music (National School of Music) in Rio, "police intervention was needed."[86] The only person to write about Nazareth while he was still alive was Mário de Andrade, who was twenty years his junior. Moreover, Nazareth was already a late composer of instrumental tangos (although the term "tango" was still employed in Brazil through the late 1920s, it was used nearly exclusively for vocal music).[87] Indeed, he began to write tangos in large numbers only in 1893, while Chiquinha Gonzaga, the genre's other great proponent, seventeen years his elder, had already been composing them since at least 1880.[88]

We can thus see that the source of Nazareth's problems concerning *tango brasileiro* was his own longevity, and the fact that his pieces continued to be played and appreciated in Brazil at a time when the meaning of the word designating their genre had changed entirely.

* * *

The first printed piece of music to be officially labeled *maxixe*, cited by Jota Efegê, is "Ora bolas!" ("Oh Nuts!") by Juca Storoni, published in 1897.[89] "Juca Storoni" was a pseudonym, yet another sign that the label of "*maxixe* composer" would not exactly be bestowed as a distinction. In 1902 the term appears in the press clearly signifying a musical genre: "the band played a maxixe that sent shivers up the spine," reports the newspaper *Jornal do Brasil* apropos of a Clube dos Democráticos party.[90] But until the mid-1890s, *maxixe* was danced to songs that were not yet labeled as such: they were polkas, *lundus*, tangos (and every combination of these names). *Maxixe* was basically anything that was written in a binary meter, had a lively tempo, and got dancers to shake their hips to the rhythm of the "syncopation."

The most common of such name combinations to provide the soundtrack to *maxixe* dancing was *polca-lundu*. But there were others: in 1883 the actor Vasques took the stage with a "comic scene" of his authorship titled *Aí, cara-dura!* (*Hey, Shameless!*). In it *maxixe* dancing is mentioned explicitly, and the stage directions indicate that the orchestra, consisting of flute, *cavaquinho*, and guitar, plays a *polca-tango*.[91] A few years earlier, in 1880, the Casa Bevilacqua was selling the "beautiful habanera-tango-lundu 'Cecília,' written especially for Carnival."[92] The BNRJ also has an anonymous "1ª habanera-polka-lundú" ("1st Habanera-Polka-Lundu") published in Pernambuco in the late nineteenth century. As late as 1913, the carnival revue *Fandanguassu* presented a tango with the following lyrics: "Não há nada / que mais me enrabiche / do que um lundu de massada / com remexidos de maxixe" (There is nothing / that gets me more / than one of those great *lundus* / mixed with *maxixe*).[93]

What is surprising in these newspaper announcements, sheet music titles, and song lyrics is the gestation of, in Mário de Andrade's words, that

> tremendous rhythmic-melodic mixture in which the danced lundus and fados of the masses of the Rio de Janeiro of the First Empire [1822–1831] contaminated the imported polkas and *havaneiras*. As a result of such great mixture, maxixes and tangos emerged that, starting roughly 1880, were the characteristic expression of Carioca dance.[94]

One of the problems generated by this "mixture" was the terminological confusion in which musicologists found themselves. Without ever quite understanding the difference between a *habanera* and a tango, a polka and a *polca-lundu*, they were often driven to make classificatory statements about what the pieces "actually" were, despite the fact that such pieces were wrapped up in so many different genre labels. Mozart de Araújo, for example, taking to heart the thankless task of establishing the difference between *maxixe* and *tango brasileiro*, writes the following:

> Both being derived from the same trunk—from the Spanish tango, from the habanera, from the polka, and from the lundu—it is not difficult to observe that the dosage of tango and habanera is much larger in the *tango brasileiro* than in the maxixe. In [the latter], to an inverse and decreasing degree, the preponderant dosage is of lundu, polka, habanera, and tango.[95]

It is difficult to know how Araújo arrived at such a highly improbable "dosage," especially when we take into account the nonexistence of precise definitions for these genres. Luciano Gallet, in a text written in 1928, also shows us the confusion to which similar attempts lead:

> I have concluded that, under the name of Tangos, he [Nazareth] conceals various well determined types of music of ours. I found—a) maxixes—b) tangos, the Brazilianized polka, without the stiffness of the original polka . . . f) puladinhos [??] . . . h) Brazilian polkas, different from tangos, etc.[96]

As such, in b) tango is defined as a Brazilianized polka, but in h) Brazilian polkas are said to be different from tangos.

Tinhorão says the tango "Chô, Araúna" ("Shoo, Araúna"[97]) was "in reality a maxixed lundu,"[98] while Mário de Andrade called the same piece an "authentic lundu danced by Negroes" (note how for this topic, expressions such as "authentic" and "in reality" recur).[99] But elsewhere the same Tinhorão recognizes "the little importance that was given to names of the dance genres, even well within the current [twentieth] century. Just as a fadinho could be a lundu . . . , the *polca-tango* Vasques requested to accompany the maxixe dance could be either a polka or a maxixed lundu, for both were often referred to simply as tango."[100]

Here we need to distinguish between the perspective of researchers and the perspective of the era and society for the music we are discussing. Researchers should not, in principle, regret the "imprecision" of a society that was indifferent to calling the same musical piece a *lundu* or a tango, nor insist that said *lundu* is "actually" a tango or vice versa. What should be expected of researchers is that they understand why, and under what circumstances, different names are given to what appear to be the same things.

The information we have suggests that this is not really a case of terminological imprecision, but rather of substantive indifference. That is, both tango and *lundu* would be, according to the reigning criteria in Rio de Janeiro during the second half of the nineteenth century, adequate and "true" names for certain musical pieces. This nominal equivalence wholly corresponds to the equivalence of rhythmic patterns evoked earlier, for these names were always attributed to pieces whose accompaniment fit within the 3–3–2 Paradigm.

Tinhorão subsequently notes that this supposed "imprecision" was specific to the "designation of songs that did not come already structured from Europe (such as the waltz, the quadrille, the mazurka, the schottisch, the polka itself)."[101] Yet *fado* and *lundu*, in certain contexts, could also be "structured" genres. The description of *fado* in Rio de Janeiro from the early nineteenth century in the novel *Memórias de um sargento de milícias* (*Memoires of a Militia Sergeant*), for example, demonstrates this quite well: "everyone knows what fado is, that dance so voluptuous, so varied, which seems the offspring of the most comprehensive study of the art."[102] The novel follows this with a description of the *fado* choreography, which conformed to precise rules that all the participants knew. This was, after all, a traditional practice, adopted collectively by a particular group of people, and for them, indeed, the terminological ambiguities are reduced to a minimum. Everyone knows what *fado* is.

The problem, it seems to me, is that starting in the 1870s, the issue of popular dances in Rio de Janeiro is placed in completely novel circumstances. Musical forms are created that are no longer the readymade dances imported from Europe, just as they no longer correspond to popular amusements inherited from the colonial period. *Fado*, whether as a choreography or a social happening, was no longer enough to meet the "modern" expectations created by urban life in the Second Empire (1840–1889). As we have seen, the intertwined couple replaces the separated couple; but the piano also replaces the *viola*, the authored composition—commercialized as sheet music—replaces the traditional or anonymous refrain, and new international fads are born. And it is in this context—the "tremendous mixture" mentioned by Mário de Andrade—that the problem of the scrambled terminologies appears, and it does not get sorted out entirely until the mid-1920s, when the "mixture" is resolved by the imposition of samba as the "characteristic and main type of Brazilian salon dance,"[103] and by the adoption of a new rhythmic paradigm. In this context, the true element of confusion ends up being the new something that was emerging, a something that was still seeking not only a definitive form but even more than that, a name.

From Bahia
to Rio

The word "samba" is found in different parts of the Americas, nearly always in connection with a Black cultural context.[1] Argeliers Léon points out a nineteenth-century Cuban engraving of a Black couple dancing, which includes the caption "Samba la culebra, sí siñó" (Samba-ing [or dancing] the snake-dance, yes sir[2]).[3] For the Río de la Plata region, Vicente Rossi makes note of "the nursery rhyme: 'Samba, mulenga, samba!,' heard from Africans."[4] Fernando Ortiz makes note of an Afro-Haitian dance in which the introductory singer is called a "samba."[5] Vicente Gesualdo cites the song "El negro blanqueador" ("The Whitening Negro"), a satire about Italian immigrants (then arriving en masse to Buenos Aires) who were beginning to take up occupations that had theretofore been reserved for the Black population:

> Neapolitan usurpers
> They are taking the work of the poor
> There are no more black bottle makers
> Nor loaders
> Because these Neapolitans
> Even work as confectioners
> In such a short time,
> Jesus, by God!
> They will be dancing *cemba* to the sound of drums![6]

This excerpt speaks of a dance accompanied by drums that is viewed as even more characteristically Black than the occupations "stolen" by the Neapolitans; but the song also says that the name of this dance was *cemba*, with an *e*, which directs us to the most cited etymology of Brazilian samba, which is what interests us here.

This etymology, which we find, for example, in the *Enciclopédia da Música Brasileira* (*EMB*, Encyclopedia of Brazilian Music) entry for "samba," once again references the African American context. It says the word comes from "the quimbundo *semba*," which would mean *umbigada*.[7] The *umbigada* is a choreographic gesture that consists of bumping abdomens, or bellies (that is, *umbigos*), and which has a specific function during certain dances, as we will see. The *umbigada* has been documented countless times in the dances of Black Brazilians. Under the name *semba*, the dance gesture was witnessed by nineteenth-century Portuguese travelers who were in Angola and the Congo,[8] and even in the 1980s, Gerhard Kubik encountered the name and the gesture being practiced in Luanda.[9] In Brazil, the most cited account is that of Aires da Mata Machado Filho, in *O negro e o garimpo em Minas Gerais* (*The Negro and Mining in Minas Gerais*): "the Negroes correct it as *semba* if someone speaks to them of *samba*."[10]

As of late, however, this etymology has been much debated.[11] We do not need to spend much time on the debate; what matters is to note the importance of the *umbigada*, documented as early as the nineteenth century in both Brazil and Africa, as a gesture around which certain Black dances are organized. In general terms, such dances consisted of the following: all of the participants form a *roda* (ring). One of them goes to the center, where he or she dances individually until choosing a participant of the opposite sex to substitute him or her (the two may execute a choreography—as a separated couple—before the first leaves the center of the ring). All of the participants clap their hands and repeat a short refrain in response to the improvised singing of a soloist. The instrumental accompaniment is provided by membranophones such as the *pandeiro*, idiophones such as the *prato e faca* (plate and knife), and less commonly by chordophones, especially the *viola*.[12] The *umbigada* is the gesture by which a dancer signals the person who will substitute him or her.

Researchers held the *umbigada* in such high regard as the characteristic gesture of certain secular Afro-Brazilian dances that in 1961, Edison Carneiro coined the expression *samba de umbigada* (that is, *umbigada* samba) as an umbrella term to designate all such dances.[13] For Carneiro, it made sense to use this name as a label for any dance with the traits described above (the presence of the *umbigada* or equivalent gestures, the participants-spectators forming a *roda*, responsorial singing, handclaps, and so forth), whether the participants or observers called it "samba," *coco*, or *lundu*, or even if there was no official name. The advantage of this terminological conceptualization is that it bypasses variations in empirical names, which often do not correspond to a real variation in local categories, nor to substantive changes observable by a researcher.

The name given by nineteenth-century Portuguese travelers to these and other African dances is *batuque*. In Brazil, there is written evidence of the word *batuque* dating to the 1700s, as we see in this eighteenth-century quote: "it does not seem very wise to tolerate that in the city streets crowds of Negroes of one or the other sex perform their barbarous *batuques* playing many and horrible *atabaques* [drums], dancing dishonestly and singing gentile songs."[14] We see here that the word does not refer to a specific dance but rather to Black celebrations in general.[15] This word's generic meaning lasted until the beginning of the twentieth century, when, as we will see, the word "samba" became more widespread.

The first printed mention of the term "samba" appears in the satirical Pernambuco newspaper *O Carapuceiro*, on February 3, 1838,[16] nearly sixty years after the first recorded mention of *lundu*.[17] Interestingly, here "samba" does not expressly appear as a dance, but rather as music—"mule-drivers' samba," which the writer, Father Lopes Gama, says ironically is "as pleasing as *Semiramis*, the *Gaza-ladra*, the *Tancredi*, etc. of Rossini."[18] The next mention we find, however, in the same newspaper, speaks of the "samba dance," referred to as an amusement of country folk, in contrast to people from the state capital (Recife), who danced not only the minuet and the comporta, but also the "beautiful sobbing landum [*lundu*]."[19] After all, by the mid-nineteenth century, there was already a wholly urbanized *lundu* accepted by "good society," while samba was a sign of rural backwardness (it was "*tatamba*,"[20] as the newspaper claims in rhyme).

That samba was limited to rural areas is confirmed by other nineteenth-century accounts. Baptista Siqueira, in *Origem do termo samba* (*Origin of the Term Samba*), offers various examples of this (although they are not enough to sustain his thesis of an Amerindian origin of the word).[21] At any rate, in Rio de Janeiro, then the country's capital, "samba" was a nearly unknown word until the last quarter of the nineteenth century. Botanist Freire Alemão, for example, upon witnessing an amusement of the Black population in the interior of Ceará in 1859, wrote that it was a "fado, which they call samba."[22] *Fado*, as we have already seen, was the name that, in Rio de Janeiro at the time, designated certain dances of disadvantaged segments of the population.[23] "Samba" would therefore have been a type of *fado*, given that this was—once again—treated as a generic name for common amusements. But in addition to *fado*, other names served as points of reference when speaking of samba in Rio de Janeiro. França Júnior, for instance, in a *crônica* about Bahia that was published in a Carioca newspaper during the 1870s, clarifies that sambas "are our *cateretês*, etc."[24] By "our," the writer is referring to the readership in Rio de Janeiro.

In these two citations we thus see that authors who are writing for a readership in the country's federal capital about facts from the provinces are obligated, when introducing an unknown word, to make reference to already known words that designate realities considered to be more or less equivalent. As such, up until the mid-1870s, although the readership in Rio de Janeiro had surely already heard of *fado* and *cateretê*, the same could not be said of samba.

Indeed, by 1868, the play *Orfeu na roça* (a parody of *Orpheus in the Underworld*, by Offenbach) contained a *cateretê*, which, furthermore, had precisely the subtitle "Fado brasileiro" ("Brazilian *Fado*"). The *roça* (countryside) mentioned in the title of the play geo-socially situates the *cateretê* and the *fado*: it is in a rural area, specifically the poorest, most destitute, most cut off from urban progress. The same idea appears in a novel published in leaflets in 1870, which discusses a mixed-race musician who was "one of those types found at parties in the countryside, amidst liquor and a group of happy wights who are unaware of the existence of grammar and prefer the *cateretê* and the *fado* to the delights of Jouvin and the scissors of Dason!"[25]

Another account along these lines is in a *crônica* published again by França Júnior, but this time in the 1880s, about a *viola* player who held a concert in the federal capital: "the *viola's* setting is the slaves' quarters, the cattleman's ranch, the little thatch house, the shop in the shed, the backyard of the farm on the night of a party" (that is, the setting of poor folks from the interior of the country). This is why it was such a surprise to see the *viola* on a theater stage, performed for an urban public; but the apparent incongruity is explained by the change in repertoire: "It [the *viola*] did not come there accompanying a *fado*, as the accomplice of a *cateretê*, or to shake itself [*requebrar*] coyly in the foot movement of a voluptuous samba. Its mission was otherwise: to become civilized!"[26] We thus see that samba, the *cateretê*, and *fado* are all common musical activities in the countryside as described above and are consequently hindrances to the goal of making the *viola* "civilized."

Some years later, in 1897, Sílvio Romero draws distinctions: "it is called 'xiba' in the province of Rio de Janeiro [that is, in the interior of the state of Rio de Janeiro and not in its capital, which has the same name], 'samba' in those [provinces] of the North, 'cateretê' in that of Minas, 'fandango' in those of the south, a popular practice of *pardos* and *mestiços* in general."[27] ("Provinces of the North" refers to what is today known in Brazil as the "Northeast," which therefore includes Bahia, an area that was predominantly rural and had, already by the nineteenth century, become economically peripheral.) And in 1906 Guilherme de Mello engages point by point with the geographical distribution proposed by Romero, making the description more precise: "[in Bahia it is called "samba" that which] in Rio de Janeiro was denominated *chiba*,[28] in the State of Minas, *cateretê*, and in the States of the South, *fandango*, it is a dance of the countryside, out in the open, in which the instruments included are guitar, steel-string *viola*, *cavaquinho*, beneath the sung melody and danced to the rhythm of handclaps, *pratos* [plates], and *pandeiros*."[29]

We thus see that samba is initially foreign to Rio de Janeiro, not only because of its social placement in the countryside, which stands in opposition to the city and in particular to the federal capital, but also because of its geographical placement in the "North" (especially in Bahia). But we must discuss a third "placement" of samba: that with which we began this chapter, that which associates it with a Black context. We see this association in the previously cited Freire Alemão excerpt; Sílvio Romero, for his part, spoke of a "popular practice of *pardos* and *mestiços* in general." But there are two other nineteenth-century accounts that unequivocally situate samba as a "thing of Blacks" (to redeploy the terminology Rossi uses in his book on tango): the chapters dedicated to the topic in the novels *Til*, by José de Alencar (1872), and *A carne (Flesh)*, by Júlio Ribeiro (1887).

Both novels take place in São Paulo, on the coffee plantations that, driven by the sweat of slaves, represented what was then the country's main economic activity. But in neither work are the enslaved people the main characters of the plot; in fact, although the authors did their best to ignore them, doing so was impossible. In the end, they are there, at least as part of the background. Ribeiro's *A carne* revolves around the love between a plantation owner's son and his female ward. Only in chapter 10 do the enslaved people occupy the scene all by themselves, and it is precisely here that there is a "samba." All of the elements with which we are already familiar are there, this time with the participants well defined: "[Black] men and women formed a wide circle, moving and clapping rhythmically, a few beating *adufes* [square tambourines]. In the centre, a dancer leapt."[30] This is followed by a description of responsorial singing and the use of the *umbigada* by the first dancer, who selects his replacement to occupy the circle.

As for *Til*, the main characters do not come from the dominant class but are rather intermediary characters, as they are servants of a type common on São Paulo plantations of the era.[31] Here, too, the only moment during which the Black characters occupy the center of the narrative is in a description of the samba. What is interesting here is that Alencar insists on the social stratification of the amusements: while the enslaved people do their samba (the title of the chapter) or *batuque* (as it is frequently referred to in the text), the "overseers and comrades," poor *mestiço* and white people, keep their distance, playing *viola* and singing *chulas*.[32]

It is worth noting, moreover, that in neither of the two novels are the descriptions of samba central to the plot. Instead, they seem to offer a picturesque element, giving readers a strong dose of exoticism and emotion. For example, Alencar writes, "the blacks dance the samba with a frenzy that touches delirium. One cannot describe, nor can one imagine this desperate shake, in which the whole body trembles, hops, shakes, spins, sways."[33] Ribeiro, for his part, portrays the dancing thusly: "[a Black man] squatted down and rose up, his arms and neck writhing, swinging his hips and beating his feet in an indescribable frenzy, with a prodigality of movement . . . which would have exhausted a white man in less than five minutes."[34]

This last phrase, however, gives us an important hint, for it shows, under the veil of the picturesque, that within the narrative, samba exercises a "differentiating" function. By insisting on describing the "prodigality of movement" in the dance of the Black characters, Ribeiro is able to measure the distance that separates them, even in physical terms, from their white masters. For him, even in their amusements, the Black figures demonstrate that they are made for manual labor. This "differentiating" function, which is even more evident in Alencar, will be revisited later.

Additionally, all of these social "placements" of samba—a thing of the countryside, of the North, of Black populations—had obvious consequences for the value attributed to it. This is the irony in the Father Lopes Gama excerpt we cited earlier: how can one compare a "mule-drivers' samba" to Italian operas? Whether the practitioners were mule drivers or enslaved people, the perceived difference was slight. Samba continued to be seen as "low," "undignified," and so forth for quite some time. On that note, it is worth citing the famous words delivered by Ruy Barbosa in the Federal Senate on November 7, 1914, just days after a celebration at the Palácio do Catete, during which the wife of the president of the Republic had played "Corta-Jaca,"[35] by Chiquinha Gonzaga:[36]

> One of the papers from yesterday was stamped with a *fac-simile* of the program from the presidential reception at which, before the diplomatic body, the finest society of Rio de Janeiro, those who should have given this country an example of the most distinct manners and of the most reserved customs, elevated "Corta-Jaca" to the heights of a social institution. But the "Corta-Jaca" I had heard of for so long, what does it become, Mr. President? The lowest, most *chula*, most vulgar of all the savage dances, the twin sister of the *batuque*, the *cateretê*, and the *samba*. But at presidential receptions the "Corta-Jaca" is performed with all the honor of the music of Wagner, and you do not want the conscience of this country to rebel, our faces to become flush, and the youth to hoot![37]

Father Lopes Gama mentioned Rossini in 1838, and Ruy Barbosa in 1914 preferred Wagner. The lyrical European drama seemed to occupy an unshakable position among Brazilian elites as the preferred model of artistic elevation. Still, the incident that motivated Senator Barbosa's discourse reveals that something was changing. First, there was a properly published piece of written music that was inspired by the *corta-jaca* folk samba dance step. Second, the piece was played at a presidential reception, even at the price of a controversy in the Senate.

Samba's "movement," going from the countryside to the city, appears very concretely in a series of letters published in the press in Salvador, the capital of

Bahia, at the beginning of the twentieth century. The letters complained of the ostensive Black presence in Carnival festivities, demonstrating effectively how anti-Black prejudices got jumbled up with the dismissal of their music:

> I think the authorities should prohibit these batuques and candomblés[38] that, in great numbers, are scattered about the streets these days, producing this tremendous racket, having neither pitch nor tone, as if we were in the Quinta das Beatas or Engenho Velho, as it is with the masquerade wearing a skirt and turban, singing that traditional samba, for all of this is incompatible with our state of civilization. . . . Moreover, if Candomblé and samba are prohibited on the outskirts and in the countryside, how can they dominate in the cities on a festive day like Carnival?[39]

Samba recalls Quinta das Beatas, Engenho Velho, the outskirts, and the countryside. But when it is heard in the cities, it provokes the readers' outrage, which reveals itself through aesthetic judgments (as in the case of Ruy Barbosa). For them, samba is a "racket having neither pitch nor tone." The object of the unpleasantness is first and foremost the physical presence of Black people during Carnival, "the way in which it has been Africanized, amongst us, this great celebration of the civilization."[40] But making matters worse is a specifically musical displeasure, which is presented as a separate issue. In the end, it is unclear if the letter writer is condemning samba because it expresses Black people's "lack of civilization" or if instead the writer is condemning the Black presence at Carnival because he or she dislikes their music.

* * *

Documented cases of the word "samba" in the city of Rio de Janeiro begin appearing in the 1870s. And from thenceforth the borders that had seemed so clear begin to dissipate; and thus little by little, samba is no longer only from Bahia, nor only from the countryside, nor only made by people of African descent.

Earlier we saw that Jota Efegê found mentions of "samba" in the Carnival club advertising published in the Carioca press in 1876 and 1877. Exactly one year later, in 1878, for the first time in the city, according to Baptista Siqueira, there is a wider dissemination of the word "samba," when the newspapers announce, outside of the Carnival period, the performance of a popular amusement with this name. One of the announcements reads like this: "Cease all that antique Muse hath sung / For now a better *fado* rears its bolder brow:[41]—samba! It is better to try it than judge it."[42] The announcement revisits famous verses from the beginning of *Os Lusíadas* (*The Lusiads*) and uses them to emphasize the novelty of the topic while at the same time also establishing yet another parallel between the "new samba" and the "old *fado*."

In the 1880s descriptions of dances that fit perfectly within the concept of *samba de umbigada* begin to appear, but their context is no longer old Bahia or the coffee plantations, being instead a variety of neighborhoods in the federal capital. The following example refers to the Festa da Penha (Penha Festival), which brought together large crowds on the outskirts of Rio on Sundays in October and was described by Raul Pompéia in 1888:

> A delirium of samba and *fados*, Portuguese *modinhas, tiranas* from the north. A *viola* rattles the beat, a *pandeiro* plays along, the accordion wails, a Negro scrapes a knife on the bottom of a plate.... The *roda* closes. In the center the *mulata* shakes her hips and sings.... The spectators clap their hands, marking the rhythm ..., watching the slow swaying, or the unbridled *umbigadas*, of the little *fados*.[43]

These are the same elements found in countless descriptions of folk sambas: *viola, pandeiro*, plate and knife, bystanders clapping, a *roda*, and a dancer who executes her individual choreography (she shakes her hips) at the center of it all.

At practically the same time, Aluísio Azevedo offered in his novel *O cortiço*, translated into English as *The Slum* (in which the author seeks to document the social life of Rio de Janeiro's poor in the 1880s),[44] a description of what he first calls *chorado baiano* (Bahian *chorado*)[45] (p. 59) but later also "samba" (pp. 78, 183, 199, 202). The accompaniment is provided by guitar and *cavaquinho*, a *roda* is formed, the spectators clap their hands ("the steady rhythmic clapping continued, unceasing in its excited, insane persistence," p. 60), and a *mulata* called Rita Baiana[46] sways in the middle.

Note that at both the Festa da Penha and in the slum of the Botafogo neighborhood of Rio described by Azevedo, participation is not limited to Black residents, in contrast to the sambas depicted by Alencar and Ribeiro. Both descriptions emphasize the heterogeneity of the economically disadvantaged sectors of what was then the federal capital. In the first, as we have seen, samba coexisted with the "Portuguese *modinhas*" and the "*tiranas* of the North."[47] In the second case, the coexistence of people who are white and mixed race, Portuguese and Bahian, is one of the book's themes and is revealed in the earliest descriptions of the characters.[48]

This difference goes hand in hand with the flagrant repositioning of samba within the narrative: in *O cortiço*, the main characters participate in the activity, and it is here that some of the decisive events of the plot take place, such as the Portuguese Jerônimo falling in love with the *mulata* Rita Baiana. Samba's move to the center of the literary text's plot parallels its movement from the periphery to the heart of social life—from the countryside to the city, from the provinces to the nation's capital, from the Black to the general population. This movement will culminate in the creation, between 1917 and the early 1930s, of urban Carioca samba.

* * *

Above I mentioned that samba had a "differentiating" function, which is detected in the novel *Til*, by José de Alencar. This idea becomes more evident when the samba of *Til* is compared with that which is described years later by Aluísio Azevedo in the aforementioned *O cortiço*.

In both novels, the samba scenes offer opportunities for lovers' quarrels. In Alencar, the quarrel ends right there, with no further consequences for the plot's development. In Azevedo, on the other hand, the dispute is one of the story's key elements. In both, the conflict calls attention to characters from different worlds. In Alencar, the slave Florência, a so-called *negra da roça* (country Black woman [that is, a direct participant in the manual labor of the coffee plantations]), fancies the page Amâncio, who is of mixed race and works in the Big House. Florência tries to attract Amâncio to the samba, which would represent a triumph over her rival Rosa, who as a maid also enjoyed a privileged status; the person of mixed race hesitates, "fearful of degrading his nobility of page by mixing with riffraff of the hoe."[49] But in the end, Amâncio gives in, which provokes the violent intervention of Rosa, followed by a full-scale conflict: "The Negroes of the countryside aided their partner, insulted by the group of pages and maids. The guards took Amâncio's side in a show of camaraderie."[50]

Alencar constructs a sociology of the São Paulo farm around samba: the "Negroes of the countryside" are those who practice samba; the overseers and companions, who are white *caipiras* (hicks), remain distant. ("The fellows wanted indeed to enter the party and throw a foot into the *batuque*; but, inhibited by the discipline of the farm, they made do with looking on.")[51] The pages and maids are Black or mixed race, but they work in the house rather than in the coffee plantation, enjoying a differentiated status thanks to their direct contact with the masters. Unlike the *caipiras*, they are not "inhibited by the discipline of the farm" and can go to the *batuque*; it is rather their own desire to differentiate themselves that moves Amâncio to hesitate. As for the masters, they are completely absent from the chapter, just as are the main characters of the plot, who are marginal to the plantation's economic activity.

Meanwhile, the stratification proposed by Azevedo is far less explicit. Samba appears as something pertaining primarily to the *mulatos*: Firmo and Porfiro, who make the music (guitar and *cavaquinho*), and Rita Baiana, who dances better than anyone else. But samba also appears to pertain to all of the inhabitants of the slum, who are attracted to the *mulatos*: the performance emanates from the *mulatos*, but others participate. Contrary to what we see in Alencar, samba here is not exclusive to anyone, but rather brings the whole slum together: "And then Florinda joined in, followed by Albino and even—who would have thought it?—solemn and circumspect Alexandre. Despotically, the *chorado* engulfed them one by one, to the despair of those who couldn't dance."[52] In the end, even the owners of the slum, "after finishing their work, wanted to have a little fun," and the rich family that lived next door "came to the windows, enjoying the sight of that rabble below them,"[53] predating thus by close to a hundred years the VIP box seats of the sambadromes.[54]

The only person who refrains from participating is the Portuguese man Jerônimo, who prefers to sing the *fados* from his land.[55] He appears at the beginning of the novel as completely unamenable to the general seduction of samba because of his typically European work ethic. It is worth spending a moment on the characterization of Jerônimo, for it contrasts so strongly that of Firmo and of Rita Baiana, characters in the novel who are more closely identified with samba. This contrast allows us to anticipate our discussion of the *malandro* lifestyle, which will be developed later.

As such, when Jerônimo argues with João Romão, the owner of the quarry, about the conditions of his hiring, his views are those of a modern and enlightened capitalist. We see a magnificent quarry lost on ignorant, lazy, and underpaid workers:

> —Your workers aren't worth a damn! . . . Look at them loafing. . . . They wouldn't take it easy with me around. I think workers should be well paid, with full bellies and plenty of wine, but if they don't do their jobs, fire them! . . . You don't need a lot of these workers. . . . Instead of all those loafers who must make around thirty mil-réis, . . . you'd be better off hiring two skilled workers for fifty who'd get twice as much done and who could do other jobs too.[56]

Azevedo highlights Jerônimo's "zeal," his "skill," "the sober, austere purity of his character and habits."[57] This good husband, good father, and God-fearing man has exemplary morality rooted in his dedication to his work:

> Jerônimo rose at four every morning, washed beneath a faucet in the courtyard while everyone else was still asleep. . . . The sound of his pickaxe called his fellow workers to order. . . . Jerônimo did not return home until late afternoon, always starving and exhausted. . . . Then, until bedtime, which always came at nine o'clock, he took his guitar and, sitting outside the door with his wife, played *fados*. At such moments he gave full rein to his homesickness, through those melancholy songs in which his exiled soul took flight, returning from the torrid Americas to the sad villages of his childhood.[58]

Azevedo makes Jerônimo a foreigner: he lives in Brazil but is Portuguese in his music, cuisine, and work ethic. The exact opposite of Firmo and Rita Baiana. In regard to Rita, here is what her fellow washerwomen have to say:

> She's crazy! . . . Imagine going on a spree like that without giving back those clothes—she'll end up with no customers! . . . It doesn't matter how much work she's got; as soon as she smells a party, she's off like a shot. Look what happened last year at that street festival by the Penha Church! . . . Now that she's hanging around with that mulato Firmo,[59] she's more shameless than ever! Didn't you see what they did the other day? They went on a drunk, her dancing and him playing the viola.[60] . . . —Even so, she's not a bad sort. Her only fault is that she likes to take it easy and have a good time.[61]

As for Firmo, it is not that he does not work, but, just like his lover, he works as little as possible: "He was a skilled turner, expert but lazy. . . . Sometimes, however, he would get lucky at dice or roulette, and then he would celebrate as he had for the past three months: spending his money on a spree with Rita Baiana."[62] His professional frustration was in never having "managed to get a job in a government office—his dream!—making seventy mil-réis and working from nine to three." The irony of this last phrase is accentuated by the fact that (as is elsewhere indicated in the novel) this amount is precisely what Jerônimo requests and João Romão is so hesitant to pay, even for a schedule that is twice as long (from five to five).[63] In the next chapter, we will return to the character of Firmo and the relationship between samba and a rejection of work.

What I want to highlight here is that in Alencar's novel, samba allowed for the establishment of a series of differentiations among workers (Blacks from the countryside, pages, guards), while in Azevedo's the only clear opposition is a "national" one: Brazilians, primarily of mixed race, perform samba, while the Portuguese man sings *fado*. What's more, it is in seeing and hearing samba that Jerônimo falls in love with Rita Baiana and begins a Brazilianization process, such that a shift in musical taste occurs in tandem with a shift in his relationship to work. Samba's seductive power is also present in Alencar's novel; it is the means by which Florência brings Amâncio closer. But in the end this seductive power is defeated by the social differentiation that samba itself also establishes. In Azevedo's novel, on the other hand, the national difference is overcome by seduction. Jerônimo kills his rival Firmo and becomes "Brazilian":

> He was utterly transformed. Rita extinguished his last memories of Portugal; . . . [drying] his last nostalgic tear, which vanished from his heart with the last arpeggio on his guitar. His guitar! She replaced it with a Bahian *violão* and . . . bewitched his dreams with songs from the north. . . . Jerônimo had passed the

point of no return; he was a Brazilian. He grew lazy, fond of extravagance and excess, . . . his love of thrift and moderation vanished. He lost all interest in saving money.[64]

We still see here the geographical placement of samba in Bahia or in the "North." But, in contrast to the excerpts cited previously, the "Bahian *violão*" appears as a national symbol: it makes the Portuguese man "Brazilian," not "Bahian." If we revisit the Sílvio Romero distribution discussed earlier, we see that there are any number of candidates that could potentially occupy the position of national musical emblem: the *fandango* from the provinces of the South, the *cateretê* from Minas, and even Rio de Janeiro's own *xiba*. But in the end, the one that rises to national symbol, in an ascension that was only just beginning, is indeed the "samba from Bahia."

We can follow samba's gradual nationalization in yet another context, in the work of theorists. For instance, when Carneiro seeks a generic name for the *umbigada* dances in his aforementioned essay from 1961, he pauses for a moment between *batuque* and "samba"; the pause echoes that of other scholars who preceded him. For Alvarenga, both names would work equally well to represent this "choreographic type," but "at least in the plume of the learned, Samba appears to have completely substituted the designation Batuque."[65] Luciano Gallet, in a book published posthumously in 1934, offers *batuque* as a generalized term and "samba" as a term specific to Bahia, Rio, and Pernambuco.[66] Arthur Ramos, in *Folclore negro no Brasil* (*Negro Folklore in Brazil*), corrects Gallet, insisting that "samba" is also widespread. But, Ramos adds, the term "samba" tends to be even more common: "It loses its primitive quality, synonym of batuque . . . to become a generic term for Brazilian popular dance. Samba thus tends to substitute maxixe."[67] For Alvarenga, too, samba "saw its meaning broadened more even than that of Batuque, being extended as a name for any popular dance, equivalent to 'função' [function], 'pagode,' 'forró,' and many others."[68]

I have already mentioned the opposition between *batuque* (an *umbigada* dance, thus of "separated couples") and *baile* (an "intertwined couples" dance). We have also seen that *maxixe* is a type of *baile*. And in Brazil, *umbigada* dances are considered to be part of traditional culture (a folk dance), while *maxixe* (which is urban, danced to the sound of printed music, by a known author) is classified as "popular."[69] Here Ramos and Alvarenga express a nearly imperceptible slippage from one area to another: unequivocally, the type of samba that substitutes *batuque* as a generic term is folk samba, *samba de umbigada* (as Carneiro would have it). But the type of samba that substitutes *maxixe* is popular samba, characteristically urban and danced in "intertwined couples" (thus without the *umbigada*), the birth of which we will study next.

Finally, "samba" also substitutes "tango" as a designation for popular song. (We have already seen that at the beginning of the twentieth century, "tango" and *maxixe* were basically equivalent.) During Carnival of 1911, a report from the newspaper *Jornal do Brasil* said that the *rancho* (Carnival group) "A Filha da Jardineira only has one samba: 'Ladrãozinho' ['Little Thief'], tango." Marília T. Barboza da Silva and Arthur L. de Oliveira Filho, who reference the report, add this: "the word samba, which had hitherto been used as a nearly perfect synonym of tango and maxixe, came into its own, substituting the other two in practice."[70]

Incidentally, in the introduction to Luciano Gallet's *Estudos de folclore* (*Studies of Folklore*), Mário de Andrade writes the following as commentary on a piece by the composer:

> What is important to notice in this "Tango-Batuque," is mainly the name, already indicating his preoccupation in specifying with clarity the form and character of Brazilian musics. It is interesting to note in the manuscript of the sheet music, dated April 1919, that Gallet first wrote in ink "Tango-Batuque," but that, later, the word "tango" was crossed out. Written in pencil, above it, is the word "samba."[71]

It would be difficult to illustrate with better clarity the substitution we are discussing. Tango was headed out, and samba was on its way in, without a change in either the musical content or its association with *batuque* (the association between tango and *batuque*, as the reader may remember, was discussed above).

We thus see that the growing significance of the term "samba" occurs in two concomitant branches, a folk and a popular: the former substitutes *batuque* while the latter, *maxixe* and tango. These two "branches" are still present today, as we can see, for example, in the *EMB* and the *DFB* entries on "samba," both of which are divided into two corresponding parts.[72] Indeed, the defining and redefining process discussed above led to a situation in which a folk and a popular meaning converge in the same word; and though samba's "branches" are treated as distinct, they remain closely related, and at times, as we will later see, unduly confused.

But the convergence of the folk and the popular in a single word expresses a novel ideological convergence forged between the two areas. When consummated, popular samba reaps the benefits of all of the prestige that so many Brazilian intellectuals attributed to folk songs since at least the publication of *O nosso cancioneiro* (*Our Songbook*) by José de Alencar in 1874.

* * *

Let's return for a moment to *O cortiço*. The novel represents an intermediate step in samba's "nationalization." In the book, samba is identified with both Bahia and

Brazil; that which comes from Bahia is treated as authentically Brazilian: the *mulata* Rita Baiana, the food she prepares, and the music to which she dances.

For this "nationalization" process to be complete, however, samba must be associated with Rio de Janeiro, which became the nation's capital in 1763, after having been transferred from Salvador (Bahia), and remained the capital until 1960. The creation of "Carioca samba," which we will study next, begins in 1917 with the success of the composition "Pelo telefone" in Rio de Janeiro. The piece's author, Ernesto dos Santos ("Donga"), the Carioca son of a Bahian woman, baptized it as "samba." Samba takes on its definitive shape at the beginning of the 1930s, with a series of rhythmic (and other) changes. Only then does samba uncontestably assume its position as national rhythm par excellence.[73] But the connection between "Carioca samba" and "Bahian samba" still needs some attention.

This connection, as one might suspect, runs parallel to, as we discussed earlier, the connection between popular samba and folk samba. The "Bahian samba" described by Carneiro, Ralph C. Waddey, and others is *samba de umbigada*, which has no official record except for that which is given to it from outsiders, by novelists or anthropologists: folklore. Meanwhile, "Carioca samba," as we have already seen, is what replaces *maxixe* and tango in sheet music titles and in the tastes of urban audiences: the popular. Ostensibly, these are two wholly distinct entities.

Still, they share the same name, diverging only in their geographical associations. Moreover, people in Brazilian culture generally assume the two are related, such that Carioca popular samba is said to have its origins in Bahian folk samba, the former being said to have developed from the latter. Consequently, on the one hand, samba is said to have been "born" in 1917 with "Pelo telefone,"[74] such that the composer Zé Keti sang these lyrics in the 1955 samba "A voz do morro" ("The Voice of the Morro"):[75]

Eu sou o samba	I am samba
Sou natural daqui do Rio de Janeiro.	I come from Rio de Janeiro.

However, samba is also said to have been "born in Bahia" (as in the lyrics of "Samba da bênção" ["Samba of the Blessing"], composed in 1966 by Baden Powell and Viniciús de Moraes). Donga himself, the author of "Pelo telefone," affirms in an interview that "samba wasn't born with me. It already existed in Bahia, well before I was born, but it was here in Rio that it was stylized."[76]

The notion of "stylization" employed here by Donga is important, for it serves to specify the difference between the "Bahian" and "Carioca" versions while also positing some continuity between the two. But in other cases, this difference is entirely forgotten. For example, the task of writing the aforementioned "Carta do samba"—which was approved at the Congresso Nacional do Samba held in Rio de Janeiro in 1961—was entrusted to Edison Carneiro, who was not only president of the Campanha de Defesa do Folclore Brasileiro (Campaign of Defense of Brazilian Folklore)[77] but also a Bahian and the creator of the expression *samba de umbigada*! This decision conspicuously demonstrates an intent to reinforce Carioca samba's folk parentage.

In his book *O mistério do samba* (*The Mystery of Samba*), Hermano Vianna shows how in the 1930s, nationalist ideologues were interested in attributing to a newborn musical product the respectability owed to time-honored, traditional things. As we will see, it was during this decade that a new kind of samba, which took on its defining traits in Rio de Janeiro roughly between 1928 and 1932, started to be consumed from the country's north to its south. Still, this new samba is nevertheless portrayed as being the most traditional musical expression of the whole of Brazil. Consequently, in a composition such as the famous "Aquarela do Brasil" ("Brazil"),[78] released by Ary Barroso in 1939, the samba that is heard is a musical production full of novelty, being in part a result of urban Brazil, of records, and of the radio. But the samba that is sung about—"Brasil, terra de samba e pandeiro" (Brazil, land of samba and *pandeiro*)—is defined by references to the era of slavery, to the "cortina do passado" (curtain of the past), to the "mãe preta no cerrado" (mammy in the *cerrado*),[79] to the "rei congo no congado" (King of Congo in the *congado*),[80] and to the *sinhá* who walks "pelos salões arrastando o seu vestido rendado" (through the halls dragging her lace garments). The implicit message is that colonial and Imperial ancestors were already familiar with a "samba" that would be, in essence, the same as that of "Aquarela do Brasil." This exceedingly easy transition from the folk to the popular, from musical traditions said to be anchored in the past to practices linked to the record industry, a mythology fueled in part by the discourse of the actors themselves and by the existing bibliography, will be discussed next by analyzing two of the prime moments in the construction of Carioca samba: that of the success of the composition "Pelo telefone," during Carnival of 1917 and, in part 2, that of the emergence, between 1928 and 1933, of the *sambistas* connected with the Carioca neighborhood of Estácio de Sá.

From the Dining Room
to the Drawing Room

During the second half of the nineteenth century, the migratory flow from the country's Northeast to the Southeast intensified in step with the regional shift in economic power that had begun a century earlier, a shift expressed moreover in the decision to move the nation's capital from Salvador to Rio de Janeiro (1763). Part of this contingent comprised free-born Black Bahians—either because they were children of freed slaves or because they were beneficiaries of the Law of the Free Womb (1871)—who even enjoyed, in certain cases, relative economic security. This group, unified by strong ties of solidarity, would constitute a "Bahian community" in the neighborhood of Saúde, in downtown Rio.[1]

This solidarity was in large part ensured by the *tias* (aunts)[2]—that is, older Bahian women who were leaders in the organization of families, religions, and leisure time. Among the well-known *tias* were Tia Amélia and Tia Perciliana, who were the mothers, respectively, of the aforementioned Ernesto dos Santos (1889–1974) and João Machado Guedes (1887–1974), who, known by the nicknames "Donga" and "João da Baiana"—as they will henceforth be referred to in this work—would come to exercise prominent roles in the Carioca music scene of the early twentieth century.[3]

But without a doubt the most famous of the Bahian *tias* was Hilária Batista de Almeida, who entered the annals of samba as Tia Ciata. The importance imputed to her by samba *cronistas* is due especially to the fact that "Pelo telefone" (unanimously considered to be the first time a composition designated as samba became a popular music hit), despite finding in Donga an official author, was actually a collective creation gestated at her home. According to Henrique Foréis

Domingues (known as Almirante), it was "the *habitués* of Tia Ciata's house . . . [who] created a musical product, which they classified as samba."[4] Tinhorão also affirms that "Pelo telefone" "had been one of the songs to emerge during the gatherings promoted by the Bahian Tia Ciata."[5] Tia Ciata's house thus takes on a nearly mythical dimension as Carioca samba's "place of origin."

But Tia Ciata was not the only person to promote nighttime musical affairs. According to João da Baiana, his mother also regularly "put on *Candomblé* parties. The Bahian women of the era liked to throw parties. . . . It was necessary to go to the police headquarters and explain that there was going to be a samba, a *baile*, a party, whatever."[6] And Donga confirms: "At home, the first *sambistas* got together, actually, no one was called a *sambista*. . . . They were definitely parties. Just like they happened at my house, they happened at the homes of all of my mother's fellow Bahians."[7]

Here we see Oneyda Alvarenga's definition of samba at work, a definition cited earlier: "any popular *baile*, equivalent to 'função' [function], 'pagode,' etc."[8] In these citations, thus, "samba" appears as a kind of *baile*, where *baile* does not signal a "dance" (and therefore different from the other meanings, as we have seen and will see again, in which "samba" and *baile* are oppositional), but rather a party, where dance, music, food, beverages, and socializing cannot be conceptualized separately.

This meaning is clarified by the two other terms mentioned by Alvarenga, *função* and *pagode*. Let's see what the *DFB* says in its entry on *função*: "Old designation for our religious festivities, and for our familial ones such as baptisms, weddings, and birthdays . . . still preserved by musicians, who thus call solemnities of any type in which they take part."[9] And on *pagode*: "Party, festive and noisy get together, party with food and drink, with or without dancing, party always of an intimate nature, in which friends participate."[10]

We thus have our first general characteristic of the turn-of-the-century "sambas" of these Bahians/Cariocas: no longer the outdoor gatherings mentioned to us by Edison Carneiro and others,[11] being instead parties of an intimate nature, with food, drinks, music, and dance, held for any variety of reasons.[12] As such, when in 1933 the Carnival *cronista* Vagalume (Francisco Guimarães, 1870?–1946) writes, in his book about samba, a chapter dedicated to the "People from the Old Times" (*Gente de outro tempo*), he uses the homes at which the sambas took place to organize his description: first, "the parties at the home of Tia Tereza," subsequently referred to as "the sambas of Tia Tereza"; then, "the sambas of João Alabá," which clearly referred not to his compositions, but rather, once again, to the parties at his home; later is the mention of "another famed samba . . . at the home of Tia Asseata [*sic*]."[13]

Born in Salvador in 1854, purportedly to freed slaves, Tia Ciata arrived in Rio de Janeiro in 1876. There she married João Batista da Silva, also a Black Bahian, who in Salvador had studied medicine for two years at Bahia's famed medical school, the Faculdade de Medicina da Bahia.[14] Later he was able to get a job in the office of Rio's chief of police—and according to his grandson, this was possible thanks to the intercession of Tia Ciata's *Orixás*,[15] who supposedly cured the ailing leg of Brazil's then president, Wenceslau Brás![16]

Tia Ciata's husband's professional "respectability" must have contributed to making her home a point of reference in the Black Carioca community in the early twentieth century. However, this can also be attributed to her own work, as Tia Ciata engaged in social activities that reinforced a particular Afro-Bahian identity while at the same time wove subtle relationships with the world of the Carioca elite. She was involved, for instance, in making and selling sweets, a trade that had already by then become common for Bahians living in Rio. Documented by Jean-Baptiste Debret as early as the first half of the nineteenth century, the *baiana doceira* (Bahian confectioner), at her traditional *tabuleiro* (serving tray), had become an integral part of the city's landscape, even filling orders placed by white families. In addition, she made *baiana*[17] costumes, widely used in official Carnival clubs. In both activities, Tia Ciata ended up with a large number of Bahian women who worked under her supervision. Another factor in her social ascent was her preeminent position in the Candomblé religion. She was an Iyá Kekerê (that is, the primary aide to the *pai de santo*, the priest) at what was then one of the most prestigious Candomblé temples in Rio, that of João Alabá, cited above by Vagalume.[18]

The sambas at Tia Ciata's house have remained in Rio de Janeiro's oral memory, as we can see in the accounts gathered by Moura (and also in the city's literary memory, as they are cited by poets such as Manuel Bandeira and Mário de Andrade).[19] In the following paragraphs, we will use these (and other) accounts to detail what we know about the sambas.

The first thing to emphasize is that the term was not only, as we have seen, a generic designation for these parties. It was also the specific name for one of the activities practiced there, as we can gather from the categorizations found in certain accounts: "the party was like this: *baile* in the drawing room, *partido-alto* samba at the back of the house, and *batucada* in the backyard" (João da Baiana).[20] "*Baile* in the front, samba in the back" (Carmem do Xibuca, interviewed by Moura when she was nearly one hundred years old).[21] "At black homes, the parties were centered around choro and samba. At black parties there was the more civilized *baile* in the drawing room, the samba in the back room, and the *batucada* in the backyard" (Pixinguinha).[22] "Samba was danced in the dining room and the *baile* was in the drawing room."[23] "The Bahians threw parties with the following characteristics: there was samba at so-and-so's house, so there would be choro too. In the back there would also be *batucada*" (Donga).[24]

And thus we come to a second meaning of the word "samba," as it is placed in contradistinction, within the context of the party, to a whole host of other activities. However, prior to examining the way in which *baile* differed from samba (which is the most significant opposition in this set of accounts), let's clarify the meaning of some of the terms employed in these accounts: *choro, batucada,* and *partido-alto* samba.

The word *choro* initially designated an instrumental ensemble that appeared around the 1870s, at the same time as *maxixe* dancing, in fact. Traditionally, the ensemble included flute, *cavaquinho,* and guitar, and its early repertoire, dances of European origin—mainly polka, but also *schottische,* waltz, and some others. As we have seen, these were dances with intertwined couples; indeed, musically speaking, the *choro* developed along with the process noted earlier, that of the working classes adopting new dance styles. The ensembles called *choros* were among the primary vehicles by which polka's rhythm was altered, as we analyzed earlier via piano sheet music. Eventually, the word *choro* becomes the name for the compositions performed by these ensembles.[25]

The word *batucada,* in this context, refers to a game of physical dexterity that was popular in Rio de Janeiro. It was a variation of *capoeira,* but might also be considered a variation of *samba de umbigada* as defined by Carneiro, for it consisted of a *roda,* with the customary handclaps and responsorial singing performed by the participants. In this case, though, the *umbigada* was replaced with a *pernada,* a kick designed to knock over an opponent, who, if able to stay standing, won the chance to give a *pernada* to the person he chose.[26] *Batucada* differed from other *sambas de umbigada*—and in particular from those that would have been practiced at Tia Ciata's house—in its violent nature, which explains, as mentioned in the cited accounts, why it was practiced outside of the house, in the backyard.

As for the expression *partido-alto* samba (that is, *samba de partido alto*), it has led to quite a bit of confusion; Nei Lopes offers a list of ten different meanings for the word.[27] Nonetheless we find a consensus that there are two basic types of *partido-alto*: the old or Bahian, and the modern or Carioca.[28] It is easier to reach conclusions if we examine each independently, for both are still practiced today; the ethnographic work of Waddey in Bahia and the work of Lopes in Rio are the best sources.[29] The latter offers the following definition for Carioca *partido-alto*: "[a] type of samba [that is] sung in the form of a duel by two or more contenders and is composed of a choral part . . . and a solo part with improvised verses or the traditional repertoire, which may or may not refer to the refrain's subject matter."[30] Lacking in this definition is an important detail, as I deduce from Lopes's own observations (and also from my own direct contact with Rio's *partido-alto*): *partido-alto* is never sung as part of a procession, but instead always in a *roda*. This distinction is important because there were sambas sung in processions that correspond to Lopes's description, but these were never considered to be *partido-alto*.

An important point to highlight is that the expression *partido-alto* is often used to emphasize the authentic, traditional character of samba. Donga speaks of his youth as the "time of the real samba, the *partido-alto* samba";[31] and Carneiro says that the "*partido-alto* that so delights the veterans of samba, is not performed for the general public. . . . This is how the elders remember the 'old days' of samba's arrival to Rio de Janeiro."[32]

It is precisely these greatly idealized "old days" that are so difficult to grasp, and they are also responsible for the profusion of definitions mentioned above. Indeed, it is difficult to know exactly what constituted the *partido-alto* practiced by the children of Bahians in early twentieth-century Rio de Janeiro. On this, the accounts we have at our disposal are unhelpful, as they are contradictory; at times the expression appears as a mere synonym of *samba de umbigada*, and at other times it seems to be a specific type of samba within a whole range of them, including *chula raiada* and *samba-corrido*—equally hazy terms. The few pre-1930 samba recordings whose labels mention *partido-alto* are also of no help, given their disparateness. Later on, I will again touch on *partido-alto* and its meaning.

As for the contradistinction between *baile* and samba, which appears with notable regularity in the accounts cited above, a part of its meaning has already been examined: it signals the cultural difference that is expressed in the way people dance, whether in intertwined couples (for *baile*) or separated couples (for samba). These oppositional relationships also coincide with the differences that distinguish *choro* from samba, though these differences must be treated cautiously, for both terms continue to be used in Brazilian music today, albeit with different meanings. *Choro*, as we have seen, went from being the name of the ensemble to the name of the musical genre, retaining very little of its relationship with the polkas from which it originated. In the 1920s *choro* musicians began to provide the harmonic support and melodic ornamentation on most commercial samba recordings, playing flutes, trombones, and so forth. As such, samba and *choro* are much more intertwined today than they were at the beginning of the twentieth century, when the overlapping was nowhere near as extensive as it later became.

But the contradistinction between *baile* and samba is also linked to another differentiation, a spatial one, between the drawing room and the dining room. We find, in Jeffrey D. Needell's book on the Carioca elite of the *Belle Epoque*, details regarding what this architectonic categorization might signify:

> The rooms were distinguished from one another by the symbolic value of European appearance. Some rooms, notably the drawing room, . . . clearly acted as the public statement of family status. . . . The family passed their time in the

bedrooms and the family dining room, where no one but very intimate relations were admitted. . . . As one stepped from one room to another, one might also move from one cultural expression, and associated statement of role, to another. One's formal Society persona was more European, one's family one, more Brazilian.[33]

When Needell places European culture, with which the Carioca elite of the *Belle Epoque* sought to identify itself, in contrast to traditional Brazilian culture, he largely defines the latter by the presence of African traces.[34] What is interesting, however, is that at the same time, he also softens the contrast, showing that such traces were present even in the homes of wealthy families, in their most intimate of rooms.

My arguments also soften the contrast, but in the other direction: the first-person accounts presented above allow us to see that at the homes of the Bahian aunts, the European traces were also quite present—in this case, in the room characterized by a higher degree of formality. In other words, at the home of Tia Ciata, too (which reproduced the general structure of the homes of the elite), a "respectable" status was attributed to the drawing room, with the intertwined couples dancing and the *choro* music, which was based on genres of European origin such as polka and waltz. In sum, the drawing room hosted the more "civilized" part of the party, in Pixinguinha's words. In contrast, the dining room was the intimate sphere, where, protected by a "cultural screen,"[35] an Afro-Brazilian type of activity was predominant.

Still, it seems quite impossible to imagine that the hermeticism of the "screen" separating the drawing room from the dining room would have been so total that the illustrious visitors would be surprised or shocked to learn what was happening in the other room. The purpose of the "screen" was not to obstruct, but rather to demarcate a border across which, given the right circumstances, there would have been a constant back and forth. Indeed, there are accounts that recall members of the white elite in the samba *rodas*, as in the composition by Pixinguinha and Cícero de Almeida:

Samba de partido-alto	*Partido-alto* samba
Só vai cabrocha que samba de fato	Only the *cabrochas*[36] who really samba go
Só vai mulato filho de bahiana	Only *mulato* children of Bahian women go
E gente rica de Copacabana.	And rich folk from Copacabana.[37]

Vagalume also references this in writing, explaining that "when the *roda* was formed, the participants were the elite, and the invitees, the hand-picked guests, who deserved to be called 'Iaiá' and 'Ioiô.'"[38] These hand-picked guests, still according to Vagalume, were people "from high up": "the baron, the commander, and the Portuguese from the corner shop and from the butcher shop."[39]

These two citations show an important characteristic regarding the appraisal of *partido-alto*,[40] which is directly related to our interests here. It is that this type of samba is made over with an "elitist" character, a term that should be understood in two senses. First, it is only the *bamba* elite, who, due to their abilities and familiarity with the tradition, may take an active part in this moment, for it is, as we have seen, the *nec plus ultra* of samba traditionalism. The only participants were, as Pixinguinha says, "*cabrochas* who really samba" and the "*mulato* children of Bahian women" or, as Vagalume would have it, the "distinguished." Second, among the white spectators of samba (or the people outside of the "world of samba," to use an expression that will be discussed below), only members of the elite are given entry—here, elite in terms of wealth and prestige.

The elitism noted in this appraisal of *partido-alto* within the turn-of-the-century Bahian/Carioca group is confirmed in the research Waddey conducted in Bahia during the 1980s. One of his informants says that *partido-alto* is the "samba of the aristocracy." The author mentions a piece of information from Professor Zilda Paim, from Santo Amaro da Purificação (a city crucial to the cultural region of the Bahian Recôncavo), according to whom "'*partido alto*' was the *samba* which the *senhores de engenho* (the owners of the sugar plantations and, of course, of the slaves) held to show off their favorite *cabrochas* . . . that is, their favorite slave mistresses."[41] This would explain one of the particularities of the Bahian version of *partido-alto*: the dance is executed by a sole dancer and accompanied by instruments alone; the singing appears only during the intervals that separate one dancer from the next.

It seems to me that the connotations attributed to *partido-alto* allow us to understand the only account we have from a participant of Tia Ciata's parties that offers a divergent explanation of how the parties were configured. This is João da Baiana's statement, published by Tinhorão: "The elders would be in the room at the front singing *partido-alto* . . . , the younger folks would be in the bedrooms singing *samba-corrido*. And in the backyard were the folks who liked the *batucada*."[42] Always this threefold division of the party, with the *batucada* in the backyard and the house spatially divided into a more outward part and a more inward one. But rather than the drawing room, we have mention of the front room, and instead of dining room, bedrooms.[43] As far as the music is concerned, instead of *baile* and samba, we have *samba de partido-alto* and *samba-corrido*.

Based on what was said above, we can deduce that *partido-alto* is to *samba-corrido* what *baile* is to samba. To confirm this supposition, the only expression whose meaning still needs clarifying is *samba-corrido*. Let's see what Waddey says on the topic: "One constant among all of these variables is the essentially European textual form of the *samba chulado*. . . . In contrast, the short pattern of solo call and group response and the indeterminate duration of the *samba corrido* are African."[44] But what is this *samba-chulado*, which Waddey places in contra-distinction to *samba-corrido*, situating the former as "essentially European" and the latter as "African"? Nothing less than another name for *partido-alto*: "each of the . . . names—'samba de chula' (or 'samba chulado'), . . . samba de partido alto, . . . identifies the same genre by a different specific aspect."[45] This, as we can see, confirms the above thesis by way of a different route: if *partido-alto* is to *samba-corrido* what Europe is to Africa, and if Europe is to Africa what *baile* is to samba, then *baile* is to samba what *partido-alto* is to *samba-corrido*.[46]

Partido-alto's place as an aristocratic form of samba gives it, and it alone, the distinction of being performed in the front room. This is an ambiguous position, inasmuch as the elitism of the Afro-Bahian tradition is confused with the elitism of the white guests who include plantation owners, barons, and commanders, and inasmuch as European elements merge more profoundly with African elements. But it is this ambiguity that grants consistency to João da Baiana's statement when compared to other eyewitness accounts, and even to other accounts given by João da Baiana himself.

* * *

While there are no detailed descriptions of how the samba music/dance was practiced in the dining room of Tia Ciata's home, bits and pieces of information in the accounts we have substantiate the hypothesis that it was a type of *samba de umbigada*. The fact that the accounts counterpose, within the activities of the samba party, the samba music/dance to the *baile*, is one such datum, for as we saw in an earlier chapter, *baile* was often employed in opposition to terms designating *umbigada* dances. There are further corroborative hints in the accounts collected by Moura: for example, references to the *roda* and attendants' handclaps.[47] An-other datum is that many of the participants showed a clear attachment to their Bahian roots, relevant when considering the importance of *samba de umbigada* in Bahia, as per the descriptions by Carneiro and Waddey,[48] among others. It seems reasonable to assume that among the many ties this group maintained to its homeland (religion, celebrations, cuisine[49]), one of them would also have been the samba practiced there. But still more important in supporting the hypothesis in question are the few choreographic descriptions we have of the parties.

Indeed, one account states that Tia Ciata "spent half an hour dancing the *miudinho* in the *roda*."[50] The *miudinho*, as defined by Renato Almeida, "is one of the steps of the [Bahian] samba. I myself was able to see, in Bahia, the women dance it in *sambas de roda*."[51] Lili Jumbemba, Tia Ciata's granddaughter, born in 1885, remembers that at the sambas her grandmother knew how "to samba just right . . . , gracefully shuffling her sandals on the tips of her toes and in the middle of a *roda*."[52] Compare this with what Gilberto Freyre says about *samba rural* (rural samba) in Pernambuco during the era of slavery: "the *mulatas*, with much movement of the hips . . . , entered into a sensual and nearly endless dance, with their sandals turned up on the tips of their toes."[53] And Donga adds this: "A *roda* formed. . . . In the middle, the people danced. . . . They danced one at a time, with excitement, performing samba with their feet."[54] The dancing was thus done in the middle of the *roda*, and the characteristic step was the graceful foot shuffle known as *sapateado* or *miudinho*. As Waddey describes it, "rapid, and at times nearly imperceptible foot movements (the '*sapateado*', also called '*repicado*', '*recolchete*', or '*miudinho*') are almost the only body movements in the properly executed *Recôncavo* style of *samba* choreography."[55] João da Baiana gives us other aspects: "We would sing a verse and people would samba, one at a time. . . . One would get out to signal another. If it were 'smooth' [*liso*] then it would be only an *umbigada*, but if it were to go 'hard' [*pegar 'duro'*], now that was doing *capoeira* [*capoeiragem*]."[56] The way in which the solo dancer chooses a substitute is broken down into *samba liso* (with an *umbigada*) and *samba duro* (or *batucada*, in which, as we have seen, the *pernada* replaces the *umbigada*).[57]

All of this now better equips us to comprehend the two meanings used for the word "samba" in the eyewitness accounts of Tia Ciata's parties. In the most general sense, it designates the party itself. Of course, not every party that took place in Rio de Janeiro during this period would have carried the designation of "samba"; Pixinguinha speaks of "black parties," and Donga of "Bahian parties." Treating this idea somewhat more liberally, we might define these as parties held at the homes of the working class, returning us thus to the concept of samba we got earlier from Alvarenga: "any popular *baile*" (that is, a *baile* of the masses).

In the most restricted sense, however, the term "samba" designates one of the musical activities practiced at the parties of Bahian transplants in Rio de Janeiro. It was a *samba de umbigada* according to the Carneiro definition we saw earlier, in which the singing and dancing introduced particular signs of Afro-Brazilian identity. It was practiced in the dining room, an area of the house characterized by a higher degree of intimacy and more restricted access.

* * *

The physical layout of Tia Ciata's house, and the use made of it, suggests that the path from the front to the back—from the exterior to the interior—reflects a polarization between public and intimate space.[58] This polarization does not occur gradually but rather in ruptures, in the separations between the rooms. As such, the drawing room could be used to receive people whose access to the dining room would have been verboten. On the other hand, in the intimacy of the dining room, people close to the family could engage in practices or behaviors that would not have been tolerated in front of more formal visitors. Separations created in this way—which we earlier called, with Sodré, "cultural screens"—act as filters, restricting and limiting access in both directions. Moreover, this filter can be conceptualized as more or less permeable, which, as we will see, implies different conceptions about the circulation of cultural practices between the intimate and public sphere and, for the issue at hand, about the creation of samba itself.

The separation between the rooms of Tia Ciata's home also suggests an analogy with the idea of "censorship" according to Freud's topographical model of the mind. A similar analogy appears in an Arthur Ramos passage concerning Praça Onze, which was the primary stage of Rio de Janeiro's Black Carnival until 1930:

> Persecuted by the white man, the Negro in Brazil hid his beliefs in the "terreiros" [temples] of the macumbas and the candomblés. Folklore was the valve by which he communicated with "white" civilization . . . primarily during Carnival. Every year Praça Onze de Junho, in Rio de Janeiro, receives an avalanche of this collective catharsis. . . . Praça Onze is a great grinder, giant mill, which refines the unconscious material, and prepares it for its entry into "civilization." Praça Onze is the censor of the African Negro unconscious. . . . It is the border between Negro and white European culture, a border without precise limits, where institutions interpenetrate one another and cultures take turns.[59]

Tia Ciata's house, then, which was not by chance located right near Praça Onze, served as this type of valve of communication between an "African Negro unconscious" and a "'white' civilization," to employ Ramos's terminology.

Yet it is problematic to transpose onto a sociological plane a theory that Freud elaborated on a psychological plane. More problematic still are the equivalences postulated by Ramos between Black culture and the unconscious. Nevertheless, the analogy formulated here turns out to be of great use in explicating two of samba's historiographical paradigms: the repression paradigm and the topographical model paradigm.

Both paradigms are immediately visible in the first phrase of the passage from Ramos: "persecuted by the white man, the Negro in Brazil hid his beliefs in the 'terreiros' of the macumbas and the candomblés." African and Afro-Brazilian beliefs—or, more generally, their social and cultural practices—would have fallen victim, in a Brazil that remained a slavocracy for three centuries, to interdictions and prohibitions: the repression thesis. To a certain extent, however, these practices survived, for they would have been hidden and restricted to specific places where the masters could not discover them: the topographical model. The image of cultural contents being placed at a distance from a repressive body's reach, and thus maintained outside of the mainstream circulation of ideas in society, serves the psychoanalytical analogy so well explored by Ramos.

Both the repression thesis and the topographical model can be understood as historiographic paradigms not only because they appear in Ramos's analogy, but also because they appear in most of the samba literature. And this is what I will show in the following paragraphs.

The repression of Carioca samba is often discussed in writings and accounts about its embryonic phase. According to Sérgio Cabral, samba was "a genre so execrated by the dominant classes of the first decades of the century that the police imprisoned anyone who sang, danced, or played."[60] This statement is undoubtedly an exaggeration, at the very least because, as we have seen, prior to 1917 samba was not yet a "genre" that was sung or played outside of very specific contexts. But it is also an exaggeration, as we will see, because it treats the relationships between "dominant classes" and popular culture as a case of complete repudiation, without a trace of nuance.

Nevertheless, Cabral is not the only author to emphasize that until the 1930s, samba was victimized by an official persecution. Much to the contrary, this is a common theme in the bibliography. Indeed, many *sambista* accounts attest to such persecution, such as in this reminiscence from Cartola: "during my time, the samba *rodas* . . . were often broken up by the police, since samba back then was for *malandros* and criminals."[61] And João da Baiana reports, "I was arrested many times for playing *pandeiro*."[62] Even Noel Rosa, a composer about whom much will be said later, reported that "at first people fought against samba. It was considered a pastime for bums."[63]

But anthropologist Hermano Vianna has shown that from early on—along with the repression—members of the elite also took an interest in, and were supportive of, popular music.[64] I agree with the basic thesis of his book *O mistério do samba* (*The Mystery of Samba*): the acceptance of the genre, in the 1930s, as "national music" was the "culmination of a gradual process . . . of encounters among various social groups that collectively, and over centuries, invented Brazilian identity and popular culture."[65] Consequently, samba—and Afro-Brazilian culture before that—was not merely an object of persecution but also a partner in a cultural dialogue from the outset.

This broad thesis needs to be substantiated by a detailed study that can elucidate the intermediations by which this process occurred (Vianna took only the first steps).[66] But one of its great strengths is in going against the current of samba's traditional historiography, which highlighted only the repressive aspect of the relationship between elites and popular culture, making its subsequent acceptance a paradox, a true "mystery," as the title of Vianna's book puts it.

Following the anthropologist, it is easy to see that the limits of the repression thesis become self-evident if we just read through to the end of the *sambistas'* own accounts. For instance, Juvenal Lopes recounts that "we were very persecuted by the police. They would come to Estácio, we would run to Mangueira, because that was where we could find Nascimento, the deputy who covered for us and we could samba more freely."[67] For every deputy who repressed, there was another who provided cover. And in an account from Tia Ciata's granddaughter, we learn that "when she held *pagodes* at home, there was colonel Costa who sent six characters."[68] Colonel Costa's "characters" were policemen who, no doubt thanks to the contacts Tia Ciata's husband had at the office of the chief of police, acted as "security."[69]

Samba's persecution was supposedly aggravated by its association with Black religions, insomuch as it upset the values of Catholicism, which was well-nigh the official religion in Brazil. We have already noted Tia Ciata's links to Candomblé, and similar links could be noted for the dominant samba figures in its early phases (until 1930). A journalist close to Sinhô, for example, wrote this of him: "zealous adept of African religions, Sinhô would never leave his spiritual father—the Prince of Alufás, the highly regarded and respected Henrique Assumano Mina do Brasil."[70] This association was recognized and perhaps even exaggerated by the white elite, as in the case of Guilherme de Mello, who writes that "every African function is based on spiritism and consists of sambas."[71]

While this link could, in some cases, work against samba, this was not necessarily the norm, as there was also ambiguity in the attitudes of the authorities who dealt with Afro-Brazilian religions. For example, according to Vagalume, João Abedé was "the only *pai de santo* who held a diploma of Doctor in the occult sciences, from a North American academy," and he promoted his *candomblés* without incident, "seeing that there was a society there of Occult Sciences, organized as a civil society, given that their police-approved Statutes included African religion and dances."[72] Already mentioned, too, was the account given by one of Tia Ciata's grandsons, according to whom his grandmother's *Orixás* were said to have cured the ailing leg of a president of the nation.

We find in Nina Rodrigues other examples of how ambiguity could characterize the relationships between official authorities and Afro-Brazilian religions. An 1896 report transcribed from the Salvador newspaper *Diário de Notícias* said that "open for six days, in a place called *Gantois*, a large candomblé. . . . We have just been informed that among the people who went to enjoy the candomblé were found to be a police authority and diverse groups of plain-clothes police and some secret groups from that same police force." The following year, *O Republicano*, a newspaper also from Bahia's capital, included this comment: "let it not surprise the public if tomorrow the press announces that inside the bureau of security there were celebrations in homage to [the deity] Xangô or any other one."[73]

Nevertheless, more than forty years later, when the Department of Culture of São Paulo, directed by Mário de Andrade, sent a Folk Research Mission to the Northeast, it found that the repression of Afro-Brazilian religions still existed. The *interventor* of Pernambuco—a federally appointed official put in place by Brazil's populist dictator Getúlio Vargas to "intervene" in state affairs when necessary—staffed politicians who were linked to the clergy and to the right-wing Catholic periodical *Fronteiras*, which severely undermined the work of the Mission. Indeed, the field researcher explains in a letter to Mário de Andrade: "The priests are holding all the cards. . . . By way of [their and of their allies'] imposition, the xangôs[74] were closed and all of the material of their sessions seized."[75] Even in 1944, Andrade affirms that "Recife, João Pessoa, and Natal[76] persecute the Maracatus, Cabocolinhos, and Bois. . . . Who is it who can [deal] with a delirious order from a policeman or from a mayor"?[77]

Also in the 1940s, in the interior of São Paulo, the clergy and the police prohibited the practice of *samba de umbigada* in Itu. Oddly, however, this samba had been performed since the nineteenth century without incident, in the square facing a church that housed an image of Saint Benedict and that was left illuminated the whole night so that the participants could come to rest inside![78]

The Itu case thus inverts what is seen as a common pattern: instead of going from elite repression of samba to acceptance, we see it go from acceptance to repression. These examples show that if, as Vianna suggests, prior to Carioca samba's ascent, there was an "interaction between elites and popular culture" that ran parallel to the persecution then even after samba's ascension, persecution continued to coexist with acceptance. People in 1940s Itu (just as in Recife, João Pessoa, and Natal) had certainly already heard the Carioca sambas broadcast on the radio and put on records, but this did not necessarily translate to a greater appreciation of local Afro-Brazilians and/or their forms of amusement, which lacked the aura ensured by technology, by the voice of an enormously successful singer such as Francisco Alves, and by the arrangements of a maestro like Radamés Gnattali.

In speaking of the creation of samba as the invention of popular Brazilian culture, Vianna turns to Hobsbawm's thesis on the invention of tradition. Samba would thus be a tradition invented by "blacks and whites (and, of course, mestiços), as well as a few gypsies—also a Frenchman here or there. Cariocas and Bahians,[79] intellectuals and politicians, erudite poets, classical composers, folklorists, millionaires . . . While some were interested in the construction of Brazilian national identity, others were merely trying to survive as professional musicians or to make a statement in the world of modern art." Samba results from the dialogue among these heterogeneous groups that, each with its own motivations and approach, end up creating the notion of a national music. Prior to and outside of this process, there would never have existed "a well-defined, 'authentic' samba genre prior to its elaboration as a national music. . . . The crystallization of the genre and its symbolic elevation were concurrent—not consecutive—processes."[80]

These statements contradict samba's other historiographic paradigm, which I called the "topographical model." Here samba would not have been invented at all, much less by "various social groups"; it would already have existed, confined to nights on the plantations, the Macumba temples, or the *morros* (hillsides) of Rio de Janeiro, prior to coming to light and winning over Brazil. Samba's "place" would be in Black culture's refuges, the nooks in which it had hidden out and resisted.

Alvarenga phrases it thus: "In Rio de Janeiro samba lives in its primitive form as a *roda* dance among the dirt-poor who inhabit the *morros* of the city. Carioca urban Samba was born of the Samba of the *morros*, which spread to the rest of Brazil."[81] And Andrade: "Fortunately, in the highest airs of the *morros*, the samba continued its beat, ignored, developing with more liberty and purity, in the fraternity of the *macumbas* and the *cordões* [Carnival groups] of carnival. And when it felt pubescent, now inhibited from suffering any new deformations to its essence, it descended onto the city, and Brazil adopted it."[82] Arthur Ramos, too: "*samba do morro* [samba from the hillsides] is the heir to the primitive Angola-Congo Negro *batuque*, and to the Brazilian slave of the plantation and mining rush."[83] Finally, Ary Vasconcelos, building on Gallet, speaks of the "famous Samba, today exported to the whole world," as a "black dance installed in Brazil."[84]

In sum, according to this point of view, samba would belong intrinsically to Afro-Brazilian culture. Intrinsic in two senses: first, because samba would not be an independent invention, a creation, with all the arbitrary components that these words evoke, but rather a form of heritage, atavism, what Mário de Andrade would call a "racial fatality." And from there it follows that samba would also be intrinsic to Black culture in a second sense, that is, in contrast to the other cultures and ethnicities that make up Brazilian society.

The first person to convincingly question this position—and in this way, he precedes Vianna's work—was Flávio Silva, who wrote the following, based on his study of the origins of urban Carioca samba: "It is thus a mistake to affirm—as is done with exceeding frequency—that 'samba came from Africa.' . . . I see no black-African trace in the recording of 'Último desejo' made by Aracy de Almeida in 1937."[85]

We can now see precisely how closely connected these two paradigms are. The more we treat Black culture as the "place," the samba *topos* par excellence, the more we see its relationship to white culture through a prism of repression. We thus arrive at a "high contrast" version, in the photographic sense, of the history of samba. The symmetrically opposed version, toward which Vianna's book leans, would see here a neutral music, stripped of any potentially conflicting cultural signs.

Here is the issue according to its logical extremes: if samba is conceptualized as exclusively Black, it is as if Tia Ciata's dining room (or other versions of this "place," such as a Macumba temple or a *morro*) had been completely sealed off from any white element; the degree of leakage into the drawing room (or, as Ramos put it, into "'white' civilization") would have been nil, and the repression to which samba would be subjected in larger society, maximal. If, on the other hand, the wall separating the two rooms were to disappear without a trace—and with it the "topographical model"—samba would be conceptualized as nothing more than just another genre performed alongside the waltz and the polka to animate the dances of a Brazil in which ethnic differences would never be expressed musically. As such, it would be a perfectly homogeneous mix, the internal composition having no majority group; a product, so to speak, that is completely artificial—an arbitrary creation, free from any heritage, atavisms, and ethnicities.

Formulated as such, both of the positions are unilateral, simplistic, and unsustainable. Yet, to different degrees of attenuation, the former has been predominant in the samba literature. Vianna writes against the supremacy of this view and thus tends toward the latter, which he also attempts to attenuate in saying he does not seek to deny the repression of samba, but only to show that it "coexisted with other types of social interaction."[86]

The attenuation of these two positions is sometimes conscious, as in Vianna's case. But at other times, it is done without the authors recognizing it, leading to the inclusion of the flip side of their argument. For example, even historians of popular music who describe Carioca samba as "Black music" nevertheless include in their books information showing that, from the outset, white people from different classes and nations participated in the music's creation. Yet we had to wait for Vianna's work to see this participation problematized—a task, moreover, that benefited greatly from those very same music history books.

But the reciprocal is also true: Vianna argues in favor of the invention of samba by various social groups while leaving hints here and there that, not unlike those whom he critiques, he also places Black Brazilians in a predominant role in the process. He affirms, for example, that "these families [that occupied downtown housing in Rio] included many black migrants from Bahia who had come to Rio after the abolition of slavery in 1888. Along with other baggage, these migrants brought with them rites of Afro-Brazilian religions like candomblé and various musical rhythms that would soon be incorporated into Carioca samba."[87] These Bahians, who were Black and mixed race, would thenceforth become the bearers of the rhythms of samba.

More problematic for his point is the statement he makes at the end of the second chapter:

> The poor black inhabitants of Rio de Janeiro favelas did not create samba in isolation from the rest of Brazilian society. . . . People of other classes, other races, even other nationalities participated in the process, *if only as active spectators who encouraged musical performances*. Hence, this study will emphasize the *"external relations," so to speak, of the sambistas' world*. (emphasis added)[88]

It is indeed true that many of the groups mentioned above by Vianna—such as the millionaires, the French, and the classical composers—did not participate as practicing musicians in the creation of samba. But to consider them exterior to the "*sambistas'* world" seems to contradict the author's efforts to abandon what I am calling the "topographical model."

He brilliantly shows us that members of such groups had a decisive role in the history of popular music as spectators and motivators. Take, for example, what Donga says in a passage Vianna does not cite: "[Irineu Marinho] was a God for the 'Oito Batutas.' If not for Arnaldo Guinle and Irineu Marinho, there would be no 'Oito Batutas.'"[89] The Oito Batutas was the first musical group organized by Pixinguinha and Donga to achieve success in Rio de Janeiro, starting in 1919. Irineu Marinho was an important journalist and newspaperman, founder of the paper *O Globo*, seed of the *Globo* companies that today heavily dominate the panorama of communications in Brazil. Arnaldo Guinle was a millionaire, a member of what, at the time, was one of the wealthiest families in Brazil. A patron of music, he financially supported not only the Oito Batutas but also Heitor Villa-Lobos, who, to show his gratitude, dedicated his "Choros no. 5 (Alma brasileira)" to him.[90] Oito Batutas is to musical groups what "Pelo telefone," which will be analyzed later, is to popular song: it represents the initial moments that a group of Black musicians achieves mass success, creating "popular music" indeed. When Donga says that without Marinho and Guinle there would be no group, he is saying that a white newspaper tycoon and a white millionaire were as important to their success as were the musicians themselves.

Yet it is not because they were not musicians that these two are considered to be external to the "*sambistas'* world." Rather, it is because their social existence is otherwise—the neighborhoods they lived in, the circles they ran in, their religious practices, and so forth. In accepting this, Vianna surreptitiously reintroduces the hierarchy he critiques throughout the book, for he is simultaneously accepting that samba possesses a world of its own, a world from which—at least in principle—other groups are excluded. Despite everything he says contrary to the idea of authenticity and in favor of the artificial and invented nature of samba, he nevertheless sees it as pertaining first and foremost to a separate and antecedent cultural space, a space with which other groups maintain relationships that, as intimate as such relationships may be, are still no less external.

In my opinion, it is better this way. These nearly imperceptible contradictions in Vianna's book, as far as his main argument is concerned, show that, in the end, the issue of authenticity is far too complex to be resolved by placing the word in quotes. What to do, then, with the "*sambistas*' world," and all of the ways it alludes to a topographical model of the topic? Perhaps we should treat it as we treat Tia Ciata's dining room, or as we treat the expressions "folk music" and "popular music," which I employ in this book. Together with Vianna and with contemporary constructionist anthropology, we should perhaps refuse to adhere purely and simply to such categories, which would imply taking them as natural realities. But recognizing the constructedness of categories still does not mean we need pay them no heed; after all, they are part of the processes being analyzed. I believe it is important to recognize that to understand these processes, we are required to take such categories into account, employing them within their own scope of validity, treating the definitions themselves as part of the analysis.

CHAPTER 5

"Pelo telefone"

In late 1916 Donga took a composition to the authors registry of Rio's National Library whose genre was indicated as *samba carnavalesco*, or carnivalesque samba. It was called "Pelo telefone," and the history of its creation has been, as far as Brazilian music is concerned, one of the topics over which the most ink has been spilled. We find the most in-depth study of the song in "Origines de la samba urbaine à Rio de Janeiro" ("Origins of Urban Samba in Rio de Janeiro), Flávio Silva's 1975 master's thesis, defended at Paris's École Pratique des Hautes Études. According to Silva, other compositions that indicated *samba carnavalesco* as their genre were registered or put on record prior to this date, but they went unnoticed, were dropped from popular memory, and were not even worthy of mention in either Edigar de Alencar's *História do Carnaval carioca através da música* (*History of Carioca Carnival through Music*) or in early twentieth-century literary accounts. Meanwhile, the composition registered by Donga is remembered to this day; it was the big hit of Carnival in 1917 and made the term "samba" incomparably more popular. Silva showed that during Carnival in 1916, the Carioca press mentioned "samba" only three times; in 1917, twenty-two times; and in 1918, thirty-seven times.[1] Thenceforth the prestige of the word increased at a dizzying rate. In the 1920s the most important popular composer, Sinhô (José Barbosa da Silva, 1888–1930), comes to be known as "O Rei do Samba" (The King of Samba). By the end of the following decade—that is, in just over twenty years—samba would come to symbolize Brazil not only all over the country but even abroad. At the inception of this all is the success of "Pelo telefone"; thus, it is important for us to spend some time analyzing the song.

We have seen that many researchers of Brazilian music attribute the creation of "Pelo telefone" to a musical evening at Tia Ciata's house. Indeed, at least a significant part of the composition is a direct result of the folk samba practiced at the turn of the century in the Carioca dining rooms of the Bahian *tias*. We know this first and foremost from accounts given by contemporaries, for the success of Donga's enterprise elicited reactions from his friends. In fact, on February 4, 1917, the newspaper *Jornal do Brasil* published a note in which Tia Ciata, Sinhô, and others protested against Donga's claims to authorship, using verses that parodied the third part of the song's recorded version (as we will later see):

Tomara que tu apanhes	Hopefully you get yours
Pra não tornar fazer isso	So you don't do this again
Escrever o que é dos outros	Write what belongs to others
Sem olhar o compromisso.[2]	Without acknowledging your debt.

Donga himself recognized, much later, in an interview with the newspaper *O Globo*, that he was not exactly the "author" of the song: "I picked up a melody that didn't belong to anyone and elaborated it."[3] The official author of the lyrics listed on the original recording, Mauro de Almeida, also relativized his "authorship" in two letters to the press, published in January and February of 1917, affirming that "the verses of the *samba carnavalesco* 'Pelo telefone' . . . are not mine. I got them from popular ballads and did as do so many *playwrites* running around today: arrange them, putting them to music, nothing more. . . . To the people, their *rolinha*, which is more theirs than mine" (emphasis in original).[4]

Elsewhere, Donga expresses himself in the following terms:

> Me and Germano . . . , and also the no-less-beloved Didi da Gracinda, we always sought out the late Hilário Jovino [all of the cited names are central figures in the Bahian-Carioca community of the era] . . . and we would talk to each other about choosing from within our own folk repertoire what would be best to introduce into society, as soon as there was an opportunity, which happened in 1916, when we began to close in. . . . Because that was the right time.[5]

The "folk repertoire," as we have seen, was limited to the dining room; introducing it into society meant making it public, moving it into the drawing room, into the "civilized" party. As Donga notes in another statement, this meant "showing those folks that samba was not what they thought it was."[6] In other words, the sung melodies in the *sambas de umbigada* could also, with certain adaptations (as we will see), be sung in Carnival festivities.

In Donga's proposed undertaking, though, this folk repertoire had to be filtered through several mediations. One Carnival alone would not be enough to "introduce into society" what samba had effectively been up to that point—that is, a musical activity that included a choreography, codes of conduct, poetic improvisation, and more. It was necessary to take these behaviors and interpersonal relationships, and highlight vestiges, objects capable of traveling between society's screens (no doubt creating, as a result of such transit, new relationships). These objects then needed to be molded into formats capable of being adapted to the mass media available at the time: commercial piano sheet music; band arrangements; printed lyrics, whose rigidity transforms all posterior improvisations into mere parodies; and recordings. But the success of this endeavor was still dependent on other factors: registering the composition at the National Library in order to preserve its authors' rights (which required bureaucratic hoops described in detail by Silva),[7] and obtaining a white ally, a journalist and important figure in the Clube dos Democráticos (one of official Carnival's main institutions at the time), Mauro de Almeida. All of Donga's efforts resulted in transforming something theretofore limited to a small community into a genre of popular song in the modern sense, with an author, a recording, press access, and widespread success in society.

As such, Donga may not have been the "author" of "Pelo telefone" in the same sense that, some years later, Noel Rosa will be said to be the author of "Feitiço da Vila" ("The Vila Spell"). However, as Silva aptly notes,[8] it is Donga who is the author of the history, it is he who invents the song and thus Carioca samba with many of the traits that still characterize it today. To use an expression from Michel Foucault, this is the first moment of the constitution of an "author function" in the universe of samba;[9] we will see other moments of this constitution later.

This image of Donga as proactive and innovative sits in contrast to the idea conveyed by João Máximo and Carlos Didier in their book, which includes a photo of him in a swimsuit, with the caption: "Donga, a lifeguard of *choro* and of samba."[10] But Donga's relationship to samba was not one of seeking to rescue something that was drowning; it was rather a relationship of innovation. He (and his friends) "created" samba as a modern genre, and it is precisely because of his proactiveness and innovativeness that he was accused by Vagalume and others not of having saved traditional samba but rather of having dug its grave.[11]

The goal of the following paragraphs is to show how textual evidence can be added to the accounts of those who affirm the partially folk origins of "Pelo telefone." I would like to show that the famous samba is a hybrid product, a lovely patchwork quilt that integrates elements understood to be as much a part of the folk sphere as of the popular.

"Pelo telefone" was recorded in January 1917 by the singer Bahiano on a Casa Edison[12] record. But the recorded lyrics were not the only ones in existence; oral and written records have shown us that there are other "unofficial" lyrics, with a different first part. I offer here both versions of the song's first stanza:

(VERSÃO GRAVADA)	(VERSÃO ANÔNIMA)
O chefe da folia	O chefe da polícia
Pelo telefone	Pelo telefone
Manda me avisar	Manda me avisar
Que com alegria	Que na Carioca
Não se questione	Tem uma roleta
Para se brincar	Para se jogar

(RECORDED VERSION)	(ANONYMOUS VERSION)
The chief of revelry	The chief of police
On the telephone	On the telephone
Sends word to me	Sends word to me
That with merriment	That in Carioca [Square]
Issue not be taken	There's a roulette wheel
In order to celebrate	For gambling

It is important to note from the outset that the question of which set of lyrics came first was quite controversial. Donga himself, depending on the interview, would sometimes espouse one of the theses, sometimes the other.[13] As for me, I tend to think the anonymous version came first, as will be seen.

The reference to the telephone, a constant in both versions, alludes to an incident that took place during a city campaign against gambling. On October 29, 1916, the newspaper *A Noite* reported that "conflicts, sometimes bloody, explode on a daily basis in the fancy gambling clubs, under the very noses of the police."[14] On October 30, the city's chief of police reacted and sent a letter (published in the papers the following day) "to the deputy of the district ordering him to issue writs of apprehension of all of the objects of the game." The published text continued, however, with this odd recommendation: "prior however to being carried out, communicate to him my recommendation *on the* official *telephone*" (emphasis added).[15]

The text, read quickly, leaves a question unanswered: did the chief of police order someone to telephone the district deputy with the intention of expediting the necessary measures, or was he suggesting a call to the clubs' directors so they could "clean up house" prior to the arrival of the authorities? It was the latter hypothesis that gained traction, given the well-known complacency of the police in relation to gambling, which, as stated, was practiced in "fancy clubs." The telephone itself, while no longer a novelty in 1916 Rio de Janeiro, was still "fancy," such that only a tiny parcel of the population had access to it.[16] Consequently, to order an apprehension "on the telephone" seems to be a means of abating the situation; as Silva notes, it is implied that when searches and apprehensions were carried out in the homes of the poor, authorities did away with such formalities.[17]

In fact, we saw that working-class forms of recreation were often subject to police persecution. There is no lack of references to the "chief of police" in the lyrics of popular Carioca songs, ranging from the *cantigas de fado* (*fado* songs) mentioned in *Memórias de um sargento de milícias*, which satirized the feared Major Vidigal,[18] to the *lundu* "Graças aos céos" ("Thank Heavens") by Gabriel Trindade (ca. 1830), with these ironic lyrics:

Sr. Chefe da polícia,	Sir Chief of Police,
Eis a nossa gratidão	Here is our gratitude
Por mandares os vadios	For sending the vagrants
À casa da correção.	To the house of correction.[19]

Another example is the quatrain sung at the 1916 Festa da Penha, cited by Silva:

O dr. Chefe da Polícia	The Chief of Police
Mandou me chamar	Called for me
Só pra me dizer	Just to tell me
Que já se pode sambar.	That we can now samba.[20]

Here the anonymous version of "Pelo telefone" merely takes up, with particular delight, what was already a century-old tradition; and it is quite understandable that the moment at which samba becomes popular all over the city—thus becoming more immune to police repression—would be a moment conducive to ridiculing the final avatar of that repression. The chief of police, who becomes a target of collective scorn, is therefore transformed into the chief of revelry, into the *Rei Momo* (King of Carnival). In the end, as with an expiatory goat, the crowd sings and dances around him during Carnival of 1917 with "merriment" and without "taking issue." The repressor is transformed into a Dionysian chief.[21] Yet it seems that the scorn was not widespread enough to be put on record. It is here, I think, that we see one of the functions of Mauro de Almeida: to filter the popular satire, leaving the chief of police discernible in the new lyrics only as the chief of revelry.

The reference to the *roleta* (roulette wheel) in Carioca Square (cited as "Carioca") also derives from this context. In May 1913 reporters of the newspaper *A Noite*, in order to reveal the ineptitude of the Rio police, installed a roulette wheel in front of the newspaper's headquarters (located at Largo da Carioca, No. 14) and invited passersby to bet; and on the following day, they published a report with the title "Gambling Is Open."[22]

I will only add, to wrap up this brief presentation of the first stanza's lyrics, that coupling two events that happened more than three years apart, as is the case with the episode of the roulette wheel in Carioca Square and that of the telephone, is effective as satire only to the extent that the chief of police in 1916 is as tolerant of gambling as he is in 1913. The new incident (the orders given on the phone) is illuminated with help from a reference to the old incident (the roulette wheel in Carioca Square). The satire turns to the 1913 roulette to ridicule even more effectively the current authority; it is as though the lyrics were saying, at one time it was the roulette, and now it's the telephone. The chiefs of police may change, but the double standard is still present in the authorities' engagement with different social classes.

Moving now from content to form, we find additional differences between the lyrics of the recorded version and the lyrics of the anonymous one. For the recorded version, each verse of the first tercet rhymes with its corresponding verse of the second tercet, constituting an "ABC-ABC" rhyme scheme; in the anonymous version, it is only the last verse of each tercet that rhymes, the scheme being "ABC-DEC." The recorded version, needing a rhyme for *telefone* (telephone), turns to the verb *questionar* (to question, or, more loosely, to take issue) (rarely employed in colloquial language, especially in this sense of "fighting"), conjugating it in the subjunctive (that is, *questione*)! The result is a second tercet that is a true syntactical wonder: "That with merriment / Issue not be taken / In order to celebrate." In other words, "that, in order to celebrate merrily (during Carnival), we mustn't take 'issue' (fight)." The equivalent tercet in the anonymous version, on the other hand, employs simple vocabulary and direct syntax, without neglecting to use the verb *ter* (to have) instead of *haver* (to exist), bucking grammarians of the era.[23]

The following discussion will require repeated reference to the rest of the lyrics of the recorded version of "Pelo telefone," which is why it seems convenient to present them here in their entirety:

I':

O Chefe da Folia	The Chief of Revelry
Pelo telefone	On the telephone
Mandou me avisar	Sent word to me
Que com alegria	That with merriment
Não se questione	Issue not be taken
Para se brincar.	In order to celebrate.

II':

Ai, ai, ai	Oh, oh, oh
É deixar mágoas pra trás,	You've got to leave your sorrows behind,
Ó rapaz	Oh man
Ai, ai, ai	Oh, oh, oh
Fica triste se és capaz,	Just try to be sad if you can,
E verás.	And you'll see.

(REPEAT II')

III':

Tomara que tu apanhes	Hopefully you get yours
Pra não tornar fazer isso	So you don't do this again
Tirar amores dos outros	Take another's love
Depois fazer seu feitiço.	To later cast a spell.

IV':

Ai, se a rolinha—sinhô! sinhô!	Oh, if the ground-dove[24]—massa! massa!
Se embaraçou—sinhô! sinhô!	Got all wrapped up—massa! massa!
É que a avezinha—sinhô! sinhô!	It's that the little bird—massa! massa!
Nunca sambou—sinhô! sinhô!	Has never samba danced—massa! massa!

Porque este samba—sinhô! sinhô!	Because this samba—massa! massa!
De arrepiar—sinhô! sinhô!	That gives goosebumps—massa! massa!

Põe perna bamba—sinhô! sinhô!	Makes legs weak—massa! massa!
Mas faz gozar.	But gives a thrill.

I":

O Perú me disse	Perú told me
Se o Morcego visse	If Morcego were to see
Eu fazer tolice	Me do something foolish
Que eu então saísse	Then I should leave
Dessa esquisitice	From this strangeness
De disse-não-disse.	Of gossip.

II":

Ai, ai, ai	Oh, oh, oh
Aí está o canto ideal,	There it is the ideal song,
Triunfal	Triumphant
Ai, ai, ai	Oh, oh, oh
Viva o nosso carnaval	Long live our Carnival
Sem rival.	[That is] unrivaled.

(REPEAT II")

III":

Se quem tira amor dos outros	If he who steals another's love
Por Deus fosse castigado	By God were punished
O mundo estava vazio	The world would be empty
E o inferno, habitado.	And hell, inhabited.

IV":

Queres ou não—sinhô! sinhô!	Whether you want or not—massa! massa!
Ir pro cordão–etc.	To go to the *cordão*[25] [Carnival group]–etc.
É ser folião	Is to be a reveler
De coração.	With sincerity.

Porque este samba	Because this samba
De arrepiar	That gives goosebumps
Põe perna bamba	Makes legs weak
Mas faz gozar.	But gives a thrill.

I''':

Quem for de bom gosto	Those with good taste
Mostre-se disposto	Should show themselves willing
Não procure encosto	Don't look for a headrest
Tenha o riso posto	Show laughter
Faça alegre o rosto	Put on a happy face
Nada de desgosto.	Not a bit of dismay.

II''':

Ai, ai, ai	Oh, oh, oh
Dança o samba com valor,	Dance the samba well,
Meu amor!	My love!
Ai, ai, ai	Oh, oh, oh
Pois quem dança não tem dor,	For those who dance neither feel pain,
Nem calor.	Nor get hot.

(REPEAT II''')

We can see that the recorded version is made up of four parts, constituting a cycle (I', II', III', IV') that repeats once (I", II", III", IV"), and a second time halfway through (I''', II'''), constituting this scheme:

I'–II'–III'–IV' / I"–II"–III"–IV" / I'''–II'''

Parts I and III are "simple," as they are sung only once within each cycle. But parts II and IV are "doubled"—that is, they are repeated (i.e., they appear twice) every cycle. The reprise of part II is outright; both the lyrics and the music are repeated within each cycle. Whereas the reprise of part IV is only musical, which is why it contains two quatrains in each cycle.

All of the parts were parodied countless times and used for the creation of innumerable anonymous versions; but only for the first part was there an anonymous version that contested the precedence of the recorded one. As such, I will not occupy space here comparing the three other parts of the recorded version with their respective parodies, as it would lead us too far off topic. Rather, I will compare the different sections of the recorded version itself, for doing so shows the coexistence, within this version, of two distinct poetic voices.[26]

We have seen that the first stanza of the recorded version (I') tended to rhyme more than its anonymous counterpart. Parts II', I", II", I''', and II''' emphasize the tendency of the recorded version to rhyme as much as possible. They adopt a repeated rhyme, the same in every verse of each stanza, and in all of the part IIs, the rhyming occurs as many as two or even three times within each verse. The first (II'):

É deixar má**goas**[27] pra **trás**, ó ra**paz**
Fica triste se és ca**paz**, e ver**ás**[28]

The first repetition (II"):

Aí está o canto ide**al**, triun**fal**
Viva o nosso Carna**val**, sem ri**val**

The second repetition (II'''):

Dança o samba com val**or**, meu am**or**
Pois quem dança não tem d**or**, nem cal**or**.[29]

Meanwhile, the part IIIs of the recorded version consist of a classic rhyme scheme found in a type of popular Brazilian poetry called a *quadrinha*, in which the second verse rhymes with the last: "ABCB."[30]

As for the part IVs, both of them are, as we have seen, "doubled," presenting two quatrains in each cycle. In the first cycle (IV'), the two quatrains consist of two alternating rhymes per stanza ("ABAB"); in the second cycle (IV"), all of the verses of the first quatrain rhyme ("AAAA"), while the second returns to the scheme "ABAB," as it is an exact repetition of the second quatrain of IV'.

As for the lyrical content, there are three observations to be made. First, only part IV contains quatrains of undoubtedly folk origins. There are five variations of them mentioned in sources independent of "Pelo telefone": the collections of folk poetry by Francisco Augusto Pereira da Costa, Afonso Arinos,[31] and Mário de Andrade;[32] the "revue" *O Marroeiro*, cited by Henrique Foréis Domingues Almirante;[33] and Vagalume,[34] who publishes verses that were sung in a Carnival club in 1916.

These variations share what Silva calls an "interior refrain," a choral response inserted after each verse.[35] In Mário de Andrade, it is *dorme, dorme* (sleep, sleep); in both Pereira da Costa and Arinos, it is *doce, doce* (sweet, sweet); in *O Marroeiro*, *sindô*, *sindô*, which derives from the previous refrain by way of syllabic inversion,[36] and which, for its part, is the source for *sinhô*, *sinhô*, which we find in the version by Vagalume and in that of "Pelo telefone." This musico-poetic technique is also part of the Carioca *partido-alto* tradition studied by Lopes, called *partido-alto cortado* (cut *partido-alto*).[37] The quatrains are as follows:

PEREIRA DA COSTA AND ARINOS:

Olha a rolinha	Look the ground-dove
Caiu no laço	Got trapped
Embaraçou-se	It got all wrapped up
No nosso amor.	In our love.

O MARROEIRO:

Olha a rolinha	Look at the ground-dove
Mimosa flor	Delicate flower
Presa no laço	Trapped
Do meu amor.	In my love.

VAGALUME:

Olha a rolinha	Look the ground-dove
Que se embaraçou	That got all wrapped up
Presa no laço	Trapped
Do nosso amor.	In our love.

MÁRIO DE ANDRADE:

Uma rolinha	A ground-dove
Que caiu no laço	That got trapped
Dais um beijinho	Give a kiss
E um abraço.	And a hug.

As for the recording of "Pelo telefone," the first time part IV is sung, we hear these verses:

Ai, se a rolinha	Oh, if the ground-dove
Se embaraçou	Got all wrapped up
É que a avezinha	It's that the little bird
Nunca sambou	Has never samba danced
Porque este samba	Because this samba
De arrepiar	That gives goosebumps
Põe perna bamba	Makes legs weak
Mas faz gozar.	But gives a thrill.

The underlying metaphors present in all of the folk variants are of love, or a beloved person, symbolized by a ground-dove, and the act of falling in love, characterized as "getting trapped." The "Pelo telefone" variants, on the other hand, returning to the dove/love metaphor, propose samba as an antidote . . . not to remedy love, but to remedy the suggested link between love and the trap, between the lovesick person and the inattentive ground-dove that allows itself to get trapped. It is an antidote that acts concretely on the body, causing goosebumps, leaving the legs weak, giving a thrill.[38] The body's irruption within the text—much more direct than the kiss and the hug of the version collected by Mário de Andrade—suggests the presence of what Muniz Sodré calls the Black Brazilian's "discursive position."[39]

The second observation is related to the dialogue we see being established among the different quatrains. When we read the treatment of the *rolinha* (ground-dove) in the folk versions and then turn our focus to the recorded version by Bahiano, the responsorial nature of the latter becomes clear; by simply hearing "Pelo telefone," however, this goes unnoticed, given that we do not hear the quatrains that would be the point of departure.[40] The same thing can be seen in the part IIIs of the recording. Here is the first quatrain (III'):

Tomara que tu apanhes	Hopefully you get yours
Pra não tornar fazer isso	So you don't do this again
Tirar amores dos outros	Take another's love
Depois fazer seu feitiço.	To later cast a spell.

And the second (III"):

Se quem tira amor dos outros	If he who steals another's love
Por Deus fosse castigado	By God were punished
O mundo estava vazio	The world would be empty
E o inferno, habitado.	And hell, inhabited.

It is immediately clear that this is a response from the *tu* (you) of the first verse. The first quatrain makes an explicit accusation against this *tu*, whose turn it is to speak in the second quatrain, as he defends himself using irony. The dialogic structure, though, is hidden by the fact that the second quatrain (III") is sung by the same singer; moreover, it appears only after a complete repetition of the song, which makes it even more difficult for the listener to make the connection.

The idea of quatrains responding to each other is reminiscent of a common practice in folk samba: improvisation and, especially when there is more than one soloist, poetic disputes.[41] According to Lopes, *partido-alto* "is sometimes also a form of *desafio* [contests/disputes], 'poetic disputes, having an improvised part and a memorized part."[42] Vagalume gives us one example of samba sung as a form of *desafio*.[43] There are also many examples of improvisatory dialogues in the *partido-alto* discography.[44]

Yet what seems to me revealing is that it is precisely the opening quatrain of part IV"—which returns, as we have seen, to the rhyme that is repeated in every verse—that circumvents the dialogic character of the other two quatrains! Here it is:

Queres ou não—sinhô! sinhô!	Whether you want or not—massa! massa!
Ir pro cordão—etc.	To go to the *cordão*—etc.
É ser folião	Is to be a reveler
De coração.	With sincerity.

This brings us to the third observation about the lyrical content. The stanzas that adopt the repeated rhyme, in addition to abstaining from the aforementioned "dialogue," either refer explicitly to Carnival or urge a merriment that, given the context, is doubtless carnivalesque.

Such a fact is especially significant when taking into account that Donga's entire endeavor was an effort to create a hit for Rio's Carnival in 1917. In early twentieth-century Rio de Janeiro, Carnival was effectively the ideal time of year for a new popular song to achieve widespread success. As such, in its countless references to Carnival, "Pelo telefone" uses its lyrics to present itself as a Carnival song, or a *samba carnavalesco*, to use an expression that was not only printed on the labels of the era's records but also found in the short introductions that, in the announcer's voice, initiate the recordings themselves. The "carnivalesque" stanzas correspond perfectly with Donga's intentions of making a hit, thus suggesting the stanzas were deliberately designed with this in mind.

Supporting this idea is the fact that in folk samba lyrics, transcribed by Carneiro and Vagalume, among others, there is no mention of Carnival. It becomes a recurring theme in samba lyrics only much later, with the development of *sambas de enredo* (sambas with story lines), written specifically for samba school competitions, which, starting in the 1950s, began to represent the height of Rio's festivities.

The allusions to Carnival in the lyrics of "Pelo telefone" are sometimes quite direct, as in stanza II", while at other times the allusions are subtler. We see such subtlety in the first quatrain of part IV", which speaks of the *cordão* and the *folião*, and of stanza I", in its mentions of "Perú" and "Morcego," which are the nicknames of two well-known Carnival figures of the period:

O Perú me disse	Perú told me
Se o Morcego visse.	If Morcego were to see.

In two other stanzas that adopt the repeated rhyme (II' and I'''), Carnival is not mentioned but is nonetheless implied, not only by the fact that they incite having fun (for example, "You've got to leave your sorrows behind, Oh man"; "Show laughter / Put on a happy face") but also by their context (the internal context, constituted by the other directly carnivalesque stanzas, and the external context, for the song was indeed a hit during the Carnival period).

Lastly, part II''' neither mentions Carnival nor incites having fun; what it does incite, however, is to "dance the samba," which, taking the song's context into account once again, ends up being the same thing. It is furthermore worth noting that in the world of Carioca samba, the correct expression is not *dançar o samba* (dance the samba) but rather *sambar* (that is, to samba or samba dance).

We still need to address one of the stanzas that directly incites carnivalesque fun, an especially important stanza, as it establishes the song's general mood right from the outset: the very first stanza, I'. The specifically carnivalesque character of the *alegria* (merriment/fun) mentioned here is ensured by the presence of the word *folia* (revelry) and the verb *brincar* (to play/to celebrate).[45] Unlike the other similar stanzas, however, it does not have the repeated rhyme, which contradicts the connection I am drawing between content and form.

However, the construction of the first stanza requires the expression *pelo telefone* (on the telephone) in the second verse, for this, as Silva has shown, was already the song's title even before it had its official lyrics. If the author of the recorded version wanted to insist on the repeated rhyme, he would have been obliged to find five words that rhymed with *telefone*, which, assuming at least minimal textual consistency, is a virtually impossible task in Portuguese. It is not surprising that he opted for three alternating rhymes, "ABCABC," which nevertheless situates this stanza within the group of "three or more rhymes," as opposed to the other group of stanzas, which has "two or fewer rhymes." As such, we end up seeing that in stanza I', too, there is a positive correlation between the greater number of rhymes and the theme of Carnival.

* * *

The goal of the analysis above was to show that within the official "Pelo telefone" lyrics, there are two sets of poetic voices: one of which I will call folk, and the other popular or, if we prefer, "authored." The "authored" stanzas (all the Is and IIs, and the first quatrain of IV") are formally characterized as having three or more rhymes; as for content, they include references to Carnival and the incitement of carnivalesque fun. The folk stanzas (the IIIs, IV', and the second quatrain of IV") have, in terms of form, two or fewer rhymes; and their content is dialogical in character.

Finally, it is important to note that while the anonymous version of I', which speaks of the chief of police, is not included in the official lyrics, it is part of what we might call the historical lyrics; it is employed, even today, every time the samba is sung in casual situations. This version is unequivocally linked to the group of folk stanzas. It has only one rhyme, and though it is not dialogical in the sense described above, it is dialogical in what is perhaps a more profound sense. Indeed, it dialogues in its own way with the chief of police and with the newspaper report from *A Noite*, constituting thus a response to the discourse of groups that held a stable position in the city's social landscape, for they had already been afforded the institutional means of making their voices heard. With "Pelo telefone" and the arrival of samba as popular music, novel figures discovered an equally novel means of participating in this dialogue, and they sent their discourses to the four winds of Rio de Janeiro—and shortly thereafter, to all of Brazil.

PART TWO

FROM ONE SAMBA
TO THE OTHER

When Did Samba
Become Samba?

According to Máximo and Didier, in the late 1920s, Rio de Janeiro had "two types of samba. One that is made, played, and danced at the home of Ciata and other Bahian 'tias.'"[1] As for the second type of samba, it "emerged a few years ago [the reference they give is 1929] in Estácio de Sá, the neighborhood situated between Rio Comprido and Catumbi, the São Carlos *morro* and the Mangue Canal zone. From there it spread to its neighbors, scaled the slopes of Saúde, Salgueiro, Mangueira."[2]

The existence of two distinct types of samba, starting around the late 1920s, has been noted by countless researchers, as we will soon see. The older samba is associated with Tia Ciata and the composers who were regularly at her house, such as Donga, João da Baiana, Sinhô, Caninha, and Pixinguinha. The more recent type is associated with a neighborhood in Rio de Janeiro—called Estácio de Sá (named for the Portuguese soldier who founded the city in 1565), or just Estácio—and with the composers who lived there or were frequent visitors, such as Ismael Silva (1905–1978), Nilton Bastos (1899–1931), Bide (Alcebíades Barcelos, 1902–1975), and Brancura (Sílvio Fernandes, 1908–1935).

The samba style said to have originated in Estácio spread quickly, influencing composers from other parts of the city, becoming not only widely popular but also synonymous with modern samba, with samba as we know it today. Everyone acknowledges the primacy of Estácio over other redoubts of Carioca samba. In the words of the famous composer Cartola, from the Mangueira neighborhood:

> Estácio's was the oldest [samba] school, let's not debate that. Outside of Carnival [season], the Estácio guys would come here to the *morro* to sing samba,

any day of the week. And we had a lot of respect for them as samba masters. One time I even wrote a samba in homage to the guys from Estácio who would come see us in Mangueira:

"Professor, chegaste a tempo / "Professor, you've come just in time
Pra dizer neste momento / To tell us at this moment
O que devemos fazer / What we should do
Me sinto mais animado / I feel more excited
A Mangueira a teus cuidados / Mangueira in your hands
Vai à cidade descer." / Is going down to the city."[3]

Regarding the Osvaldo Cruz neighborhood, where the eminent Portela Samba School originated, the composer Candeia put it this way:

It's worth pointing out that Ismael Silva, Baiaco, Brancura, and other Estácio composers participated in the samba gatherings ... in Osvaldo Cruz. Of course we don't want to downplay the process of legalization and recognition, before the court of public opinion, which is undeniably owed to Estácio.[4]

The samba literature offers no detailed description of the musical divergences between the two types. For the Brazilians who have researched samba's history— journalists, musicians, and others—the difference is recognizable "by ear." Cabral puts it like this: "it's easy: to recognize the difference between the two samba styles one needs only compare an old recording of a samba by Sinhô (or of 'Pelo telefone' itself) with another recording of a samba written by one of the Estácio de Sá composers."[5] "One needs only compare"—that is, one only needs to hear one recording after the other; the difference leaps out at you, making it superfluous to even talk about it.

Cabral's words, of course, are those of an insider to the world of samba, a person for whom the stylistic distinctions are natural and self-evident. But we are not talking about a minor difference, such as that which might exist between two composers or among the varieties cataloged in the entry on "samba" in the *EMB*.[6] Rather, we are talking about a substantial difference, which addresses, as Vianna put it, "the true samba,"[7] its definitional essence. As such, despite Cabral's nonchalant take on the issue, his remarks have incited countless specialists to comment and attempt to offer explanations. Here I will present a critical review of the discussion.

Perhaps the most important perspective on the issue, cited by nearly every author who has since alluded to it, comes from an interview conducted by Cabral himself with two composers, Donga and Ismael Silva, who are regarded as symbols, respectively, of the samba style that was dominant until the late 1920s and of the one that became popular starting in the 1930s (which will henceforth be referred to as the "old style" and the "new style"). Cabral asked both of them the same question: What is samba? Donga offered up "Pelo telefone" as an example, and Silva disagreed: "That's a maxixe." For him, real samba was "Se você jurar" ("If You Swear") (which he composed with Nilton Bastos in 1931). Now it was Donga who disagreed: "That's not samba, that's a march."[8]

Most critics agreed with Ismael Silva. While I know of no critic who would refuse to categorize "Se você jurar" as a samba, the same cannot be said of "Pelo telefone." Máximo and Didier unhesitatingly call it a "maxixed" samba (*samba "amaxixado"*).[9] Much earlier, Mário de Andrade was already thinking along similar lines:

> One of the newest *mães de santo* . . . of fame was tia Ciatha [*sic*], a woman also said to be musically tenacious. She would spend her days with guitar in lap creating maxixed melodies and much biting gossip says that many of the maxixes found in Brazil with the names of other Negro composers were hers and were more or less brazen appropriations.[10]

The allusions to "Pelo telefone" and to Donga are clear. In fact, on the same page, two lines below, Donga is cited as the author of a different "maxixe."

Silva and Oliveira Filho also felt that the old-style sambas were, rather than "maxixed," just *maxixes* plain and simple. The culprit for the confusion appears to be Donga, who baselessly referred to "Pelo telefone" as a samba. Because of the composition's success, "the word samba, which had hitherto been used as a nearly perfect synonym of tango and maxixe, came into its own, substituting the other two in practice."[11] For Alvarenga, who thought along the same lines, "not only 'Pelo telefone,' but also all of the works written by Sinhô, the first great samba creator, are not truly distinct from the sung maxixe."[12]

The opinion of Flávio Silva is slightly different: "'Pelo telefone' is not a samba. It is much closer to maxixe than to urban samba, which only effectively appeared in the late 1920s, thanks primarily to Sinhô."[13] The difference between the two points of view is in how Sinhô's final compositions are understood: already sambas or still *maxixes*? This question will be addressed later. But for now, let's simply keep in mind that Silva also considers "Pelo telefone" and every other "samba" up to the mid-1920s to be fraudulent sambas.

Donga himself, in an interview he gave a few years after his meeting with Cabral, acknowledged that his famous composition was somewhat influenced by *maxixe*: "I created this samba [song], trying not to distance myself too much from maxixe, [a style of] music that was very popular."[14]

In answering the question raised in the title of this section—"when did samba become samba?"[15]—we thus see a preliminary response taking shape. Even though samba had already begun to be used as a designation for a genre of popular music starting in 1917, the predominant opinion among Brazilian critics insists that such a designation is unbefitting prior to the late 1920s, for only thenceforth has samba been samba.[16]

Still, not every author sees the difference between the old and new style as an issue of either samba or *maxixe*. The first two books published on samba—*Na roda do samba* (*In the Samba Roda*), by Vagalume, and *Samba*, by Orestes Barbosa, both from 1933—use the same word, "samba," to refer to compositions that would later be identified as pertaining to one style or the other. It is worth taking our time with these books, for they were written "in the heat of the moment" by people who, as we will see, maintained close relationships with the protagonists of this history. Above all else, however, the books give us a different perspective by which to understand our object of study, the distinction between the two styles.

* * *

Not only were Vagalume and Barbosa journalists, but both were also well connected within samba and popular music circles. The first of the two was likely born around 1870, according to a biographical note published in 1916[17] (and as can be inferred by certain references in his text, such as that which he makes to Brazilian *fado*, on page 27, showing his knowledge of certain amusements that were already extinct by the late nineteenth century). He was a police reporter but established himself primarily as a Carnival *cronista*; his nickname, Vagalume (Firefly), began as the name of his column for the *Jornal do Brasil*, in which he wrote about Carnival. A person of mixed race, as is clear from the photo published on page 7 of his book, Vagalume was a friend of Donga and especially of Sinhô, to whom he dedicated his book (with other dedicatees being the popular singer Eduardo das Neves, who had died in 1919, the aforementioned Hilário Jovino Ferreira, and the religious leader Henrique Assumano Mina do Brasil, all of whom were prominent figures in the Afro-Carioca cultural milieu of the early twentieth century).

The second author was born in 1893. His journalistic activity was more diverse, and he commanded more prestige than did Vagalume. Barbosa's articles "criticized events and authorities of the period, with fearlessness and irony."[18] He published a number of books, including poetry collections, and in 1922 ran (unsuccessfully) for a place in the Brazilian Academy of Letters. A white man, Barbosa began to embrace popular music in the late 1920s, becoming a lyricist and collaborating with Noel Rosa and Sílvio Caldas, among others. With the latter, the journalist penned at least one classic Brazilian song, "Chão de estrelas" ("Starry Ground," 1937).

The generational differences between Vagalume and Barbosa, as well as their different life experiences, are expressed, in their respective books, in an implicit support for either the old style (Vagalume) or the new style (Barbosa). For Vagalume, one style represents "tradition," while the other "commercialization." He saw samba as something being "perverted" by the greed of those who saw in it a source of income. His book staunchly advocates for the "true" samba, which the author situates either in the past or in the "morro," a present that seems to be frozen in time. (As we will see later, in samba mythology, the *morro*—or certain *morros* in Rio de Janeiro—occupies a privileged position as a place of origin and purity, and is honored by Vagalume in a series of stories in the second part of his book.)

Vagalume's condemnation of what he calls "the samba industry" spares not even composers who are identified with the old style, beginning with Donga, whom he accuses of having unduly appropriated "Pelo telefone," "poached from the home of tia 'Asseata' [*sic*]. . . . Donga takes it, leaving everyone behind."[19] He then takes Sinhô to task: "for an easy victory, he used a clever trick: his lover was a pianist at a music shop on the Rua do Ouvidor, and, who is it who would go there to choose songs, she would, primarily playing what was written by her sweetheart."[20] Regarding another important old-style composer, Caninha (José Luís de Morais, 1881–1961), Vagalume insists that if a particular organization, which was then in the process of being created to combat plagiarism, decides to extend "its investigations into the samba *roda*, 'Caninha' will be the first to take off running."[21]

Vagalume's harshest invectives, however, were reserved for the singer Francisco Alves. In the early 1930s Alves was the premier radio and recording star in Brazil, having been the figure most responsible for the widespread dissemination of Estácio sambas (an issue that will be discussed at length later). And it seems that he was the first to take full advantage of a phenomenon we will also discuss in detail in the next chapter, the purchase of sambas. In one of the book's most scathing passages, although never mentioning Alves by name (but in a reference that would be obvious to anyone who had read the rest of the book), Vagalume ruminates about those who "are very well off, exploiting the inexperience, the need, the destitution of modest and unknown men, paying a mere pittance for their works, hiding their names, assuming authorship of these precious creations, because they have taken great care in establishing a monopoly over record making."[22] As for the composers most directly identified with the new style—"I. Silva, N. Rosa, Alcebíades Barcellos"—though Vagalume mentions them on only one occasion, he calls them "industrial *sambistas* of Victor Recordings" and denies their familiarity with the "samba *roda*."[23]

This is, as is evident, a militant book that observes the changes affecting samba ("today . . . samba has been adopted within the fancy *roda*, . . . it is played on the phonograph and figures as part of radio programs"[24]) and unyieldingly lambasts them. "Where will samba die?" the author asks. "In the abandon to which it is condemned by the proud *sambistas*, when it leaves the mouths of those of the *roda* and ends up on phonograph records."[25] Vagalume clearly sees samba's commercialization—or, if we prefer, its transformation into "popular music"—as a process that affects everyone, from Donga to Francisco Alves; on this point, his sweeping indictment of *sambistas* who make records is indiscriminate. At the same time, however, he specifies that among the *sambistas*, there are those who are from the samba *roda* and others who are not. Here is where he shows his preference for the old-style composers (Sinhô is absent from the following list, for an entire chapter is reserved for him): "Donga—This one is the son of a fish.[26] . . . He was born in the samba *roda*. . . . Caninha—He is the son of samba and *maladragem*.[27] . . . João da Baiana—He is right up there with Donga and Caninha, for he was raised in the same *roda* and knows, as do they, all of samba's secrets. . . . Heitor dos Prazeres—He knows samba and is from the *roda*." And his reticence regarding the few figures he mentions who are linked to the new style: "Ary Barroso— . . . is not a *sambista* in the [true] sense of the word. . . . He is a vulgar presence in the samba *roda*. . . . Francisco Alves—Is not from the *roda*, nor does he know the rhythm of samba."[28]

Barbosa's book offers an entirely different point of view. We can look at how the book's preface introduces the author: "A quality *sambista*. Originator of samba's most recent phase—urban samba. For it was truly Orestes Barbosa who variegated the emotion of the *morro* by giving samba the civilized note of the silk *abat-jour*, of the imposing skyscraper, of the caressing *manteaux* [sic], of the intoxicating aperitif, of the service telephone."[29] The "civilization" to which the prefacer refers is bourgeois modernity, with the customary French and North American fetishes upon which it was remade in Brazil (*abat-jour*, *manteaux*, skyscraper). This could not be further from the traditionalist discourse of Vagalume, who wrote, "Samba is a tradition of our farms. . . . We should respect samba, as one of the Brazilian traditions."[30]

For the old-style composers, Barbosa devotes attention only to Sinhô, whom he considers the greatest of "samba's dead."[31] Pixinguinha, Donga, and João da Baiana are mentioned in passing, as if they were from a past era: "they do not allow the memory of the group to die[, a group] that was, twenty years ago, the precursor to the victory of popular music."[32] But the real focus of the book is on those linked to the new style: Noel Rosa and Francisco Alves (who receives, in a perfect counterpoint to Vagalume's book, the most praise), Ismael Silva, Nilton Bastos, and Brancura, among others.

The book begins with a categorical assertion: "samba is Carioca."[33] The fact that Barbosa does not mention Bahia as a source or origin stands in stark contrast to Vagalume, who insists, "According to our great-great-grandparents, samba comes from Bahia. . . . Bahians, with due pride, call themselves the fathers of samba."[34] Another dissimilarity is in how the book refers to those linked to samba. In Barbosa, the term *malandro* (hustler), which will be discussed in detail later, is omnipresent. For him, this is the ideal designation for the type of person who creates samba. This music belongs to the *malandro*. And *malandro* is not used only as a descriptor or generic name; the figure is personified, emerging as a flesh-and-bones person who sees, knows, loves, writes, speaks, sings, expresses faith, and to whom "should never be denied the Carioca glory that is samba."[35] In Vagalume, by contrast, the word *malandro* is quite rare;[36] in its place, the term that often appears is *bamba*. This terminological shift is not neutral, for, as we will see, the association between *malandro* and *sambista* was an important theme in the emergence of the new style.

Although neither of these two books explicitly addresses any difference between two types of samba, or between samba and *maxixe*, both nevertheless offer revealing contrasts in their approaches to the subject (one extoling tradition, the other modernity), the distinct values they attribute to the two groups of composers (Tia Ciata's group and the Estácio group), their divergent views regarding samba's provenance (Bahia and Rio), their understandings of samba's symbolic figures (the *bamba* and the *malandro*). All of these contrasts correspond perfectly to the broader stylistic difference between the two types of samba that was asserted by the authors cited earlier.

* * *

We will now examine how scholars have attempted to explain what they see as the stylistic difference. Sérgio Cabral adopts an explanation that comes from an interview with Ismael Silva: "When I started, the carnival groups couldn't parade down the street with the samba of that time. . . . The style wasn't good for parading."[37] Clarifying the point, Máximo and Didier, who also interviewed the *sambista*, note that "according to Ismael, the samba from Estácio de Sá and its characteristics come from the *blocos*' [Carnival groups'] need to sing their songs while *marching* rather than *dancing*" (emphasis in original).[38]

This explanation alone seems unconvincing to me, for there is no immanent reason that would impede the use of the old style as a means of animating a procession; the relationship between music and dance is more flexible than Ismael suggests. In theory, no given musical style can intrinsically determine the corresponding choreography, nor can a musical style be derived from a choreographic necessity. But if Ismael's account "does not put the issue to rest"—as Máximo and Didier themselves subsequently admit—it does point us in an important direction.

After all, we must consider that Ismael is not speaking "in theory," but rather from his own experience. It is likely that for him and his friends it was indeed impossible (or not exciting enough) to march to the sound of the old style, which was, as we have seen, associated with *samba de umbigada*, which has no procession, for it is danced individually within a *roda*. With the success of "Pelo telefone" and the transformation of the samba into a Carnival song, the choreographic context shifted: no longer a *roda*, but rather a *bloco*, a group of people going out into the street, in which everyone dances at the same time. The old style may still have been, at least in some circles, too inextricably linked to the *roda* context to be effectively used in a procession. As such, the choreographic transformations may indeed have played a role, as Ismael would have it, in why the "*maxixed*" sambas were abandoned.

But let us examine other attempts at explanation. For Máximo and Didier, "the rhythmic dissimilarities are perhaps due to [the new style] having been created from the refrains sung in the improvisations and in the *rodas* of *batucadas*." For such *rodas*, the accompaniment would have been

> performed essentially by percussion instruments, most of which were constructed by the percussionists themselves or invented by them. While in Cidade Nova [i.e., the old style] the music of the festivities is performed by trained musicians, skilled performers of the piano, flute, clarinet, strings, and brass, in Estácio de Sá, except for a guitar or *cavaquinho* here or there in inept hands, it is all *tamborim, surdo, cuíca*, and *pandeiro*. Or even more rudimentary accompaniment, hands clapped together rhythmically or [used to] beat on tables, chairs, cups, bottles.[39]

For Máximo and Didier, the difference is primarily that of instrumentation. The old style seems to be characterized by the use of European instruments, and the new style by instruments of African origin (such as the *cuíca*)[40] or those invented in Brazil (such as the *surdo*). But implied in the above citation is another difference. The Cidade Nova musicians are said to have training and be skilled performers. Those of Estácio de Sá are said to have inept hands and practice a rudimentary form of accompaniment. As such, a difference in technical capacity is implied as existing between the two sambas. The European instruments go hand in hand with a specialized training while the Afro-Brazilian instruments seem to correspond to a "savage" musicality, so to speak, in which, as with Claude Lévi-Strauss's *bricoleur*, the musicians make use of objects they happen upon: chairs, cups, bottles.[41]

Meanwhile, Silva and Oliveira Filho approach the issue not by way of musical instruments, but rather by way of the musicians' social origins. But they reach essentially the same conclusion:

> The word samba, therefore, designated for some time two musical genres of distinct origins and quite clearly defined [from each other]. For the profes-

sionally trained musicians, who generally knew how to read music, were lower middle class, regular attendees in *ranchos* [Carnival groups] and at popular theaters, such as Donga and Sinhô, samba was synonymous with maxixe, the final phase of the Brazilian version of the European polka. For the blacks and *mestiços* descended from slaves, it was a new genre, the most recent phase of the Brazilianized Angolan *batuque*, which they sought to teach the nation's society by way of the samba school movement.[42]

On the one hand is the middle class (albeit lower middle class). On the other, descendants of slaves. The former have professional training that includes learning to read music, possessing a European-like musical knowledge, and a consequent stylistic link to polka. As for the latter, they perpetuate in their music their ancestors' lack of professional qualifications; their salvation, though, appears to be their paradoxical capacity to create a genre that is somehow both new and also the most recent phase of the Angolan *batuque*.

Such polarizations no doubt oversimplify the relationship between music and social class. In fact, the examples cited by Silva and Oliveira Filho end up serving, in part, as their own counterexamples. Although Donga and Sinhô became professional musicians, they had nothing close to what could be called "professional training," nor even any type of training by which they would have learned to read music.[43] Even if their music was recorded and performed in theaters by orchestras, they were not themselves orchestral musicians, conductors, or arrangers. What's more, they were both descendants of slaves, which, according to the authors, would place them in the new-style camp.

Indeed, the crucial problem underlying this explanation is that even if "trained musicians" performed Donga's and Sinhô's compositions on theater stages and recording studio dates, they rarely—if ever—did so in Tia Ciata's dining room. From our discussion of "Pelo telefone" and its origin, we know that this samba, too, was born out of improvisations and *rodas*, to the sound of rhythmic handclaps and instruments invented by the musicians themselves (such as the *prato e faca*), all of which, according to these authors, would serve to define the new style. If the gatherings hosted by the famous Bahian *tia* were in fact regularly attended by "skilled performers of the flute, clarinet," and so on, they would typically be in the drawing room, where *choro* was played for the *baile*. Very rarely do any firsthand accounts make note of European instruments, aside from guitars and *cavaquinhos*, being played at the Bahian *tias'* samba *rodas*. I know of only one mention of a clarinet, which comes from Tia Ciata's grandson,[44] and of a few mentions of a flute, which, based on at least one person's recollection, was not a common instrument to see: "Back then, when a flute would appear at a samba party, it was a novelty.... The whole week everyone would be commenting:—'Oh! Man,

Bambala played a samba right there! . . . There was even a flute!—What do you mean?!—I swear, by the light[45] of God.'"[46]

The only old-style musician who seems to fit perfectly within Silva and Oliveira Filho's parameters is Pixinguinha, who was indeed not only well-versed in music theory but also an orchestral musician, a conductor, and an arranger. But in the context of Tia Ciata's house, he was much more a man of *choro* than of samba: "Samba is João da Baiana's thing. Samba wasn't mine. They would play their samba in the backyard and I would play my *choros* in the drawing room. Sometimes I would head out to the backyard to play a countermelody on the flute, but I didn't know anything about samba."[47]

In the 1930s Pixinguinha ended up writing the orchestral parts for countless samba recordings, in both the old and new style. Moreover, he authored a number of compositions that were recorded with the genre indicated as samba. His claim of being foreign to samba is only explicable if we consider the difference between the categories of folk samba and popular samba, or in other words, homemade samba and recording studio samba. While Pixinguinha understood the latter, he considered João da Baiana to be the true specialist in the former.

* * *

The explanations heretofore proposed to delineate the differences between the two types of samba are not conclusive. After all, both styles can be performed by white or Black musicians, by orchestras and *batucada* groups, in theaters or at informal residential gatherings. Tinhorão understood this when he proposed an alternative explanation for the difference:

> All of the sambas recorded during this first phase that goes from 1917 to 1927 retain the sonic imprint of their kinship with the *partido-alto* sambas of the Bahians. . . . It was thus necessary for a new generation of talents, this time emerging from Rio's lower stratum that was also heir to a local tradition of call-and-response samba *rodas*, . . . to make its entrance onto Rio de Janeiro's popular arts scene with the definitive contribution to the genre's commercial career: the drummed and marched samba from Estácio.[48]

The problem is that although the Bahian traditions that are said to have spawned the first type of samba have to some extent been documented, the same cannot be said for the supposed "[Carioca] tradition of samba *rodas*." According to the scholarly consensus, as we have seen, folk samba was brought to Rio in the late nineteenth century, rather than having originated there. And if there were other musical practices that could have been assimilated into samba, which seems quite probable, we know nothing of them.

Furthermore, the old style is already a Bahia-Rio hybrid (not to mention the additional contributing factors we still know little about, such as those of Roma people, an influence we will later discuss). Sinhô was a Carioca and turned attacking Bahians into one of his favorite topics. João da Baiana, despite his name, was also born in Rio and used to say he was proud of having "beat out" his Bahian-born siblings. As for the new style, Lopes has shown how significantly it was shaped and impacted by musicians and musical traditions from other states (Minas Gerais, Pernambuco, among others).

One way to circumvent these objections is to note that the inhabitants of Rio had already created a new modality of folk samba by the 1920s, building on both the Bahian-brought samba and the other available influences, and were therefore not its heirs, as Tinhorão would have it, but rather its innovators.

This is precisely the position Ismael Silva takes in his interview with Cabral: he claims to have invented the new style, as a necessity born out of the practice of parading.[49] Pointing in a similar direction is also Bucy Moreira's statement, again to Cabral, as he tells him of the time he came upon a group that had gathered near Estácio to sing sambas: "I went up to them and asked: 'what's this?' And they said: 'it's a modern samba by Rubem.'"[50] In this case, "Rubem" refers to Rubem Barcellos, Bide's brother, who died prematurely and is said to have been one of the first to compose in the new style. Defining this samba by Rubem as "modern" suggests that its uniqueness results not from its link to some existing tradition but rather from having been something new.

Clearly, the "reasons" the new-style samba is different from the old are multiple and varied. These may include aesthetic innovations as well as the transition from the folk to the popular, as Tinhorão suggests. Indeed, the diverse categories according to which, at any given moment, society carves up its musical universe are mutually influential, in what can be seen as a continual process of reciprocal repercussions, with certain elements being selected over others. Moreover, these categories experience their own processes of transformation, not only because of the influence of other categories, but also because of their own dynamics, which are rooted, as we have seen, in both the creativity of the musicians and in all sorts of other musical and extramusical factors. It is this complex process I seek to explain regarding samba's transformations in Rio de Janeiro.

In the subsequent chapters I will examine samba's stylistic change from a number of different angles: the locations at which samba begins to be performed, its status as an object of economic exchange, its form, its content, its association with emblematic characters of the city. All of these topics will offer, I hope, a frame through which to understand the social meaning of this shift in the rhythmic paradigm.

7

Of Birds and Commodities

Just as the old style was associated with Tia Ciata's home, the new style, too, had its preferential social spaces, crucial to fully understanding the style itself. Of these spaces, the *bloco* (literally block, or Carnival group) and the *botequim* (bar, plural: *botequins*) strike me as particularly noteworthy. *Blocos* were the immediate predecessors of samba schools. They brought together, as they still do today, celebrants, usually from the same neighborhood, who brandished a decorated banner (*estandarte*) as they sang and paraded through the streets. Other labels for such groups were *cordões* (cordons) and *ranchos* (ranches). While the first of these designations fell into disuse in the 1910s, the latter would, a bit later, be used to refer to much smaller musical groups. The term *bloco* became popular in the 1920s. In fact, in 1926 Rio's press, which always promoted different parade groups, created, for Carnival, the "Day of the *Blocos*."[1] Some *blocos* sang only the year's hits, while others performed songs composed by their own participants. Regarding these original pieces, it was quite common during the 1930s, as we will soon see, for compositions to consist of only a refrain that was sung by the whole group. Then, in performance, these composed refrains were followed by soloists who would improvise verses.[2]

As for the *botequim*, it is Rio de Janeiro's equivalent of the pub in London or the café in Paris. It is, first and foremost, a gathering spot, a place to socialize. In new-style *sambista* biographies, there are countless references to *botequins* as the preferred location for samba making: Apolo, where the Estácio group would congregate,[3] and Carvalho, a favorite haunt of Noel Rosa,[4] not to mention so many others. One of the best descriptions of a *botequim* is in the samba "Conversa de botequim" ("*Botequim* Chit Chat"), by Noel Rosa and Vadico,[5] in which they humorously list all of the things a waiter at a *botequim* is expected to do: in addition to serving that traditional cup of coffee and some buttered bread, he is also supposed to report the results of the soccer game; fetch cigarettes, a card, and an envelope; arrange for an umbrella; place phone calls; lend money; and finally, open a tab.[6]

For the era's *sambistas*, the *botequim* was such a routine destination that it was sometimes called "the office" (*escritório*), appearing under this moniker elsewhere in the lyrics of the samba just cited, as well as in Ismael Silva's biography.[7] In this way, the *botequim* combined play with work. After all, it was also here that the *sambistas* could be found by possible "employers" (in the 1930s, most of the *sambistas* who had begun working as professional musicians did not have telephones, nor could they receive—in contrast to Tia Ciata—important people at their own homes). Incidentally, Pixinguinha remarked of Bar do Gouveia, where he was given his own reserved seat after years of patronage, "I don't like going from spot to spot. . . . It's like a job. You go there and you'll find me."[8] This was another way in which *botequins* replaced the homes of Bahian *tias*, which also acted as gathering spots and places to take care of minor services. As Vagalume noted, "it was by way of Tia Tereza's home that *sambistas* kept themselves informed. Whatever event there was, you had to go there—to the information bureau."[9]

Blocos and *botequins* share at least one important characteristic: both are more public and more socially open than Tia Ciata's dining room. At the Bahian *tia's* home, as we have seen, the white guests in attendance were "hand-picked" and, for one reason or another, had the privilege of being granted access to these intimate spaces. Yet in the case of the *blocos* and *botequins*, practically anyone could participate. Both of these carved out an exceptional space in Carioca society where diverse groups of people who were typically segregated by profession, wealth, religion, culture, or skin color were here able to interact. And samba was able to circulate within these new social spaces with unprecedented mobility.

An illustrative example is the backstory of "É bom parar" ("You'd Better Stop"), a huge Carnival hit in 1936, discussed in detail by Máximo and Didier.[10] At a *botequim*, Francisco Alves runs into a group of friends who are singing a refrain by the professional boxer Rubens Soares (1911–1998). Excited, Alves learns the refrain and sets out in search of a professional composer (in this case, Noel Rosa) who can create the second part.[11] He finds him, where else, but in another *botequim*. With the second part done, Alves records the samba and works to promote it at a "confetti battle" (*batalha de confetes*), a street party that brings together a number of different Carnival *blocos*:

> People come from all over Rio to participate in the parade of open cars, showered in confetti and streamers. Each *bloco* goes by with its *baianas*[12] and per-

cussionists. Composers—the city's best—come out to sing their sambas and marches, or to listen to what others have made. . . . How many people participate? It's impossible to count. Thousands, many thousands cover the sidewalks on both sides, while the cars pass by.[13]

Rubens Soares's refrain[14] is a *samba de rua* (that is, street samba), which he created at a time when he was not yet a professional composer (though he would later become one, serving thus as a further example of the social circulation I mentioned above). Nonetheless, snatched up by the successful Alves—a regular at the *botequim*—the refrain soon finds itself in the hands of a professional composer, where it receives a second part that, as we will see, is precisely what it needs in order to enter the world of radio broadcasts and records. For its entry to be productive, however, it is crucial that it be legitimized by the confetti and streamers alongside the Carnival *blocos*. Here, everything circulates: the open cars, the composers, the city's neighborhoods, the social classes. This broad new context for circulation, which revolves around samba while also being the space within which samba itself circulates, replaces the old circulation of the *roda*. There is only one remnant of Tia Ciata's recondite dining room, the Carnival figure of the *baiana*, which even today has an important role in samba school processions.[15]

* * *

The "openness" of the *botequim* made it ideal, too, for less scrupulous activities, such as the theft of sambas. Máximo and Didier remark on some of the tricks employed by dishonest musicians who stole "fragments, often whole sambas, heard at the Mangue *botequins* [that had been created] by anonymous composers who will remain in anonymity forever."[16] But of interest to us here is understanding the ways in which many of these composers were in fact able to shed their anonymity.

One of the defining traits of the notion of "folk music" is the absence of any known author. Yet it should be noted that even in a folk context, such as that which is described in Vagalume's account, the idea of authorship can be relevant: "Aimoré . . . around daybreak, after showing much jealousy,[17] improvised this samba: . . . whether because of Aimoré's popularity, or because the samba was really the 'thing,' it stuck around for a long time. Even today it is a hit, when someone remembers it and says: '—Aimoré's samba!'"[18]

Still, the move from "anonymity" to "authorship" is perfectly observable *in what has been written about samba*. The aforementioned writings on *samba de umbigada*, from the nineteenth century on, as we have seen, describe the participants, the dance steps, the whole event. In striking contrast, the Carioca samba literature, starting in 1917, omits such topics, focusing instead on the "authors" and their texts. There is no better example to illustrate this than the samba "Pelo telefone": its two major controversies, causing rivers of ink to be spilled, were, first, who its true authors were, and second, what its original lyrics were. Very little was written about the song's performance contexts.

The debate over the "true author" of "Pelo telefone" is, in fact, just the first in a series of controversies surrounding samba authorship. In the 1920s the most famous of such issues seemed to involve Sinhô, who is associated with the phrase "samba is like a bird, it belongs to whoever catches it."[19] The idea expressed here is that countless anonymous refrains were sung throughout the city with not a soul seeming to care who had composed them. The metaphor at the heart of the phrase attributed to Sinhô is the same as that which is implied in the treatment of folk melodies as things that can be "harvested" (*coletadas*), an expression employed liberally by authors such as Mário de Andrade and Oneyda Alvarenga.[20] In both cases, popular song is treated as a natural object—a bird in one, a plant in the other.

Sinhô's modus operandi seems to have been widely known, and even considered normal. In a 1935 interview, Noel Rosa puts it this way: "No one knows where samba was born. . . . Today, it has a school. Originators of style. J. B. Silva, the famous Sinhô, he was one of them. Sinhô went up to the *morro*, collected a bunch of samba refrains and stylized them to great success."[21] Pixinguinha, when asked about the "*cigano* [gypsy[22]] camps in the neighborhood of Catumbi," notes the following: "I spent some time with them because they liked me. But, in terms of music, the person who could tell you more, were he alive, is Sinhô. He was the one who was always there with them to get their melodies and publish them. . . . He didn't make them partners because back then that wasn't a thing."[23] In other words, the issue of authorship did not seem to be a problem, as the "author function" had not yet been fully established in the samba world.

In a *crônica*, poet Manuel Bandeira also tells of his experience at a party in late 1929, when Sinhô introduced a new samba he claimed to have just composed, "Já é demais" ("That's Enough"). Years later, Bandeira came across a *lira* (as collections of lyrics to popular songs were called) that included a song titled "Já é demais":

> Below it was this information: "Lyrics and music by *seu* Candú." Now, there it was, the refrain of Sinhô's samba. . . . I was immediately sure that the plagiarism could not be *seu* Candú's, for the publication was from 1927 . . . and there was moreover the note below the title that "Já é demais" was a carnival choro from 1925, which was there so clearly proven by the lyrical content, just filled with references to revolutionary facts of '24. . . . In any case, it is clear that Sinhô had exploited *seu* Candú's refrain.[24]

Neither *seu*[25] Candú nor the Roma mentioned by Pixinguinha made any known attempts to defend their intellectual property rights, their author's rights (*direitos autorais*), suggesting that they did not in fact think of themselves as "authors." However, Sinhô's way of doing things did not go entirely unopposed. Heitor dos Prazeres claimed authorship of two big hits that had been credited to Sinhô, "Ora vejam só!" ("Hey, Take a Look!," 1927) and "Gosto que me enrosco" ("I Get a Kick Out of It," 1928).[26] As for the latter, Prazeres once remarked in an interview, "When I went to talk to him [Sinhô] to complain that he hadn't given me credit on the recording, he defended himself by saying that he didn't know the song was mine. He thought it was a common melody with no author."[27] (We will later discuss in more detail Heitor dos Prazeres and Sinhô's quarrels regarding authorship.) Meanwhile, Prazeres was himself accused of the uncredited appropriation of a samba by Antonio Rufino, "Vai mesmo" ("Go Ahead").[28]

(It is worth noting, if only in passing, that in the case of both "Gosto que me enrosco" and "Ora vejam só!," Prazeres accuses Sinhô of stealing only the first part of the samba—that is, the refrain.[29] This strongly suggests to me that folk samba primarily took the form of a refrain with added improvisations whose lyrical content did not necessarily have any intrinsic relationship to the initial composition. The autonomy between refrains and verses during this period is also evident in the case of "Já é demais," given that the revolutionary facts referenced in *seu* Candú's verses had no thematic connection to the amorous refrain, taken up by Sinhô. These issues will be discussed in detail later.)

While sambas, for Sinhô, were products of nature to be harnessed and published by whoever happened upon them first, the late 1920s was marked by the emergence of a new commercial approach to the genre: the buying and selling of sambas. Noel Rosa, in an interview given in late 1932, affirmed the following: "Are there composers who buy sambas? I can say for certain that there are. I speak from my own personal experience. I've sold a lot of sambas."[30] The most well known, perhaps the first, of the samba buyers (known also as *comprositores*[31]) was singer Francisco Alves, who had already bought and recorded a samba by Bide, "A malandragem" ("The Malandro Lifestyle"), as early as Carnival of 1928. This date, as we can see, was right around the same time as the Sinhô-Prazeres disputes.

There were a number of different types of samba purchase. The most drastic type of purchase was that in which the author, in exchange for a fixed sum, gave up not only his author's rights but also any official recognition of his authorship—that is, his name appeared on neither the record nor the sheet music. In other cases, a composer sold his author's rights, but his authorship continued to be recognized, whether on the record, on the sheet music, or on both. Finally, there were cases in which a singer would negotiate a deal according to which he would agree to record the samba in exchange for his name being included as coauthor, and he would, accordingly, receive a share of the author's rights.

The relationship established in this last case was considered to be a type of "partnership" (*parceria*). In such partnerships, authorship of a samba is split between two or more individuals. A type of partnership I will call "nominal," as in the case just mentioned, is when the partnership was given or purchased within the practices of the commercial samba market; whereas a "real" partnership would refer to those cases in which the partners worked together in composing the samba, even if the contributions of each party were not necessarily equal. Partnerships in popular music became increasingly important starting in the late 1920s, marking thus an important transition from one compositional phase to another. After all, while Sinhô, the most prominent composer of the phase that ended during this period, rarely relied on partnerships, all of the important composers of this next phase routinely participated in partnerships, whether real or nominal.

In the case of a pure and simple samba purchase, it was the singer alone who was jeopardizing his name and his money if the song was unsuccessful. Yet in the last case discussed, that of shared authorship, it seems that the composer receives, at least from the point of view of today's music industry, only the disadvantages: he gives up part of his author's rights, and if the song is unsuccessful, he gets no money in return. As such, it is perhaps surprising that in their statements to Cabral, both Ismael Silva and Bide, who relied heavily on this type of partnership system in their transactions with Francisco Alves, show a preference for it over the direct sale of their songs, and speak up when the interviewer confuses the two:

(Cabral:)—You sold how many songs to him [to Alves]?
(Ismael:)—Just two.... For the others, he was a partner and we split the money that the song made....
(Cabral:)—How much did you sell the samba for?
(Bide:)—No, I didn't sell it....
(Cabral:)—But Francisco Alves made himself a partner.
(Bide:)—You don't think he should have? ...
(Cabral:)—Did you sell your songs, Bide?
(Bide:)—No, never. I knew that a lot of people did.[32]

When Bide retorts with "you don't think he should have?," he is indicating how obvious it seemed to him that Francisco Alves's contribution was paramount to the samba's success, and thus how fair it seemed to him that he be made a partner. The same point of view is evident in Bucy Moreira's recollections: "He [Alves] would go up into any *morro* to find a good samba. So they said that he was buying sambas, but it wasn't like that at all. He would give a little something to the author to hold the samba. So you can see how ungrateful these people are. They still put the guy down."[33]

In his eagerness to defend the singer, Bucy omits that Francisco Alves's name is listed on the labels of the records and on the covers of the sheet music as a co-author—and in some cases as the sole author—of sambas for which he "would give [the author] a little something." This view seems to reflect a belief that Alves's role was positive and that he somehow deserved the authorship he was given.

This reveals a conceptualization of "authorship" that is broader than what has been developed by modern theorists of intellectual property. Even today, this broader conceptualization can still be found among samba schools, as is expressed in the 1992 words of a member of the directorship of the samba school Mocidade Independente de Padre Miguel: "there's you who created the samba, the guy who thinks up the lyrics, the other guy who has money [for promotion], another guy who's a friend of the [School's] directorship, so they include everyone as a partner."[34] It is worth asking if this conceptualization is not, at its core, in fact more realistic, when taking into account the whole chain of mediations that leads to a samba's existence as popular music, instead of limiting authorship to lone creators up in the *morro* or the recording studio.[35]

Bide, Ismael, and Bucy had not yet become professional composers in a competitive market; they were "blueprints of a [professional] artist" (*ante-projeto de artista*), as Paulo da Portela (Paulo Benjamin de Oliveira, 1901–1949), using an inimitable blend of ingenuity and irony, puts it in his samba "Cidade mulher" ("The City Is a Woman," 1935).[36] They were, in other words, composers to whom the doors to earning a living with their music were opened for the first time. As such, it seems that Francisco Alves's contribution was not so much in creating sambas as it was, perhaps more importantly, in creating "samba composers," in the concept's modern and professional sense.[37]

However, as Bucy phrased it, "you can see how ungrateful these people are." Indeed, by 1933, as we have seen, Vagalume was already attacking Francisco Alves, accusing him of being "the *enshrined author* of works by humble men, who, hounded by necessity, are forced to *burn them* for 20$000 and 30$000" (emphasis in original).[38] The composer Cartola recounts an incident with a higher figure: "It was in 1931. Mário Reis came up here to the *morro* [because] he wanted to buy a samba of mine. . . . He asked me how much I wanted. I didn't know what to say. I was going to ask for something like fifty *mil-réis*, but Clóvis whispered to me that I should ask for five hundred. So I asked for three hundred. And he gave it to me."[39] Cartola's words are from 1974, more than forty years after the fact; so it is hardly inconceivable that he might misremember the exact figures. But at any rate, he gives us an account of his nonplus upon being asked to attribute a monetary value to his sambas, and it is a higher value than he at first assumes.

The practice was widespread. Even Bide, who did business with Francisco Alves, bought, together with João de Barro, the samba "Vem meu amor" ("Come,

My Love"), by Mano Décio da Viola and Ernani Silva, as noted by Suetônio Valença and Raquel Valença. The authors further add, "the first songs composed
by Mano Décio, ... such as those by other popular composers, were sold by their
authors so that they could get some spare change."[40] Noel Rosa went so far as to
use samba as a form of currency in paying Alves for a car he bought from him.[41]
And there is a story about the aforementioned Bucy Moreira, told with disarm-
ing casualness by a cousin of his: "He was always down there at *Praça Tiradentes*
[Tiradentes Square] making those sambas. . . . He was a mess, he would sell a
samba to one guy, then he would sell that same samba to someone else."[42]

More than a few observers considered the commerce in sambas to have been a
unilateral form of exploitation, in which the wily purchasers, white and bourgeois,
always got the better of the naive sellers, Black and working class. As we have
seen, this is the view of Vagalume, who said the buyers "got in with the *sambistas*,
stealing their names, draining their sweat, exploiting their work, withholding their
profits, and always leaving them in the depths of oblivion!"[43] We can see another
example of this view in the film *Rio, Zona Norte* (*Rio, North Zone*), by Nelson
Pereira dos Santos (1957), which portrays the exploitation of a poor Black *sambista* by his white counterpart in a nominal partnership. But the truth seems to
have been far more complex, for popular music composers also benefited from
discovering that monetary value could now be attributed to something that just a
few short years earlier had been considered to be of the public domain. The most
revealing narrative concerning this issue can be found in *sambista* Raul Marques's
words to Sérgio Cabral:

> (Cabral:)—Did everyone sell sambas to César Brasil? (Marques:)—Yes, ev-
> eryone did. I even remember a samba that Zé Pretinho sold him that had al-
> ready been recorded. Zé Pretinho comes up with this story: "Dang, César, we
> couldn't get your name on the record. But the next time the samba's recorded,
> your name's going to be there. Don't worry." And César Brasil, believing him,
> gave him a bill of ten-*mil réis*. . . . There were times we'd be talking in a hotel and
> some samba would come on the radio. "Hear that, César?"—Jota Piedade would
> ask. "Yeah, and it's really good." "Then, from here on out, you're my partner on
> it." And he'd get some cash for a samba that Piedade had never even heard.[44]

The samba market was also enabled by the fact that many of the *sambistas* had
become aware that it was they who had a unique know-how, allowing them to reap
certain benefits and to place themselves—albeit sometimes anonymously—into
the burgeoning modern cultural market. Such a practice yet again distinguishes the
new-style composers from the old-style composers. After all, for the latter group,
the "author function" was still very much at a rudimentary stage, dismissing monetary intermediation and settling on the pure and simple method of appropriation.

* * *

Early 1930s Carioca street samba, according to existing firsthand narratives about it, consisted of a refrain sung by the *coro* (chorus, or group of people), whose repetitions were punctuated by soloists singing improvised verses. Since these improvisations were ephemeral, always changing, and often unrelated to the subject matter of the refrain, they cannot be used to identify a given samba. We can therefore say that while sambas were always understood to include improvised verses, a given samba was conceived of independently of them, since they were not specific to it.

In the previous chapter we examined accounts attesting to the importance of improvisation during the embryonic stages of Rio's samba. But improvisation was still quite vibrant in the 1930s. This was the case, for example, during Carnival processions, as we will see to follow; but this was true outside of such contexts too, as is clear in "O século do progresso" ("The Century of Progress"), a samba composed by Noel Rosa in 1934:

A noite estava estrelada	It was a starry night
Quando a roda se formou	When the *roda* took shape
A lua veio atrasada	The moon was late to arrive
E o samba começou.	And the samba began.

This is about folk samba: performed at night, in a *roda*, outdoors, bathed in moonlight. The song portrays improvised verses, as the following sequence shows:

Entretanto, ali bem perto	However, quite nearby
Morria de um tiro certo	Dead by a sure shot
Um valente muito sério.	Was a very serious tough guy.

In other words, just as the samba is taking place, a death occurs, and such a dramatic event invites a sung commentary:

Chegou alguém apressado	Someone arrived in a hurry
Naquele samba animado	To that lively samba
Que cantando assim dizia:	Who, in song, said it like this:
"No século do progresso	"In the century of progress
O revólver teve ingresso	The revolver came along
Pra acabar com a valentia."	To end valor."

The last tercet is precisely the sung commentary of someone who has just witnessed the death of the tough guy; it is a line improvised in response to an immediate situation. "O século do progresso," like so many of Noel Rosa's compositions, is a samba about samba, and more specifically a popular samba about

130

folk samba. It is not improvised, but it masterfully portrays the improvisation and its circumstances, of which it acts as a witness. What's more, it puts improvisation on the scene, using quotation marks and loaning its own voice to the voice of the improvisor "who, in song, said it like this." In so doing, however, it highlights a move that, pulling from Sodré, I call "transitive-indirect discourse" to "transitive-direct discourse":

> The lyrics of traditional samba [are] a transitive-direct discourse. In other words, the verbal text of a song is not limited to speaking about [transitive-indirect discourse] social existence. Rather, what it says is the existence. . . . The words in traditional samba have an operationality in relation to the world, whether in insinuating a philosophy about the practice of daily life, or as social commentary.[45]

The situation described by Noel Rosa in his samba is precisely an example of this direct transitivity: the improvisor sings what he just experienced, extracting from the death of the tough guy a life lesson appropriate to the practice of everyday life in the *morros* of Rio. The final tercet cannot be read as "pure poetry"; it assumes that all of the people in the *roda* also heard the gunshot, and this information is necessary to fully understand the verse. If someone arrives late to the *roda* without having heard the gunshot, the person will not understand the tercet; but conversely, if someone leaves the *roda* before hearing the tercet, that person will not understand the gunshot. But if both the gunshot and the tercet can still be heard by us today, it is because there is a samba that tells the story, a specific samba song called "O século do progresso." With its quotation marks, it tells us about something that is not part of our—readers' or listeners'—life experience. The song's "indirect transitivity" goes hand in hand with its nature as a "composed," rather than improvised, samba.

Hence the advent of popular music in Brazil carried with it a world of immutability, a world in which the role of improvisation was drastically reduced. Recordings, publications, and author's rights all created a demand for a second part in addition to the refrain, both of which would be the "property" of a given samba. This second part needed to be "exclusive" in two senses. First, its verses could not appear in any other samba; second, its verses were expected to be only those, to the exclusion of other possible ones, closing itself off to the theretofore welcome practice of improvising new verses.

As such, we see the appearance of a new category in the vocabulary and practice of samba in the 1930s: the "second part" (in Portuguese, *segunda parte*, or simply, *segunda*). In relation to the refrain, the second part exercises the same role as that of the improvisations: it is sung by a soloist rather than the group, with lyrics that vary, while the refrain is by definition invariable. (For this reason, the second part is often referred to in the plural: "second parts" or, in Portuguese, *segundas partes*.) Moreover, each of the stanzas of the second part is sung only once, unlike the refrain, which is always repeated.

Splitting up samba into refrain and second part enabled a specific type of real partnership, where one of the partners composes the refrain and the other, the second part. This is quite distinct from the types of partnerships that have been common in Brazil since *bossa nova*, in which one person composes the music and the other, the lyrics (for example, Antonio Carlos Jobim and Vinícius de Moraes, João Bosco and Aldir Blanc, Chico Buarque and Edu Lobo).[46]

Máximo and Didier insist that Noel Rosa, who had countless partnerships with *sambistas* who were on their way to becoming professionals, was in fact the one who sought out such partnerships.[47] Noel would create the second parts to already existing refrains. The refrains already existed, and a professional composer was the one who invariably offered his services to "complete them" with the second parts, which suggests that as refrains, these sambas did not need anything else in order to work perfectly well in *bloco* parades or samba schools or to be sung, for example, by Rubens Soares and his friends in a *botequim*. And in all of these performance contexts, in addition to singing the composed refrains, people would also improvise verses. They were thus already whole, complete sambas; the idea that a second part was "missing" resulted from music's emergent new professional context, of which Noel Rosa was an integral part.

As such, "Não faz, amor" ("Don't Do That, Love")—by Noel and Cartola— had been Mangueira samba school's refrain in the Carnival procession of 1932 prior to being put on record.[48] "Sorrindo sempre" ("Always Smiling")—partnership of Noel with Gradim—also "began as one of the [Carnival] procession refrains [for Mangueira] in 1932."[49] "Fita amarela" ("Yellow Ribbon," 1932) was originally an anonymous refrain well known in Estácio and in São João de Meriti,[50] for which Noel created the second parts. Another case is "De babado" ("With Frills," 1936), a common refrain that, like so many others, was already well-known all over Rio de Janeiro in the 1930s. Noel claimed to have heard it "he doesn't remember where. The other day, asking João da Baiana if he knew whose it was, he got a prompt response: —*It's by João Mina.* [João] da Baiana explained to Noel that Mina was a samba improviser from the *morro* of São Carlos." But "there are also those who say that the refrain isn't his, but by some [guy] Papai da Cancela."[51] Regardless of who in fact created the refrain, Noel composed the second parts, which he subsequently recorded.

It is worth examining the case of two Noel Rosa sambas: "Felicidade" ("Happiness," 1932), whose refrain was by René Bittencourt, and the aforementioned "É bom parar," whose refrain was by Rubens Soares. According to Máximo and Didier, both Bittencourt and Soares always denied having been Noel's partner.[52]

This seems astounding from today's perspective, as sambas are nowadays viewed as single entities made up of two indissolubly linked "parts"; but the paradox quickly unravels when recognizing the refrain as a self-contained entity, which is coupled with a second part only as it makes its way to the recording studio. Consequently, the second part was often created by someone who did not have the slightest contact with the author of the refrain. This is what transpired in the case of these two Noel Rosa sambas.

In the case of "É bom parar," putting it on record was clearly the motivation behind the creation of the second part. Other such cases are "Vai haver barulho no chatô" ("There Is Going to Be an Uproar in This Chateau," 1932),[53] a refrain by Walfrido Silva for which singer Mário Reis, enthusiastic about the samba, asked Noel to compose a second part so that Reis could record it;[54] and "Escola de malandro" (*"Malandro* School," 1932), a refrain by Orlando Luís Machado that was "completed" by Noel and Ismael Silva in order to put it on record.[55]

The case of "Só pra contrariar" ("Just to Be a Naysayer," 1932), a samba coauthored with Manuel Ferreira, is an interesting *counterexample*: "So as not to break with convention, the idea for the partnership came from Noel. After hearing the refrain written by Manuel Ferreira, he asked him:—*Will you let me add a second part to this?* So surprised and content was the *sambista* that he didn't even want to tell Noel that he had already made the second part."[56] This incident demonstrates that the absence of a second part seemed to Noel to be beyond question: nonprofessional *sambistas*, such as this one, composed only refrains, and not "sambas" with a first and second part. As he himself says in "Quem dá mais?" ("Do I Hear More?," 1932),[57] the samba that comes from the neighborhood of Salgueiro and the city's other *morros* is made "without an introduction and without a second part"; "it has only a refrain."[58] Yet, as the Manuel Ferreira case shows, "spontaneous composers,"[59] too, began composing their own second parts, making their sambas perfectly ready for the recording studio.

At the Prazer da Serrinha samba school, in Madureira, it is said that "all of the sambas [up to 1946] had only a first part, with the second part improvised in the *roda* that took shape."[60] With regard to the Deixa Falar samba school, which existed between 1928 and 1933 and is generally recognized as "the first samba school," Bide notes, in his previously cited interview with Sérgio Cabral, "—Do you remember any Deixa Falar sambas? . . .—I do. Mine: [Bide sings a quatrain]. Afterwards, we created the verses."[61] In other words, what the author created was the refrain ("mine"), whereas "the verses," or the solo part, are consigned to an indeterminate subject ("we"), the community or its mouthpieces, the improvisers. Around the same time, for the Portela samba school, "the sambas only had the first part, since the second part was provided by the improvised and intuitive versification of the composers."[62] This is confirmed by Alvaiade, a composer from the school, in an interview with Sérgio Cabral: "—When was the first time that Portela sang one of your sambas in a procession at Praça Onze?—It was around 1934. [Alvaiade sings the refrain]. Then everyone improvised. Back then, second parts weren't done."[63] Well, yes they were, but only for the sambas by Noel Rosa, Ary Barroso, and other professional composers.

Mangueira too, in the early 1930s, "usually parades with three sambas, or rather, three refrains, since the verses of the second parts are left to the improvisers."[64] "Three sambas, or rather, three refrains"—this phrase encapsulates wonderfully this difference between folk samba and popular samba. For Máximo and Didier, as well as for other authors and popular music professionals, a "refrain" is not yet truly a "samba." Consequently, a book published in 1984 about Salgueiro samba school says of the samba "Arrependimento" ("Regret"), by Antenor Gargalhada (composed in the 1930s and recorded in the 1970s), that it had its "second part created 40 years later by the composer João Melo, for the author had left it *incomplete*" (emphasis added).[65]

However, if samba schools indeed identified themselves as such, it is clear that, for them, what they created were in fact sambas, and not, as others would have it, "refrains," "samba fragments," or "incomplete sambas." These expressions, so common today in the literature discussing Carioca samba songs of the 1930s, are patent anachronisms. We are dealing with a conceptual difference: folk samba, as we have seen, was first and foremost a festivity; but it was also each of the sung refrains, which were followed by improvisations (and such improvisations would not identify the sambas, as they were not permanently attached to a given refrain). In the professional context, on the other hand, samba is reified. It becomes autonomous in relation to the people who produce it—this is what creates the conditions for its theft and eventual purchase. As an independent object, it needs to delimit its borders; space is no longer left open for improvisation. Instead, samba's two parts are defined once and for all, the lyrics and music duly notated, published, and recorded.

From *Malandro* to Composer

In our discussion of Orestes Barbosa's book, we saw that the author considered samba to be the living expression of a notable figure on Rio's social scene: the *malandro* (hustler). The *malandro* is defined primarily by way of his evasive relationship with the world of work: he works as little as possible, supporting himself by gambling, relying on women who are willing to pay his way, and taking advantage of *otários* (suckers or chumps), the well-behaved counterparts to *malandros*.

Orestes was hardly alone in associating samba with *malandros*. Indeed, during the period under investigation here—the late 1920s to the early 1930s—this association was quite common among the general population, as well as in Rio's local press outlets and in the lyrics of the songs themselves.

But the characteristics that define this figure were not exactly novel. Rather, it would be more realistic to conceive of him as the final (or perhaps just the latest) avatar of a lineage traceable to at least the nineteenth century. As such, we will begin our investigation of the *malandro* by visiting his previous incarnations. Doing so will, I hope, make him easier to understand.

* * *

In 1830 Gabriel Fernandes Trindade published a *lundu* for voice and piano titled "Graças aos céos," with these lyrics:

Graças aos céos de vadios	Thank heavens [that] of vagrants
As ruas limpas estão	The roads are clean
Deles a casa está cheia,	Of them the house is full,
A casa da correção	The house of correction

	(Refrain:)
Já foi-se o tempo de mendigar,	'Tis gone the era of begging,
Fora vadios, vão trabalhar	Get out vagrants, get to work

II	II
Sr. Chefe da polícia,	Sir Chief of Police,
Eis a nossa gratidão	Here is our gratitude
Por mandares os vadios	For sending the vagrants
À casa da correção	To the house of correction
	(Refrain)

III	III
Sede exato, pois Senhor	Be exacting, indeed, Sir
Em tal deliberação,	In such a deliberation,
Que muita gente merece	For many people deserve
A casa da correção.	The house of correction.

In this *lundu's* lyrics we already see the appearance of one of the many important figures of Brazilian popular song. Known by different names in different eras, he is perennially marked by a fundamental trait: an aversion to the world of work. The position that such a figure occupies within the discourse of popular song also varies. In the case of this *lundu*, he is called a *vadio* (vagrant) and is here part of someone else's discourse; it is not he who employs the word. Rather, the text is enunciated by a nonvagrant, perhaps even an antivagrant, who apparently delights in the fact that all of the vagrants have been imprisoned. At first glance, the text seems to have a moralistic tenor, directly opposing the satirical vein of the *lundus* examined in the previous chapter.

The final stanza, however, introduces an element that challenges just such a casual reading. If indeed all of the vagrants have already been hauled off to the house of correction, why ask the chief of police to be exacting in his deliberation? In saying that "many people deserve the house of correction," the *lundu* unequivocally suggests that the grievance is not only about the vagrants *stricto sensu* but also about countless others who reap the benefits of someone else's labors. With this in mind, if we return to the first stanza, we see that the construction is ambiguous enough to leave the reference to the "house" entirely vague. "Of them the house is full," is the line, only later specifying, perhaps with a wink from the narrator, that it is "the house of correction."

This second reading of the text, in which the moralism is transformed into satire, would no doubt have been reinforced by the appropriate gestural and scenic performance. At the same time, it also conforms perfectly to the chosen musical genre, which, as we have seen, often uses its humor to express sympathy for society's disenfranchised. (In some cases, this meant enslaved people; in this case, it is vagrants. Both were faces of a society in which working is not a way of life, but of violent oppression.)

Yet at other times it is easy to perceive, without any double entendre, the mutual affection that popular music and the vagrant had for each other. Both are kept under the watchful eye of the chief of police while simultaneously arousing the interest of a public privileged enough to acquire a piano and purchase sheet music. "Those who spend their lives playing *viola* and drinking *cachaça* [sugarcane alcohol], have no other choice but to cause disorder"; this phrase appears in an 1885 novel, the words spoken by a colonel.[1] In the context of Brazilian culture, the logic is irreproachable—the antecedents are the *viola* and the *cachaça*, and the consequent disorder. The link between the first two of these is such that neither can be substituted without risking unintelligibility; it would not work, for example, to say "playing piano and drinking *cachaça*," or "playing *viola* and drinking champagne." The *viola* and *cachaça*, the instrument and the drink of the masses, are icons of the vagrant, whose refusal to work in a slavocracy is tantamount to inciting disorder.

One important incarnation of the vagrant was the *capadócio* (literally Cappadocian, here meaning tough guy, bully, or hustler), of whom we have a good description in a novel from 1875:

> It remains for us to outline another type that we have already discussed elsewhere; the singer and *viola* player at *batuques*, the—*capadócio*—. The *capadócio*, as the name suggests, lived in holy sloth, had an easy life and was on a perpetual vacation; he was usually a tough guy [*valentão*] and a swordsman; beyond these qualities he had other gifts that made him a complete natural and a fixture of the amusements we are discussing. He would play the *viola*, guitar, and mandolin more or less perfectly, he was masterful in lundu, in *fado*, that which we call *rasgado*,[2] and for the corresponding songs he performed sung duels, improvising.[3]

The author subsequently adds that these *capadócios* "lived at interminable parties," because "the invitations were so many and so insistent that the only difficulty was in choosing." We find another description of the *capadócio* in *Memórias de um sargento de milícias*:

> There was a convivial malefactor, absolute exemplar of the capadócios[4] of the era, whom the major [Vidigal, the chief of police] had had his eye on for months. . . . He enjoyed a reputation as a clever and entertaining fellow, and there was no festivity of any kind to which he was not invited. He spent all his time corresponding to such invitations. . . . He played the viola and sang *modinhas* extremely well; he danced the fado with great perfection.[5]

As such, the *capadócio* links disorder ("tough guy and swordsman," "convivial malefactor") to the *viola*; as for the *cachaça*, even though it is not explicitly mentioned, it is implicit in the reference to the interminable parties. The abundance of invitations ("the only difficulty was in choosing") is a clear symptom of the *capadócio*'s popularity, perhaps even among those who were more economically privileged ("parties of any type"). This is a theme reappearing much later, in the 1930s, in Noel Rosa's biography: "Noel approaches. He takes a handful of papers out of his pocket. They are cards, prints, clippings, loose sheets that he reads and separates. '—Do you know what I have here? A heap of invitations to parties. Downtown, in Grajaú, in Tijuca.'"[6] The difference is that, as we will soon see, in Noel's era the *viola*, *cachaça*, and disorder had already become more independent of one another. Popular music was becoming professionalized. In his time, moreover, people no longer spoke of the *capadócio*. The new name for the vagrant was *malandro*.

The oldest printed *malandro* reference of which I am aware comes from 1904, and even here it is linked to popular music: it is in the title of a collection of *modinhas* and *lundus* by Eduardo das Neves, *O trovador da malandragem* (*The Troubadour of the Malandro Lifestyle*).[7] But only in the late 1920s does *malandro* begin appearing as a recurrent theme in samba lyrics, popularizing this figure and turning him into a near synonym of the *sambista*. When, in 1932, the newspaper *O Mundo Sportivo* promoted the first official samba school competition, it announced the event in the following way: "The princes of the *malandro*'s melody, samba's 'highest ranks' will compete in the big championship.... The public who knows the *malandro* from the records may not yet have tasted the flavor of the melody from the mouth of the *malandro* himself."[8] Samba is thus defined as the "*malandro*'s melody," as the musical expression of this character, precisely as in Orestes Barbosa's previously cited book. Another report, this one published in 1933 in the *Diário Carioca* newspaper, asserted that "the *morro* is samba's cathedral. It is there, on the picturesque simplicity of its battered banks that its faithful—the *malandros*—go to deliver their fervent prayers at moments of affliction and misfortune."[9]

The link between *sambista* and *malandro* is established at precisely the moment that the stylistic transformation that concerns us is taking place. This has already been noted by Cláudia Matos, who has written that "the notion of the *malandro* has been associated with that of the *sambista* since the 1920s. The association is concurrent with the process by which samba splintered off into its rhythmically 'modern' version, that which began to be disseminated in the late 1920s through the creations of the Estácio group."[10]

Matos also notes that "the existence of a rather large group of people able to survive at the expense of others (of the '*otários*'), employing more or less illicit devices, is not exclusive to the 1930s and 1940s, nor to Rio de Janeiro, nor even to the working class."[11] Indeed, equivalents of the Brazilian *malandro* and the *capadócio* are the *milonguero* of Buenos Aires, the *negro curro* of Cuba, or the *guapo* from Andalusia.[12] All of these figures share certain characteristics: an aversion to work, delinquency, and their own personal set of "ethics." Still, the uniqueness of *malandros*—and their importance in the context of the present work—derives from their association with samba and, more precisely, with the modern version of samba. What I will try to show in the remainder of this chapter is, first, that this association was not just extrinsically ascribed to them, for we see it in the samba texts themselves; and second, when viewed from the perspective of the texts themselves, the association reveals itself to be problematic. Contrary to what both Barbosa and the general public seem to have thought, this wily samba, a *malandro* in its own right (what might be called, in Portuguese, a *samba-malandro*), was also a samba that was uneasy with the *malandro* lifestyle.[13] Nevertheless, we will see that it is impossible to dissociate the new élan that samba was taking on in the 1930s from its *malandro* theme, which was decisive in characterizing the new style.

* * *

We will begin by analyzing a group of eight sambas, all of which were recorded between 1927 and 1931 by Francisco Alves (with the exception of one, which was recorded by Mário Reis). The first of these has already been mentioned: it is a samba supposedly written by Sinhô, known as "Ora vejam só!," which was the big Carnival hit of 1927. Here is the refrain:

Ora vejam só	Now look at this
A mulher que eu arranjei!	The woman I got!
Ela me faz carinhos até demais	She cares for me almost too much
Chorando, ela me pede:	Crying, she begs me:
"Meu benzinho,	"My love,
Deixa a malandragem se és capaz."[14]	Quit this *malandro* lifestyle if you can."

Vagalume discusses this samba and even transcribes the lyrics; but the title he gives it, one which he repeats four times over the course of two pages, as if it were the only one he knew, is "A malandragem" ("The *Malandro* Lifestyle").[15] However, the first recorded samba by an Estácio composer had this exact title. It was composed by Bide and released (also by Francisco Alves) in early 1928.[16]

"Ora vejam só!" (claimed by Sinhô) is connected to the Estácio group not just because of its date, theme, and title but also because of the dispute surrounding its authorship. As we have seen, Heitor dos Prazeres—who at the time had the nickname "Lino do Estácio" (Lino from Estácio) because he indeed lived in the

Estácio neighborhood—attested to having composed the refrain, and gave it yet another title: "Deixa a malandragem se és capaz" ("Quit This *Malandro* Lifestyle, If You Can").[17]

We already know that this was not the only samba whose authorship Sinhô and Heitor dos Prazeres disputed. In 1927 Francisco Alves records a *maxixe* claimed by Sinhô and Bastos Tigre called "Cassino maxixe" ("Casino *Maxixe*"). The composition is unsuccessful. Sinhô creates new verses and changes the title and genre. It becomes the samba "Gosto que me enrosco," claimed by Sinhô alone, which is recorded by Mário Reis and becomes a big hit the following year.[18] And yet once again, Heitor dos Prazeres claims authorship of the samba, the refrain on Mário Reis's recording.[19] This claim to authorship appears to be well founded: Sinhô's biographer, Edigar de Alencar, in fact affirms that Prazeres was paid a part of the author's rights that were owed to him for the samba.[20] This partnership is also documented in the *EMB*.[21] Here is the section of the lyrics said to have been written by Prazeres:

Não se deve amar sem ser amado	One shouldn't love without being loved
É melhor morrer crucificado	It's better to die crucified
Deus me livre das mulheres de hoje em dia	God save me from these women of today
Desprezam o homem só por causa da orgia.	They brush aside men just for the *orgia*.

Here the "*orgia*" (literally orgy, or life of excess),[22] as in countless other Estácio sambas, is a synonym for the bohemian lifestyle, which was so treasured by the *malandro*. In this context, therefore, *orgia* is almost synonymous with *malandragem*, the *malandro* way—always meaning a lifestyle. In the case just cited, the focus is on the object, while in the next case, the focus is on the subject/actor:

A malandragem	The *malandro* lifestyle
Eu vou deixar	I'm going to leave it
Eu não quero outra vez a orgia.	I don't want this orgy anymore.

This is the beginning of Bide's aforementioned samba.

The two refrains claimed by Heitor dos Prazeres share a common theme: a woman who rejects the protagonist's adopted way of life. In one case, she asks him to quit the *malandro* lifestyle, and in the other, she pushes him aside for the *orgia*. The only change is the tactic, plaintive in the first ("Crying, she begs me: / 'My love'"), pure and simple disregard in the second. But the incompatibility between "woman" and "*orgia*" is firmly established in both.

This incompatibility is a recurrent theme in Estácio sambas, making it possible to categorize these two sambas as pertaining to a specific thematic group of sambas that highlight this incompatibility in regard to love/relationships. Pertaining also to this thematic group is "Não é isso que eu procuro" ("This Isn't What I'm Looking For") (Silva-Alves, 1928). Here is its refrain:

Eu juro que hoje em dia	I swear that today
Mulher sendo da orgia	Women of the *orgia*
Não quero mais.	I don't want [them] anymore.

Here again is the incompatibility between the two terms, but this time taking a different shape. The hypothetical involvement of women in the *orgia* is rejected by the man, just as, in the previous examples, he says that the woman rejected his involvement in the *orgia*. The symmetry is reinforced by the expression "hoje em dia" (today, or nowadays), for whereas "Gosto que me enrosco" insists that "these women of today brush aside men just for the *orgia*," in "Não é isso que eu procuro," the protagonist is a man of today who brushes the woman aside for the *orgia*.

Finally, in the refrain of "Se você jurar" ("If You Swear") (Silva-Bastos-Alves, 1931), we hear the following:

Se você jurar	If you swear
Que me tem amor	That you love me
Eu posso me regenerar	I can resuscitate myself
Mas se é	But if you're just
Para fingir, mulher	Feigning, woman
A orgia assim não vou deixar.	I won't quit this *orgia*.

Here "resuscitate" should be understood to mean quitting the *malandro* lifestyle. In this case, either the woman leaves the *orgia* behind and swears to love the protagonist, or he considers her attitude to be feigned and drops this illusion of love, the dissolute life persevering. In both cases, the male protagonist's involvement with the woman implies leaving the *orgia* behind (without it mattering whether it is he or it is she who leaves it behind), and vice versa, the involvement of either of them in the *orgia* implies leaving the amorous union behind.

It is, moreover, worth considering what comes after the refrain of "A malandragem" (Bide-Alves, 1928), the first three verses of which we saw above:

Mulher do meu bem querer	My darling woman
Esta vida não tem mais valia.	This life no longer has any worth.

The protagonist had begun by affirming that he would leave the *malandro* lifestyle behind; two verses later we see that he is now committed to a woman, and he thus no longer values the *orgia*.

A second thematic group of Estácio sambas deals with another incompatibility: the *malandro* lifestyle and work. The most straightforward example is "O que será de mim" ("What Will Become of Me") (Silva-Bastos-Alves, 1931):

Se eu precisar algum dia	If I one day need
De ir pro batente	To punch the clock
Não sei o que será	I don't know what will become [of me]
Pois vivo na malandragem	For I live the *malandro* lifestyle
E vida melhor não há.	And there is no better life.

This samba complements another one by the same authors, from the same year, "Nem é bom falar" ("Don't Even Say It"):

Nem tudo que se diz se faz	Not everything one says can actually be done
Eu digo e serei capaz	I'm saying it and quite possibly
De não resistir	I wouldn't survive
Nem é bom falar	Don't even say it
Se a orgia se acabar.	If the *orgia* ends.

The protagonist says he might die if the *orgia* ends, but he does not say why it would end in the first place. In the previous samba, on the other hand, he does not say what would happen to him if he were obliged to work, but he makes it clear that this eventuality is stalking his *malandro* lifestyle. Both sambas deal with a fatal threat to the *orgia*; the first mentions only the cause, the second only the consequence. The part missing in each is replaced with a negation: in the first case, "I don't know what will become [of me]"; in the second, "don't even say it." In both cases, the negations constitute the titles of the sambas themselves. It is as if the entire utterance were too frightening to be contained in a single samba.

Finally, I turn to a samba by Gradim, who was from Mangueira, an area whose composers, not unlike those from other *morros* in Rio de Janeiro, were heavily influenced, as we have seen, by Ismael Silva and his friends. Here we have "Nem assim" ("Not Even Like That"), in which the protagonist finally leaves the *malandro* lifestyle behind, only to regret it soon thereafter:

Ai, minha vida	Ah, my life
Oh Deus, tenha pena de mim	Oh Lord, take pity on me
Deixei a maldita malandragem	I left the damned *malandro* lifestyle
Para ver se endireitava	To see if I straightened up
Mas, nem assim.	But, not even like that.

In this samba's refrain, we see the negative effects of the *malandro* lifestyle (we do not see this in the other sambas of this thematic group). It is deemed to be damned and is in part to blame for the bad situation in which the protagonist finds himself ("Oh Lord, take pity on me"), leading him to leave the *malandro* lifestyle behind and join the workforce. Unlike "Nem é bom falar" and "O que será de mim," in which such a possibility seems to be a kind of threat, in this samba there is a dimension of rational choice. The protagonist tries it "to see if he straightens up"—that is, if he can improve his life. The "not even like that" of the title indicates that not even this extreme measure worked. In the second parts, as one might expect, he announces his about-face:

Vou voltar à vida antiga	I'm going back to my old life
Pra tornar a ser feliz.	To be happy again.

Disappointment with the world of work transfigures the previous situation, and the *malandro* lifestyle goes from being "damned" to being a source of happiness.

Having presented these eight sambas in two separate thematic groups, let's see what they all have in common. It is not so much in the fact that all of them deal with the *malandro* lifestyle (that is, *malandragem*) and/or the *orgia*. Instead, my view is that in the Estácio sambas, *malandragem* is more than a word; it is, rather, its own theme, for it is enmeshed in a web of interconnected issues. The *malandro* theme that we find in these two groups of sambas is, in fact, that of the end of the *malandro* lifestyle, as is articulated by a lyric speaker who identifies with it. In four of the eight sambas studied here ("Ora vejam só!," "A malandragem," "Se você jurar," "Nem assim"), the protagonist's action is literally "to leave the *malandro* lifestyle behind," or the *orgia*, as is the case in the third samba. The action is demanded of him ("Ora vejam só!"), it is something he intends to do ("A malandragem"), it is something he would like to do if a certain condition is met ("Se você jurar"), and finally he actually does it despite paying the price of regret ("Nem assim"). These four sambas are therefore syntagmatic variants of the "I am going to leave the *malandro* lifestyle behind" archetype.

In the others, as I hope to have shown, although the expression "leave the *malandro* lifestyle behind" does not literally turn up, the presence of the same archetype can be deduced quite easily. In the two sambas of the thematic group related to work, the hypotheses around which the refrains are constructed are "if I need to punch the clock" ("O que será de mim") and "if the *orgia* ends" ("Nem é bom falar"), which are translations of "if I (am obliged to) leave the *malandro* lifestyle behind." Both of the remaining sambas ("Gosto que me enrosco" and "Não é isso que eu procuro") belong to the love group, discussed above. In both cases, it is either the man or the woman who is dismissed by the other because of his or her involvement in the *orgia*—that is, because he or she does not want to leave the *malandro* lifestyle behind, as seems to be the stipulation of "today."

* * *

In the preceding paragraphs we saw not only the importance of the *malandro* lifestyle as a theme in the new style but also its fundamentally problematic nature, wherein leaving the *malandro* lifestyle behind altogether is a constant concern.

We can now examine the role of this theme, if it had any at all, in the work of old-style *sambistas*. Let's begin with Sinhô. "Ora vejam só!" and "Gosto que me enrosco" are two of Sinhô's most successful sambas, and they address the *malandro* lifestyle, but in light of what was just discussed in the preceding paragraphs, we now have new arguments supporting Heitor dos Prazeres's claims to authorship. Consequently, they will not be dealt with here. But Sinhô also mentions the *malandro* lifestyle in other sambas, among which the most well known is "A Favela vai abaixo" ("Favela Is Being Razed"):

Minha cabocla, a Favela vai abaixo	My love, Favela is being razed
Quanta saudade tu terás deste torrão ...	You will miss this soil so ...
Que saudades ao nos lembrarmos das promessas	What nostalgia in remembering the promises
Que fizemos constantemente na capela	That we always made at the chapel
Para que Deus nunca deixe de olhar	So that God never stops watching
Para nós da malandragem e do morro da Favela.[23]	Us of the *malandro* lifestyle and of the *morro* of Favela.

Clearly, this lacks all of the typical ingredients of the *malandro* theme as I have defined it. With its references to missing soil and to the promises at the chapel, this song could not be further from the Estácio sambas. Furthermore, the protagonist and his love both belong to the *malandro* lifestyle, without either of them protesting or dismissing the other. In fact, the *malandros* only appear in this samba because, according to a commonplace notion of the era, the *morros* of Rio de Janeiro were inhabited by them.

Another example is "Ave de rapina" ("Bird of Prey"), recorded by Francisco Alves in 1930. One of the second parts says this:

Tenho certeza	I am sure
Que o mundo vai te ensinar	The world will teach you
A malandragem	The *malandro* lifestyle
Não tarda muito a acabar.	Will soon end.

As with the Estácio sambas, the end of the *malandro* lifestyle is announced; what makes it different, however, is that the individual in the text celebrates this. But there is an important detail. This samba had already been in circulation since Carnival of 1924, but at this earlier date it did not mention the *malandro* lifestyle. The corresponding stanza, rather, was this:

Formaste pulo	You leaped
Como a onça mais ligeira	Like the nimblest jaguar
Fizeste capa	You made the cloak
Da nossa pura bandeira.[24]	Out of our noble flag.

When Francisco Alves revisits the song in 1930, the *malandro* trend influences this change in lyrics, a decision that was perhaps made by the singer himself, for as we have seen, he was no stranger to the theme.

The *malandro* lifestyle is also mentioned in "Alta madrugada" ("Wee Hours of the Night"), a song of the genre known as *cena cômica* (comic scene), recorded in 1930. Likewise, *orgia* is referenced in "Que vale a nota sem o carinho da mulher" ("What Good Is Money without a Woman's Affection"), a samba from 1928. In "Fala macacada" ("Say It, Gang," 1930), Sinhô uses the word *malandro* in connection with the aforementioned *batucada* game of dexterity:

REFRAIN:

Leva, leva, se tens perna pra levar	Do it, do it, if you have the legs to do it
Não há malandro que possa me derrubar (bis)	There is no *malandro* who can take me down (repeat)

SECONDS:

I	I
Eu sou é bamba	I am a *bamba*
Ô macacada	Hey, gang
Eu sou do samba	I come from samba
E também da batucada	And also from the *batucada*

II	II
Sou carioca	I am a Carioca
Da velha guarda	Of the old guard
Não uso arma	I don't use a gun
Tenho fé numa pedrada.	I'm confident in my kick.

In the *batucada*, one contender stays still while the other attempts to take him down with a kick to the leg (called a *pernada*). This is what is referenced in the refrain. The second verse is a response from the contender awaiting the kick, boasting that no one can take him down. In the final verse of the second stanza, *pedrada* is used in place of *pernada*, the term that eventually replaces *batucada* (at least in Rio de Janeiro) as the name for the game itself.[25] Given the association of the game with gambling and the *malandro* lifestyle, it is possible that the change from *pernada* to *pedrada* in this song was a form of censorship exercised by Sinhô himself.

This samba does not fit into the archetype described above, but given that the *pernada* was the *malandros'* preferred sport in 1930s Rio de Janeiro—and since we are already familiar with Sinhô's modus operandi—I would float the hypothesis that the samba derives from an actual *batucada* refrain, which seems plausible when compared to refrains cited by other researchers.[26]

We thus see that Sinhô, in the late 1930s, partially adopts the vocabulary that would come to characterize the new style, though he does so without possibly confusing it with his actual style of composing. In fact, he insists on distancing himself from the new style in an interview from 1930:

> The evolution of samba! Frankly, I don't know if we should call what we are now seeing evolution. Take a good look at the songs of this year. Their authors, wanting to introduce new things and dress them up, they completely disregard samba's rhythm. . . . And always with the same thing. "Woman! Woman! I'm going to leave the *malandro* lifestyle." "I left the *malandro* lifestyle behind."[27]

In this interview, Sinhô points out precisely what I have sought to demonstrate: the link between the stylistic change (in which, as he notes, the rhythmic change is decisive) and the *malandro* theme. In fact, the abovementioned samba, "Fala macacada," can also be read as an affront to the newcomers by a "Carioca of the old guard," by a "bamba," who sings, with utmost self-assurance, "there is no *malandro* who can take me down."

Donga, another representative of the old style, also gives us a samba that references the *malandro* lifestyle: "Foram-se os malandros" ("The *Malandros* Are Gone"), recorded by Francisco Alves in February 1928.[28] It is divided into two clearly distinct parts. The refrain is a quatrain that leads me to believe it is another of Donga's folk melody appropriations:

Minha casa foi abaixo	My house has been razed
Meu cachorro se perdeu	My dog got lost
A mulher que eu mais amava	The woman I loved the most
De desgosto já morreu.	Has already died of dismay.

Instead of continuing with the list of grievances or explaining the reasons for such misfortunes, the second parts shift the angle, taking up a position external to the figure who is suffering, a figure who is now called a *malandro*:

Os malandros da Favela	The *malandros* of Favela
Não tem mais onde morar	Have nowhere else to live
Foram uns pra Cascadura	Some went to Cascadura
Outros para Circular.	Others to Circular.

This samba, not unlike the aforementioned "A Favela vai abaixo," by Sinhô, considers the inhabitants of the *morro* of Favela, whose "house has been razed," to be *malandros*.[29] But this includes the people of other *morros* too:

Os malandros de Mangueira	The *malandros* of Mangueira
Que vivem da jogatina	Who live a gambling life
São metidos a valentões	Like to play tough guy
Mas vão ter a mesma sina.	But will suffer the same fate.

This is where the song begins to express a certain aversion to *malandros* that becomes blatant in the final stanza:

Mas eu hei de me rir muito	But I'll laugh a lot
Quando a Justiça for lá	When the Law goes up there
Hei de ver muitos malandros	I'll see many *malandros*
A escorrer, a se mudar.	Empty out, move away.

The lens through which Donga views *malandros* in this samba is clearly negative. The same can be said of João da Baiana in his statement to the Museu da Imagem e do Som, in which he claims to have declined a trip to Europe in 1922 with the group Os Oito Batutas in order to avoid trading in his employment security for an uncertain adventure—a seemingly anti-*malandro* attitude. Indeed, the interviewer follows with a question: "So you mean that this whole *sambistas*-are-*malandros* deal isn't your thing?" João responds without hesitation: "Of course not!"[30]

Still, there is an important detail. The job João da Baiana did not want to lose was as an inspector at the docks, something he explained elsewhere in that same interview.[31] Yet according to Moreira da Silva's account, obtained by Cláudia Matos, the job of dock work inspector, which did not require one to "do the heavy lifting," is precisely what a "*malandro*'s profession" would be![32] This shows that the "objective" profile of João da Baiana corresponds perfectly with that of the *malandro*: mixed-race, from an economically underprivileged background, a partyer, a *sambista*, imprisoned "many times for playing *pandeiro*,"[33] earned a living without doing "the heavy lifting." Nevertheless, he and his generational cohort chose not to adopt the *malandro* label in defining their own identity. It is thus clear that the *malandro* lifestyle is not just an objective position but also an imagined construction by which a group both recognizes itself and is socially recognized.

A Respectable Spell

As has already been noted, the generation of *sambistas* responsible for creating and developing the new style did not adopt the *malandro* lifestyle as a defining trait of their identity without some conflict. One such conflict has already been analyzed: we saw the *malandro* appear in a significant number of sambas, though the songs were often about leaving the *malandro* lifestyle behind. The other conflict I would like to discuss—one that will occupy our attention for a bit longer—came to life in a debate, carried out via samba lyrics, between Noel Rosa and Wilson Batista.

In 1933 Batista composed the samba "Lenço no pescoço" ("Handkerchief around the Neck"), which begins with a physical description of the archetypal *malandro*:

Meu chapéu de lado	My hat to the side
Tamanco arrastando	Clogs shuffling
Lenço no pescoço	Handkerchief around the neck
Navalha no bolso	Knife in the pocket
Eu passo gingando	I strut by with my *ginga*
Provoco e desafio	I instigate and confront
Eu tenho orgulho	I am proud
De ser tão vadio.[1]	Of being such a vagrant.

Here the *malandro* is seen in his typical clothing and bodily attitude: hat, clogs,[2] handkerchief, pocketknife, and the famous *ginga*, in which the walker struts, swaying his body. We should begin by noting that this description accurately corresponds to the description of the *capadócio* we found in the aforementioned novel *O cortiço*. The character Firmo was, already in the late nineteenth century, using a "hat to the side" ("straw hat he had cocked at a rakish angle over his left ear"), a "handkerchief around the neck" ("and around his neck, protecting his collar, a white perfumed handkerchief"), and a "knife in the pocket" ("and then the mulatto . . . raised his right hand, in which a knife[3] glittered").[4] Despite all of these commonalities, Firmo is defined as a *capadócio*,[5] not as a *malandro*.[6] It is thus clear once again that the definition of *malandro* is far more complex than merely an assemblage of superficial traits. But let's return to "Lenço no pescoço":

Eu sou vadio	I am a vagrant
Porque tive inclinação	For I had the predisposition
Eu me lembro, era criança	I remember, I was a child
Tirava samba-canção.	I would sing samba songs.[7]

One of the essential ingredients of the *malandro*, much like the *capadócio*, is musical. The natural predisposition for the *malandro* lifestyle is understood by way of a predilection for samba starting at an early age. Now, although Firmo is said to have "been born in Rio de Janeiro," his music is said to be "Bahian."[8] Indeed, perhaps the only trait missing from the characterization of the *capadócio* that would allow us to call him a *malandro* is the undeniably Carioca aural emblem that will be given to him with the stylistic change under analysis. Consequently, treating the *malandro* as a distinct character of Carioca culture goes along with a novel treatment of samba itself: the creation of the new style first identified with the Estácio de Sá neighborhood.

I spoke of a conflict, set off by "Lenço no pescoço," that erupted between its author and Noel Rosa, revolving around the issue of the *malandro* lifestyle as identity defining. This is because Batista makes his character unabashedly proud of the most visible signs of his identity: he instigates, confronts, and scatters to the four winds his pride in being the way he is. Noel, for his part, reveals in some of his sambas a preference for a more discreet strategy. The samba that most clearly shows this is "Feitiço da Vila" ("The Vila Spell," Vadico-Noel Rosa, 1934), possibly his most famous samba.[9] It pays homage to Vila Isabel—a neighborhood located in the north zone of Rio de Janeiro that served as home and birthplace to the song's composer—as well as to the characteristics of the samba practiced there:

A Vila tem	Vila has
Um feitiço sem farofa	A spell without *farofa*
Sem vela e sem vintém	Without candles and without coins
Que nos faz bem	Which does us good
Tendo nome de princesa	Having the name of a princess

Transformou o samba	It transformed samba
Num feitiço decente, que prende	Into a respectable spell that takes hold
a gente.[10]	of us.

Samba is here directly identified as a *feitiço*, a spell.[11] This word is also used in Brazil to designate the offerings left at crossroads for magical ends, generally within the context of Afro-Brazilian religions.[12] These offerings often consist of food (*"farofa"*[13]), candles, and coins. The "name of a princess" alludes to Princess Isabel, the daughter of Brazilian Emperor Pedro II, who signed the 1888 decree that eradicated slavery in Brazil (a year before the Proclamation of the Republic).

"Feitiço da Vila" insists, thus, that there is a relationship, by way of her name, between "Vila" Isabel and "Princess" Isabel. This relationship explains why the former would have transformed samba, which, for its part, is placed in a relationship with the spell—the spell (*feitiço*) being, to the eyes of the Brazilian elite, a representation of why Afro-Brazilian practices were so threatening. What remains implicit is that what Vila Isabel does with samba is somehow akin to what Princess Isabel did with the Black population by abolishing slavery. It is an analogy concerning the right to citizenship for both Black Brazilians and samba.[14]

Let's examine more closely the transformations that, according to Noel, Vila effected in samba. Though never ceasing to be a spell, it ends up being stripped of its exterior characteristics: the *farofa*, the candles, and the coins. It became a more spiritualized spell, as in a homeopathic remedy, in which the physical absence of the active substance can mean an increase in its energetic presence, distilled, purified, and thus altogether more potent. The spell thus gains in force what it loses in appearance, in materiality. Without candles, *farofa*, or coins, the spell is in a pure state, an exceedingly subtle spell, making it more difficult for even the bewitched to protect themselves from it. What could this spell be if not music itself?

And so, samba is transformed: a spell, but *decente*—that is, "respectable" or "decent." The word *decente* primarily denotes social acceptance; the princess's seal of approval tells us that there is nothing wrong with enjoying samba. It is not something to be prohibited from the living rooms of even the most aristocratic families. But all of the changes Noel sees in samba do not alter, according to him, its bewitching essence, its capacity to "take hold of us." This phrase, which closes the stanza, serves as an antithesis to the initial idea that we proposed (the parallel between Vila and Isabel, the redeemer). The sweet revenge of formerly enslaved people is in performing a music that enslaves those who hear it; samba is respectable, but a spell nonetheless.

These observations indicate the broader problem with the relationships between so-called "Black culture" and Brazil's dominant culture. The end of slavery has obvious consequences for these relationships: the legal equality of Black and white people as citizens, as an undifferentiated mass population, and soon thereafter as members of a republic. Yet the consequence as far as music is concerned, a few decades later, is the emergence of "popular music," which in this sense stands in opposition not just to "folk music" but also to "Black music." But for this to take place, it requires a collapsing of boundaries, starting with those erected within the country itself. This can be seen in another section of "Feitiço da Vila":

Lá em Vila Isabel	There in Vila Isabel
Quem é bacharel	Those who are bachelors
Não tem medo de bamba	Aren't afraid of *bambas*
São Paulo dá café,	São Paulo bears coffee
Minas dá leite	Minas bears milk
E a Vila Isabel dá samba.	And Vila Isabel bears samba.

The bachelor (as in a bachelor's degree)—in Brazil, a symbol of literate, white, European culture. The *bamba*—the bachelor's equivalent in the culturally mixed milieu of Rio de Janeiro. Vila is treated as a utopian space in which the two fraternize, a space that is soon projected onto the whole country. Samba is just one more "product," another resource after milk and coffee, which were already the main products of the states of Minas Gerais and São Paulo, respectively. Samba defends its right to participate in the market, to mount the shelves of national heritage. It is no longer a sign of exclusion, of separation, but rather of positive difference. At the same time, it mitigates the overly drastic contrast between coffee, which is black, and milk, which is white, proposing itself as a mixture.

The idea of a respectable spell is paradoxical in the framework of Brazilian culture. Similar paradoxes appear often in Noel's sambas. We have already seen one such example in "Feitiço da Vila," as it suggests that the *bamba* and the bachelor fraternize. In the following paragraphs, I will examine similar cases, allowing us to better understand Noel's disagreement with the samba "Lenço no pescoço." We begin with an interview from 1935:

At first, samba ... was considered a pastime for bums. But samba was fortunate. It came down from the *morro*, wearing clogs, with a handkerchief around the neck, it wandered the streets with a cigarette butt in the corner of its mouth and its hands stuffed into empty pockets and, suddenly, there it is in a cutaway coat and white gloves in the salons of Copacabana.[15]

Here the sartorial signs of the *malandro* are contrasted with those of elegance (cutaway coat and white gloves) while also being mapped onto geographical signs: the *morro* corresponds to the handkerchief around the neck, and Copacabana to the elegant vestments. I have already addressed the matter of clothing and will address it again later, but here let's spend some time on the geographical aspects.

Rio's *morros* were, from the beginning of the twentieth century, occupied by low-income groups evading the increasingly expensive rent prices of the city's older neighborhoods. Bereft of basic utilities (water, electricity, sewage system), with very little policing, and with no schools, churches, or health centers, they developed as communities apart, viewed with wariness. Although they were technically part of the city, given that they were located within city limits, they lacked everything that categorically defined the city, beginning with paved roads and brick homes. They were, starting in the 1920s, privileged sites for samba. In his 1933 book *Na roda do samba*, Vagalume dedicates all of the second part (pp. 139–233) to "life in the *morros*": that of Querosene, Mangueira, São Carlos, Salgueiro, Favela (the last of these being the oldest, whose name subsequently became a generic designation for all *morros*).

Copacabana, on the other hand, was a fancy part of Rio at the time, and the few homes there were owned by wealthy families. The neighborhood is also mentioned in the samba "O 'x' do problema" ("The Crux of the Problem," 1936), and the meaning is roughly the same:

Você tem vontade	Your hope is
Que eu abandone o Largo do Estácio	That I leave Estácio Square
Pra ser a rainha em um grande palácio	To be queen in a grand palace
E dar um banquete uma vez por semana	And host a banquet once a week
Nasci no Estácio	I was born in Estácio
Não posso mudar minha massa de sangue	I can't change what's in my blood
Você pode crer que palmeira do Mangue	Believe me, a palm tree from Mangue
Não cresce na areia de Copacabana.	Doesn't grow in the sand of Copacabana.

The Mangue Canal, next to the Estácio neighborhood, was also a red-light district.[16] Copacabana, where the rich had grand palaces and hosted weekly banquets, is offered here as a contrast, just as it is contrasted above with the *morro*. What Estácio had in common with the *morro* was the presence of samba. In the lyrics of his samba, Noel highlights the difference and even the incompatibility of the two neighborhoods, metonymic representations of two ways of life: that of the bourgeoisie and that of the *malandro*.

Yet in the above-cited interview, he emphasizes samba's capacity to circulate, personified in the figure of the *malandro* who leaves the *morro*, changes clothes (as circumstances require), and goes to Copacabana, which does not entail, clearly, leaving Estácio Square behind.

The same idea is expressed in the samba "Cem mil réis" ("One Hundred *Mil Réis*, 1936), whose title evokes the amount of money necessary to buy a *soirée* (that is, an elegant dress, to attend *soirées* of high society) and a *tamborim*. The person in question circulates freely in both contexts but has to behave in the manner appropriate to each:

Não custa nada	It doesn't cost a thing
Preencher formalidade:	To meet the formality:
Tamborim pra batucada	*Tamborim* for the [samba] percussion
Soirée pra sociedade.[17]	*Soirée* for [high] society.

But the classic formulation—not only in the works of the author who is the focus of our attention, but in samba lyrics generally (even in broader Carioca culture)—of the opposition that has hitherto appeared as *morro*/Estácio versus Copacabana is expressed in another samba, which is one of Noel's most famous. Its title evokes yet another paradox, as it compares a samba song to a prayer. Indeed, the title of the samba "Feitio de oração" (Vadico-Rosa, 1933) translates as "Shape of a Prayer," with the implication being that the singing of samba is akin to praying:

O samba, na realidade	Samba, in fact
Não vem do morro, nem lá	Comes neither from the *morro*,
da cidade.	nor the city.

The *"morro"* and the "city": this opposition reappears in countless other sambas, before and after "Feitio de oração," ranging from the previously cited "A Favela vai abaixo" (Sinhô, 1927) to "O morro não tem vez" ("The *Morro* Has No Chance," Jobim and Moraes, 1963). It appears too in the famous 1932 headline with which the newspaper *O Mundo Sportivo* announced the first official samba school competition: "The Sonorous Soul of the *Morros* Will Make Its Way Down to the City."[18]

If samba "comes neither from the *morro*, nor the city," it is because a place exists that is neither, or is both at the same time; a place where this divide—which was unfortunately as evident to Rio's citizens in 1933 as it is for them today—finally ceases to make sense. In part, this place is Vila, not the real Vila but a utopic one that Noel invents in the lyrics and music of his sambas (and, in the same gesture, transforms this utopia into something real, at least inasmuch as history allows). But the place of samba's origin is also, as is explained elsewhere in "Feitio de oração," the composer's heart:

O samba, então,	Samba, then,
Nasce do coração.[19]	Is born in the heart.

Noel plays with the common notion that music is the direct expression of sentiments. In so doing, he offers a reminder that the *sambista*'s work, in the end, results in "music"; indeed, contemporary culture finally recognizes that samba is just as much "music" as is a symphony, both duly represented in the *New Grove Dictionary*.[20]

Still, it is important not to forget that Noel is speaking for himself, against the dominant view of samba as exclusive to the *morro*, for he was not from there. He was, as we already know, from Vila Isabel, a geographically flat (i.e., not a hillside) neighborhood that was "predominantly middle class, petite-bourgeois, concerned with social ascension, conventions, rules";[21] and furthermore, he was from a family with the means not only to pay for his studies at São Bento, a very well-reputed religious school, but also to get him into medical school, the career path taken by his great-grandfather, grandfather, and uncle.[22] In other words, he was from the part of Vila Isabel that, as far as his social conditions were concerned, was farthest away from the *morro*.

Consequently, choosing samba over medicine, something that would have been unthinkable a generation earlier, was even in 1930 a disappointment to Noel's family and a surprise to his friends. At the time, having a university diploma was of great value in Brazil. Those who held them were the aforementioned "bachelors," or "doctors." But he was not the only one in this type of situation to make such a decision, as he notes in an interview: "When people talk about being a doctor of samba [as was the moniker of singer Mário Reis, who had a law degree] it's not in vain. There is no lack of doctors and lawyers who can elevate samba. So there they are, doctors Joubert de Carvalho, Ary Barroso, Olegário Mariano, and many others."[23]

In another interview, Noel remarks on the fact that samba had become increasingly able to attract people whose social positions would previously have limited them to being, in the best-case scenario, mere admirers of samba:

> Samba has evolved. The rudimentary voice of the *morro* has become, little by little, an authentic artistic expression.... The spontaneous poetry of our people has won the battle against the spell of academism to which the intellectuals of Brazil have lived for so many years ingloriously enslaved. Authentic poets, ankylosing in the hands of the sonnet, depleted by the torturous lapidation of sonorous decasyllables and alexandrines, have felt the truth in time. And samba has overtaken some of them.... The public's taste has improved. Other poets have come along saying, in clean and beautiful language, marvelous things. ... It is necessary, though, to stress that these poets, too, have had to change themselves, leaving behind a host of literary prejudices. They have influenced the public but were also influenced by it. Out of the reciprocal action of these two tendencies came the elevation of samba, as an artistic expression, and has

resulted in the humanization of poets condemned to stagnation due to the spell of academism.[24]

The evolution of samba, to which he refers, gets mixed up with the evolution of each of the two parties involved: the public, whose taste improves, and the poets, who free themselves from the spell of academism. Samba's shift—from "rudimentary voice of the *morro*" to "artistic expression"—thus reveals itself to be an expression of a larger societal shift, a circular flow made up of reciprocal influences, which are produced not directly but rather through the intermediation of this catalyzer.

The reciprocity between intellectuals and the masses is moreover reinforced by the choice of the metaphors "spell" and "enslaved." Just as precisely a year and a half earlier, in "Feitiço da Vila," Noel had spoken of samba as a "spell" that became respectable through its contact with Princess Isabel, who was said to be the redeemer for having signed the law that ended slavery in Brazil, here it is samba that liberates the poets from the spell that had enslaved them.

* * *

Allow me to make a small interjection here, which I do not believe will interrupt the flow of the argument. In 2008 I was part of an internet controversy after watching a video posted by the singer and composer Caetano Veloso, in which he called the song "Feitiço da Vila" racist. The main idea of the video was that, in calling Vila Isabel's samba *decente* (respectable), Noel Rosa was implicitly accusing other sambas of being unrespectable. I wrote an article in response, "Vídeo infeliz" ("Unfortunate Video"), which was first published online and later included as an appendix to the second Brazilian edition of my book. Here I summarize my arguments from that article.

Caetano missed the mark in at least two respects. First, Noel's praise of Vila is not an effort to differentiate it from the *morros*, from the other places samba was being made. Instead, his aim is to bring Vila closer to the *morros* by placing it within the context of the neighborhood rivalries so common in the samba world. Second, and most important: the paradoxical character of the expression "feitiço decente" (respectable spell) inexplicably escaped Caetano, a composer so well versed in paradoxes, contradictions, and antitheses. *Feitiço* is a Portuguese word whose main use (albeit far from its only use) has always been accusatory. As such, it is not only "Feitiço da Vila" (and many other sambas that could easily be mentioned) that seeks to distance itself from *farofa*, from candles, and from coins. *Feitiço* (spell) and *feiticeiro* (sorcerer), in Brazil and elsewhere, are categories of accusation. We are willing to say our enemies are *feiticeiros*, but we do not call ourselves *feiticeiros*, nor, moreover, are we willing to say that being a *feiticeiro* is a positive thing. And if we act in this way, it is not because of racism but rather because of the way the system of sorcery works, not only in postslavery Brazil, but in Africa too, as E. E. Evans-Pritchard demonstrates in his classic book on witchcraft among the Azande.[25]

Noel Rosa's work expresses, as I hope this chapter demonstrates, a concern for Brazilian society's acceptance of the rights and the value of samba and Afro-Brazilian cultural expressions. This acceptance was much more precarious in 1934 than it is today; and I doubt there was, in 1930s Brazil, a better way to bring *feitiço* to the surface, to insert it into society at large, than by way of this type of Zen *koan*. The "respectable spell" is a paradox, an impossible thing, a logical short circuit. And this is precisely where Noel Rosa's genius is (and that of Caetano Veloso, too, though not in his unfortunate 2008 video): creating impossible objects, pipe dreams, utopias, and a spell that is capable of transforming our lives.

* * *

Let's return to Noel Rosa's understanding of the role the *malandro* lifestyle played in defining the *sambista*'s identity, and how this differed from that which we see in Wilson Batista's "Lenço no pescoço." If, in Noel's utopia, the movement between Estácio and Copacabana was a two-way street and the movement between the *morro* and the city was free and unimpeded; if the bachelor did not fear the *bamba* (which, as we have seen, is another name for *malandro*); and if the identity of the latter was not taken to be an affront but rather a subtle spell, then it should come as no surprise that Noel was not a fan of Batista's samba. In it, after all, the *malandro* prefers the label of *vadio* (vagrant) to that of professional composer; he not only wears a hat, clogs, and a handkerchief but also carries a pocketknife that he is ready to use against the first bachelor who crosses his path.

Indeed, Noel did not like the song and wasted no time, quickly composing a samba that responded, point by point, to Batista. The samba is called "Rapaz folgado" ("Idle Boy," 1933):[26]

Deixa de arrastar o seu tamanco	Stop shuffling your clogs
Pois tamanco nunca foi sandália	For clogs were never meant to be sandals
E tira do pescoço o lenço branco	And take the white handkerchief from your neck
Compre sapato e gravata	Buy shoes and a tie
Jogue fora esta navalha	Throw away your pocketknife
Que lhe atrapalha	'Cause it gets in your way
Com chapéu de lado deste rata	With your hat to the side you've erred
Da polícia quero que escapes	I want you to evade the police
Fazendo samba canção[27]	Making samba songs

Eu já lhe dei papel e lápis	I've already given you paper and pencil
Arranja um amor e um violão	Get yourself a love and a guitar
Malandro é palavra derrotista	*Malandro* is a defeatist word
Que só serve pra tirar	Only good for undermining
Todo o valor do sambista	All of the *sambista*'s worth
Proponho ao povo civilizado	My proposal to the civilized people
Não te chamar de malandro	Is that they no longer call you *malandro*
E sim de rapaz folgado.	But rather an idle boy.

Máximo and Didier, Noel's biographers, find it difficult to make sense of these lyrics in the context of the *sambista*'s life, as he had always shown great affection for *malandros*, regularly keeping their company. The way the authors deal with the issue is to turn the composition into a personal attack on Wilson Batista.[28] However, the lyrics of Noel's samba are clearly more generic when they level accusations of defeatism against—not the *malandro*, as he is careful to specify, but rather—the word *malandro*. The same idea is repeated in the samba "Se a sorte me ajudar" ("If Luck Helps Me," 1934), composed with Germano Augusto, who was himself a *malandro*:

A palavra "malandragem"	The word *malandragem*
Só nos trouxe desvantagem	Has only done us a disservice
E você não vai dizer que não.	And you can't say it hasn't.

Has only done a disservice to whom? Who is "us"? The *malandros* themselves, of course! For Máximo and Didier to see Noel as a critic of the *malandro* lifestyle would be the equivalent of seeing him as a moralist, an adept of the very bourgeois values that the *malandro* way of life evaded;[29] but it is precisely because of Noel's affinity for *malandros* that he proposes they be defined as composers. His biographers, moreover, present us with all the elements necessary for a broader, more generalized (and entirely consistent) understanding of the verses of "Rapaz folgado." They list, for example, the countless number of times Noel offered to work as a partner with *malandros*, in which he completes the second parts, transforming what were mere refrains from the perspective of popular music into sambas ripe for the record industry. The authors also mention the adjustments he made to the *malandros*' sambas (with their consent), changes the *malandros* themselves called "corrections."[30]

What Noel Rosa does, therefore, is to clear a path that was surely not an invention of his own; it was a path available to a group of people who liked samba and had few options for survival beyond the precarious life of the *orgia*. The path, ultimately, was from *malandro* to composer. Noel does this, as he himself says, by "giving paper and pencil." That is, he encourages the documentation of samba, in two concomitant senses: as a written document that plucks samba from the sphere of pure orality, transforming the improvisations into definitive second parts; and as an authored document, transforming the samba composer into a virtual colleague of Beethoven.

Finally worth noting is that despite what Noel says, the word *malandragem*— and once again, his attention is indeed focused on the word itself—brought with it at least one advantage. I am referring to the most obvious of all the advantages: the word was in vogue, and it helped the commercial success of sambas written by Ismael Silva, Bide, and others. Even Sinhô benefited from this trend, thanks in part to the refrains by "Lino do Estácio"—the same Sinhô who, already having become a professional composer by the early 1920s, did not really use the *malandro* theme in his own work. Of the seventeen Sinhô songs released by Casa Wehrs between 1926 and 1928, "Ora vejam só!" and "Gosto que me enrosco" were by far the best selling: these two alone sold 11,089 copies versus the 11,259 that was the sum of the other fifteen put together![31]

Indeed, perhaps the *sambistas'* only real and decisive *malandro* move, their only true "hustle," was in conveying to the record-buying public and to popular music consumers an idealized image of their own existence, which they were able to use, when lucky enough, to overcome some of their material difficulties. This idea shines some light on the issue from another angle: it explains why leaving the *malandro* lifestyle behind was expressed, in the Estácio sambas, by way of the *malandro* theme.

* * *

Let's return once again to the controversy with Wilson Batista, which is serving as the common thread in our journey through Noel Rosa's sambas. We have seen the way in which "Rapaz folgado" positions itself against the exterior signs of the *malandro* lifestyle: the hat, clogs, pocketknife, handkerchief around the neck. Notice that these objects are to the *malandro* precisely what *farofa*, candles, and coins were to the spell in "Feitiço da Vila." In both cases, the objects are what I called visible signs of an identity; and in both cases, Noel suggests suppressing them so that samba can serve as their replacement. The spell, made respectable by turning into samba, and the *malandro* made into a *sambista* by way of paper and pencil, are both clearly the same type of transformation, which in both cases is facilitated by the suppression of objects that index a given identity.

Still, what cannot be overemphasized is that it is not the identity itself being suppressed. Rather, it is sublimated into the music: "The *malandro* didn't disappear. It was merely transformed, with its *cabrocha*,[32] to trick the police."[33] Now, music also expresses itself through objects. The next step is thus to look at the musical objects—for instance, the instruments—and signal which ones allow for the elaboration of a list that corresponds, in the case of samba, to the spell, on one hand (*farofa*, candles, coins); and to the *malandro*, on the other (hat, clogs, handkerchief).

Let's do this by beginning with Noel Rosa once again. In an interview published in 1935, when asked about which instruments would be "samba's own," he says this: "They've just started coming around, and aren't yet everywhere. The *cuíca* that growls [*ronca*]. The *tamborim* clamoring [*repicando*] around the heart that is the *barrica*."[34] *Barrica* is an older name for the bass drum known today as the *surdo*. The term still appears in 1948, in the samba "Adeus América" ("Goodbye, America"), by Haroldo Barbosa and Geraldo Jacques, which mentions the same three instruments remembered by Noel. The lyrics speak of a U.S.-based Brazilian whose homesickness is so great that he decides to return to his homeland, saying:

Eu vou voltar prá cuíca	I'm going back to the *cuíca*
Bater na barrica	Beat the *barrica*
Tocar tamborim.[35]	Play the *tamborim*.

In the interview cited above, Noel Rosa says that the *cuíca* was not prevalent in Rio de Janeiro in the early 1930s. Judging from a report published in *O Mundo Sportivo* in 1932, on the occasion of the first official parade of samba schools, he is right: "The public will have the opportunity to hear various instruments not well known by most in the city. This is the case, for example, with the *cuíca*, whose sound stands out from all the others as it is singular and unmistakable."[36] Moreover, in 1933 *O Globo*, which was promoting the second parade, reported this: "we are satisfied at having afforded the city the strangest show of the year."[37] It is likely that adding to this strangeness would have been the instruments, to which the public was not generally accustomed.

Indeed, in all of the references to samba instruments prior to the late 1920s, not only the *cuíca* but also the *tamborim* and the *surdo* (or *barrica*) are strikingly absent. In Vagalume's already cited book, there is no mention of *surdos*; the *tamborim* is spoken of only once (included on a list);[38] and regarding the *cuíca*, "it no longer satisfies nor fits with the harmony of the *samba chulado*."[39] In the previously cited descriptions of folk sambas, including those from the house of Tia Ciata and the Festa da Penha at the turn of the twentieth century, there is not the slightest reference to the *cuíca* or *surdo*, and the *tamborim* is rarely mentioned.[40]

The instruments that most commonly provided the rhythmic accompaniment for folk samba up until the beginning of the twentieth century appear to have been the *pandeiro*, *prato e faca*, and handclaps. This ensemble appears in aforementioned passages from Guilherme de Mello and Raul Pompéia, among others.

On the other hand, an examination of the instrumentation of the professional groups created by Pixinguinha, Donga, and João da Baiana reveals that the rhythm section also lacked *cuícas* and *tamborins*. In Os Oito Batutas, during the 1920s, we have a *ganzá*, *pandeiro*, and *reco-reco*;[41] in the group Velha Guarda, created in the 1950s, *pandeiro*, *prato e faca*, and *afochê*.[42] The *pandeiro* is a constant, and the apparent variety in the other four instruments is merely superficial, for the *reco-reco* and the *prato e faca* substitute each other, as both are scraped idiophones, while the *ganzá* and the *afochê* serve as types of shaken idiophones.[43]

Note that in the above-cited interview with Noel, when asked about specific samba instruments, he does not mention the *pandeiro* or *prato e faca*, which are perhaps the two most cited in the literature concerning both pre-1917 folk samba and old-style popular samba. Rather, he speaks as if samba did not have its own unique instruments until the 1930s—and in so doing, he anticipates the researchers we have already discussed, according to whom a key difference between the old and new style is that the former was based on (European) "orchestra" instruments while the latter was based on (African or Brazilian) "percussion" instruments. As I see it, this deliberate negation of the *pandeiro* (among other instruments) as a samba instrument is linked, at least in Noel's case, to a recognition of the emergence of the new paradigm. The *pandeiro* was indeed used, as it still is today; but a samba without at least one of the instruments from among the *cuíca-surdo-tamborim* series was simply not samba.

Meanwhile, samba *cronistas* give us many references to *Estácio-linked sambistas* who invented, or introduced into samba, instruments that would later be viewed as the most characteristic of the new style: "The creator of the *tamborim* was Bide and Bernardo, from the time they were little boys they always had a *tamborim* with them, they invented it. And the one who introduced the *surdo* into samba was Bide."[44] Regarding the *cuíca*, its introduction "into the percussion of the [samba] schools" is attributed to João Mina, "from the *morro* of São Carlos"[45] (the *morro* that bordered Estácio).

Cuíca, *surdo*, and *tamborim* appear together again in the lyrics of the classic Ismael Silva samba "Antonico" (1950). The lyrics elaborate a plea for help, which is directed toward someone—the Antonico of the title—who, it seems, has the means of interceding on behalf of another figure, Nestor, who is in turn defined in two ways—negatively, by the difficult situation in which he finds himself:

Está vivendo em grande dificuldade	He is living with a lot of trouble
Ele está mesmo dançando na corda bamba.	He is really dancing on a tightrope.

And positively, due to the virtues that make him deserving of Antonico's help:

Ele é aquele	He is that guy
Que na escola de samba	Who in the samba school
Toca cuíca, toca surdo e	Plays *cuíca*, plays *surdo*, and *tamborim*.
tamborim.[46]	

The "negative" definition of Nestor makes use of the verb *estar* (to be), which in Portuguese denotes incidental, temporary situations; but the "positive" definition makes use of the verb *ser* (to be), which denotes permanent characteristics, identities. As such, in response to the question "Who is Nestor?," the samba tells us he is that guy who "plays *cuíca*, plays *surdo*, and *tamborim*," which assures that Nestor will be recognized as a unique *sambista*—after all, as the lyrics later say,

No samba,	In samba,
Ninguém faz o que ele faz.	No one does what he does.

It has been suggested that Nestor is a representation of Ismael himself.[47] True or not, the text indeed postulates an equivalence between the two, saying, in its final verse, "faça por ele como se fosse por mim" ("do for him as you would for me"). Now, Ismael Silva, as the reader will already have noted, has taken on nearly mythic proportions in the history of samba as the great composer of the Estácio group, which has been such a major focus of our attention. When he defines himself (by way of his alter ego Nestor) as the guy who plays *cuíca*, *surdo*, and *tamborim*, we have good reason to see here yet another indication of the emblematic value of these three instruments for the new style.

Consequently, it seems reasonable to consider these three instruments to be icons of identity, making thus the *cuíca*, *surdo*, and *tamborim* syntactically equivalent to *farofa*, candles, and coins, as well as to the hat, clogs, and handkerchief. At the same time, we should note that they are not selected as such because of any practical links to the spell, as in the former, nor to *malandro* fashion, as in the latter, but rather because they are musical objects. This gives us another set of correspondences, for these instruments replace, as we have seen, the *pandeiro*, *prato e faca*, and *ganzá*. This double substitution can be illustrated in a diagram where we see that the three objects in question are found precisely at the intersection between music and identity:

> **Identity:**
> *farofa, candles, coins*
>
> :
>
> *hat, clogs, handkerchief*
>
> :

Music: *pandeiro, prato e faca, ganzá*   :   *cuíca, surdo, tamborim*

* * *

In "Rapaz folgado," Noel Rosa put it this way:

Da polícia quero que escapes	I want you to evade the police
Fazendo samba-canção.	Making samba songs.

It was not just the police who threatened Noel's *malandro* friends. Deep down, he must have hoped that with samba's help they would also be able to evade other threats that were equally frightening, or were perhaps even worse. For many, such evasion was unattainable. Canuto, for example, Noel's partner on "Esquecer e perdoar" ("Forget and Forgive," 1931), lived in the *morro* of Salgueiro and died of tuberculosis in 1932, before his thirtieth birthday. Another Salgueiro resident (in fact, one of the neighborhood's leaders), Antenor Gargalhada, who partnered with Noel on "Eu agora fiquei mal" ("Now I'm in a Bad Spot," 1931), died of tuberculosis in 1941. Ernani Silva, Noel's partner on "Primeiro amor" ("First Love," 1932), had "two vices: samba and cards"; he died at twenty-eight, shot from atop the *morro* of Favela by distrustful opponents. Gradim, author of the aforementioned "Nem assim," wrote "Sorrindo sempre" (1932) with Noel and found death as "a young man with ruined lungs."[48]

The Estácio group also had its share of early deaths. Bide's brother, Rubem Barcelos, credited by some as the first to compose sambas in the new style, died of tuberculosis at twenty-three. Nilton Bastos, who partnered with Ismael Silva on some of the sambas analyzed previously, died of the same illness at thirty-two. Mano Edgar was killed at thirty-one during a fight that broke out while gambling.[49] Brancura and Baiaco also died early, the former at twenty-seven, of insanity, the latter at twenty-two, of an ulcer.[50]

All of these premature deaths were no doubt seen by those who were hostile toward *malandros* as the fatal effects of the inescapable association linking *violas, cachaça,* and disorder. But the professionalization developing in popular music would partially contribute to dismantling this association, especially as far as disorder was concerned. As for old-style *sambistas,* who already enjoyed relatively comfortable professional positions by the early 1920s, the only one to die of tuberculosis was Sinhô, at forty-two. Pixinguinha, João da Baiana, Donga, and Caninha all lived well into their seventies, with their *cachaça* and all.

Ismael Silva was a new style representative who did evade these dangers. But he hit some rough patches along the way. Between 1935 and 1937, he spent two and a half years in prison for attempted homicide.[51] Yet on at least one occasion, samba saved Ismael from a mix-up with the police. The incident took place on the island of Paquetá, located an hour from Rio by boat,

> where a policeman, and composer, Roberto Martins, lived, whom the local commissioner, Policarpo, called:—*Stop by here, Roberto. I arrested this skinny*

*black kid [*crioulinho*] for cheating in a game, and he says he's a composer. He swears he knows you.—What's his name?—Ismael Silva.—Ismael? No, it can't be, Poli. But if it is, he's the author of*... And Roberto Martins sang some of Ismael's sambas on the phone, "Se você jurar," "Para me livrar do mal," "Não há," "Nem é bom falar," "Novo amor," "Adeus." When it was over, the commissioner was confused:—*But all of those are his? It'd be better if you came, Roberto.* Roberto Martins went there. From the gated door of the prison, he saw Ismael inside. ...—*But you don't need this, Ismael! You're a great composer! In any case, let's do something: you hop on the first barge and we'll keep this all between us.*[52]

It is by being "a great composer," instead of a "skinny Black kid" who cheats in a game, that Ismael Silva becomes "a real somebody." And he simultaneously becomes a figure capable of resorting to a form of conduct that is classic in Brazil, the "do you know who you are talking to?" approach, a phrase that was the focus of a fine study by anthropologist Roberto DaMatta.

This is an utterance employed in situations for which a person's position, considered to be superior, prevails over complying with the law. Although it is perhaps true that in every country powerful people can resort to their prestige when attempting to transcend the law, in DaMatta's view, in Brazil this practice takes on such proportions that it can be thought of as being a veritable ritual. It is precisely this ritual to which Ismael resorts, for upon being imprisoned for cheating, rather than claim his own innocence, he instead relies on the fact that he is a composer and has a friendship with an authority figure, which ends up being much more efficient.

His case fits into one of the types examined by DaMatta, which he calls a "revelation of social identity":

> The situation reaches its climax with the emphatic representation of another social identity—one which is generally pertinent and may even be essential, but in a different social domain.... [By presenting this revelation] the abstract figure involved becomes a concrete, complete human being with power and prestige, with beauty and grace, and, above all, with relations or connections to powerful people "at the top," as we like to say. Ceasing to be a [*sic*] merely a *cidadão brasileiro* (Brazilian citizen) or *indivíduo* (individual)—universalizing social roles that confer no rights in the given situation—the person becomes an *alguém*, a "real somebody": a deputy, lawyer, army officer, government official or, even better, a relative or friend (that is, someone with *substantive, untransferable* ties) to an important personage.[53]

DaMatta's analysis exposes the profoundly hierarchical character of Brazilian society, according to which certain social positions assure relative indifference toward the law. It is worth adding only that in Ismael Silva's "do you know who you are talking to?" moment, his position of power would not necessarily ensure impunity but is merely a means of attempting to circumvent an imminent punishment. Still, it is a difference only in degree.

But our chief interest here is in confirming the surprising fact that the samba composer was able to reach a condition of relative prestige, one which allowed him this recourse. This is novel, even when considering Hermano Vianna's argument that personal connections already often ensured immunity for *sambistas*.[54] In such cases, the only element of impunity was that of patronage. But in the case of Ismael, his primary claim is that he is a composer; being the police officer's friend is secondary. And the officer acts less as a patron or protector than as an earwitness to Ismael's real identity as the author of the popular hits he mentions. When Roberto Martins cites the compositions, it is as if he were explaining to Commissioner Policarpo how important the person he arrested is; it is as if he were listing his medals.

Of course, while this recourse can momentarily resolve Ismael's situation, it does no more than confirm the prevailing social mechanisms. This newfound prestige allows the two to "keep this all between us"; the law applies only to the anonymous.

The game that Ismael was playing was the *jogo da chapinha* (bottle cap game). We find a good description of the game in the samba "Jogo proibido" ("Prohibited Game"):[55]

Não quero outra vida	I want no other life
Senão jogar chapinha	Except that of playing *chapinha*
(Da cerveja Cascatinha)	(Of Cascatinha beers)
Navalha no bolso	With a pocketknife
Lenço no pescoço	Handkerchief around the neck
Chapéu de palhinha	Straw hat
. . .	
Esta ganha esta perde	This one wins, this one loses
Na voltinha que eu dou	With my little turn
E o otário não sabe	And the *otário* doesn't know
Onde a bolinha ficou.	Where the ball went.

I present here Claúdia Matos's explanation:

[The game] consisted of controlling three bottlecaps, one of which had a small balled up piece of bread underneath it. The *malandro* would quickly switch the placement of the little ball, and the *otário* who was betting would try to guess which bottlecap was hiding the little ball, but it was almost always a losing bet, for in the agile handling of the bottlecaps the *malandro* would slip the little ball under his nail.[56]

Note that the fourth and fifth verses repeat verbatim Wilson Batista's description of the *malandro* in "Lenço no pescoço." In fact, this samba adds an extra detail to that description, for Batista's samba includes no mention of the game.

There is a moment in Noel Rosa's life that is directly related to the *jogo da chapinha*. As a teenager, he appears to have taken a beating from a player who refused to pay up when Noel discovered the little bread ball under his nail.[57] Such an episode further elucidates Noel's relationship with *malandros*. He is not one of them—that much is clear. And he is also not an *otário*, as he was shrewd enough to call the *malandro* out on his tricks. The gambler with whom he had this altercation could have been Ismael Silva himself, or any other *malandro sambista*. Máximo and Didier convincingly demonstrate that Noel befriended countless *malandros*, revealing how fascinated he was with their way of life (probably the same fascination that motivated him to watch the gambler relentlessly enough to learn the trick). But I hope to have shown that Noel understood the limits of the *malandro* lifestyle, and that he encouraged those who lived it to become professional composers. Just like Deputy Roberto Martins, Noel could very well have told Ismael Silva, "you don't need this. You're a great composer!"

As everyone in Brazil knows, Noel Rosa died in 1937, at twenty-six years old, of tuberculosis.

On the
Gramophone

Everything thus far presented has suggested that when the Estácio group supplanted Donga and Sinhô's group, samba underwent a decisive change. Indeed, this is, as we have seen, a consensus among Brazilian music historians. However, we still have yet to hear from a very important group of witnesses before we take a position on the subject: recordings from the era.

The use of recordings in the historical study of popular music raises various types of problems. The first is that, even if records are the only audio documents we have from a given period, they are not necessarily faithful representations of the music in question. In other words, just as the nineteenth-century *lundu* sheet music for piano and voice is not the same as the *lundus* that were heard in the musical activities of those who neither read music nor owned pianos, the sambas heard on recordings from the 1920s and 1930s are not necessarily the same as what would have been heard at Tia Ciata's house or in the Estácio *botequins*. As with sheet music, records convey only certain aspects of the musical interactions prevalent at a given time and place, aspects that take on more or less importance in any particular case.

The samba recorded in the studio is not the same as what was performed outside of it—this does not mean, though, that the two are unrelated or that we cannot make inferences about the sound of the samba to which we have such limited access (what was not recorded) by way of that to which we have more access (what was recorded). Still, these inferences must always be made with the utmost prudence.

Nevertheless, the fact is that the analysis proposed in this section focuses on the samba performed in the recording studio. I believe this kind of analysis is important not only because of the inferences it allows us to make regarding what happened outside the walls of the studio but also because in Rio de Janeiro and especially in the twentieth century, recorded music was indeed tremendously relevant both artistically and socially.[1]

The second problem I would like to address is more specific. This concerns the difficulty of conducting research with historical recordings in a country that has only quite recently begun to invest in public sound archives. As early as 1946, this shortcoming had already motivated Oneyda Alvarenga to write the following:

> The exact moment of samba's rhythmic-melodic differentiation, felt for some time now, can be perceived through a careful analysis of the nation's discographic production. However, such an analysis is, unfortunately, difficult to do. I believe that the masters of the old records no longer exist and it is nearly impossible to acquire copies of those that are by chance still preserved somewhere.[2]

On this point, Oneyda was overly pessimistic. The truth is that in different parts of Brazil, the individual efforts of a handful of aficionados have allowed for the creation of important 78 rpm record collections. It was thanks to the support of such collectors that the research presented in this book was possible. In particular, I would like once again to mention Jairo Severiano and the late Ary Vasconcelos, who generously gave me access to their magnificent sound archives.

This is all well and good. Now with access to the recordings, and a researcher who is aware of the methodological prudence necessary in dealing with them, we still have a problem to resolve: which records should be listened to? The fact is that from the 1920s to the 1930s, the Brazilian phonographic industry was already producing a quantity of sambas that would make it impossible for a lone researcher to work with all of them. As such, there needs to be a preliminary selection process.

Among the numerous possible criteria for this selection process, I chose to listen to all of the recordings of one singer: Francisco Alves (1898–1952). One of the most famous Brazilian singers of all time—also called "Chico" Alves, "Chico Viola,"[3] and "Rei da Voz" (King of the Voice)—Alves was the primary vehicle for the widespread dissemination of the earliest compositions by Ismael Silva and his friends.

Thanks to the help of Severiano, I was able to listen to every samba recorded by Francisco Alves between July 1927 ("Passarinho do má" ["Bird of the Sea"], by Duque, Odeon 10.001) and August 1933 ("Feitio de oração," by Vadico and Noel Rosa, Odeon 11.042). Given that it was not until early 1928 that Alves recorded a samba by an Estácio composer ("A malandragem," by Bide), my chosen start date not only marks the inauguration of Odeon's 10.000 Series (the first in Brazil to be recorded through the "electric" system)[4] but also made it possible to listen to the sambas that immediately preceded the Estácio group's rise to popularity. The ending date corresponds to the year during which Alves stopped recording Ismael Silva's sambas.[5]

Still, because my intention is to delineate contrasts between the Estácio samba style and the old style, it is also necessary to listen to sambas written by composers who identify with the latter. As for the "Pelo telefone" era, there is one clear advantage: there are far fewer recorded sambas. The famous Donga composition, which marks the beginning of the commercial recording of sambas, was released by Casa Edison in January 1917, as number 121.322 in the Odeon Series 121.000. From that moment on, until 1921, when the series ends (with number 121.999, constituting a total of 678 recordings), Casa Edison released seventy-four sambas. I was able to listen to forty-one of these, which are in Ary Vasconcelos's collection. These numbers show that samba's earliest years represent no more than a tiny fraction of the era's discographic production.

On the other hand, between 1927 and 1930, a period coinciding with the emergence of the Estácio group, Sinhô, undoubtedly the most prominent old-style composer, was still active, even finding himself at the height of his creative forces. In order to study this phase of Sinhô's work, I turned to a three-CD collection released on the Revivendo label, which, devoted entirely to the composer, contains sixty original recordings from the period.

As such, I approached the old style from two different points of reference: the initial phase, with "Pelo telephone" and the sambas recorded during the four subsequent years; and the final phase, with the recordings made during the four years prior to Sinhô's death. Furthermore, we also find, in what is the most extensive corpus of the research—that is, Franciso Alves's 1927–1933 recordings—a number of sambas by old-style composers, which were also studied.

1917–1921

The first thing to note is that the way in which the samba recordings of Odeon series 121.000 are divided up would already surprise anyone familiar with the genre and its more modern characteristics, for they are separated into sung and instrumental sambas. The vocal sambas are performed by Bahiano (Manoel Pedro dos Santos, 1887–1944), who had the honor of recording "Pelo telefone," and Eduardo das Neves (1874–1919), one of the people to whom Vagalume dedicated his book Na roda do samba, as well as the main figure in one of the book's chapters. Both had worked for Casa Edison from the inception of commercial recordings in Brazil, in 1902. Their repertoire up to 1917 basically consisted of *modinhas* and *lundus* (no longer the printed *lundus* of the preceding century but rather orally transmitted *lundus*, whose specific features we cannot analyze here). For these recordings, the musical accompaniment was provided by a guitar, and sometimes also a *cavaquinho*, with the help of a flute or clarinet for intros or solos.

The nonvocal recordings consisted of instrumental versions of the same sambas, but these were performed by a type of small ensemble that we have already mentioned, *choros*. The *choros* of series 121.000 adhere to the classic model, generally made up of a *cavaquinho*, guitar, and two or three wind instruments, one of which acted as soloist (flute or clarinet), while another, such as an ophicleide or tuba, played the bass part. In the left corner of the labels on the records, we see either "canto" (singing) or "choro," indicating whether the record is the sung or the instrumental version of the samba.

A second type of instrumental samba was put on record by *bandas de música* (that is, brass and wind bands). In series 121.000 there are sambas performed by Banda da Casa Edison (Casa Edison Band), by Banda do Corpo de Bombeiros (Band of the Fire Brigade), by Banda do Batalhão Naval (Band of the Naval Battalion), and by Banda do Primeiro Batalhão da Polícia da Bahia (Band of the First Police Battalion of Bahia). Such bands had already been an important part of musical life in Rio since the late nineteenth century and were highly active in the recording studio from 1902 onward.

We can see that from the perspective of the performers, the sambas of series 121.000 do not represent any sort of rupture in relation to the musical genres or instrumentation that had theretofore been in practice. The entrance of Donga and his friends into the medium did not at first introduce new performers or new types of instruments onto the recordings. And this trend is clearly in step with the musical continuities we have observed between early samba and its preceding genres.

There are many samba composers in series 121.000. As we have seen, with the success of "Pelo telefone," the term itself became a widely successful designation. Consequently, professional composers, such as Freire Júnior and Marcelo Tupinambá, who had nothing to do with Tia Ciata's house or with the cultural context described previously, labeled some of the compositions they contributed to the series as "sambas." This was also done by composers who otherwise left no documented historical record, such as José Napolitano, who is listed as the author of six sambas, and Francisco Antônio da Rocha, author of the samba "Cangerê,"[6] recorded in three versions: one vocal version by Bahiano (Odeon 121.728) and two instrumental versions, one by Banda da Casa Edison (Odeon 121.735) and another by the *choro* known as Grupo do Além (Group from the Beyond) (Odeon 121.732).[7]

But among composers of the Odeon Series 121.000, we also find the names of those with whom we are already quite familiar: Sinhô (the author of seven sambas), Caninha (ten sambas), Pixinguinha (three sambas), and of course, Donga (seven sambas).

What are the main characteristics we can hear on samba recordings from the era? In what ways are they different from the post-1930 sambas? The first notable thing is the way in which old-style sambas were structured. We have seen that "Pelo telefone" consists of four parts that have little or no relation to one another. The evidence suggests that this structure is linked to a need to make sufficiently long recordings out of relatively short musical units, which are precisely what folk samba refrains and improvised quatrains/couplets were.

The idea that these musical units were "small" when placed into a popular music context crops up in the words of the historical actors themselves. Indeed, Pixinguinha, interviewed by Sodré, reminisces about when he first began performing professionally: "the truth is that I liked *choro* because it was more refined, with three parts, each having sixteen measures and not just eight, like in samba."[8] Heitor dos Prazeres also discusses the issue in an interview with Sodré: "My first compositions were motivic sambas. . . . At first, the lyrics were very short or else a bundle of short motives."[9] Donga himself, in discussing the composition "Pelo telefone," affirms: "Nor did I make some small thing, like samba is."[10]

We can see that among the pioneers of Carioca samba there was something of a consensus that samba was "small," whether from the point of view of a flute virtuoso who was already a professional musician (Pixinguinha), or from the point of view of *sambistas* who were on their way to becoming professional composers (Heitor dos Prazeres and Donga). For Pixinguinha, the issue is resolved by a preference for *choro*, which not only consisted of three sixteen-measure parts but also already had a harmonic sophistication that was absent from early sambas; while for the *sambistas*, the issue was remedied by seeking out techniques that could extend a samba's duration. The first such technique, as can be seen in "Pelo telefone," and as we will see in other sambas of the same period, is the aggregation of various melodies, or "motives," as Heitor dos Prazeres put it. As such, the form of early Carioca sambas was of a "rhapsodic" type.

This definition speaks not only to the fact that the motives were short and put together without much concern for continuity, but also to the fact that their very content exhibits, in many cases, signs of their folk origins.

We have already seen how this occurred in "Pelo telefone." But I would like to add some more specifically musical observations to what was said about Donga's samba.

* * *

In our earlier discussion of the famous samba, we saw that the lyrics could be divided up into four parts (I, II, III, and IV). The musical divisions accompany the poetic divisions, with the caveat that there is an exclusively musical component that adds a new datum: the introduction. This term should not be taken in a literal sense, for samba introductions are not limited to the beginnings of the recordings; they are also repeated prior to each repetition of the whole piece and then again at the end. In the case of "Pelo telefone," moreover, the introduction also appears in the middle of the samba, separating parts I and II from parts III and IV.

"Pelo telefone" is sung by Bahiano as well as, in parts II and IV, a chorus of men and women. The accompaniment is provided by guitar, *cavaquinho*, and clarinet.

The guitar's rhythmic accompaniment is a rendition of the "characteristic syncopation." The melody of the introduction, played by the clarinet, is constructed over the same rhythmic figure, but without the first sixteenth note, as seen in the transcription.[11]

Clarinet:

Guitar:

Part I presents the "characteristic syncopation" at the beginning of each tercet:

O Che - fe da Fo - li - a pe - lo te - le - fo - ne man - dou me'a - vi - sar

Que com a - le - gri - a não se ques - ti - o - ne pa - ra se brin - car

Part II, which begins with three commetric sixteenth notes, also strongly contrasts the rhythmic style that becomes predominant in samba starting around 1930; serving as proof is the fact that on the other two recordings of Donga's samba I was able to consult, that which was made in 1940 for the record *Native*

Brazilian Music and the version by Martinho da Vila, the same part is instead sung with a syncopation at the end, as seen in the example below:

Part III most clearly shows the influence of the "characteristic syncopation" in its rhythmic organization (which is in line with what was said in chapter 5 regarding its folk origins):

As for part IV, it is built on a two-measure pattern, the first measure for the soloist and the second for the chorus, in a practice Andrade called "line and refrain" (*verso e refrão*),[12] which also has folk origins. The influence of the "characteristic syncopation" is notable:

On the other hand, the most striking aspect of the contrametricity on Bahiano's recording, when compared to the nineteenth-century *lundus* discussed previously, is how much more frequent sixteenth-note syncopations are between the measures, as can be observed in the section of the first part cited above.

* * *

Now let's look at how the creation of sambas by way of grouping small motives (to employ Heitor dos Prazeres's expression) plays out in the Sinhô sambas recorded on Odeon Series 121.000. I will begin by looking at "Confessa, meu bem!" ("Confess, My Love!"), which Alencar claims was a "great success during Carnival of 1919."[13] Here, the number of motives is five. The harmony essentially consists of the tonic and the dominant. The guitar's rhythmic accompaniment pattern, as in the case of "Pelo telefone," is based on the "characteristic syncopation," and this is true for the accompaniment patterns on all of the sung sambas recorded as part of series 121.000.

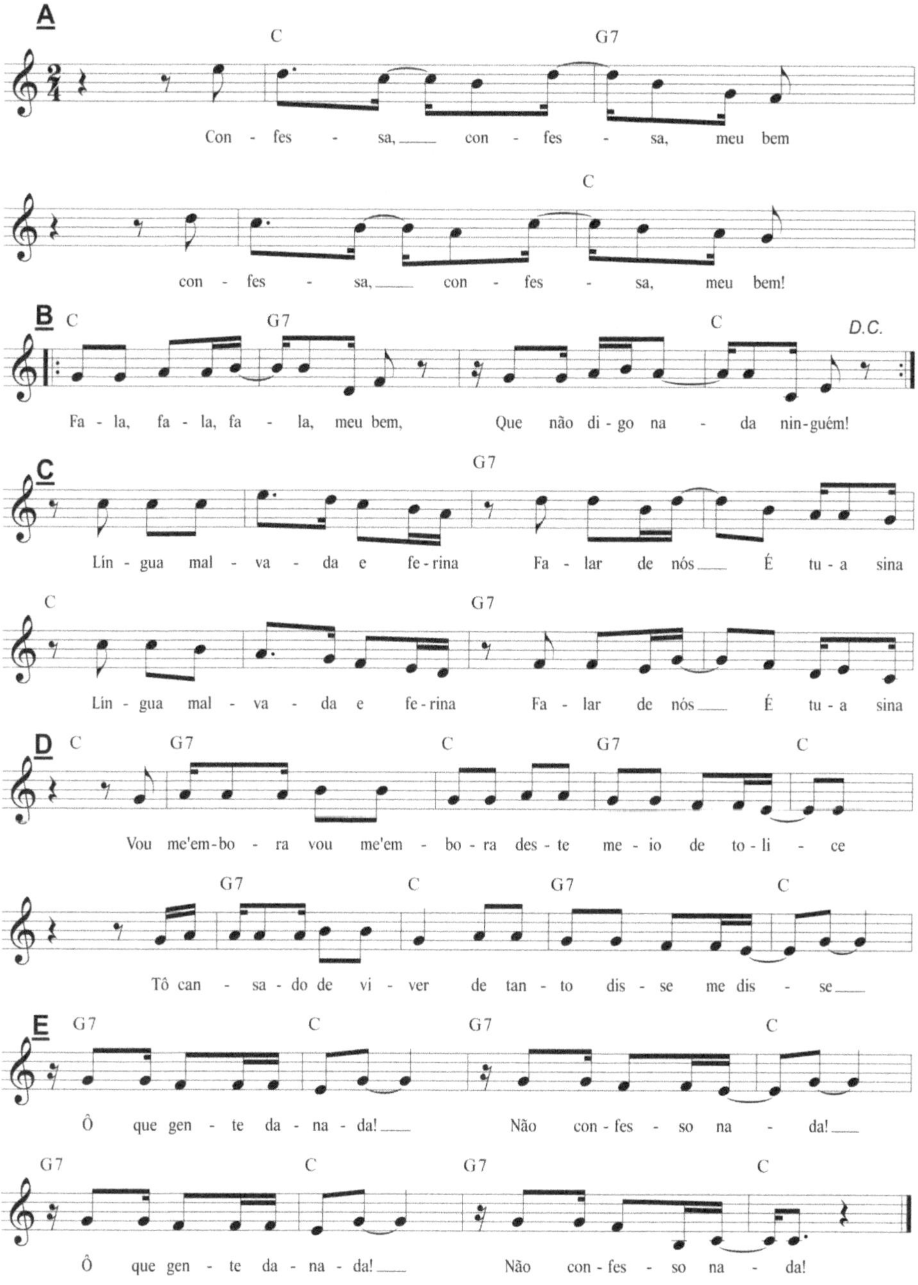

"Confessa, meu bem!" (Sinhô, 1919)

Generally speaking, as with "Pelo telefone," we see a significant increase (compared to the *lundu* sheet music we examined) in the syncopations between measures, sixteenth-note syncopations in particular. Such syncopations, however, are superimposed over a rhythmic structure in which traces of the old "characteristic syncopation" still prevail. This observation is true for parts B, D, and E of the samba examined here. Furthermore, in the second measure of part D, we see the "characteristic syncopation" in all its purity, putting to music (not coincidentally) a ready-made verse from Brazilian folk poetry, "vou me embora, vou me embora" (I'm leaving, I'm leaving).[14]

Another Sinhô samba, "Quem são eles?" ("Who Are They?"), is also broken up into several independent parts by its music and lyrics. Here is the first stanza:

A Bahia é boa terra,	Bahia is a good land,
Ela lá e eu aqui, iaiá	She's there and I'm here, *iaiá*
Ai, ai, ai	Oh, oh, oh
Não era assim que o meu bem chorava	This was not how my love cried
Não precisa pedir, que eu vou dar	You need not ask, 'cause I'll give [it] to you
Dinheiro não tenho, mas vou roubar	I don't have any money, but I'll steal it
Carreiro, olha a canga do boi	Rancher, look at the yoke of the ox
Toma cuidado que o luar já se foi	Be careful, for the moonlight has gone
Ai! Que o luar já se foi![15]	Oh! For the moonlight has gone!

Using double spacing, I have separated the four "motives" of the samba, which are bound by the poetic phrases as well as by each motive's corresponding musical phrase.

Regarding the lyrics, notice first the negative reference to Bahia, for Sinhô was from Rio, and as has already been mentioned, he whipped up controversy with the group from Bahia at the beginning of his career. In the heat of this controversy, Hilário Jovino Ferreira (who was himself from Pernambuco) offered Sinhô a response: the samba "Entregue o samba a seus donos" ("Give Samba Back to Its Owners"), the first quatrain of which is worth introducing here:

Entregue o samba a seus donos	Give samba back to its owners
É chegada a ocasião	The occasion is upon us
Lá no Norte não fazemos	There in the North we don't make
Do pandeiro profissão.	A profession out of the *pandeiro*.

174

A

A Ba - hi - a'é bo - a ter - ra e - la lá e eu a - qui ia - iá!___

B

D.C.

Ai, ai, ai! Não e - ra'as - sim que meu bem cho - ra - va

C

Não pre - ci - sa pe - dir que vou dar di - nhei - ro não te - nho mas vou rou - bar

D

Car - rei - ro'o - lha'a can - ga do boi! Car - rei - ro'o - lha'a - can - ga do boi!

E

To - ma cui - da - do que'o luar já se foi, ai!___ Que'o lu - ar já se

foi, ai!___ Que'o lu - ar já se foi!

"Quem são eles?" (Sinhô, 1919)

The idea that samba has "owners" is made explicit here; indeed, samba belongs to a specific group linked to the "North," or Bahia, as is clear from the lyrics.[16] Sinhô, conversely, is accused of making the *pandeiro* a profession and of transforming samba into a commodity that circulates indiscriminately among geographic groups, as long as they have the money to pay for it.

Despite such conflicts, however, it is quite clear how closely related this samba is to the old style practiced by the descendants of Bahians. "Characteristic syncopations" abound in the melody. The second verse begins with an "Ai, ai, ai!" articulated in three commetric sixteenth notes that are inescapably reminiscent of part II of "Pelo telefone." The references to the "rancher," "ox," and "moonlight" evoke the same rural atmosphere that appears in some of Donga's other compositions, such as "Patrão, prenda o seu gado" ("Boss, Secure Your Cattle") and "Passarinho bateu asas" ("The Bird Took Off").

If people who hear or read these sambas today feel the lyrics sometimes appear to lack coherence, it is perhaps due to the veiled references to figures or situations of the era. This is the case with the title of "Quem são eles?," which appears to be entirely unrelated to the lyrics. But Edigar de Alencar tells us that this samba, whose original title was "A Bahia é boa terra" ("Bahia Is a Good Land"), ended up taking the name of the *bloco* created by Sinhô during Carnival of 1918, a *bloco* that was the composition's main outlet.[17] Even more enigmatic references are suggested on the sheet music's cover page, which shows "a person with a top hat, well dressed, wearing gloves, in a lone boat sailing serenely along with the flag of Feninanos [the Carnival club to which members of the *bloco* Quem são eles? belonged] on the mast. Nearby, a black man yells for help, as if he were drowning to death. The guy with the top hat couldn't care less."[18] As such, the lyrics, title, and illustration together create not just a hodgepodge, as is the case with the lyrics of "Pelo telefone," but a veritable puzzle that might be solvable only by someone who participated in Rio's Carnival that year. This seems to be another example of the principle of direct transitivity, of what Sodré described as "operationality in relation to the world": total intelligibility of the discourse is dependent on its link to a "here and now." This trait, which we can find in many of Sinhô's other sambas, is yet another way in which they are more closely related to common folk music practices than to compositions from the 1930s.

Let's look at what happens in the Donga sambas, other than "Pelo telefone," that were recorded on Odeon series 121.000.

We begin with "O malhador" ("The Beater"), composed in 1918 by Donga, Pixinguinha, and Mauro de Almeida. Its form is simpler than in the previous examples—there are only two well-defined, albeit short, parts. The first part comprises rhythms that appear to derive directly from a *lundu* of the previous century: "characteristic syncopations," "habanera rhythms," no syncopation between beats or measures:

While the first part is sung by a soloist, the second alternates between soloist and chorus, in the already mentioned pattern that was baptized by Mário de Andrade as "line and refrain":

In the second part, in addition to the chorus, there is an unidentified percussion instrument—a nod to the title, since *malhar* is employed here to mean "beating."

176

The instrument's rhythmic pattern (which is the oldest example I could find of a percussion instrument on a samba recording) is a variation of the 3–3–2 Paradigm, a "habanera rhythm" without its last eighth note:

The repetition of the first part, on the other hand, offers a slightly more contrametric treatment of the melody, with sixteenth-note syncopations appearing between measures, in the same style already confirmed for Sinhô's sambas:

The harmony is once again basically a movement between the tonic and the dominant.

Another of Donga's compositions, "O veado à meia-noite" ("The Deer at Midnight"), is also in two parts, each consisting of four measures. Although the label on the record says "samba carnavalesco" (that is, carnival samba), a voice at the beginning of the recording announces it as "*batuque*." Understanding the lyrics is difficult due to the poor technical quality of the recording, but the poetic meter is similar to that of an *embolada*, a poetic form defined by one Brazilian folk poetry specialist as an "ottava rima [*oitava*] accompanied by a refrain . . . in which the first and fourth verses have four syllables while the others have seven."[19] In this case, each stanza of "O veado à meia-noite" corresponds to half an ottava rima of an *embolada*—that is, each corresponds to a quatrain in which the first verse has four syllables, and the others, seven. But if we put the two quatrains together (which, in the samba, are separated by the refrain), we have the rhyme scheme mentioned by the author we just cited: ABBCDAAC.[20]

It is not only an *embolada* in its poetic form but also in its musical form. The melodic rhythm of the solo stanza is entirely composed of repeated sixteenth notes while the choral refrain, repeated twice for each cycle of the samba, employs longer rhythmic values, the articulations of which fit perfectly within the 3–3–2 Paradigm:

The last of the old-style composers with sambas in Odeon series 121.000 that I will mention here is Caninha.[21] As for the first Caninha samba I will discuss, the title indicated on the label is "Quem vem atrás fecha a porta" ("Whoever's

Last Closes the Door"). It is introduced by the announcer as "Quem vem atrás fecha a porta, 'seu' Rafael" ("Whoever's Last Closes the Door, 'Seu' Rafael"), but it became generally known as "Me leve, 'seu' Rafael" ("Take Me, 'Seu' Rafael"), which is the phrase of the refrain:

Me leve, me leve "seu" Rafael	Take me, take me *seu* Rafael
Me leve, me leve lá pro Pará (bis).	Take me, take me to Pará (repeat).

The refrain is repeated by the chorus and is followed by the soloist singing his quatrains, which make reference to *Iaiá* and to Bahia:

Quero que Iaiá me leve	I want *Iaiá* to take me
Lá na beira do caminho	There by the roadside
Tem paciência Iaiá	Be patient, *Iaiá*
Me leve devagarinho	Take me slowly
Eu chegando na Bahia	As I got to Bahia
Fiquei perdido de amor	I lost myself in love
Por ver tanta bahianinha	When I saw so many Bahian women
Na terra de São Salvador.	In the land of São Salvador.[22]

This samba's form exhibits perfectly the characteristics Vagalume attributed to the sambas practiced at the beginning of the twentieth century in the homes of the Bahian *tias*: a short refrain ("a quatrain or just two verses") followed by improvisations.[23] Clearly, this mention of improvisation refers to a way of performing, to a behavior, something that resists being transformed into an object. Still, certain formal characteristics of fixed verses can serve as good indications that they were originally linked to the practice of improvisation.

Indeed, the quatrains I cited from "Me leve, 'seu' Rafael" demonstrate the formal characteristics of the improvisations that, according to Lopes, were part of the earliest phase of Rio's *partido-alto*: "at first, *partido-alto* solos were performed most commonly in . . . quatrains . . . nearly always in heptasyllabic verses . . . and with obligatory rhyming only for the even verses."[24]

In Lopes, we also learn of a folk samba that was collected in the Bahian backlands in 1949 that reproduces almost verbatim the refrain of Caninha's samba:

Não me leva, não me leva,	Don't take me, don't take me, *seu*
"seu" Rafaé	Rafa[el]
Não me leva, não me leva para	Don't take me, don't take me to the
o "quarté."[25]	barracks.

In this instance, as in so many others, this is not a case of figuring out who influenced whom, but rather of noting the formal and thematic proximity to folk music, which was so much a characteristic of old-style samba, beginning with "Pelo telefone."

The rhythm of "Me leve, 'seu' Rafael" is likewise based on the "characteristic syncopation," albeit ornamented with some syncopations between beats and between measures:

Me le - ve, me le - ve, seu____ Ra - fa - el! Me le - ve, me le - ve, lá____ pro Pa - rá

The existence of the other title, "Quem vem atrás fecha a porta" ("Whoever's Last Closes the Door"), seems confounding, given that nowhere in the lyrics is there any reference to a "door" or to anyone who might be "last." However, the previously mentioned case regarding Sinhô's samba "Quem são eles?" suggests to me that here too, the composition's alternate title may have come from the *bloco* that sang the samba during Carnival. Indeed, "Quem vem atrás fecha a porta" is perfectly acceptable as a name for a Carnival *bloco* (it is similar, for example, to "Quem fala de nós tem paixão" [Whoever Speaks about Us Is Passionate], Sinhô's 1917 Carnival *bloco*).

This is, moreover, another indication that during this era sambas were more "stuck" to their circumstances than were those created by the Estácio composers. In fact, it seems that in these cases, the samba was so clearly identified with the group that sang it that the song would be known by the name of the performers, even if the name had nothing to do with the lyrics of the composition. This is also a reminder that before the 1930s, the primary channel for the dissemination of popular music was neither the radio nor records, but rather live performances—the bands and *blocos* that performed during special occasions such as Carnival and the Festa da Penha, as well as in theater revues throughout the rest of the year.

Another samba by Caninha is "Esta nega 'qué' me 'dá'" ("This Woman Wants to Give It to Me"),[26] whose refrain is as follows:

Esta nega qué me dá,	This woman wants to give it to me,
Eu não fiz nada pr'apanhá.	I didn't do anything to deserve a whooping.

The quatrains below illustrate the same pattern as that which is mentioned above—that is, they are heptasyllabic with the rhymes in the even verses:

Nega, tu não faz feitiço	Woman, you won't cast a spell
Que eu tenho o corpo fechado	Because I have a protected body[27]
Pancada de amor não dói	Getting hit by love doesn't hurt
Por isso apanho calado	That's why I take my beating

Eu quero fugir da nega	I want to flee from my woman
Custe lá o que custar	At whatever cost
Nosso Senhor está com pena	Our Lord feels bad
De ver a nega me dar.	When he sees my woman give it to me.

Here we find one of the most blatant displays of the anti-*malandro* inclination of old-style sambas. The man in the lyrics gets beaten by his "woman," whereas the *malandros* had a reputation for beating their partners, at least since Heitor dos Prazeres's 1932 samba "Mulher de malandro" ("*Malandro*'s Woman"). And in Caninha's case, what is perhaps even worse is that he repeatedly recognizes, in the refrain, that he "didn't do anything to deserve a whooping."

As for its rhythmic characteristics, "Esta nega 'qué' me 'dá'" is very similar to "Me leva, 'seu' Rafael."

Finally, it is worth noting the harmonic simplicity of these two sambas, as they are both limited almost entirely to the tonic and the dominant.

1927–1933

In our study of the 3–3–2 Paradigm in "Musical Premises," a strong emphasis was placed on the rhythmic accompaniment patterns. Likewise, when the Estácio Paradigm was introduced, I primarily concerned myself with the patterns used in the rhythmic accompaniment of the percussion instruments.

My initial intention, in studying the sambas from the 1927–1933 period, was to do as I did in the two preceding cases and turn most of my attention to the patterns used in the rhythmic accompaniment. However, I quickly realized that doing so would be far from possible, an observation that needs clarifying.

I first noticed the rhythmic difference between the old and new styles when I heard how different the guitar accompaniment pattern on sambas such as "Jura" ("Swear," Sinhô, 1928) and "Pelo telefone" was from the samba rhythm I myself learned as a guitarist, the rhythm that is still associated with samba in Rio de Janeiro today.[28]

The guitar is perfectly audible in recordings of the "Pelo telefone" era, and it is also audible in many samba recordings made much later, from 1960 onward (when the earliest, stripped down recordings of *sambistas* such as Nelson Cavaquinho and Cartola began appearing). But when I began listening systematically to the recordings from the 1927–1933 period, I realized that the overwhelming majority were made with orchestral accompaniments.

This made it impossible for me to base my research on the rhythm played by the guitar, for the instrument can be heard clearly only when it is part of small ensembles. As such, it is as if we were able to see only two ends of a process that lasted years: we know what guitarists did around 1920 and what they did from 1960 on, but we are unable to see how, or exactly when, one thing became the other.

To make matters worse, on many of the recordings that interested me, I could not even clearly hear the *cavaquinho*, the piano, or the percussion instruments—in short, none of the instruments of the rhythm section, the ones that would give some sense of the rhythmic accompaniment pattern.

However, what at first seemed to be a hindrance to my project ended up being a source of unexpected revelations. Indeed, when I listened to the recordings, despite the rhythm section's nebulosity, the sense that I was hearing a new-style samba was nevertheless entirely there. Intrigued, I began to transcribe the melodies of the sambas, which made me realize that they were built on the rhythmic framework of the Estácio Paradigm. In other words, the syllables of the melodies are articulated not at the places favored in a 2/4 meter but rather at those anticipated by rhythmic oddity. As such, the rhythm of the syllabic articulation implies that of the percussion instruments and contributes just as much to characterizing the new style.

Popular singers who are influenced by Afro-Brazilian culture are known to phrase song lyrics in such a way that the syllables (or most of the syllables) fall outside of the downbeats suggested by Western music theory's notions of meter.[29] But there is not, in the samba literature with which I am familiar, any recognition of a "system" according to which this contrametricity is organized. Brasílio Itiberê even affirms that "what is found in popular [Brazilian] song is multiple variations of a free, spontaneous, happened-as-it-happened rhythm."[30] Yet in studying the aforementioned time period, I instead discovered, and not without some surprise, that the melodies of a large number of sambas tended to be organized in a rhythmically fixed way, rather than randomly. Not only did they tend to oppose the metric hierarchy of the 2/4 time signature in which they are generally notated, but their contrametricity also tended to recur at the same points within a given period and not at others. That is, it tended to occur in a systematic, cyclical way.

This idea regarding the correspondence between a rhythmic pattern and the sung rhythmic articulations was first introduced by Alejo Carpentier, who asserted that "the rhythm of the *claves*, as Emilio Grenet has intelligently observed, *is the only one that can always adjust itself, without variation, to all the types of Cuban melodies*, thereby constituting a type of constancy in rhythmic phrasing" (emphasis added).[31] As such, just as Cuban melodies would be built on the rhythm of the *claves*,[32] the melodies of certain sambas would be built on the rhythm of the *tamborim*.

This idea also turns up in Kazadi wa Mukuna's work, in which he associates one of the typical *tamborim* rhythms (indeed, one rendition of our Estácio Paradigm) with J. H. Kwabena Nketia's time line concept. For Nketia, the time line is "a constant point of reference by which the phrase structure of a song as well as the linear metrical organization of phrases are guided."[33] Such an observation would be, according to Mukuna, wholly applicable to samba, where "this pattern fits quite well with the divisions of the phrases in the melodic lines. For each melodic segment, there is a complete rhythmic cycle."[34] My observations have shown that this rhythmic cycle corresponds to the melody not only in terms of phrase length but also in terms of internal shape: the rhythmic articulations of these samba melodies "fall" on the emphases anticipated by the logic of rhythmic oddity.

I do not intend for this claim to stand for all Carioca samba, let alone for the many sambas practiced in other parts of Brazil. The study presented here was exhaustive only in relation to the commercial recordings of Francisco Alves's sambas in Rio de Janeiro from 1927 to 1933. Within this corpus, the melodies whose rhythmic articulation tends to outline the new paradigm are, not coincidentally, primarily those that were written by the Estácio de Sá composers and their friends (especially Noel Rosa). But an unsystematic look suggests this might also be the case for other periods and composers, leading me to believe that further studies will be able to demonstrate the existence, even if not exclusively, of the same "phrasing model"[35] in other types of samba.

* * *

We have already discussed a group of eight sambas whose texts allowed us to establish the characteristics of the *malandro* theme: "Não é isso que eu procuro," "A malandragem," "Nem é bom falar," "O que será de mim," "Nem assim," "Se você jurar," "Ora vejam só!," and "Gosto que me enrosco." I will begin with these sambas in order to show the emergence of the Estácio Paradigm in the transitional period from the 1920s to the 1930s.

It is important to note, from the outset, that five of the sambas share one especially significant commonality. This commonality is mainly found in the poetic technique of the second parts, whose verses are all made up of two quatrains of heptasyllabic verses—with emphases generally falling on the third and seventh syllables—rather than just one quatrain, as had been preferred in earlier sambas.

This shared poetic meter creates the conditions for strong rhythmic similarities in the melodies of the second parts. Indeed, each of their eight verses occupies a rhythmic cycle of two measures in 2/4, and the articulations correspond to different versions of the Estácio Paradigm. Each of the five sambas contains two eight-verse second parts, giving us a total of eighty verses. And the rhythm of nearly every one of these eighty verses conforms to one of three basic patterns, presented here in order from the most commetric to the most contrametric:

If we consider each second part, constituted by eight two-measure cycles, to be a syntagmatic chain, we see that each of the three rhythmic types identified here can appear in any one of these eight positions. The positional variations appear not only from one samba to another but also from one second part to another within the same samba. The way it plays out makes it seem as if the singer could seek out alternatives from within a small repertoire of equivalent rhythmic variations and from among them—and only them—choose which to sing.

As an example, I offer here the musical transcription of two verses taken from the second parts of each samba.

Não di - go que te - nho rai - va

Por vo - cê ser da or - gi - a

"Não é isso que eu procuro," second part, second stanza, verses 1 and 2

Quan - do che - ga'o car - na - val____

A mu - lher lhe dá o suí - te

"A malandragem," second part, second stanza, verses 3 and 4

A mi - nha vi - da'é bo - a

Não te - nho'em que____ pen - sar____

"Se você jurar," second part, first stanza, verses 5 and 6

Não vou a - trás de nin - guém____

Hei de vi - ver sem - pre'as - sim!____

"Nem assim," second part, second stanza, verses 7 and 8

Tra - ba - lhar, só o - bri - ga - do

Por gos - to nin - guém____ vai lá!____

"O que será de mim," second part, second stanza, verses 7 and 8

We have already seen that rhythmic oddity interpolates groups of two and three pulsations. These can be presented in two ways: aggregated (where the groups of two are represented by eighth notes, and groups of three, by dotted eighth notes) or subdivided into sixteenth notes, which are themselves grouped by way of accents, changes in timbre, or other types of demarcations.

The most common versions of the Estácio Paradigm in the accompaniment patterns comprise, as we saw above, aggregated binary groups, and ternary groups subdivided into a sixteenth note plus an eighth note. Given that there are, in the sixteen-pulse cycle of the paradigm, five binary and two ternary groups, we have a total of nine articulations (as in the three variations of the above example): seven eighth notes and two sixteenth notes.

For these types of rhythmic patterns to be reproduced in the sambas, the melodies of which demonstrate virtually no vocal prolongations, one syllable would be needed for each rhythmic articulation, totaling nine; yet there is not a single nine-syllable verse in any of the second parts transcribed here. Most of them have either eight—when the last syllable is atonic—or seven syllables.[36] These versions of the paradigm must therefore leave out one or two of the articulations, which spawns new variations, built on each of the three mentioned above.[37] In the first case, one of the groups of three is aggregated into a dotted eighth note. In the other case, this same group of three is replaced by a rest. On the other hand, in the second parts of "Se você jurar," the majority of the verses have only six syllables, which, moreover, results in the disappearance of an eighth note from the pattern. Effectively, what matters in characterizing the paradigm is not the presence of all the articulations, but rather that the existing ones always "fall" at the positions anticipated by it.

There is great rhythmic uniformity in the second parts, and the same structure can be observed in a number of other second parts of the period, such as "Para me livrar do mal" ("To Free Me from Evil," Ismael Silva-Noel Rosa, 1932), "Me faz carinhos" ("She Gives Me Affection," Ismael Silva-Francisco Alves, 1928), and many others. On the other hand, the rhythm of their refrains is more diverse. But this diversity nevertheless always fits within the Estácio Paradigm.

Let's begin by seeing what happens in the refrain of "O que será de mim." In the transcription below, the first nine measures are juxtaposed with the corresponding version of the paradigm. We can see that the rhythm of the melody, once again, coincides perfectly with the paradigm's points of articulation, even if not every single point of articulation appears in the melody. There are only three exceptions to this rule, duly indicated: the two notes at the beginning and the commetric quarter note used to sing the word "pois," in the ninth measure, after the long rest. Such exceptions appear systematically, at similar moments, in the sambas of the period: the commetricity tends to substitute the contrametricity at a song's outset or after a prolonged rest. This seems to suggest that to the musical sensibilities of the *sambistas*, the start (or upon restarting after a long rest) was where all of the rhythmic articulations should coincide, and this was easier to coordinate through commetricity than contrametricity, even at the expense of momentarily abandoning the paradigm.

In the transcription of the refrain of "Nem assim," we see the same juxtaposition of melody and paradigm, which shows the same conformity. Here, however, there are no exceptions, and even the beginning is aligned with the paradigm's contrametricity.

The refrain of "Se você jurar," on the other hand, demonstrates some divergences from the Estácio Paradigm. The first two phrases are sung by Francisco Alves (here together with Mário Reis) in a way that is close to the old style, for we hear an inverted "characteristic syncopation."

"O que será de mim," the refrain compared to the corresponding versions of the Estácio Paradigm

"Nem assim," the refrain compared to the corresponding version of the Estácio Paradigm

Now, in 1956 Ismael Silva himself made a recording on which he sings his own compositions, including some of his hits from the period under investigation. In rhythmic terms, he begins his version of the samba by syncopating the second and third syllables of each verse, and this minor modification changes the feel of the section entirely: it places us squarely into Estácio territory, with not a trace of the old style. This suggests to me that Alves's rhythmic treatment might best be interpreted as a sign of the difficulties involved in learning the new style.

To support this assertion, I think it is instructive to add to our comparison a much more recent version of "Se você jurar," recorded in 1994 by singer Teca Calazans.

"Se você jurar," comparison of three different versions, that of Alves/Reis (1931), of Ismael Silva (1956), and of Teca Calazans (1994)

We thus see that the two most recent versions (Silva and Calazans) overlap much more than the two oldest versions (Silva and Alves), even though thirty-eight years separate the two most recent, while the two oldest are separated by only twenty-five years. I think that anyone familiar with samba singing would agree that it would be surprising to hear someone today sing the beginning of "Se você jurar" with the rhythm Alves uses in his version.

So far I have limited myself to five of the eight sambas whose lyrics were analyzed in my discussion about *malandragem*. I will now discuss the sixth, "Nem é bom falar." The original recording of this samba is especially interesting, for in the final repetition of the refrain, we can hear—albeit not without quite a bit of difficulty—a percussion instrument playing a version of the Estácio Paradigm. The rhythmic versions chosen by the singer, however, are more contrametric than the version played by the percussionist, which is shown in the sections below.

"Nem é bom falar," refrain

We thus see that even if these sambas' refrains are more rhythmically varied than their second parts, they nevertheless adhere, in the end, to the "constancy in rhythmic phrasing" (to revisit Carpentier's expression), constituted by the Estácio Paradigm. Still, it is important to recognize that the difference in the way the refrain expresses this constancy versus the way the second parts do is pronounced and systematic enough to be considered significant.

I believe this difference is related to a contextual difference I have already noted: unlike the refrains, the second parts were originally improvised by soloists. Now, there are countless improvisatory singing styles in Brazilian music, and in these, free poetic invention is commonly regulated by a certain musical standardization. This is the case, for example, with the northeastern duelers (*repentistas*), who use melodic formulas for their singing style. This is also the case—closer to the subject at hand—with the improvisation found in other types of Carioca samba, such as *partido-alto*. This does not mean that new melodies could not be invented in these contexts, but verbal improvisation (improvising words) within a fixed meter takes precedent over musical variation, leading singers to adopt ready-made melodic-rhythmic formulas. It seems to me that the high degree of melodic-rhythmic standardization in the Estácio sambas' second parts, in contrast to their refrains, could reasonably be linked to these factors. Initially, then, the second parts would have been composed in a manner that strongly adhered to the improvisational practices of the time, only later adopting a greater freedom of melodic-rhythmic invention.

The only two sambas of the group of eight we have not yet discussed are "Ora vejam só!" and "Gosto que me enrosco." It is precisely these two whose authorship was, as we have already seen, disputed by Heitor dos Prazeres and Sinhô. By analyzing their lyrics, I reached the conclusion that they were written by the former, for they were about the *malandro* lifestyle and the *orgia*, important themes for the Estácio composers. A musical analysis, however, suggests contributions from Sinhô.

Among old-style composers, Sinhô was, without a doubt, the one who traveled farthest along the path of samba's transformations. The contrametricity of his melodies is much more varied than in the work of Donga, Caninha, or João da Baiana; in fact, some of his melodies, such as in "Dá nele" ("Give It to Him")[38] and "Amostra a mão" ("Show Your Hand"), and in the refrains of "Sem amor" ("Without Love") and "Reminiscências do passado" ("Reminders of the Past") (all recorded in 1930, sometimes with percussion accompaniment), fit perfectly within the Estácio Paradigm. Sinhô also paved the way for Ismael Silva and his friends by adding greater harmonic sophistication and constructing longer parts (as in his classic "Jura," from 1928, with its modulation to the dominant and its thirty-two-bar refrain).

Most of Sinhô's work—even that of his late period—continues, though, to owe a debt to the old style.[39] In this respect, the 3–3–2 pattern is the most important element at his disposal, heard in a number of his recordings as the accompanying rhythmic pattern, played on the *cavaquinho* or the piano. The 3–3–2 pattern is especially evident, for example, in the second part of the original recording of "Jura" and on the recording of "Amar a uma só mulher" ("To Love Just One Woman," 1928).

In this sense, other elements at his disposal are the melodic responses played in the bass—or *baixarias*, as Carioca musicians say—heard on most of Sinhô's samba recordings. These responses, which we are unable to study in detail here—and which have already been noted by Flávio Silva as being an important characteristic of *maxixe*—are one of the most striking characteristics on the recordings, and they rely almost obsessively on the "characteristic syncopation."

"Ora vejam só!," second part

The melodies of "Ora vejam só!" and "Gosto que me enrosco" (p. 191) demonstrate greater and more varied contrametricity than the old-style sambas heretofore discussed. Moreover, they are closer to the new style in their more elaborate harmony and in the length (sixteen measures) of each of their parts. But neither in their melodies nor in their accompaniments do we find the rhythmic patterns typical of the Estácio Paradigm. Clearly then, both of these sambas are rhythmically distinct from the other six of the same group. We thus find confirmation yet again of the invariability of the association, which I want to show, between the new style and the Estácio Paradigm: the only two sambas of the group in which one of the authors is associated with the old style are also the only two in which the paradigm is absent.

* * *

"Gosto que me enrosco," second part

I spoke a bit ago about obstacles to learning the new style. This is thus the moment to cite evidence of a learning curve, which involves none other than Francisco Alves, who was the primary figure responsible for bringing the new style to samba recordings. The following account comes from an episode I have already mentioned, in which the singer discovers a new samba:

> Francisco Alves, Nonô, the boxer Rubens Soares, and some of his friends were talking while at one of the tables at Café Trianon. At a certain point, Rubens's friends began to sing a refrain: "Why do you drink so much, man ... etc." Francisco Alves, with good reason, cheered. . . . With that infallible intuition for success, he soon saw that the guys had a winning ticket in their hands.—"Which of you wrote this samba?" Rubens, somewhat timid, responded: "Me. But for now it's just a refrain." . . . Francisco Alves indeed [got] excited: "Repeat the refrain for me, Rubens. And with that same *bossa* that the guys put on it. I want to learn it just as you did it." Rubens repeated it. One, two, several times, until Francisco Alves memorized the lyrics and assimilated that *bossa* of the refrain.[40]

We cannot know exactly what this "bossa" was,[41] which kept the professional singer there for hours learning with "the guys"; but we can presume that the rhythmic articulation was part of it. This account of the quasi-ethnographic zeal of the singer in learning the song "just as the composer did it" is especially telling when we learn that it was in fact the author of this samba, Rubens Soares, who recounted this incident to Máximo and Didier.

Starting in the 1920s, as has already been noted, samba recordings began to adopt, in addition to instrumental introductions, an instrumental version of the melody, usually coming right before the final sung repetition of the samba. As such, the same melody, on a given recording, is introduced several times, but by different enunciators: sometimes by the main singer, sometimes by different orchestral instruments, and still other times by the chorus. This made it possible to hear that Francisco Alves employed, in his versions of the melodies, rhythms closer to the Estácio Paradigm or, in more general terms, more contrametric rhythms than those of the instrumentalists. This is perhaps due to the fact that Alves, and possibly other singers of the era, were close to the "sources"—so to speak—thus differentiating them from other professionals involved in the production of samba recordings, such as arrangers and orchestra musicians.

Consequently, the rhythm of the melodies once again reveals itself to be a privileged area for the study of changes to the rhythmic paradigm, for it enables us to confirm that this change took place at a different pace for each enunciator. The various rhythmic treatments of the melody that are on each recording show in detail the steep learning curve—in its various stages—faced by performers as they were laying the groundwork for what would, in subsequent years, become samba's "natural" rhythm.

To support this idea, I offer the words of singer and radio personality Paulo Tapajós (b. 1913):

> Radamés [Gnattali, composer and arranger] really used to enjoy talking about the particularities of Brazilian rhythm, notably samba rhythm, and it is important to say here that it was [drummer] Luciano Perrone who suggested to Radamés that he write his samba arrangements with the rhythmic division of the *tamborins*. This happened at a time when samba had a style of instrumentation that was unsuited for the division done by singers. They weren't musicians, but their intuition led them to a rhythm with a much tastier accentuation than that which was on paper. The singing and the orchestra seemed to fight. Radamés composed, with Luciano, "Ritmo de Samba na Cidade" ["Rhythm of Samba in the City"], which stood as a great watershed moment for the patterns that had been adopted up to then, so much so that samba orchestration came to be defined as being before or after "Ritmo de Samba na Cidade."[42]

Tapajós employs the term "division" (*divisão*), which is a category used in Brazilian popular music to designate the variations of rhythmic-melodic articulation that are employed in songs. In this way, Tapajós suggests that the *tamborim* has a typical rhythmic articulation ("the rhythmic division of the *tamborins*"), which was adopted by the singers but not by the orchestra or the "paper"—that is, the score. *Tamborins* and singers are counterposed to the orchestra and the score (they "seemed to fight"); some were from the sphere of oral tradition (for he claims the singers "weren't musicians"), while others, the written tradition. It is the former who articulated the rhythm in a way that is aesthetically valued by Tapajós: "much tastier."

Unfortunately, I was unable to gain access to the recording mentioned by Tapajós. But my research allows me to affirm that this process was not quite as simple as he makes it out to be: the adoption of the new rhythmic division by all of those involved in the recordings was not the result of a single recording, but rather of a learning process—a creative learning process, to be sure—which took years.[43]

I offer two examples that demonstrate the gap that existed between the way in which the singers performed the rhythmic articulations and the way in which the instrumentalists did: the second parts of "Não é isso que eu procuro" and of "És ingrata, mulher" ("You're Ungrateful, Woman," Loló Verbo, 1930). The first of these follows the pattern already described, with its heptasyllabic verses and its three variations of the Estácio Paradigm. When the orchestra introduces the same melody, however, the result is an almost entirely commetric version, in which the new style is no longer recognizable. The only syncopations we hear are between the beats (expressed as sixteenth note–dotted eighth note), which sound something like a clumsy attempt at imitating Alves's style.

"Não é isso que eu procuro," the sung version of the second part compared with the instrumental version of the second part

Meanwhile, in "És ingrata, mulher," Alves's singing, despite being quite heavily contrametric, does not give us perfect versions of the paradigm, except for the section between the ninth and twelfth measures. The orchestra, however,

"És ingrata, mulher," the sung version of the second part compared with the instrumental version of the second part

shows its tendency once again toward commetricity, systematically distorting Alves's syncopations.

We saw above that this formal feature—the greater or lesser commetricity of the various versions of a given melody—might bear some relation to how close the enunciator is to oral traditions or to Western classical music traditions. In other words, the distinct rhythmic versions are not socially neutral. In fact, we can take this association between social and musical variables even further.

Indeed, if we take a given group of sambas recorded by Francisco Alves in Rio de Janeiro in 1931, we see that in the orchestral sections, whenever there is a clear separation between the string and brass parts, the former is nearly always more commetric than the latter. As I see it, this is related to differences in the social positions of these two types of instruments, and these are differences, moreover, that still exist today. If, for example, we look at the names of the orchestral musicians who played on a recent Brazilian music CD, we have on strings Giancarlo Pareschi, Marie Christine Springel, Michel Bessler, Jacques Morelenbaum; and on brass, Serginho do Trombone, Formiga, Bidinho, Paulinho do Trompete.[44] Playing strings are conservatory (or equivalent) trained musicians who are listed according to their full names, the children or grandchildren of Europeans; on brass, "popular" names: diminutives (Serginho), a name incorporating his instrument (*do Trombone*, or of the Trombone), nicknames (*Formiga*, literally Ant), and no

"Oh! Dora!," comparison of the melody of the refrain performed by instruments and voice

surnames are mentioned. Brass instruments have been common in Brazil since the nineteenth century, played by musicians being recruited from the disadvantaged strata of society, musicians who are not trained in conservatories but rather in the army or in *bandas de música*—that is, groups who played for popular dance parties, ranging from turn-of-the-century *choros* to today's street carnivals.

We can hear such differences in the samba "Oh! Dora!," by Orlando Vieira, recorded by Francisco Alves in 1931. The melody of the first part, in the singer's treatment, is heavily contrametric. The saxophone then turns the same melody less contrametric, but the violin's treatment is the least contrametric of them all.

But it is not as though contrametricity has some popular essence, or that darker skin automatically makes its assimilation easier. To return to Mário de Andrade's metaphor, it is not "blood" but rather "social milieu" that makes the Estácio Paradigm so much easier to assimilate for musicians trained in the Afro-Brazilian popular tradition than for musicians trained in the European classical tradition. After all, the former are more adept at dealing with this type of rhythm because it is with such rhythms that they earn their daily musical bread. For the others, conversely, contrametricity is the exception ("syncopation"), requiring the graphic duplication of a tied note, and the analytical resource of counting.

The progressive adoption of samba's new rhythmic paradigm over the course of the 1930s therefore reflects a novel capacity, on the part of official Brazilian culture, to accept much more contrametric rhythms than those expected in the old 3–3–2 Paradigm. Starting in the late 1930s, written music, recorded music, record studio orchestra musicians, arrangers, record label artistic directors, the record and sheet music buying public—all of that which we can call "official musical culture"—began not only to accept the new musical paradigm but also to see it as true samba. That is, new-style samba was, precisely at that time, beginning to be viewed as the premier musical expression of the nation.

Conclusion

I would like to underscore three main points I believe I have covered in this work. First, I reviewed the prevailing concepts and interpretations regarding samba. Given that this genre is so popular in Brazil, much ink has been spilled over it, naturally. The invaluable contributions of those—from Vagalume to Sérgio Cabral—who used their intimacy with the world of samba to trace its history sometimes suffer from the inherent limitations of a point of view that is overly close to its subject. It is thus necessary to "clean house": this had already been initiated in the works of Samuel Araújo and Hermano Vianna in the early 1990s, and I believe I have taken it a bit further—especially with respect to the analysis of the discourse of samba pioneers and the characterization of 1930s Carioca samba.

Second, by analyzing recordings, I found data to support the fact that samba underwent a stylistic change around 1930. I would nevertheless like to emphasize that those who experienced and lived this history had already carried out this analysis, albeit in their own way. Clearly, Donga, Ismael Silva, Sérgio Cabral, Tinhorão, and others who spoke or wrote about the difference between "modern samba" and "samba-*maxixe*" also understood this difference in musical terms. We can see this, for example, in the following excerpt from the famous interview Sérgio Cabral conducted with Ismael Silva:

> (Cabral):—Were you Estácio guys aware that you were introducing a new type of samba? (Ismael Silva): . . .—Samba was like this: *tan tantan tan tantan*. It didn't work. . . . So, we started playing a samba like this: *bum bum paticum-bumprugurundum*.[1]

Ismael "demonstrates" which musical traits strike him as important in distinguishing the two styles; he does this by singing the rhythms, as if drumming with his voice. It is a perfectly adequate method to meet his needs. If he had taken this a bit further, it could even have been formalized, following the example of Indian musicians and others who have created systems of rhythmic syllables.

Cabral, for his part, translates Ismael's singing into written syllables that are incapable (in the absence of other information) of revealing the totality of the musical content. But Cabral is a Carioca journalist, and his audience is samba's audience; in this context, saying any more than he did would in some ways have been redundant. The efficacy of his discourse can be measured by the fact that the expression "bum bum paticumbumprugurundum" returned to the world of samba in 1982, when it was used as the theme for Império Serrano samba school's performance (their *samba-enredo*), which won that year's Carnival competition.

Yet if my own discourse regarding the recognition of the difference between the two styles is not redundant, as I hope it is not, this is because the systematizing, critiquing of sources, and formalizing that guided it led to results that would otherwise have been impossible to obtain. These results, I think, also merit being part of the larger conversation on samba that was initiated by Cabral and Ismael Silva, among others.

Finally, I have attempted to situate samba's transformations within a more general history of Brazilian popular music. The assimilation of old-style samba to the 3–3–2 Paradigm allowed us to see it as a beneficiary of a musical and ideological universe that dates to well before 1917—a universe whose first written records come from the late eighteenth century, with the manuscripts of the Biblioteca da Ajuda, discussed in part 1.

Broadening our perspective allows us to understand samba's stylistic change in the 1930s as a true turning point in Brazilian popular music. It was the end of an era that spanned not just from 1917 to 1930; the era effectively began in the nineteenth century. As such, throughout this work we have explored not one but *two* cycles of transformations: one *short* cycle, which leads from samba's old style to its new style, and a *long* cycle, which leads from the 3–3–2 to the Estácio Paradigm.

* * *

One of the most successful Brazilian Carnival hits in the 1930s was a *marchinha* by Lamartine Babo called "História do Brazil" ("History of Brazil"):

—Quem foi que inventou o Brasil?   —Who was it who invented Brazil?
—Foi seu Cabral! Foi seu Cabral!   —It was *seu* Cabral! It was *seu* Cabral!
No dia 21 de abril,   On the 21st of April,
Dois meses depois do carnaval!   Two months after Carnival!

"Seu Cabral" is Pedro Álvares Cabral, the Portuguese navigator who on April 22, 1500, arrived in what would become Brazil. Perhaps one of the reasons for the success of Lamartine Babo's *marchinha* is that it highlights a Brazilian identity that *predates* Cabral. Given that in Brazil the Portuguese navigator has, until recently, been treated as the "beginning" of the country's history, a Carnival predating him would be seen as ahistorical, eternal. *After* Cabral (the lyrics subsequently tell us) came the great novelist José de Alencar (1829–1877), the great opera composer Carlos Gomes (1836–1896), *feijoada* (meat and bean stew), *guaraná* (soft drink), and *cachaça*; in sum, these are the achievements of Brazilian civilization, everything we could "invent," as is said in the first verse.[2] But if something already existed *before* Cabral, it would need to be on the order of the atemporal, predating all inventions; it would define us even more profoundly.

Throughout this work I used words that are not unlike "Carnival," as defined in this *marchinha*, as they evoke, for so many Brazilians (and I count myself as one of them), deep layers of identity: words such as "samba," "folk music," "Brazilian popular music." These are words that speak to us not just about music but also about our sentiments, behaviors, and even political convictions.

Over the course of these pages, we have learned that however much we may enjoy Lamartine's *marchinha*, words such as these do not designate timeless concepts. Still, a claim like this would be empty if it did not motivate us to show, in as much detail as possible, the process by which the phenomena designated by such words are socially constructed and assume the identity-marking roles to which I have referred. This is what I sought to do in the case of samba.

This case seems to me rich in implications for the study of culture in Brazil. Indeed, among other reasons, it shows particularly well that the invention of the country the song tells us about—the social construction of a Brazilian identity—is not an arbitrary process but rather one shaped by the deliberate selection and elaboration of historical materials that support their claims to timelessness. Rhythmic patterns, musical instruments, terminology, religious creed, and so forth are some of the aspects by which, in the molding of Carioca samba, creativity found an echo in the past.

In other words, to understand our topic, it is not enough to simply say that samba was part of a socially constructed identity; this is true, but it is far too general. My task consisted of shining a light on the social and musical details of this construction, showing how its efficacy partially lies in the selective harnessing, in novel contexts, of characteristics that were already in existence.

In terms of the musical aspects, I dedicated special attention to rhythmic traits of African origin. But I did not concern myself with trying to trace given rhythms to one or another ethnicity or region of Africa. Instead, I showed that the two paradigms—the 3–3–2 and the Estácio—can be described satisfactorily by way of the concept of "rhythmic oddity," a concept that emerges from the context of

African music research. What matters is to recognize that at different moments and in different circumstances, two types of rhythmic oddity are plucked from within the Afro-Brazilian musical heritage to indicate identity in a novel context, the context of popular music.

On the other hand, the study of the transition from one paradigm to the other contributes something new to studies that have heretofore been conducted on samba. Such studies have repeatedly emphasized the "whitening" of the genre, its progressive assimilation by the status quo.[3] Yet if we accept, along with the majority of researchers, that the tendency toward contrametricity is, in the music of the Americas, a trait of African origin, it would instead be necessary to see this transition as an "Africanization," for the Estácio Paradigm is much more contrametric than the 3–3–2.

The Brazilian slave trade ended in the mid-nineteenth century. To see in the Estácio Paradigm a trait of African origin thus implies supposing that it already existed in the country well before 1930—but in a latent state, so to speak, as far as records of official culture go. Supporting this hypothesis is the fact that we can find the same rhythmic model in other orally transmitted Afro-Brazilian musics. An investigation that is far from exhaustive has revealed the presence of this model, for example, on *samba de viola* recordings from Bahia, and in a type of *candomblé de Angola* practiced in Rio de Janeiro.[4]

If we accept the hypothesis that this rhythmic model was already practiced in Afro-Brazilian music before 1930, two questions arise. First, why did it take so long to appear in written and recorded music given that by the nineteenth century, the 3–3–2 had already set the groundwork? Second, why is it that when the Estácio Paradigm finally reached popular music, it made so much of a mark—much more so than its presence in folk music would have had us expect? In other words, why, within the tremendous rhythmic diversity of Afro-Brazilian music, did the new version of Carioca samba in the 1930s choose precisely this model as its rhythmic icon, as its "beat"?

As for the first question, I believe that the second paradigm took longer to become conspicuous in sheet music and recordings because it was much more contrametric than the other. This considerable contrametricity elicited at least three levels of repression. First, cognitive repression, for in a given musical culture, the ear tends to reject or reinterpret information that is excessively different from habitual patterns. Second, social repression, for the Estácio Paradigm's "excessive difference" ascribes the quality of being unknowable, uncontrollable, indomitable onto those who practice it—Black people, enslaved until 1888 and marginalized since then. Finally, the rhythm in question was also submitted to what we might call an aesthetic repression, for, showing all too conspicuously the mark of "Black music," it brought upon itself the same inferiority attributed to its practitioners.

There are countless examples of all these "attributions" in the literature. These are verbal manifestations of the repression of Afro-Brazilian music. Likewise, the fact that these "exaggeratedly" contrametric rhythms were not documented prior to 1930 is a musical manifestation of this repression.

But this repression is, once again, only part of the story. *Lundu*, as we have seen, had already, more than a century earlier, begun to show that there was also an intercultural dialogue in Brazil. But the primary musical element by which *lundu*—and *polca-lundu* and *maxixe* after it—flaunted its subdued Blackness was the use of rhythmic patterns based on the 3–3–2 Paradigm. Being much less contrametric, it was easier for Western rhythm to accept, especially when it was transformed into the "habanera rhythm" by a providential sixteenth note.

The second question is more difficult to answer. But everything that has heretofore been said seems to suggest that the Estácio Paradigm was a possible compromise between Afro-Brazilian polyrhythms and the musical language of the radio and the record industry. This compromise also allowed people such as Ismael Silva, Cartola, and other *malandros* who were on their way to becoming professional composers/artists to showcase their difference, asserting that their music was samba, and not *maxixe*. Finally, the paradigm played a role in helping Brazil, where slavery had ceased to exist a mere forty years earlier, transition to another phase of its cultural identity, integrating things it had theretofore excluded.

In 1939, a few years after the period that has received most of our attention, composer Ary Barroso expressed this redefined identity in a musical emblem by introducing his celebrated samba "Aquarela do Brasil" ("Brazil"): and there it was, the Estácio Paradigm in all its glory, played by a full Western orchestra . . . and without rhythmic hesitations.

Glossary

General Terms

Bamba (n.m.)—The term that meant *sambista* in the early twentieth century; another name for *malandro*, though without the negative baggage *malandro* could sometimes carry. (See "Musical Premises," note 41.)

Batucada (n.f.)—A game of dexterity similar to *capoeira*. In this game, one partner remains standing while the other tries to knock him down using a *pernada* (kick). This game was practiced (in particular by *malandros*) in a *roda* (ring), to the sound of short refrains similar to those of certain folk sambas.

Bloco (n.m.)—Literally, "block." A group of friends, neighbors, and so forth who parade together during Carnival. The *blocos* were the immediate predecessors of samba schools. (See chapter 7.)

Botequim (n.m., plural: *botequins*)—This is Rio's equivalent of the English pub and the Parisian café. People go to a *botequim* to have coffee, drink beer, eat the day's special, meet up with friends, and make music. (See chapter 7.)

Cachaça (n.f.)—A very popular Brazilian sugarcane-based alcohol.

Caipira (adj.)—Initially this word designated the people who were from geo-cultural rural areas of São Paulo. Today it is a synonym for "hick" or "redneck."

Candomblé (n.m.)—An African-derived religion common in Brazil (and especially in the state of Bahia). Associated with the worship of deities from West Africa (primarily those of Yoruba- and Gbe-speaking peoples). The term *Candomblé* refers to the religion while *candomblé(s)* refers to the group/temple/gathering.

Capadócio (adj.)—A hustler, bohemian, party animal, someone who likes fighting and music. See also *malandro*. (See chapter 8.)

Capoeira (n.f.)—A martial art invented or developed by Afro-Brazilians, probably in the nineteenth century. It is a "game" (*jogo*) that incorporates music and dance with kicks and (often) acrobatics. (See chapter 2 and "Musical Premises," note 24.)

Carioca (adj.)—A person or thing from the city of Rio de Janeiro.

Cerrado (n.)—Vast tropical savanna of Brazil mostly in the plateaus of the nation's central region.

Congado (n.m.)—A traditional Brazilian "dramatic dance" (to use an expression from Mário de Andrade). It is also a festival in which, notably in the nineteenth century, a "Black King" was crowned among Afro-Brazilians. *Congados* continue to thrive in the state of Minas Gerais, in Southeast Brazil. (See chapter 3, note 80.)

Cordão (n.m., plural: *cordões*)—Literally, "long rope." A group of friends, neighbors, and so forth who parade together during Carnival. A rope or cord separates the members from onlookers and other *cordões*. The term is equivalent to *bloco*, but is older.

Feitiço (n.m.)—Literally, "fetish." However, the word is best understood here to mean "spell" or "enchantment." (See discussion of the term in the translator's foreword and chapter 9.)

Festa da Penha—A festival held on Sundays in October starting in the nineteenth century, near the Church of Penha, in the suburb of Rio called Penha. This festival was very popular at the beginning of the twentieth century, especially among Afro-Brazilians, who deeply venerated Our Lady of the Rosary, to whom the festival was dedicated.

Folião (adj., plural: *foliões*)—A term used to describe a person who actively participates in Carnival festivities.

Ginga (n.f.)—A type of swaying strut often associated with *malandros*. (See chapter 8.)

Iaiá, ioiô (n.f., n.m.)—See *sinhá, sinhô*.

Macumba (n.f.)—An Afro-Brazilian religious tradition. A type of Candomblé practiced in the state of Rio de Janeiro.

Mãe de santo (n.f.)—Literally, "mother in saint." The name of the Candomblé priestess.

Malandragem (n.m.)—The *malandro* lifestyle. (See chapter 8.)

Malandro (adj.)—A hustler, bohemian, party animal, someone who likes fighting and music. The *sambistas* who created new-style samba in the early 1930s were in many cases *malandros*, and at that time the terms *sambista* and *malandro* were, whether accurately or not, associated with each other. (See chapter 8.)

Morro (n.m.)—Literally, "hill." The city of Rio is rich in *morros*, which, especially starting in the early twentieth century, were inhabited by the poorest strata of the population. Some of the *morros*—such as that of Mangueira and that of Salgueiro—are especially important in the samba world.

Nhanhá, nhonhô (n.f., n.m.)—See *sinhá, sinhô*.

Orgia (n.f.)—Literally, "orgy." Here it means life of excess, life of the *malandro*. Thus a synonym of *malandragem*. (See chapter 8.)

Orixá (n.m.)—The gods of the Yoruba pantheon imported to the Americas and venerated in many Candomblé temples. Sometimes written in English as *Orisha*.

Otário (n.m.)—A sucker or chump. The *otário* is the victim of the *malandro*. A person who is naive, who is systematically tricked.

Pai de santo (n.m.)—Literally, "father in saint." The name of the Candomblé priest.

Pernada (n.f.)—Literally, "kick." It was the main move in the *batucada* game, and it was also one of the names by which the game was known.

Rancho (n.m.)—A group of friends, neighbors, and so forth who parade together during Carnival. Larger and more organized than *cordões* and *blocos*, *ranchos* are at the origin of certain characteristics of today's samba schools (such as the floats). (See chapter 7.)

Réis (n.m., generally as *"mil-réis"*)—Old Brazilian currency, used until 1942.

Sinhá/Sinhô (n.f./n.m.)—Caricatured speech that was said to depict the way in which enslaved people would say *senhora* (ma'am, miss) and *senhor* (massa, mister). (See chapter 1.)

Tambor de Mina—An Afro-Brazilian religious tradition. A type of Candomblé practiced in the state of Maranhão.

Tia (n.f.)—Literally, "aunt." It was the name reserved for older women who exercised leadership among Bahian immigrants to Rio at the turn of the twentieth century. The term is still in use today in the samba world. (See chapter 4.)

Xangô (n.m.)—An Afro-Brazilian religious tradition. A type of Candomblé practiced in the state of Pernambuco.

Musical Terms

Adufe (n.m.)—A type of tambourine used in samba at the beginning of the twentieth century.

Agogô—A type of struck idiophone (single or multiple bell).

Baile—The generic name for a dance; also refers to a specific kind of intertwined couples dancing.

Batuque (n.m.)—The designation (generally in the nineteenth century) used by the Portuguese and Brazilians to refer to Black dances and musical festivities.

Barrica (n.f.)—Literally, "barrel." The former name for *surdo*.

Cateretê (n.m.)—A musical-choreographic genre supposedly of Amerindian origin.

Cavaquinho (n.m.)—A small four-string guitar of Portuguese origin (roughly the size of a ukulele); very popular in Brazil.

Choro (s.m.)—A small instrumental ensemble created in Brazil during the second half of the nineteenth century. The basic ensemble consisted of flute, guitar, and *cavaquinho*. Starting in the 1920s, the word begins to designate the style of music played by ensembles of this type.

Chula (adj.)—Literally, "vulgar." In Bahia, the *chula* is the sung part of a folk samba. It is also the name of a style of samba in Bahia.

Coco—A type of *umbigada* dance popular in Northeast Brazil.

Corta-jaca—The expression literally means "to cut the jackfruit," and it indicates a basic folk samba dance step.

Cuíca (n.f.)—A friction membranophone. An important percussion instrument in samba and emblematic of new-style samba.

Desafio (n.m.)—A poetic and musical competition in which improvisation plays an important role.

Fado (n.m.)—This word was used in Brazil starting in the early nineteenth century to designate a popular dance accompanied by singing and guitars. The word *fado* also refers to the popular Portuguese musical genre, but this use in Portugal only begins to be documented in the late nineteenth century. The relationship between old Brazilian *fado* and Portuguese *fado* has been an object of controversy.

Ganzá (n.m.)—A shaken idiophone common in samba percussion.

Lundu (n.m.)—(1) A popular dance in Brazil and Portugal first documented to the late eighteenth century; (2) A comic salon song often alluding to Afro-Brazilians. Hundreds of these comic *lundus* were published in Brazil between 1830 and the beginning of the twentieth century. (See chapter 1.)

Maracatu—Carnival groups built around the crowning of a king and queen, said to be rooted in Central African traditions. Although these are viewed as secular groups, they have important links to Afro-Brazilian religions. The *maracatu* tradition is most closely associated with the state of Pernambuco.

Marchinha (n.f.)—Literally, "little march." A genre of Carnival music created in Rio in the 1920s. It is usually considered more bourgeois than samba.

Maxixe (n.m.)—A popular dance created in Rio probably in the 1870s. The oldest documented cases of the word come from around 1880. Subsequently, *maxixe* came to denominate the genre of music performed for the *maxixe* dance.

Miudinho (adj.)—Literally, "very small." It is the designation of one of the main folk samba dance steps, one in which the feet make very small shuffling movements.

Modinha (n.f.)—A romantic song created by Brazilians and Portuguese at the end of the eighteenth century. (See chapter 2.)

Pandeiro (n.m.)—A type of tambourine. One of the most common of all samba instruments. (See chapter 3, note 12.)

Polca-lundu (n.f.)—A genre of instrumental music created in Brazil around 1870. It was played by *choros* and pianists; we are able to find traces of this music in the sheet music whose genre is indicated as *polca-lundu*.

Prato, prato e faca (n.m.)—Literally "plate," "plate and knife." These kitchen utensils have become a musical instrument (in this case a scraped idiophone) quite common in Bahia, especially in folk samba.

Quebrar (v.)—To shake the hips. The most famous gesture of certain Afro-Brazilian choreographies (variation of *requebrar*). (See chapter 2.)

Reco-reco (n.m.)—A scraped idiophone that is a common samba percussion instrument.

Requebrado/Requebrar (adj./v.)—Hip shake/To shake the hips. The most famous gesture of certain Afro-Brazilian choreographies (variation of *quebrar*). (See chapter 2.)

Roda (n.f.)—Literally, "circle" or "ring." Symbolic of folk samba, as it is in a *roda* that participants gather in order to perform, with one or more dancers in the middle while the participants forming the *roda* clap, play instruments, and/or sing.

Roda de samba (n.f.)—Literally "samba circle" or "ring of samba," meaning a samba gathering. In the context of Rio de Janeiro, the term refers generally to a gathering of musicians who play samba. The term is also used with a similar connotation for other genres, such as *choro* (i.e., *roda de choro*), or even for nonmusical events such as a *roda de conversa* (conversation ring), which might be understood in English as a group discussion, a Q&A, or any type of relatively informal venue for conversation. As for the circular nature of the *roda*, this can be more or less strict. In the context of Rio de Janeiro, a *roda de samba* is often imagined as musicians sitting around a table as they perform.

Samba-canção (n.f.)—Literally, "samba-song." The most common meaning is a kind of samba characterized by a slow tempo and the expression of suffering in love. However, the term can also simply refer to samba as a song (as opposed to samba as a celebration).

Samba-chulado (n.m.)—A type of folk samba characterized by a longer sung part. See *chula*.

Samba-corrido (n.m.)—A type of folk samba that might be described as the opposite of *samba de partido-alto* due to its relative simplicity. (See chapter 4.)

Samba de enredo (n.m.)—Samba specifically composed for samba school Carnival parades. The lyrics of the *sambas de enredo* summarize the theme (*enredo*) of the samba school's parade in a given year.

Samba de partido-alto (n.m.)—(1) In Bahia, a type of folk samba characterized by, among other things, the fact that the singing and the dancing alternate. (2) In Rio, a folk and popular samba form, characterized above all by short choruses and improvised parts.

Samba de roda (n.m.)—A type of folk samba practiced in Bahia, characterized by the participants gathering in a *roda*.

Samba de umbigada (n.m.)—A general term for the folk dances in which the *umbigada* is found.

Sambista (n.m.)—The protagonist of the samba world. He dances, sings, plays, and composes sambas. Professional samba composers are not necessarily considered *sambistas* because some of them are not part of the world of samba; the same is true for singers and instrumentalists.

Sapateado (n.m.)—Used interchangeably with *miudinho*, this term is derived from *sapato* ("shoe") and describes a foot shuffle characteristic of folk samba.

Segunda / segunda parte (n.f.)—Literally, "second" or "second part." The solo part sung after the refrain in new-style samba. (See chapter 7.)

Surdo (n.m.)—A bass membranophone of a cylindrical shape. Dimensions: about 60 cm (23.5 in) in diameter and 75 cm (30 in) long. The instrument is said to have been invented by Bide, one of the *sambistas* from Estácio. It is one of the main percussion instruments in new-style samba.

Tamborim (n.m.)—A small frame drum. Dimensions: about 15 cm (6 in) in diameter and 4 cm (1.5 in) deep. One of the main percussion instruments in, and emblematic of, the new style of samba.

Umbigada (n.f.)—Literally, "belly bounce." One of the most characteristic gestures of a variety of Afro-Brazilian dances, a gesture also present in certain central African dances. It is by way of the *umbigada* that a person dancing in the middle of the *roda* chooses the person who will next occupy the center.

Viola (n.f.)—A type of guitar with ten steel strings (often arranged in five double courses) used in rural areas of Brazil. It corresponds, in terms of its origins and organology, to the European guitar of the early eighteenth century. (See chapter 3, note 12.)

Notes

Introduction to the English Translation

1. This section on "popular music" in Brazil is an edited version of an article I wrote and published after teaching a seminar at the University of Texas at Austin: Carlos Sandroni, "Hitting a 'Popular' Note: Musical Contrasts in Brazil and the US," *Portal* 2 (2006–2007), 48–49. https://repositories.lib.utexas.edu/handle/2152/61826.

2. Philip Yampolsky, "Commercial 78's: A Rediscovered Resource for Ethnomusicology," in *This Thing Called Music: Essays in Honor of Bruno Nettl*, ed. Victoria Lindsay Levine and Philip Bohlman (Lanham, MD: Rowman & Littlefield, 2015), 302–314.

3. Yampolsky, "Commercial 78's," 306.

4. Yampolsky, "Commercial 78's," 309.

Original Introduction

1. The first and second chapters also present some technical passages in sidebars, so that readers who wish to skip them may do so.

2. The term *carioca* is in Merriam-Webster's online dictionary. However, its definition, which says it refers to "a native or resident" of Rio de Janeiro when capitalized and to a variation of samba (likely a reference to the 1933 film *Flying Down to Rio*), is hardly as ample as it will be used here. I will use it, in capitalized form, as an adjective referring to anyone or anything from Rio de Janeiro. In other words, I will use it as I would the word "Californian," or, more related to this book, the word "Bahian" to mean a person or thing from the Brazilian state of Bahia.—Trans.

3. The same type of reflection could be made in relation to more recent samba transformations, such as *pagode* or *samba-reggae*. But this would be a subject for another book.

Musical Premises

1. The term *sambista*, which will appear repeatedly in the following pages, refers to performers of the type of samba discussed in this book. The term is widespread in Brazil, but there are notable exceptions. In traditional samba of the Bahian Recôncavo, for instance, samba performers are known as *sambador* (man) and *sambadeira* (woman).—Trans.

2. Edison Carneiro, *Folguedos tradicionais* (Rio de Janeiro: Conquista, 1974), 161.

3. The translations of Carneiro's words and the cited portion of the "Carta" are adapted from the unpublished translation of the "Carta do samba" done by Francesca Negro and Ananya Jahanara Kabir. I thank both scholars for graciously sharing this with me.—Trans.

4. Carneiro, *Folguedos tradicionais*, 162.

5. Mário de Andrade is still today considered to have been one of the most important Brazilian writers of the twentieth century. He is perhaps most well-known for his classic rhapsody *Macunaíma*, but he was also central to the study of Brazilian music as well as a pioneer of Brazilian ethnomusicology.—Trans.

6. Mário de Andrade, *As melodias do boi e outras peças* (São Paulo: Duas Cidades, 1987), 382.

7. José Cândido de Andrade Muricy, "Ernesto Nazareth (1863–1963)," *Cadernos Brasileiros* 5 no. 3 (1963), 42.

8. Marc Honegger, *Dictionnaire de la musique—science de la musique*, vol. 2 (Paris: Bordas, 1976).

9. Alberto Basso, ed., *Dizionario della musica* (Torino: Tipografia Sociale Torinese, 1971), 1124.

10. Willi Apel, *Harvard Dictionary of Music*, 2nd ed. (Cambridge, MA: Belknapp Press of Harvard University Press, 1974), 827.

11. For a summary of ideas about rhythm and meter in Western theory, see Jean-Jacques Nattiez, *Musicologie générale et sémiologie* (Paris: Christian Bourgois, 1987), 311–332; for a more recent and in-depth discussion of the topic, see Justin London, *Hearing in Time: Psychological Aspects of Musical Meter* (New York: Oxford University Press, 2012).

12. Simha Arom, "Du pied à la main: Les fondements métriques des musiques traditionelles d'Afrique Centrale," *Analyse musicale* 10 (1988), 19–21.

13. Simha Arom, *African Polyphony & Polyrhythm: Musical Structure and Methodology*, translated by Martin Thom, Barbara Tuckett, and Raymond Boyd (Cambridge: Cambridge University Press, 1991), 250.

14. The most recent general panorama of African music, Kofi Agawu's *The African Imagination in Music* (2016), uses the word "syncopation" not a single time in 373 pages. On the other hand, there is no prevailing prohibition, as far as I am aware, on using measures in transcriptions of African music. Various contemporary authors, posterior to Arom and Kubik, might use meters in their transcriptions. I myself, as will be seen, use a 2/4 meter in my samba transcriptions while still emphasizing samba's connections to African rhythm. This is due to the advantages of ample legibility, which the use of measures offers, in many cases making up for the possible advantages of alternative notations (as Agawu argues, *Representing African Music*, p. 66–67).

15. See, for example, Oneyda Alvarenga, "A influência negra na música brasileira," *Boletim latino americano de música* 6, no. 1 (1946), 357–407; Eurico Nogueira França, "Le noir dans la musique brésilienne," in *La contribuition de l'Afrique à la civilization brésilienne*, Ministério das Relações Exteriores, n.d.; and Renato de Almeida, "A influência da música negra no Brasil," *Revista de etnografia* 4, no. 2 (1965), 325–331.

16. Andrade, *As melodias do boi e outras peças*, 397, 409, and 416.

17. The continued relevance of Mário de Andrade's observation is evidenced by two articles from 1991 and 1989: Denis-Constant Martin, "Filiation or Innovation? Some Hypotheses to Overcome the Dilemma of Afro-American Music's Origin," *Black Music Research Journal* 2, no. 1 (1991), 24–26 and throughout; and Philip Tagg, "'Black Music,' 'Afro-American Music' and 'European Music,'" *Popular Music* 8, no. 3 (1989), 289–290.

18. Margareth J. Kartomi, "The Processes and Results of Musical Culture Contact: A Discussion of Terminology and Concepts," *Ethnomusicology* 25, no. 2 (1982), 233.

19. A. M. Jones, *Studies in African music*, vol. 1 (London: Oxford University Press, 1959), 210–213 and throughout (incidentally, the author makes approximations between African music and Brazilian samba on pages 114–115). See also J. H. Kwabena Nketia, *The Music of Africa* (New York: W. W. Norton, 1974), 131. For a more recent (and critical) discussion of the proposal of African rhythm as "additive," see Kofi Agawu, *Representing African Music: Postcolonial Notes, Queries, Positions* (New York: Routledge, 2003), 86–91.

20. Arom, *African Polyphony & Polyrhythm*, 246–248.

21. J. H. Kwabena Nketia, *African Music in Ghana* (Evanston, IL: Northwestern University Press, 1963), 78–87.

22. Arom, *African Polyphony & Polyrhythm*, 39–40 and 298.

23. *Tambor de mina, Xangô*, Candomblé, and *Macumba*, all mentioned here, are terms that designate Afro-Brazilian religious traditions that incorporate the veneration of deities originally said to come from Africa, deities that possess their devotees at specific moments (especially during celebrations and other acts of devotion). Without a doubt, Candomblé is the most well known of these and is today perhaps the most commonly used designation all over Brazil. The other two practices that Sandroni mentions here may have religious implications but are not explicitly religious. *Maracatu* is a Carnival tradition associated primarily with Pernambuco. It is a public celebration of Black kings and queens with links to Afro-Brazilian religious practices. *Capoeira*, increasingly known around the world, is an Afro-Brazilian "game" (*jogo*) that incorporates music and dance with kicks and (often) acrobatics. *Capoeira* is practiced by two opponents at a time within a ring formed by the participants, who sing, clap, and play instruments, waiting their turn to enter the ring.—Trans.

24. There are some authors who have made, over the course of the twentieth century, reference to patterns such as these in Brazilian music: Luciano Gallet, *Estudos de folclore* (Rio de Janeiro: Carlos Wehrs, 1934), 55; Kazadi wa Mukuna, *Contribuição bantu na música popular brasileira: Perspectivas etnomusicológics* (São Paulo: Terceira Margem, 2006), 82; Ralph C. Waddey, "'Viola de Samba' and 'Samba de Viola' in the 'Reconcavo' of Bahia (Brazil) Part II: 'Samba de Viola,'" *Latin American Music Review* 2, no. 2 (1981), 271.

25. The composer Guerra-Peixe—when researching the *maracatus* of Recife in the early 1950s, and without using any African music scholars in his bibliography—referred to the

"gonguê," an externally struck bell, in the following terms: "Its musical function is to main-tain an unvaried rhythmic scheme, ensuring a regular reference for the polyrhythm of the percussion instruments. . . . In the *maracatu* orchestra more than one *gonguê* is never used, so that in the event that the musicians get off they do not diverge following one [musician] or the other. 'This instrument is like the requinta [E-flat clarinet] in a marching band,' the *rainha Santa* [the *maracatu* queen] informed the musicians, on occasion of one of the re-hearsals, clarifying that the *gonguê* should be accompanied by the rest of the instruments as if it were a melody" (Guerra-Peixe, *Maracatus do Recife*, 74).

26. Cited by Solomon Glades Minkowsky, *Ignacio Cervantes y la danza en Cuba* (Havana: Letras Cubanas, 1988), 57.

27. John Blacking, *How Musical Is Man?* (Seattle: University of Washington Press, 1973), 21–23.

28. The term *tresillo* is employed to refer to the figure in question, for example, by Arge-liers León, *Del canto y el tiempo* (Havana: Letras Cubanas, 1984), 283; and by Minkowsky, *Ignacio Cervantes*, 66.

29. Coriún Aharónian, e-mail to the author, July 17, 2006.

30. Jerry D. Metz, "Cultural Geographies of Afro-Brazilian Symbolic Practice: Tradition and Change in Maracatu de Nação (Recife, Pernambuco, Brazil)," *Latin American Music Review* 29, no. 1 (2008), 68. Concerning the *gonguê*, Metz explains that it "is a single, clap-perless iron bell, one to three feet long, considered fundamental to the performance of traditional *maracatu* music. In the historical record of Brazil, reference to the bell seems to appear only in Pernambuco." *Samba de roda* and *coco* are both types of Afro-Brazilian music/dance in which people dance in the middle of a ring formed by the participants. Despite important similarities, the instruments used in each are generally different, as are the specific rhythms and dances. As for *partido-alto*, Sandroni explains this in detail at dif-ferent points in the book.—Trans.

31. Sheet music reproduced in Baptista Siqueira, *Três vultos históricos da música brasileira* (Rio de Janeiro: D. Araújo, 1969), 39–40.

32. For example, León, *Del canto*, 283. León explicitly associates the *cinquillo* with the *tresillo*.

33. León, *Del canto*, 283.

34. Nogueira França, "Le noir," 79.

35. The fact that I highlight, in relation to the Brazilian repertoire from the second half of the nineteenth century to circa 1930, the importance of the 3–3–2 rhythmic pattern in contrast to the usual binarism of 2/4, does not preclude the obvious fact that the two rhythmic feels are simultaneous (as shown by Coriún Aharónian in "Factores de identidad musical latinoamericana," a text from the early 1990s). It is this simultaneity that makes the 3–3–2 pattern of Brazil (and of other countries) "contrametric," as discussed above. It also differentiates it from what Bartók called "Bulgarian rhythms" and what Francophone ethnomusicology calls *aksak* rhythms (a Turkish word for "lame"). In these cases, the 3–3–2 pattern is commetric, without any underlying binarism. On this last point, see Bela Bartók, "El denominado ritmo búlgaro," in *Escritos sobre música popular* (Mexico City/Madrid: Siglo XXI, 1979), 164–173; Constantin Brailoiu, "The Aksak Rhythm," in *Problems of Ethnomusi-*

cology (Cambridge: Cambridge University Press, 1984), 133–167; and Jérôme Cler, "Pour une théorie de l'aksak," *Revue de musicologie* 80, no. 2 (1994), 181–210.

36. The term *batuque* could actually be defined in several different ways, as we will see throughout the text. It can be the name of a specific dance or the generic name given to all Afro-Brazilian drumming/dancing (especially by outsiders) during the nineteenth century (not to mention other meanings), as is described by Sandroni in the following note. For our general purposes here, what matters most is that the term always refers explicitly to Black practices, and here Black dance/music practices.—Trans.

37. Since the nineteenth century, the word *batuque* was used by the Portuguese and by Brazilians to refer to the percussive music of enslaved Africans and their descendants.

38. I choose to maintain the Portuguese word *mestiço*, usually translated in English as "mixed-race" or even *mestizo*. *Mestizo*, in particular, would seem a convenient cognate for *mestiço*, as it suggests common ground with a Spanish-language term quite broadly understood (in English) as racially mixed. However, the reason to choose *mestiço* over *mestizo* is because of the specificity of the term in the Brazilian context, and particularly in areas of large Afro-Brazilian populations. I will not delve into the rather complex connotations and overtones of the term and what it tells us about race in Brazil. This is done much better by others, such as Patrícia de Santana Pinho, "White but Not Quite: Tones and Overtones of Whiteness in Brazil," *Small Axe* 13, no. 2 (2009), 39–56. I will say only that *mestiço* rarely implies a mixture that does not involve African ancestry, especially in the Brazilian regions (Bahia, Rio, Pernambuco) receiving Sandroni's focus in this book. In other words, though it could, *mestiço* does not automatically suggest a generic "mixture" of, say, Indigenous and Italian ancestry, or Japanese and European. It is thus unlike *mestizo*, which seems generally to point toward a type of Amerindian mixture.—Trans.

39. This does not preclude the possibility that these same words might have different definitions in different contexts.

40. Here the term *bamba* means a *sambista*. The term can also refer more broadly to a hustler or to the *malandro*, a term we will become quite familiar with later on in the book. However, *bamba* never has the negative connotation sometimes attributed to *malandro*.—Trans.

41. Carlos Didier, "O samba que veio do Estácio," *O Catacumba* 1, no. 1 (1984), 3. Didier revisited the subject—albeit without explicit mention of the rhythmic patterns—in an unpublished 1996 text, "A formação do samba: De Donga e Sinhô à turma do Estácio," and naturally in the book *Noel Rosa*, which he cowrote with João Máximo, and which I will cite repeatedly in part 2.

42. The fact that the *sambistas* cited by Didier, all of whom grew to prominence in the 1930s, began in the "Estácio de Sá" neighborhood of Rio de Janeiro explains, as we will see in more detail in part 2, why I have used this name to baptize the group of rhythmic patterns they introduced into samba.

43. Mukuna, *Contribuição bantu*; Samuel Araújo, "Acoustic Labor in the Timing of Everyday Life" (PhD diss., University of Illinois, Urbana-Champaign, 1992); Gerhard Kubik, *Angolan Traits in Black Music, Games and Dances of Brazil* (Lisbon: Junta de Investigações Científicas do Ultramar, 1979).

44. Mukuna, *Contribuição bantu*, 92.

45. Mukuna, *Contribuição bantu*, 91.

46. Mukuna, *Contribuição bantu*, 82.

47. Mukuna, *Contribuição bantu*, 127–128 and throughout.

48. Mukuna, *Contribuição bantu*, 92.

49. Mukuna, *Contribuição bantu*, 199.

50. Mukuna, *Contribuição bantu*, 92.

51. Araújo, "Acoustic Labor," 146–147.

52. Kubik, *Angolan Traits*, 13.

53. The the *cuíca's* skin may be tightened by the instrumentalist during the performance, generating two principal pitches. As such, the transcriptions have been notated using two pitches.

54. The word *roda* in reference to samba is generally translated as "ring" or "circle." In the Rio de Janeiro context, it refers generally to a gathering of musicians who would play samba. The term is also used with a similar connotation for other genres, such as *choro*, or even for nonmusical events such as a *roda de conversa* (conversation ring), which might be understood in English as a group discussion, a Q&A, or any type of relatively informal venue for conversation. As for the circular nature of this *roda*, this can be more or less literal. In the context of Rio de Janeiro, a *roda* is often imagined as a group of musicians performing while seated around a table. But this is hardly a rule.—Trans.

55. I refer any reader interested in the issue to two articles I published in *Cahiers de musiques traditionnelles*, "La samba à Rio de Janeiro et le paradigme de l'Estácio" (1997) and "Le tresillo" (2000); to the article "Mudanças de padrão rítmico no samba carioca, 1917–1937," made available online by *Trans—revista transcultural de música* (1996): https://www.sibetrans .com/trans/articulo/286/mudancas-de-padrao-ritmico-no-samba-carioca-1917-1937; or to my English-language piece, "'I Got Phrasing': Changes in Samba's Melodic Rhythm, 1917–1933," in *A Latin American Music Reader: Views from the South*, ed. Javier León and Helena Simonett (Urbana: University of Illinois Press, 2016), 250–257.

Chapter 1. "Sweet *Lundus*, for Massa to Dream"

The title of this chapter is a verse, the original of which is "Doces lundus, pra nhonhô sonhar," from "Bancarrota blues" ("Bankruptcy Blues"), a song by Edu Lobo and Chico Buarque.

1. Generations of Brazilian music researchers have written, erroneously, "Conde de Pavolide" (Count of Pavolide): Oneyda Alvarenga, Mozart de Araújo, and José Ramos Tinhorão, among many others. (I also committed the same error in the two Brazilian editions of this book.) Josias Pires Neto, to whom I owe my thanks, wrote the name correctly as "Povolide" in his PhD dissertation, "Música e dança afro-atlânticas: (Ca)lundus, batuques e sambas—permanências e atualizações" (PhD diss., Universidade Federal da Bahia, 2020), 116 and elsewhere.

2. José Ramos Tinhorão, *Fado, dança do Brasil, cantar de Lisboa* (Lisbon: Caminho, 1994), 30.

3. Nicolau Tolentino, *Sátiras* (Lisbon: Seara Nova, 1969), 64.

4. *Entremeses*, like Italian *intermezzi*, were short, one-act performances that were popu-

lar on the Iberian Peninsula generally. Edward Mullen defines the *entremés* in the Spanish context: "a short one-act play or skit normally performed for comic relief between the acts of the three-act Spanish *comedia.*" He adds, it "was an enormously popular genre in seventeenth-century Spain." Edward J. Mullen, "Simón Aguado's *Entremés de los negros*: Text and Context," *Comparative Drama* 20, no. 3 (1986), 238.—Trans.

5. José Ramos Tinhorão, *Os negros em Portugal* (Lisbon: Caminho, 1988), 289 and 296.

6. José Ramos Tinhorão, *Pequena história da música popular* (São Paulo: Art, 1991), 54.

7. *DMB*, "Lundu," 434. See also Alvarenga Oneyda, *Música popular brasileira* (São Paulo: Duas Cidades, 1982), 170; Tinhorão, *Pequena história*, 48.

8. Mário de Andrade, "Cândido Inácio da Silva e o lundu," *Latin American Music Review* 20, no. 2 (1999 [1944]), 255.

9. Mozart de Araújo, *A modinha e o lundu no século XVIII* (São Paulo: Ricordi, 1963), 11.

10. I have chosen to leave the term *mulata* in Portuguese rather than the now-outdated and frowned upon English "mulatto" or even a more current terminology (such as "mixed race" or "biracial") because of the important baggage the term itself carries in the Brazilian academic context (Eakin claims *mulata* is "the most potent image of Brazilian sexuality"). Marshall C. Eakin, *Becoming Brazilian: Race and National Identity in Twentieth-Century Brazil* (Cambridge: Cambridge University Press, 2017), 108. I furthermore have used *mulata* given the term's broader presence in the Atlantic world, perhaps most notably in the Cuban context. Select book titles alone may give a good idea of the symbolic weight of the Cuban *mulata*, such as Alison Fraunhar, *Mulata Nation: Visualizing Race and Gender in Cuba* (Jackson: University Press of Mississippi, 2018); and Melissa Blanco Borelli, *She Is Cuba: A Genealogy of the Mulata Body* (New York: Oxford University Press, 2016).—Trans.

11. José Ramos Tinhorão, *Os sons dos negros no Brasil* (São Paulo: Art, 1988), 54 and subsequent pages; Paulo Castagna, "Herança ibérica e africana no lundu brasileiro dos séculos XVIII e XIX," article presented at VI Encuentro Simposio Internacional de Musicología / VI Festival Internacional de Música Renacentista y Barroca Americana "Misiones de Chiquitos," Santa Cruz de la Sierra, Bolívia, April 25–26, 2006. Proceedings published by Asociación Pro Arte y Cultura (2006), 26–29. Castagna's article is based, moreover, on the analysis of the scant directly musical sources we have from the early nineteenth century that contain instrumental *lundus*. The musicologist shows the presence of Iberian elements in these sources.

12. Tinhorão, *Os sons dos negros*, 36.

13. Mário de Andrade, *Modinhas imperiais* (São Paulo: Martins, 1964), 12.

14. Bruno Kiefer, *A modinha e o lundu* (Porto Alegre: Movimento, 1977), 42.

15. Araújo, *A modinha e o lundu*, 11.

16. It is Tinhorão who cites this passage from the *Compêndio narrativo do peregrino da América*, in *Pequena história*, 12. On this point see also, José Ramos Tinhorão, "O tempo das modas novas," in *As origens da canção urbana* (Lisbon: Caminho, 1997), 113–118.

17. *DFB*, "modinha," 484–485.

18. This use can still be found well into the twentieth century, for example in the song "A jangada voltou só" ("The Raft Returned Alone") (Dorival Caymmi, 1941), which has the verses "Bento cantando modas / Muita figura fez" (Bento singing *modas* / He did it very well).

19. The oldest reference I have found in which the word *modinha* alludes to music is in a poem by the Portuguese writer Correia Garção. It is within Soneto XXXV, which appears in *Obras Poéticas* (*Poetic Works*), published in 1778: "Quem? O Padre António, que tocava / Diversos minuetes e modinhas" (Who? Father António, who played / Various minuets and *modinhas*). Given that Garção died in 1772, this sonnet precedes the success of Caldas Barbosa in Lisbon.

20. Marcos Magalhães, "A modinha e géneros relacionados, desde suas origens até 1833" (PhD diss., Universidade Nova de Lisboa, 2018), 94.

21. Magalhães, "A modinha e géneros relacionados," 97.

22. As Edilson de Lima notes in "A modinha e o lundu: Dois clássicos nos trópicos" (PhD diss., Universidade de São Paulo, 2010), 17–18, *modinha* and *moda* were synonymous in *Jornal de Modinhas* and in other Portuguese sources from the 1780s and 1790s. Contrary to *moda*, however, the word in its diminutive form, *modinha*, is not found in rural contexts; its dissemination accompanies the expansion of urban song and printed music.

23. Heinrich Friedrich Link, *Travels in Portugal: And through France and Spain. With a Dissertation on the Literature of Portugal, and the Spanish and Portugueze Languages* (London: T. N. Longman and O. Rees, 1801), 393.

24. William Beckford, *The Journal of William Beckford in Portugal and Spain 1787–1788*, ed. with an introduction and notes by Boyd Alexander (London: Rupert Hart-Davis, 1954), 228–229, referring to October 15, 1787. This reference is cited by countless authors, among them Manuel Veiga, "O estudo da modinha brasileira," *Latin American Music Review* 19, no. 1 (1998), 69.

25. José Ramos Tinhorão, *Domingos Caldas Barbosa—o poeta da viola, da modinha e do lundu* (São Paulo: Editora 34, 1997), 17–41.

26. In Portugal, this Arcadian movement started in the mid-eighteenth century, when in 1756 the Arcádia Lusitana or Olissiponense (Lusitanian or Lisbon Arcadia) was created, and in 1790, this commitment to academic neoclassicism was reaffirmed with the Nova Arcádia (New Arcadia). Arcadian poets "adopted literary pseuds. [*sic*] under which they wrote and published, a gesture meant to erase social distinctions and promote a literary form of aristocracy. The realities of daily bourgeois life were a favorite theme." J. Blackmore, "Portugal, Poetry of," in *The Princeton Handbook of World Poetries*, ed. Roland Greene and Stephen Cusman (Princeton: Princeton University Press, 2017), 444.—Trans.

27. In the end, was Caldas Barbosa also a musician, or just a poet? The most recent work on the topic tends toward affirming that he was indeed a musician, but with no definitive conclusions: "according to the current state of historical documents, it is not possible to find conclusive evidence of Caldas having been a type of 'cantautor' [singer-composer] avant-la-lettre," in Marcos Magalhães, "A modinha e géneros relacionados, desde suas origens até 1833," 166. Arguments against the hypothesis are put forth by Manuel Morais, *Domingos Caldas Barbosa: Muzica escolhida da viola de Lereno (1799)* (Lisbon: Estar Editora, 2003), 69–73. The most recent argumentation in favor of his having been a musician can be found in Márcia Taborda, "A viola e a música de Domingos Caldas Barbosa: Uma investigação bibliográfica," Anais do XVI Congresso da ANPPOM (2006), 558–562; and Lino de Almeida

Cardoso, *Americana Cantilena: A canção e a construção da nacionalidade no Brasil* (Campos do Jordão, São Paulo: Edição do Autor, 2019).

28. *Arcadismo* (Arcadism) was an eighteenth-century European literary movement whose poetry was characterized by bucolic themes and the use of Latin references.

29. *DFB*, "moleque," 486.

30. *DFB*, "iaiá-ioiô," 365.

31. Andrade, *Modinhas imperiais*, 34.

32. Tinhorão, *Pequena história*, 49.

33. Domingos Caldas Barbosa, *Viola de Lereno*, vol. 2 (Rio de Janeiro: INL, 1944), 36.

34. Barbosa, *Viola de Lereno*, vol. 2, 99–100.

35. Domingos Caldas Barbosa, *Viola de Lereno*, vol. 2 (Rio de Janeiro: INL, 1944), 32–36. However, someone like Araújo, who is an authority on the subject, does not hesitate to consider "Doçura de amor" a *lundu* in affirming that "Caprice pour le pianoforte sur un londú brésilien" by Sigismund Neukomm might have that song as a source. Mozart de Araújo, *Rapsódia brasileira* (Fortaleza: Universidade Estadual do Ceará, 1994), 144.

36. Gérard Béhague, "Biblioteca da Ajuda (Lisbon) Mss. 1595/1596: Two Eighteenth-Century Anonymous Collections of Modinhas," *Anuário do Instituto Interamericano de Pesquisa Musical* 4 (1968), 44–81. *Modinhas do Brazil* were published, with an introductory study, by Edilson de Lima in *As Modinhas do Brasil* (São Paulo: EDUSP, 2001).

37. "Massa" is my translation of the word *nhonhô*. However, I also use the same term as the translation for variants of the term: *ioiô* and *sinhô*. This is despite the fact that there are subtle differences among them in tone, playfulness, and even frequency in popular parlance. However, they are all built on the same term by which enslaved people were caricatured to refer to their *senhor* ("master," though also "sir") and, as such, can fit under the umbrella of "massa" in a way that resonates with an English-reading audience better than other translations such as "sir," "mister," and "master."—Trans.

38. Béhague, "Biblioteca da Ajuda," 58, note 23; *Aurélio (Novo dicionário Aurélio da língua portuguesa)*, "sinhá," 1316.

39. Béhague, "Biblioteca da Ajuda," 54.

40. Béhague, "Biblioteca da Ajuda," 63.

41. Béhague, "Biblioteca da Ajuda," 59, 62, 68.

42. My translation of the title in the preceding paragraph is different from Béhague's. I opted for the preposition "in" because I believe it allows more effectively for the kind of ambiguity suggested in the original Portuguese *pela*, which is important to Sandroni's analysis. After all, it gives us Béhague's more geographic understanding of the term (i.e., "in" a place) while also permitting it to work (though admittedly much less fluidly) with Tinhorão's stylistic interpretation (i.e., "in" a style).—Trans.

43. Tinhorão, *Os sons dos negros*, 60.

44. Béhague, "Biblioteca da Ajuda," 62.

45. Béhague, "Biblioteca da Ajuda," 63.

46. Cited by Tinhorão, *Pequena história*, 68–69.

47. References to the techniques of *rasgado* and *ponteado* in Brazil are traceable to the

seventeenth century, where they can be found in a poem by Gregório de Matos (cited in *DMB*, "ponto," 407).

48. Joaquim José da França Júnior, *Folhetins* (Rio de Janeiro: Jacintho Ribeiro dos Santos, 1926), 447.

49. The metaphor implied by the use of the verb *rasgar* (to tear) refers to the hand gesture, which strikes the strings more aggressively than in the case of the *ponteado*—as if it were really going to tear them. But the same metaphor is employed for the word "syncopation," which, according to the respective entry in the *Dictionnaire de musique* by Riemann, in the French edition under the direction of André Schaeffner, comes from the Greek word for "lacerate," "tear." Hugo Riemann, *Dictionnaire de musique* (Paris: Payot, 1931).

50. This meaning should, however, be taken with caution, for while the term *rasgado* is associated with Afro-Brazilians since at least the nineteenth century, we cannot be sure that this was also the case in eighteenth-century Portugal.

51. On Leal, see Ary Vasconcelos *Raízes da música popular brasileira (1500–1889)* (São Paulo: Martins; Brasília: INL, 1977), 83–84. The second *lundu* mentioned in this source appears under the name "Esta noite, oh céus, que dita" ("Tonight, Oh Heavens, What Luck").

52. *Canjica* might be described as a hardened corn porridge, though much less firm than corn bread.—Trans.

53. *Vatapá* is an Afro-Brazilian dish (or perhaps more accurately, an Afro-Bahian dish) often associated with the Candomblé religion. It consists of a paste of *manioc* (or flour) that is seasoned with shrimp, palm oil, ginger, cashews, and other spices.—Trans.

54. Although the word *quindim* (plural: *quindins*) may today be known throughout Brazil as the name of a very popular dessert, it originally meant "particular and characteristic movements, typical grace of a girl or young woman" (*DFB*, "quindim," 641). The word appears with precisely this meaning in another *lundu* of the collection edited by Doderer: "Minha Lilia quem desfruta teus quindins e teus miminhos etc" ("My Lilia Who Enjoys Your *Quindins* and Your Cuddles, etc." Gérard Doderer, *Modinhas luso-brasileiras* (Lisbon: Fundação Calouste Gulbenkian, 1984), 9.

55. Andrade, "Cândido Inácio da Silva," 31–32.

56. Andrade, "Cândido Inácio da Silva," 32–33.

57. Andrade, "Cândido Inácio da Silva," 37.

58. Andrade, "Cândido Inácio da Silva," 37.

59. Andrade, "Cândido Inácio da Silva," 27–28.

60. Andrade, "Cândido Inácio da Silva," 31.

61. Andrade, "Cândido Inácio da Silva," 29 and 31.

62. *Aurélio (Novo dicionário)*, "brasileirismo," 283.

63. Andrade, "Cândido Inácio da Silva," 31.

64. While it is probably evident from the context, it is worth making clear that the use of the term "mixed race" here and throughout the text should be understood specifically as biracial or a Black (African)-white (European) "mix."—Trans.

65. Arvellos Filho was of mixed race, as is recounted by a German traveler cited by Vasconcelos, *Raízes da música popular brasileira*, 162. Garcia was the son of Father José Mau-

rício, one of the most important figures of nineteenth-century Brazilian music, and also of mixed race, as is well known.

66. The idea that the bourgeois *lundu* is a "marked *modinha*" is also demonstrated, as I see it, in the fact that the word *modinha* never completely lost the generic usage it had in the eighteenth century, even sometimes encompassing *lundus*. As such, many "collections of modinhas" were published that included some *lundus*. This practice reached Mário de Andrade, who included a *lundu* in his collection *Modinhas imperiais*.

67. Dating these is no easy task. Very few of them carry the printing date, and most do not even have a printing plate number. To reach an approximate date, the main source employed was the excellent encyclopedia entry written by Mercedes Reis Pequeno for the *EMB*, "Impressão musical no Brasil" ("Printed Music in Brazil"). Here we have a list of the main music publishers working in Rio de Janeiro in the nineteenth century, with the dates they were in operation, whether they operated independently or as part of multi-publisher associations, and when they were at a given address. As such, just as sheet music covers tended to include the name and address of the publication firm, it is possible to estimate the period within which each *lundu* was published. Other useful sources for dating some of the *lundus* were Vasconcelos, *Raízes da música popular brasileira*, and for the *lundus* sung in vaudeville revue shows, the "Cronologia" (Chronology) at the end of Roberto Ruiz, *Teatro de revista no Brasil* (Rio de Janeiro: INACEN, 1988).

68. This is a reference to the famous book of poetry *Marília de Dirceu*, by Tomás António Gonzaga. Given the book's continued popularity, Marília would thus be, to this day, the most famous Brazilian poetic muse.—Trans.

69. Cited by Araújo, *A modinha e o lundu*, 115–117.

70. "Sou Democrata" here is a play on words: it means being part of the Clube dos Democráticos, one of the main Carioca Carnival groups, and at the same time it alludes, as part of a seduction strategy, to the *democracia amorosa* (amorous democracy) in which white men and mixed-race women would fraternize during the reign of Momo (that is, during the Carnival period).

Chapter 2. *Maxixe* and Its Antecedents

1. The Mangue Canal (or Canal do Mangue) was a specific area of Rio de Janeiro: "Starting right to the west of the Rocio Pequeno (later renamed Praça Onze de Junho), the canal extended for around 1,200 yards parallel to Aterrado Street, allowing for the elimination of the Sentinela Lake and the São Diogo swamps." Bruno Carvalho, *Porous City: A Cultural History of Rio de Janeiro (from the 1810s Onward)* (Liverpool: Liverpool University Press, 2013), 28.—Trans.

2. Cited by Jota Efegê, *Maxixe, a dança excomungada* (Rio de Janeiro: Conquista, 1974), 23.

3. In a 1926 article included in Mário de Andrade, *Música, doce música* (São Paulo: Martins, 1976), 128.

4. Efegê, *Maxixe, a dança excomungada*, 23.

5. Efegê, *Maxixe, a dança excomungada,* 26.

6. Efegê, *Maxixe, a dança excomungada,* 27.

7. Melo Morais Filho, cited by Eneida de Moraes, *História do Carnaval carioca* (Rio de Janeiro: Civilização Brasileira, 1958), 48.

8. At the time, tango in Brazil was nothing like modern Argentine tango. Mention of this genre in the context of Lima Barreto's short story is significant, and we will return to the subject.

9. In *Antologia do carnaval,* ed. Wilson Louzada (Rio de Janeiro: O Cruzeiro, 1945), 123.

10. Andrade, *Música, doce música,* 128.

11. The idea that balls at Carnival clubs had dancing of a particular style that was inappropriate for young women has already been noted by Tinhorão. He cites a novel published in 1894 that contains the description of a bourgeois ball, whose waltzes and polkas are danced with frenzy by the ladies but dismissed by the actresses, "who, regarding the balls, only appreciated those of Carnival, at the Fenianos and Democráticos." José Ramos Tinhorão, *A música popular no romance brasileiro* (Belo Horizonte: Oficina de Livros, 1992), 163.

12. Frederico-José de Sant'Anna Néry, *Folk-lore brésilien* (Paris: Perrin et Cie., 1889), 76.

13. Cited by José Ramos Tinhorão, *Música popular de índios, negros e mestiços* (Petrópolis: Vozes, 1972), 128–145.

14. Regarding the reception of *maxixe* in Europe, see, in addition to Jota Efegê's book, the article by Enrique Camara Landa, "Escandalos y condenas: La recepción del tango en Itália," presentation given at the II Encontro de Etnomusicólogos Íbero-Americanos, Barcelona (1995), 7 and elsewhere. Sheet music of many *maxixes* published in France around 1910 is found in the Bibliothèque Nationale de France in Paris.

15. I thank Ananya Jahanara Kabir and Francesca Negro for their input regarding the translation of these terms. I have borrowed the term "closed-hold couples" for intertwined couple (*par enlaçado*) from Ananya Jahanara Kabir (e-mail, 2019), who further characterizes what Sandroni here calls "separated couples" (*par separado*) as a type of "open-hold group dance" (and hence my use of "open-hold couples"), given that the couples subordinate to the larger group of participants. For a helpful analysis of Caribbean quadrille couples dances that are tied to this topic, see Ananya Jahanara Kabir, "Creolization as Balancing Act in the Transoceanic Quadrille: Choreogenesis, Incorporation, Memory, Market," *Atlantic Studies* 17, no. 1 (2020), 135–157.—Trans.

16. Carlos Vega, *Danzas y canciones argentinas* (Buenos Aires: Ricordi, 1936), 82–86.

17. Cited by José Ramos Tinhorão, *A música popular no romance brasileiro* (Belo Horizonte: Oficina de Livros, 1992), 164.

18. Tinhorão, *A música popular no romance brasileiro,* 196.

19. *Figuradas,* as Carlos Sandroni explained to me, are dances such as the square dance, which have group choreographies (*figuras*). As such, they are most typically different from dances such as waltz or polka, in which each couple dances independently of the other couples.—Trans.

20. Machado de Assis, *Philosopher or Dog?,* trans. Clotilde Wilson (New York: Noonday Press, 1954), 100. The citations in this paragraph are taken from this English translation of *Quincas Borba.* Although the names are Anglicized in the translation as Maria Benedicta

and Sophia, I have maintained the Portuguese spellings (Maria Benedita and Sofia) here. Sandroni's original citation, however, was not Machado de Assis, but rather Tinhorão, *A música popular no romance brasileiro*, 158.–Trans.

21. Assis, *Philosopher or Dog?*, 92.

22. Assis, *Philosopher or Dog?*, 113.

23. It may be worth noting that *batuque* here means something different from the *batuque* we see crop up throughout this book. Here it designates this specific dance practiced in the interior of São Paulo. It is different, therefore, from the nineteenth-century examples in which *batuque* is the term outsiders use to refer generically to Afro-Brazilian musical practices.—Trans.

24. Rossini Tavares de Lima, *Da conceituação do lundu* (São Paulo: n.p., 1953), 4.

25. Cited in *Brasil, 1° tempo modernista—1917–29*, ed. Marta Rosseti Batista (São Paulo: IEB, 1972), 337.

26. Thomas Lindley, *Narrative of a Voyage to Brazil* (London: J. Johnson, St. Paul's Church-Yard, 1805), 277.

27. According to Efegê, *Maxixe, a dança excomungada*, 26.

28. Mário de Andrade, "Cândido Inácio da Silva e o lundu," *RBM* 10 (1944), 39.

29. Cited by Efegê, *Maxixe, a dança excomungada*, 159.

30. Efegê, *Maxixe, a dança excomungada*, 117.

31. Efegê, *Maxixe, a dança excomungada*, 121.

32. Efegê, *Maxixe, a dança excomungada*, 31.

33. The use of the terms *requebrar* and *quebrar* appears, like certain dance verbs in English (such as "jump," "shuffle," "shake"), to have been born specifically out of Black contexts. Even today, the terms seem to suggest at least some relation (however implicit) to Black music/dance.—Trans.

34. The title is translated literally, but it betrays the double entendre of the word "mallard," which here refers to both the bird and a woman's genitalia.—Trans.

35. Cited by Ary Vasconcelos, *Raízes da música popular brasileira (1500–1889)* (São Paulo: Martins; Brasília: INL, 1977), 109.

36. *Cateretê* is a Brazilian folk dance said to be of Amerindian origin.—Trans.

37. I suggest the reader turn to the best study of Brazilian *fado*, José Ramos Tinhorão, *Fado, dança do Brasil, cantar de Lisboa* (Lisbon: Caminho, 1994).

38. José Ramos Tinhorão, *Pequena história da música popular* (São Paulo: Art, 1991), 67.

39. Cited by Lima, *Da conceituação do lundu*, 6.

40. Cited by Francisco Augusto Pereira da Costa, *Folclore pernambucano* (Rio de Janeiro: Revista do Instituto Histórico, 1908), 209.

41. *Cronistas* were writers and journalists who chronicled daily life in what were known as *crônicas*, which were, according to Amy Chazkel, "a hybrid form of expression halfway between literature and journalism. In their approach to writing about the city, the authors of these *crônicas* [the *cronistas*] belong equally to the cults of mystery, fact-finding, and reporting." Amy Chazkel, "The Crônica, the City, and the Invention of the Underworld: Rio de Janeiro, 1889–1922," *Estudios Interdisciplinarios de América Latina y el Caribe* 12, no. 1 (2014), 79.—Trans.

42. The term *crioulo* is not quite a cognate of what in English is called "creole," which has a number of very specific meanings (usually relating to mixture in one way or another). The meaning here, derived from the Spanish *criollo*, referring mainly to people or animals born in the New World, is a person of African descent who was born in Brazil rather than in Africa. On the history of the term "creole," see Philip Baker and Peter Mühlhäusler, "Creole Linguistics from Its Beginnings, through Schuchardt to the Present Day," in *Creolization: History, Ethnography, Theory*, ed. Charles Stewart (Walnut Creek: Left Coast Press, 2007), 84–107.—Trans.

43. Luiz Heitor Corrêa de Azevedo, *150 anos de música no Brasil* (Rio de Janeiro: José Olympio, 1956), 147.

44. Unlike in other South American countries, the waltz never became a popular dance in Brazil, where popular trends instead favored binary rhythms. The Brazilian popular waltz is always unchoreographed and is usually a slow song with romantic lyrics, as with the classic "Rosa," by Pixinguinha, or more recently "Valsa brasileira" ("Brazilian Waltz"), by Chico Buarque and Edu Lobo, the latter of these suggesting, by way of its title, that it is indeed a characteristically Brazilian waltz. Regarding the fact that the waltz, as a dance, was never able to free itself from a certain aristocratism in Brazil (contrary to the polka), see Tinhorão, *A música popular no romance brasileiro*, 156 and later.

45. Alejo Carpentier, *Music in Cuba*, trans. Alan West-Durán (Minneapolis: University of Minnesota Press, 2001), 146.

46. Joaquim José da França Júnior, *Folhetins* (Rio de Janeiro: Jacintho Ribeiro dos Santos, 1926), 31–38.

47. José Ramos Tinhorão, *Os sons dos negros no Brasil* (São Paulo: Art, 1988), 62 and 67.

48. The term *pianeiro* was created by Basílio Itiberê to designate early twentieth-century popular music pianists in Rio.

49. My pluralizing of this and other like terms follows the Portuguese standard, as I am using the original Portuguese terminology, in which the first term (the noun) in the hyphenated word (in this case, *polca*) is the one that is modified to make it plural. Thus we have *polcas-lundu* rather than *polca-lundus*, as might be expected in English.—Trans.

50. Vicenzo Cernicchiaro, *Storia della musica nel Brasile* (Milano: Fratelli Riccioni, 1926), 523.

51. França Júnior, *Folhetins*, 37. One may also see in this title a link to the Bahian "Samba da chave" ("Keys Samba"), described by Oneyda Alvarenga, *Música popular brasileira* (São Paulo: Duas Cidades, 1982), 152; and Edison Carneiro, *Folguedos tradicionais* (Rio de Janeiro: Conquista, 1974), 62.

52. The titles of the Brazilian polkas appeared to have been interested in exhausting all of the possibilities of a given pattern, not unlike the myth groups studied by Lévi-Strauss, *Le cru et le cuit* (Paris: Plon, 1964), 338–339 and throughout. The series inaugurated by "Capenga," for example, would bring about "Dentuça não fecha a boca" ("The Bucktoothed Does Not Close Her Mouth"), "Barrigudo não dança" ("The Pot-Bellied Do Not Dance"), "Careca não vai à missa" ("The Bald Do Not Go to Mass"), and "Corcunda não perfila" ("The Hunchbacked Do Not Profile"), and it might have continued were it not prudently stopped by "Lamúrias do capenga e do careca" ("Grumblings of the Lame and the Bald"). Not all paradigms, however, were so fertile, as we can see in the trio "Como se morre" ("As

One Dies"), "Como se vive" ("As One Lives"), and "Como se pula" ("As One Dances"), or in the magnificent conciseness of the duo "Moro longe" ("I Live Far Away") and "Mude-se para perto" ("Move Close").

53. Tinhorão, *Pequena história*, 71.

54. Joaquim Maria Machado de Assis, *A Chapter of Hats: Selected Stories* (London: Bloomsbury, 2014), 207–220.

55. Machado de Assis, *Chapter of Hats*, 208.

56. As has already been noted, the imperial period dates from 1822 until 1889.—Trans.

57. In the song title the verb is conjugated as *bula* (which is the imperative tense), but indeed the infinitive of the verb is *bulir*.—Trans.

58. There are clear sexual overtones for the term *balaio*, here a reference to a woman's behind.—Trans.

59. Machado de Assis, *Chapter of Hats*, 212–213.

60. Indeed, I located in the archives of the BNRJ a reference to a polka called "Ai! Candongas" ("Oh, Darlings") by a certain M.S.

61. José de Alencar, *Til* (Rio de Janeiro: Ediouro, 1980), 128.

62. Augusto Meyer, *Cancioneiro gaúcho* (Porto Alegre: Globo, 1952), 17. A "*balaio*" samba appears also in Carneiro, *Folguedos tradicionais*, 62. Both authors suggest sexual overtones for the image of the *balaio*.

63. Júlio Ribeiro, *A carne* (Rio de Janeiro: Ediouro, [1992?]), 128.

64. Andrade, *Música, doce música*, 126.

65. Carlos Vega, "Las especies homónimas y afines de 'Los orígenes del tango argentino,'" *Revista musical chilena* 101 (1967), 51.

66. Vicente Gesualdo, *Historia de la música en la Argentina*, vol. 3 (Buenos Aires: Beta, 1961), 903 and subsequent pages.

67. Cited by Vega, "Las especies homónimas," 51.

68. Efegê, *Maxixe, a dança excomungada*, 22.

69. The original term here is *jogo*, which I have translated as "game" because it best describes the elasticity of *jogo* in the context of *capoeira*. After all, a game can be quite serious (as at a Las Vegas poker table), quite important (as in a professional sporting event), or quite playful (as in a board game), while also possibly being all these things at once. Indeed, the *jogo* in *capoeira* is often described as a martial art/sport/game, but the fact is "game" itself is a term that is sufficiently ambiguous to encapsulate the competitive activity. Also, it is worth noting that today a person who practices *capoeira* is no longer known as a *capoeira* but rather as a *capoeirista*.—Trans.

70. *DFB*, "capoeira," 181–182.

71. Tinhorão, *Pequena história*, 208–209.

72. Until the nineteenth century, *batuque* was a generic designation for any African or African-descended dance in Brazil. The term will be discussed more in depth later.

73. There is no good English translation here that does not involve an explanation. The term *gaúcho* might be translated as "gaucho" (understood as a sort of cowboy), but it also means someone or something from the southern state of Rio Grande do Sul. The term *corta jaca* is explained by Sandroni in the text.—Trans.

74. *EMB*, "corta-jaca," 204.

75. Brasílio Itiberê, "Ernesto Nazaré na música brasileira," *Boletim latino americano de música* 6, no. 1 (1946), 310.

76. Andrade, *Música, doce música*, 124. Nonetheless Andrade, on the following page, ends up agreeing with Nazareth's nomenclature, a move not adopted by the rest of the writers, as we will see.

77. Renato de Almeida, *História da música brasileira* (Rio de Janeiro: F. Briguiet, 1942), 61.

78. Azevedo, *150 anos*, 51.

79. Eurico Nogueira França, "Le noir dans la musique brésilienne," in *La contribuition de l'Afrique à la civilization brésilienne* (Ministério das Relações Exteriores, n.d.), 81.

80. Efegê, *Maxixe, a dança excomungada*, 28.

81. Efegê, *Maxixe, a dança excomungada*, 36.

82. Baptista Siqueira, *Ernesto Nazaré na música brasileira* (Rio de Janeiro: Aurora, 1967), 76.

83. Cited by Efegê, *Maxixe, a dança excomungada*, 22.

84. Maria Tereza Mello Soares, *São Ismael do Estácio* (Rio de Janeiro: Funarte, 1985), 80.

85. Alvarenga, *Música popular brasileira*, 24 and 336.

86. Andrade, *Música, doce música*, 319.

87. Tinhorão, *Pequena história*, 102.

88. This is the date of one such *tango brasileiro*, noted by *EMB*, "apêndices," 1129.

89. Efegê, *Maxixe, a dança excomungada*, 108.

90. Efegê, *Maxixe, a dança excomungada*, 112.

91. Efegê, *Maxixe, a dança excomungada*, 72–74.

92. Efegê, *Maxixe, a dança excomungada*, 28.

93. Efegê, *Maxixe, a dança excomungada*, 89.

94. Andrade, *Música, doce música*, 321.

95. Cited by Antonio Adriano Blanc Nascimento, "A influência da habanera nos tangos de Ernesto Nazareth" (master's thesis, São Paulo, ECA-USP, 1990), 56–57.

96. Luciano Gallet, *Estudos de folclore* (Rio de Janeiro: Carlos Wehrs, 1934), 22–23.

97. *Araúna* is a type of bird, known in English as giant cowbird (*Molothrus oryzivorus*).—Trans.

98. José Ramos Tinhorão, *Música popular, teatro e cinema* (Petrópolis: Vozes, 1972), 16.

99. *DMB*, "tango," 510.

100. Tinhorão, *Pequena história*, 69.

101. Tinhorão, *Pequena história*, 69.

102. Manuel Antonio de Almeida, *Memoires of a Militia Sergeant*, trans. Ronald W. Sousa (New York: Oxford University Press, 1999), 27.

103. In the words of Alvarenga, *Música popular brasileira*, 344.

Chapter 3. From Bahia to Rio

1. The main exception is the Argentine *zamba*. But its name indicates its association with the earlier Peruvian *zamacueca*, whose possible Black origins are even aired by the Argentine

musicologist Carlos Vega, whom no one would accuse of having Africanizing tendencies. Vega, *Danzas y canciones argentinas* (Buenos Aires: Ricordi, 1936), 107–146.

2. I am not entirely sure of my translation of this Spanish. However, as Sandroni explained to me, the engraving's caption offers a clarifying point: "a dance of congos, possibly that called 'de la culebra' [of the snake]." And the corresponding image shows the couple dancing as if imitating a snake.—Trans.

3. Argeliers León, *Del canto y el tiempo* (Havana: Letras Cubanas, 1984), 69.

4. Vicente Rossi, *Cosas de negros* (Buenos Aires: Hachette, 1958), 117. Rossi idiosyncratically writes "samba," for the correct spelling in Spanish is "zamba." In the Río de La Plata region, however, both are pronounced in the same way.

5. Cited by Janheinz Jahn, *Muntu: African Culture and the Western World* (New York: Grove Press, 1961), 84.

6. "Napolitanos usurpadores / Que todo oficio quitan al pobre / Ya no hay negros botelleros / Ni tampoco changador . . . / Porque esos napolitanos / Hasta pasteleros son . . . / Dentro de poco / Jesus, por Diós! / Bailarán *cemba* en el tambor!" Published in *El carnaval porteño*, Buenos Aires, February 1876, and cited by Vicente Gesualdo, *Historia de la música en la Argentina*, vol. 3 (Buenos Aires: Beta, 1961), 869.

7. *EMB*, "umbigada," 683.

8. A good summary of the accounts of these travelers concerning the subject is in Edison Carneiro, *Folguedos tradicionais* (Rio de Janeiro: Conquista, 1974), 28–31.

9. Gerhard Kubik, "Drum Patterns in the 'Batuque' of Benedito Caxias," *Latin American Music Review* 11, no. 2 (1990), 161.

10. Aires da Mata Machado Filho, *O negro e o garimpo em Minas Gerais* (Belo Horizonte: Itatiaia; São Paulo: EdUSP, 1985), 140.

11. Especially by Marília T. Barboza da Silva and Arthur L. de Oliveira Filho, *Cartola—os tempos idos* (Rio de Janeiro: Funarte, 1989), 43–44; and by Dominique Dreyfus, who kindly allowed me access to her unpublished research on the topic.

12. Arguably, all of these instruments have reasonably comprehensible English-language translations: *pandeiro* = tambourine; *prato e faca* = plate and knife; *viola* = ten-string guitar (five double courses). However, their specificity in the context of Brazilian music makes translating them seem almost silly. After all, a "tambourine" would never evoke, in the general English reader's mind, the amazing distinction and ingenuity of what the *pandeiro* is in the Brazilian context. Not to mention that "tambourine" is far too easily confused with *tamborim* (a small frame drum). And translating *prato e faca* as "plate and knife" seems to banalize it, taking away its symbolic power as a legitimate and quite common musical instrument in the Brazilian context. As for *viola*, cognate for the Spanish *vihuela*, it is often translated as "guitar," which seems a terrible disservice (even though leaving it as *viola* does seem to lend itself to confusion with the European bowed concert "viola"). After all, though not unrelated, the guitar is indeed a different instrument from the *viola*; the instruments are different not just organologically but also symbolically. Judging by twenty-first-century ethnographic accounts, for instance, the *viola* is viewed as distinct from the guitar in terms of symbolic power, technical mastery, and musical function. Furthermore, historical accounts such as those cited in this book regularly reference the *viola* (not the guitar), and thus consistency in this regard is

important. More to the point, one might say that the difference between *viola* and "guitar" aligns nicely with the difference between "folk" and "popular" samba, which makes blurring their differences misleading. On some of these points, see Cássio Nobre, "Samba de viola machete: Considerações sobre tradição e transformação no samba de roda do Recôncavo Baiano," in *Diversidade cultural afro-brasileira: Ensaios e reflexões,* ed. Carlos Alves Moura (Brasília: Fundação Cultural Palmares, 2013), 29–44; Ralph C. Waddey, "'Viola de Samba' and 'Samba de Viola' in the 'Reconcavo' of Bahia (Brazil)," *Latin American Music Review* 1, no. 2 (1980), 196–212; and Waddey, "'Viola de Samba' and 'Samba de Viola' in the 'Reconcavo' of Bahia (Brazil) Part II," *Latin American Music Review* 2, no. 2 (1981), 252–279.—Trans.

13. In an essay with this exact title, "Samba-de-umbigada," reprinted in Carneiro, *Folgue-dos tradicionais,* 27–57.

14. Luís dos Santos Vilhena, *A Bahia no século XVIII,* cited by José Ramos Tinhorão, *Música popular de índios, negros e mestiços* (Petrópolis: Vozes, 1972), 122.

15. Which is also evident in *DFB,* "batuque," 105.

16. It is worth noting that recently Josias Pires Neto has found earlier mentions of the term "samba," one from 1830 and another from 1831. Josias Pires Neto, "Música e dança afro-atlânticas: (Ca)lundus, batuques e sambas—permanências e atualizações" (PhD diss., Universidade Federal da Bahia, 2020), 28, 214–216, 223–225, and elsewhere.

17. José Ramos Tinhorão, *Os sons dos negros no Brasil* (São Paulo: Art, 1988), 70.

18. Here I have left the titles of the Gioachino Rossini operas untranslated, spelling them as in the newspaper cited by Sandroni. This is because there is an inconsistency in the way the newspaper treats the titles. Specifically, in one case it seems to be translated (from *La gazza ladra* to *Gaza-ladra*), whereas in another it is simply wrong. The correct title of the Rossini opera based on Voltaire's eighteenth-century tragedy *Sémiramis* is in fact *Semiramide* rather than "Semiramis," as it says here in the original Portuguese-language newspaper. Finally, *Tancredi* is indeed the title of Rossini's opera.

19. Tinhorão, *Os sons dos negros,* 70–72.

20. The term *tatamba* means generally a primitive or brute person, or someone who speaks poorly.—Trans.

21. Throughout this work, the term "Amerindian" refers to indigenous people of the Americas.—Trans.

22. Tinhorão, *Os sons dos negros,* 73.

23. On *fado* dance in nineteenth-century Rio de Janeiro, see José Ramos Tinhorão, *Fado, dança do Brasil, cantar de Lisboa* (Lisbon: Caminho, 1994).

24. Joaquim José da França Júnior, *Folhetins* (Rio de Janeiro: Jacintho Ribeiro dos Santos, 1926), 207.

25. Cited by Tinhorão, *Fado, dança do Brasil, cantar de Lisboa,* 55.

26. França Júnior, *Folhetins,* 443 and 446.

27. Cited by Baptista Siqueira, *Origem do termo "samba"* (São Paulo: IBDC, 1978), 132.

28. Though the spellings are different (in Romero it is *xiba* while in Mello it is *chiba*), in Brazilian Portuguese, the pronunciation of the two is identical.—Trans.

29. Guilherme Teodoro Pereira de Mello, *A música no Brasil* (Salvador: Tipografia São Joaquim, 1908), 31–32.

30. Júlio Ribeiro, *Flesh*, trans. William Barne (London: Modern Humanities Research Association, 2011), 56.

31. The original term here was not "servant" but rather *agregado*, which, as Richard Graham explains, was a social type "commonly to be found in the sugar zone of the north-east as well as in the coffee regions of Rio de Janeiro and São Paulo. An *agregado* depended upon someone else, especially for housing or at least a space in which to live. He or she could be a family member, even a respected parent, sister, or brother who lacked an independent source of income; more often, however, the *agregado* was a poverty-stricken agricultural worker, or single mother, sometimes a freed slave, to whom the landowner granted the right to raise subsistence crops on some outlying patch of the large estate. In exchange, the *agregado* proffered occasional services, but especially loyalty." Richard Graham, "1850–1870," in *Brazil: Empire and Republic*, ed. Leslie Bethell (Cambridge: Cambridge University Press, 1989), 126–127.—Trans.

32. José de Alencar, *Til* (Rio de Janeiro: Ediouro, 1980), 128.

33. Alencar, *Til*, 127.

34. Ribeiro, *Flesh*, 56.

35. Literally "cut the jackfruit," but here it is a reference to the samba dance step described by Sandroni in chapter 2.—Trans.

36. In 1901 Chiquinha Gonzaga wrote an already mentioned tango, which was extremely successful, whose title, "Corta-Jaca," makes reference to what is, according to the *EMB*, one of the "three basic steps" of Bahian samba (p. 684).

37. Jota Efegê, *Maxixe, a dança excomungada* (Rio de Janeiro: Conquista, 1974), 161.

38. The term *candomblé* (with a lowercase *c*) here refers not to the religion specifically (which I have translated as "Candomblé," uppercase *C*) but rather to the gatherings of those who practice the religion (including their celebrations), though in historical sources the term can also refer to their places of worship.—Trans.

39. Cited by Raymundo Nina Rodrigues, *Os Africanos no Brasil* (São Paulo: Companhia Editora Nacional, 1945), 255–256.

40. Rodrigues, *Os Africanos*, 255–256.

41. Luís de Camões, *Os Lusíadas* (*The Lusiads*), trans. Richard Francis Burton (London: Tinsley Brothers, 1880), 6. All words but *fado* in this citation come from the famed sixteenth-century epic poem. Here I use Burton's nineteenth-century translation, published during roughly the same period as the announcement Sandroni gives us.—Trans.

42. Cited by Siqueira, *Origem do termo "samba,"* 104. Jota Efegê also mentions the subject in *Figuras e coisas da música popular*, vol. 1 (Rio de Janeiro: Funarte, 1978), 171.

43. Cited by Tinhorão, *Música popular de índios*, 195.

44. Aluísio Azevedo, *The Slum*, trans. David H. Rosenthal (Oxford: Oxford University Press, 2000).

45. The word *chorado* designates a dance that, in the description of *O cortiço* and others (for example, *DFB*, "chorado," 207–208), fits perfectly within the concept of *samba de umbigada*.

46. Her name here indicates her place of origin: Bahia. (Here, though, I have spelled it as in the Portuguese-language book.) This is, of course, quite significant to Sandroni's argument and the move of "samba" from Bahia to Rio.—Trans.

47. A *tirana*, according to the *EMB* (p. 752), is a dance from Spain, which is said to have arrived in Brazil in the late eighteenth century. Guilherme de Mello says that it represents the Hispanic component of the "three popular types of Brazilian musical art"—the other two would be *lundu* (African) and *modinha* (Portuguese). Mello, *A música no Brasil*, 29.

48. Azevedo, *The Slum*, 21–30.

49. Alencar, *Til*, 129.

50. Alencar, *Til*, 129.

51. Alencar, *Til*, 128.

52. Azevedo, *The Slum*, 60.

53. Azevedo, *The Slum*, 61.

54. Sambadromes (or *sambódromos*) are the arenas used today for samba schools to process during Carnival.—Trans.

55. The reader will have noted that the word *fado*, as it appears here, unlike when we last saw it just a few pages earlier, refers to typical Portuguese song. In the time between the publication of *Memórias de um sargento de milícias* (1854), cited earlier, and *O cortiço* (1890), cited here, the meaning of the word would have changed completely for the Brazilian reader.

56. Azevedo, *The Slum*, 36–37.

57. Azevedo, *The Slum*, 40.

58. Azevedo, *The Slum*, 42.

59. In this case, I have overridden the published English-language translation (which somewhat inexplicably uses the N-word in place of the term *mulato*) and substituted for it the word used in the original Portuguese-language text, whose racial connotation—and its linked cultural baggage—is clearly distinct. In this case, using the original is far more accurate.—Trans.

60. Here, too, the original Portuguese is different enough to receive my intervention. In the English-language translation, *viola* (from the original Portuguese) was rendered "guitar." However, in the context of the current book, as already mentioned in an earlier note, this is not a neutral substitution, and as such it seemed necessary to correct.—Trans.

61. Azevedo, *The Slum*, 28.

62. Here I have adjusted the published English translation, which writes Rita's name "Bahiana." I choose instead to use "Baiana" to reflect its spelling in the original Portuguese.–Trans.

63. Azevedo, *The Slum*, 51.

64. Azevedo, *The Slum*, 174.

65. Oneyda Alvarenga, *Música popular brasileira* (São Paulo: Duas Cidades, 1982), 151–152.

66. Luciano Gallet, *Estudos de folclore* (Rio de Janeiro: Carlos Wehrs, 1934), 61.

67. Arthur Ramos, *Folclore negro no Brasil* (Rio de Janeiro: Civilização Brasileira, 1935), 138. Implicit in Ramos's phrase is the attribution of a generic value to *maxixe*, too. The idea finds support in Mário de Andrade, "Originalidade do maxixe," *Ilustração musical* 1, no. 2 (1930), 45, and in Gallet, cited by Ramos, *Folclore negro*, 143.

68. Alvarenga, *Música popular brasileira*, 152.

69. It is worth reminding the reader that the term "popular" here and generally in the book retains the Portuguese-language (and in this case specifically Brazilian) meaning as

described by Sandroni in the Introduction to the English Translation. Indeed, one of the primary distinctions ever-present in this book is between "popular" and "folk." We see it here explicated with wonderful clarity as it relates to samba.—Trans.

70. Marília T. Barboza da Silva and Arthur L. de Oliveira Filho, *Cartola—os tempos idos* (Rio de Janeiro: Funarte, 1989), 45.

71. Mário de Andrade, "Introdução" to Gallet, *Estudos de folclore,* 17.

72. *EMB,* "samba," 683–685; *DFB,* "samba," 675–677.

73. An excellent study of the ideological implications of this is in Hermano Vianna, *The Mystery of Samba: Popular Music and National Identity in Brazil,* trans. John Charles Chasteen (Chapel Hill: University of North Carolina Press, 1999).

74. As in a report by Sérgio Cabral, published in the magazine *Realidade* in August 1967, titled "Então nasceu o samba" ("And So Samba Was Born"), which commemorated the fiftieth anniversary of "Pelo telefone." It is also this author, undoubtedly one of the greatest authorities on Carioca samba, who elsewhere writes that "samba was born and raised in downtown Rio de Janeiro." Preface to Hermano Vianna, *O mistério do samba* (Rio de Janeiro: Jorge Zahar/Universidade Federal do Rio de Janeiro, 1995), 11. Another indisputable authority on the topic, Ary Vasconcelos, published in 1958 a story titled "O samba nasceu na Praça Onze" ("Samba Was Born at Praça Onze") cited in J. Muniz Jr., *Do batuque à escola de samba* (São Paulo: Símbolo, 1976), 36.

75. "Morro" is a reference to the hillsides from which samba is often said to have come. See Sandroni's description of the Carioca *morros* in chapters 4 and 9.—Trans.

76. In Muniz Sodré, *Samba, o dono do corpo* (Rio de Janeiro: Codecri, 1979), 51.

77. The Campanha de Defesa do Folclore Brasileiro was the first permanent governmental organ dedicated to Brazilian folklore. It was founded in the late 1950s.—Trans.

78. While the literal translation of the song title is "Watercolor of Brazil," the traditional translation of the song in English—as it appears, for instance, in Walt Disney's *Saludos Amigos* (released in the United States in 1943)—is simply "Brazil."—Trans.

79. A *cerrado* is a vast tropical savanna found mostly in the plateaus of Brazil's central region.—Trans.

80. As described by Suzel Ana Reily, "*Congados*—or *congos*—are drum-based music and dance ensembles that typically perform during festivals in honor of Our Lady of the Rosary, Saint Benedict the Black, and other popular Catholic saints. *Congados* are common in many small Brazilian towns, particularly in the southeastern regions of the country." Reily, "To Remember Captivity: The 'Congados' of Southern Minas Gerais," *Latin American Music Review* 22, no. 1 (2001), 4–5.—Trans.

Chapter 4. From the Dining Room to the Drawing Room

Throughout this chapter, I use the term "drawing room" as the translation for what Sandroni (and the sources he cites) calls *sala de visitas.* A "drawing room" is a formal room for receiving guests and entertaining, not unlike what English-speakers today might call a "living room."—Trans.

1. The most important study on this topic was conducted by Roberto Moura, *Tia Ciata e a pequena África no Rio de Janeiro* (Rio de Janeiro: Funarte, 1983).

2. Without getting into the complexities of Brazilian kinship relations, I will say only that "aunts" is perhaps not the best translation here, for these *tias* were not so called only by blood relations. The term *tia*, certainly in Bahia even in the twenty-first century, tends to be used by people to refer to women who are elders and with whom a certain intimacy is felt without regard for whether or not the person is an actual relative. It is in some ways thus an honorific (as if to say "miss"), but its use suggests far more intimacy (more even than some might want) than the more common honorific *dona*. Perhaps the way in which English speakers use "auntie" may be similar to the way in which *tia* is best understood, recognizing, however, that "auntie" has its own Brazilian version as *titia*.—Trans.

3. Donga and João da Baiana long outlived the other Carioca samba pioneers, and in the 1960s, together with Pixinguinha (Alfredo da Rocha Vianna Jr., 1898–1973), began to be revered as the founding fathers of samba. The accounts they gave to the Museu da Imagem e do Som (Museum of Image and Sound) were made into a book that I will cite repeatedly: *As vozes desassombradas do museu.*

4. Henrique Foréis Domingues Almirante, *No tempo de Noel Rosa* (Rio de Janeiro: Francisco Alves, 1963), 17.

5. José Ramos Tinhorão, *Música popular, teatro e cinema* (Petrópolis: Vozes, 1972), 116.

6. Antonio Barroso Fernandes, ed., *As vozes desassombradas do museu, 1: Pixinguinha, Donga, João da Baiana* (Rio de Janeiro, MIS, 1970), 51–52.

7. Fernandes, *As vozes desassombradas*, 74.

8. Oneyda Alvarenga, *Música popular brasileira* (São Paulo: Duas Cidades, 1982), 152.

9. *DFB*, "função," 334.

10. *DFB*, "pagode," 553.

11. Edison Carneiro, *Folguedos tradicionais* (Rio de Janeiro: Conquista, 1974), 64.

12. The use of the word "samba" to mean a party long outlived the context noted here, as is shown in the recurrence of the expression *ir ao samba* (go to the samba). It appears in the 1930s in a famous composition that asked "Com que roupa / Eu vou / Ao samba que você me convidou" (With what clothes / Will I go / To the samba you invited me to), and again, more recently, in the Paulinho da Viola composition that says "Eu vou ao samba / Porque longe dele não posso viver" (I'm going to the samba / Because I can't live being away from it).

13. Vagalume (Francisco Guimarães), *Na roda do samba* (Rio de Janeiro: Funarte, 1978), 80, 85, 86, and 87.

14. This was the institution's name for most of the nineteenth century, though its name has been changed a handful of times over the course of its long life (founded in 1808, it is the oldest school of medicine in Brazil). Today it is officially the Faculdade de Medicina da Bahia da Universidade Federal da Bahia.—Trans.

15. *Orixás*, also written in English as Orishas, are the African-derived deities (brought by enslaved Africans to Brazil from Yoruba-speaking areas of West Africa) that are the primary gods venerated in the Nagô/Ketu nation of the Candomblé religion (also called, in Cuban *Regla de Ocha, Orichás*).—Trans.

16. Account cited in Moura, *Tia Ciata*, 97.

17. The *baiana* is a figure used in Carnival processions even today. Because this is the name of the figure, I have left it in Portuguese (and thus with a lowercase *b*, as it is not an adjective describing a person's origin, which I translate here as "Bahian" with an uppercase *B* and an *h*, to indicate the state (Bahia) of provenance.—Trans.

18. The information about Ciata is in Moura, *Tia Ciata*, 96–106.

19. Moura, *Tia Ciata*, 161–163.

20. Cited by Moura, *Tia Ciata*, 160.

21. Moura, *Tia Ciata*, 158.

22. Moura, *Tia Ciata*, 83.

23. Fernandes, *As vozes desassombradas*, 85.

24. Fernandes, *As vozes desassombradas*, 77.

25. For a relevant English-language source on the topic, see Tamara Elena Livingston-Isenhour and Thomas George Caracas Garcia, *Choro: A Social History of a Brazilian Popular Music* (Bloomington: Indiana University Press, 2005).

26. The term *batucada* will receive another connotation starting in the 1930s. For a good description of the term's meaning as a game of skill, see Marília T. Barboza da Silva and Arthur L. de Oliveira Filho, *Cartola—os tempos idos* (Rio de Janeiro: Funarte, 1989), 32–36. We will discuss the topic again later in dealing with the theme of the *malandro* lifestyle.

27. Nei Lopes, *O negro no Rio de Janeiro e sua tradição musical* (Rio de Janeiro: Pallas, 1992), 47–51.

28. Lopes, *O negro no Rio de Janeiro*, 51; *EMB*, "samba," definition no. 10; "samba-de-partido-alto," 685.

29. Ralph C. Waddey, "'Viola de Samba' and 'Samba de Viola' in the 'Reconcavo' of Bahia (Brazil) Part II: 'Samba de Viola,'" *Latin American Music Review* 2, no. 2 (1981), 252–279; Lopes, *O negro no Rio de Janeiro*.

30. Lopes, *O negro no Rio de Janeiro*, 51.

31. Interview with Muniz Sodré, *Samba, o dono do corpo* (Rio de Janeiro: Codecri, 1979), 51.

32. Carneiro, *Folguedos tradicionais*, 50.

33. Jeffrey D. Needell, *A Tropical* Belle Epoque: *Elite Culture and Society in Turn-of-the-Century Rio de Janeiro* (Cambridge: Cambridge University Press, 1987), 150–151.

34. For example, on page 48: "*Carnaval*, after all, with its *entrudo* and *cordões*, partly expressed a whole Afro-Brazilian culture of which the Europhile elite were ashamed." And on page 165: "The explicit models for the Ouvidor [a street in Downtown Rio frequented by the elite] were the streets for fashionable concourse in Paris or London. . . . What could be, was brought over intact and implanted proudly, in edged contrast to the rest of the old port city and its largely Afro-Brazilian population."

35. As Sodré writes in *Samba*, 20.

36. The term *cabrocha* has two general meanings, one that is broader, being any mixed-race person, while the more specific meaning is a woman (especially mixed race) who samba dances. These are slightly different though only in specificity, not general tone, from the definition found in the Waddey citation Sandroni gives us later on, which is of a "slave mistress."—Trans.

37. Cited by J. Muniz Jr., *Do batuque à escola de samba* (São Paulo: Símbolo, 1976), 28. According to the *EMB*, page 1101, this is a samba from 1932.

38. The use of the terms *iaiá* and *ioiô*, versions of *sinhá* and *sinhô*, respectively, is explained by Sandroni in chapter 1.—Trans.

39. Vagalume, *Na roda do samba*, 78.

40. Although Vagalume does not mention the expression *partido-alto* in the excerpt I cited here, it appears countless times in his book as a synonym for traditional samba (for example, page 93).

41. Waddey, "'Viola de Samba' Part II," 262.

42. Cited by José Ramos Tinhorão, *Pequena história da música popular* (São Paulo: Art, 1991), 307.

43. Which ends up being the same thing, both under the prism of architecture (from the front to the back) and under that of the social structure (from the formal to the intimate).

44. Waddey, "'Viola de Samba' Part II," 259.

45. Waddey, "'Viola de Samba' Part II," 252.

46. I am aware that the expression *samba-corrido* has been given a number of differing definitions: for example, Alvarenga, *Música popular brasileira*, 152; Lopes, *O negro no Rio de Janeiro*, 51; and João da Baiana's account in Fernandes, *Vozes desassombradas do museu*, 55. But Waddey's definition has, in my opinion, the best ethnographic support. Moreover, it is in step with the use of the expression *corrido* as I have observed it used countless times by *capoeira* practitioners.

47. Moura, *Tia Ciata*, 148 and 161.

48. Carneiro, "Samba de roda," in *Folguedos tradicionais*, 59–64; Waddey, "'Viola de Samba' Part II."

49. Regarding the religious links Tia Ciata and her Bahian friends had, see Moura, *Tia Ciata*, 93 and 98; and Fernandes, *As vozes desassombradas*, 63. Regarding the festive associations called *ranchos*, which in Bahia were celebrated on Kings Day, and in Rio are transferred to Carnival, see Moura, *Tia Ciata*, 88. Regarding the maintenance in Rio of Afro-Bahian cuisine, see Moura, *Tia Ciata*, 103–104.

50. Moura, *Tia Ciata*, 100.

51. Cited in *EMB*, "miudinho," 491.

52. Moura, *Tia Ciata*, 148.

53. Cited by Muniz Jr., *Do batuque*, 27.

54. Interview with Sodré, *Samba*, 51.

55. Waddey, "'Viola de Samba' Part II," 254.

56. In Fernandes, *As vozes desassombradas*, 53.

57. The expression *samba duro* as a synonym of *batucada* also appears in Lopes, *O negro no Rio de Janeiro*, 135 and 138; and in Marília T. Barboza da Silva and Arthur L. de Oliveira Filho, *Cartola—os tempos idos* (Rio de Janeiro: Funarte, 1989), 32.

58. A reconstruction of the floor plan of Tia Ciata's home is in Moura, *Tia Ciata*, 102.

59. Arthur Ramos, *Folclore negro no Brasil* (Rio de Janeiro: Civilização Brasileira, 1935), 274–275.

60. Preface to Hermano Vianna, *O mistério do samba* (Rio de Janeiro: Jorge Zahar/Universidade Federal do Rio de Janeiro, 1995), 11.

61. Silva and Oliveira Filho, *Cartola*, 46.

62. Fernandes, *As vozes desassombradas*, 63.

63. João Máximo and Carlos Didier, *Noel Rosa—uma biografia* (Brasília: UnB, 1990), 357.

64. Hermano Vianna, *The Mystery of Samba: Popular Music and National Identity in Brazil*, trans. John Charles Chasteen (Chapel Hill: University of North Carolina Press, 1999), 17–31.

65. Vianna, *Mystery of Samba*, 15.

66. For an important furthering of the discussion on this topic, see Marc A. Hertzman, *Making Samba: A New History of Race and Music in Brazil* (Durham, NC: Duke University Press, 2013), especially chapter 2, "Beyond the Punishment Paradigm," 31–65.

67. Cited by Lopes, *O negro no Rio de Janeiro*, 16.

68. Moura, *Tia Ciata*, 101 and 146.

69. In citing examples that support Vianna's thesis, I chose ones that differ from those he used in the hope of enriching the discussion.

70. Vagalume, *Na roda do samba*, 53.

71. Guilherme Teodoro Pereira de Mello, *A música no Brasil* (Salvador: Tipografia São Joaquim, 1908), 15.

72. Vagalume, *Na roda do samba*, 87.

73. Cited by Raymundo Nina Rodrigues, *Os Africanos no Brasil* (São Paulo: Companhia Editora Nacional, 1945), 379 and 382.

74. *Xangô* was, like the word *candomblé*, both the name of the religion as well as the temple. In this case, it is left with a lowercase *x* because it designates the groups/temples. *Xangô* is what Candomblé in Recife was typically called (at least in academic literature) during the first half of the twentieth century. Today the term seems to be used increasingly less.—Trans.

75. Letter from Luís Saia to Mário de Andrade, February 16, 1938. Original documents of the Missão de Pesquisas Folclóricas, Discoteca Pública Municipal de São Paulo. Cited in Carlos Sandroni, *Mário contra Macunaíma* (São Paulo: Vértice, 1988), 125.

76. These are the respective capitals of Pernambuco, Paraíba, and Rio Grande do Norte, located in Brazil's Northeast.—Trans.

77. Mário de Andrade, *Danças dramáticas do Brasil*, vol. 1 (Belo Horizonte: Itatiaia; Brasília: INL, 1982), 70. *Maracatus, cabocolinhos*, and *bois* are not, of course, Afro-Brazilian religions but rather traditional cultural expressions of the Northeast of Brazil, subjected to the same types of restrictions as were noted for the Afro-Brazilian religions cited earlier.

78. Otávio Ianni, "O samba de terreiro em Itu," *Revista de história* 26 (1956), 403–426.

79. In this case, I have adjusted the original translation. In John Chasteen's translation of Vianna's work, the term is left as "Bahianos," a confounding Anglicizing of the Portuguese *baianos*. In order to avoid confusion, though, I have changed this to conform to the term I use throughout the book: "Bahians."—Trans.

80. Vianna, *Mystery of Samba*, 112.

81. Alvarenga, *Música popular brasileira*, 152.

82. Mário de Andrade, *Música, doce música* (São Paulo: Martins, 1976), 323.

83. Cited by Lopes, *O negro no Rio de Janeiro*, 1, in an epigraph to a chapter titled "Da África à Praça Onze" ("From Africa to Praça Onze").

84. In Rita Cáurio, ed., *Brasil musical* (Rio de Janeiro: Art Bureau, 1988), 34.

85. Flávio Silva, "'Pelo telefone' e a história do samba," *Revista Cultura* 8, no. 28 (1978), 72.

86. Vianna, *Mystery of Samba*, 15.

87. Vianna, *Mystery of Samba*, 80.

88. Vianna, *Mystery of Samba*, 16.

89. Fernandes, *As vozes desassombradas*, 95.

90. Regarding Guinle's support of Villa-Lobos, see Gérard Béhague, *Heitor Villa-Lobos: The Search for Brazil's Musical Soul* (Austin: Institute of Latin American Studies, 1994), 10, 16, and 82. Regarding his support of the Oito Batutas, see Fernandes, *As vozes desassombradas*, 88–90.

Chapter 5. "Pelo telefone"

1. Flávio Silva, "Origines de la samba urbaine à Rio de Janeiro," vol. 1 (master's thesis, Paris: École Pratique des Hautes Études, 1975), 235.

2. Cited by Henrique Foréis Domingues Almirante, *No tempo de Noel Rosa* (Rio de Janeiro: Francisco Alves, 1963), 22.

3. Silva, "Origines de la samba urbaine," vol. 2, 304.

4. The discovery of Almeida's letters is one of the many contributions of Silva's work, and it is from here that the citation was extracted: Silva, "Origines de la samba urbaine," vol. 2, 270–271. The complete text of the letters is reproduced by Silva himself in "'Pelo telefone' e a história do samba," *Revista cultura* 8, no. 28 (1978), 70.

5. Cited by Flávio Silva, "1917—questão social e carnaval," *Informativo Funarte* (1983).

6. Antonio Barroso Fernandes, ed., *As vozes desassombradas do museu, 1: Pixinguinha, Donga, João da Baiana* (Rio de Janeiro: MIS, 1970), 80.

7. Silva, "Origines de la samba urbaine," vol. 2, 247–252.

8. Silva, "Origines de la samba urbaine," vol. 2, 334.

9. Michel Foucault, "Qu'est-ce qu'un auteur?" *Bulletin de la Société Française de Philosophie* 63 (1969), 83.

10. João Máximo and Carlos Didier, *Noel Rosa—uma biografia* (Brasília: UnB, 1990), 206.

11. Vagalume, *Na roda do samba* (Rio de Janeiro: Funarte, 1978), 30–32.

12. Casa Edison was founded by Frederico (Fred) Figner in 1900. It would later go on to make the first Brazilian sound recording, in 1902.—Trans.

13. In Fernandes, *As vozes desassombradas*, 83, he said that the recorded version is the original. The other would be "a parody made for the report in the newspaper *A Noite*." But to Ary Vasconcelos and to Sérgio Cabral, he claimed that the anonymous version preceded it and that the recording was a self-censored version (see Silva, "Origines de la samba urbaine," vol. 2, 302–303).

14. Silva, "Origines de la samba urbaine," vol. 2, 296.

15. Reproduced in Almirante, *No tempo de Noel Rosa*, 19–20.

16. According to Flávio Silva, the first telephone lines were installed in Rio de Janeiro in 1877; in 1915 the city was said to have 11,181 lines. Silva, "Origines de la samba urbaine à Rio de Janeiro," vol. 2 (master's thesis, Paris: École Pratique des Hautes Études, 1975), 298.

17. Silva, "Origines de la samba urbaine," vol. 2, 297.

18. Manuel Antonio de Almeida, *Memoires of a Militia Sergeant*, trans. Ronald W. Sousa (New York: Oxford University Press, 1999), 149.

19. Gérard Doderer, *Modinhas luso-brasileiras* (Lisbon: Fundação Calouste Gulbenkian, 1984), 19. I will return to this *lundu* later.

20. Silva, "Origines de la samba urbaine," vol. 1, 182.

21. I am inspired, clearly, by Sigmund Freud, *Totem and Taboo* (Mineola, NY: Dover Publications, 2018), and by René Girard, *Violence and the Sacred* (Baltimore: Johns Hopkins University Press, 1977).

22. The correct date was established by Jota Efegê in a newspaper article published in 1972; prior to this the dominant version, adopted by Donga and Almirante, was that the roulette wheel had been installed by the newspaper only in 1916, just before the success of the samba song. See Silva, "Origines de la samba urbaine," vol. 2, 299.

23. In colloquial Portuguese, it is quite common for people to use the verb "to have" in the place of "to be/exist." For example, instead of "there is a building on the corner" (*há um prédio na esquina*), it is quite common to hear/say "there has a building on the corner" (*tem um prédio na esquina*). In fact, and this goes to Sandroni's point, it is far more common for people to use "to have" (*ter*) than "to be/exist" (*haver*).—Trans.

24. The bird here is, in Portuguese, *rolinha*, which is a type of dove (*Uropelia campestris*).—Trans.

25. Sandroni offers an explanation of the term *cordão* in chapter 6.—Trans.

26. Silva has already shown this coexistence, but I believe his demonstration can be improved. This is what I attempt to do here.

27. Because of the melody, the word *mágoas* is here pronounced like *maguás*.

28. The rhyming here is of "as" and "az," which can be pronounced in a number of different ways, depending on the regional accent. In any given accent, however, the "as" and "az" sound would always be pronounced in essentially the same way.—Trans.

29. Here there is no translation of the lyrics because the rhyme scheme is the primary focus. As such, I have not crowbarred in some sort of rhyming English-language translation. Doing so would not only be entirely artificial, it would also be useless, for Sandroni's argument refers to the way in which the rhymes play out in Portuguese.—Trans.

30. Nei Lopes's *partido-alto* research is full of examples constructed like this. For instance, see the seven quatrains cited in *O negro no Rio de Janeiro e sua tradição musical* (Rio de Janeiro: Pallas, 1992), 93.

31. Silva, "Origines de la samba urbaine," vol. 2, p. 319.

32. Mário de Andrade, *As melodias do boi e outras peças* (São Paulo: Duas Cidades, 1987), 231.

33. Almirante, *No tempo de Noel Rosa*, 16.

34. Vagalume, *Na roda do samba*, 115–116.

35. Silva, "Origines de la samba urbaine," vol. 2, pp. 326–327.

36. The "syllabic inversion" mentioned here by Sandroni is the flipping of *doce* to *sindô*. Indeed, it is worth noting that in Brazilian Portuguese, *doce* would be pronounced as *doh-see*, and thus flipping it would give us *see-doh*.—Trans.

37. Lopes, *O negro no Rio de Janeiro*, 98.

38. The original term here, *"gozar,"* is (at least to twenty-first-century ears) a thinly veiled double entendre suggesting both having fun and sexual climax. It is uncertain whether this double entendre would have been as salient a century ago, though it is entirely possible, especially if we remember the tradition of wordplay in the *lundus* Sandroni discussed earlier.—Trans.

39. Muniz Sodré, *Samba, o dono do corpo* (Rio de Janeiro: Codecri, 1979), 6 and 34–35.

40. For this observation, we are indebted to Silva, "Origines de la samba urbaine," vol. 2, 320.

41. Silva, "Origines de la samba urbaine," vol. 1, 119.

42. Lopes, *O negro no Rio de Janeiro*, 95; here he cites the *DFB*, "desafio," 275.

43. Vagalume, *Na roda do samba*, 223–224.

44. Such as "Barracão é seu" ("The Shack Is Yours") (João da Gente-Clementina de Jesus, 1966) and "Quatro crioulos" ("Four *Crioulos*") (Elton Medeiros, 1965).

45. The actions of the celebrant during Rio's Carnival are defined by the verb *brincar* ("to play," though translated elsewhere in the chapter, for the reader's ease, as "to celebrate"). One need only think of the old march sung during every Carnival, which says "Este ano não vai ser igual àquele que passou / Eu não *brinquei*, você também não *brincou* . . . / Este ano, meu bem, tá combinado / Nós vamos *brincar* separados" (This year won't be like last / I didn't *play* [*celebrate*], you didn't *play* [*celebrate*] either . . . / This year, my love, it's agreed / We're going to *play* [*celebrate*] apart).

Chapter 6. When Did Samba Become Samba?

1. João Máximo and Carlos Didier, *Noel Rosa—uma biografia* (Brasília: UnB, 1990), 138.

2. Máximo and Didier, *Noel Rosa*, 118.

3. Marília T. Barboza da Silva and Arthur L. de Oliveira Filho, *Cartola—os tempos idos* (Rio de Janeiro: Funarte, 1989), 46–47. The cited samba is called "Velho Estácio" ("Old Estácio"), and its full lyrics are transcribed on page 178 of their book.

4. Antônio Candeia Filho and Isnard Araújo, *Escola de samba—árvore que esqueceu a raiz* (Rio de Janeiro: Lidador, 1978), 57.

5. Sérgio Cabral, *As escolas de samba* (Rio de Janeiro: Fontana, 1974), 21.

6. Mentioned here are *samba de breque* (break samba), *samba-canção* (melodic samba), *samba-enredo* (story line samba), and *samba-exaltação* (samba of proudness), among others (*EMB*, 684–685).

7. Hermano Vianna, *The Mystery of Samba: Popular Music and National Identity in Brazil*, trans. John Charles Chasteen (Chapel Hill: University of North Carolina Press, 1999), 89.

8. Cabral, *As escolas de samba*, 21–22. The excerpt has become a classic, as it is cited by, among others, Maria Tereza Mello Soares, *São Ismael do Estácio* (Rio de Janeiro: Funarte, 1985), 94; Cláudia Matos, *Acertei no milhar: Samba e malandragem no tempo de Getúlio* (Rio de Janeiro: Paz e Terra, 1982), 40; José Ramos Tinhorão, *História social da música popular brasileira* (Lisbon: Caminho, 1990), 232; Roberto Moura, *Tia Ciata e a pequena África no Rio de Janeiro* (Rio de Janeiro: Funarte, 1983), 123–124; and Rita Cáurio, ed., *Brasil musical* (Rio de Janeiro: Art Bureau, 1988), 129.

9. Máximo and Didier, *Noel Rosa*, 118 and 138.

10. Mário de Andrade, *Música de feitiçaria no Brasil* (Belo Horizonte: Itatiaia; Brasília: INL, 1983), 154.

11. Silva and Oliveira Filho, *Cartola*, 45.

12. Oneyda Alvarenga, *Música popular brasileira* (São Paulo: Duas Cidades, 1982), 343.

13. Flávio Silva, "Origines de la samba urbaine à Rio de Janeiro," vol. 2 (master's thesis, Paris: École Pratique des Hautes Études, 1975), 348.

14. In Antonio Barroso Fernandes, ed., *As vozes desassombradas do museu, 1: Pixinguinha, Donga, João da Baiana* (Rio de Janeiro: MIS, 1970), 80.

15. This converts the title of a Caetano Veloso song, "Desde que o samba é samba" ("Since Samba Became Samba"), into a question.

16. My own experience with popular musicians today who perform the older repertoire suggests that they tend to make the same distinction. For example, Luís Otávio Braga's guitar method book says the following: "notable are the maxixes by composer J.B. da Silva (Sinhô), among them the well-known 'Jura.'" Luís Otávio Braga, *O violão brasileiro* (Rio de Janeiro: Escola de Música Brasileira, 1988), 81.

17. Reproduced in Vagalume, *Na roda do samba* (Rio de Janeiro: Funarte, 1978), 241–242.

18. *EMB*, "Barbosa, Orestes," 71.

19. Vagalume, *Na roda do samba*, 31 and 129.

20. Vagalume, *Na roda do samba*, 32.

21. Vagalume, *Na roda do samba*, 42.

22. Vagalume, *Na roda do samba*, 131.

23. Vagalume, *Na roda do samba*, 101–102.

24. Vagalume, *Na roda do samba*, 19.

25. Vagalume, *Na roda do samba*, 30–31.

26. This refers to a popular Brazilian saying about how progeny are like their progenitors: "the child of a fish is a little fish" (*o filho de peixe, peixinho é*), which is not unlike the English-language saying, "the apple doesn't fall far from the tree."—Trans.

27. The sense here is that if samba and *malandragem* had a child together, it would be Caninha.—Trans.

28. Vagalume, *Na roda do samba*, 92–96.

29. Martins Castello, preface to Orestes Barbosa, *Samba* (Rio de Janeiro: Funarte, 1978), 9.

30. Vagalume, *Na roda do samba*, 134.

31. Barbosa, *Samba*, 20.

32. Barbosa, *Samba*, 36.

33. Barbosa, *Samba*, 11.

34. Vagalume, *Na roda do samba*, 23 and 27.

35. Barbosa, *Samba*, 61, 63, 64, 65, 81, 93, and 96.

36. *Malandro* appears only three times (pp. 156 and 217) and *malandragem*, twice (pp. 42 and 93).

37. Interview with Cabral, *As escolas de samba*, 28.

38. Máximo and Didier, *Noel Rosa*, 118.

39. Máximo and Didier, *Noel Rosa*, 117.

40. See the entries on "cuíca" in *DMB*, 166–167; and in *DFB*, 256–257.

41. Claude Lévi-Strauss, *La pensée sauvage* (Paris: Plon, 1962), 30.

42. Silva and Oliveira Filho, *Cartola*, 46.

43. Regarding Donga's music theory limitations, see Soares, *São Ismael do Estácio*, 79. On Sinhô's limitations, see Ary Vasconcelos, *A nova música da República Velha* (self-published, Rio de Janeiro, 1985), 196 and 197–198.

44. Interviewed by Nei Lopes in *O negro no Rio de Janeiro e sua tradição musical* (Rio de Janeiro: Pallas, 1992), 105.

45. The original Portuguese phrase here is "por essa luz que está me alimiando [*sic*]," which is about the light (of God) that illuminates.—Trans.

46. Vagalume, *Na roda do samba*, 77.

47. Fernandes, *As vozes desassombradas*, 20.

48. Tinhorão, *História social*, 229.

49. Cabral, *As escolas de samba*, 28.

50. Cabral, *As escolas de samba*, 92.

Chapter 7. Of Birds and Commodities

1. Eneida de Moraes, *História do Carnaval carioca* (Rio de Janeiro: Civilização Brasileira, 1958), 122; this work was my principal source of information on *blocos, cordões,* and *ranchos*.

2. See, for example, João Máximo and Carlos Didier, *Noel Rosa—uma biografia* (Brasília: UnB, 1990), 125.

3. Maria Tereza Mello Soares, *São Ismael do Estácio* (Rio de Janeiro: Funarte, 1985), 50.

4. Máximo e Didier, *Noel Rosa*, 95.

5. "Vadico" was the nickname of pianist and composer Oswaldo Gogliano (1910–1962).

6. The original lyrics here are "pendure essa despesa no cabide ali em frente" (hang this charge on the rack at the front), which is a reference to the "hanging" of a check. It referred either figuratively or literally to the hanging (with a nail) of the unpaid check somewhere within the establishment.—Trans.

7. The full lyrics of "Conversa de botequim" are transcribed in Máximo and Didier, *Noel Rosa*, 398–399; the references to the *escritórios* (offices) of Ismael Silva are in Soares, *São Ismael do Estácio*, photographic supplements, iii and iv.

8. Antonio Barroso Fernandes, ed., *As vozes desassombradas do museu, 1: Pixinguinha, Donga, João da Baiana* (Rio de Janeiro: MIS, 1970), 31.

9. Vagalume, *Na roda do samba* (Rio de Janeiro: Funarte, 1978), 85.

10. Máximo and Didier, *Noel Rosa*, 410–411.

11. Later we will discuss in detail the importance of the creation of the "second part" in samba's transformations.

12. The *baiana*, as Sandroni briefly mentions later on, is a costumed figure representing the old Bahian *tias*, wearing the traditional Afro-Bahian clothing (especially the clothing associated with Candomblé temples). See chapter 4, note 17.—Trans.

13. Máximo and Didier, *Noel Rosa*, 411.

14. There are at least three terms that Sandroni uses interchangeably for "refrain": *refrão,*

estribilho, and *coro.* The last of these, most literally translated as "chorus," explicates well Sandroni's point that refrains were sung by groups (in opposition to the improvised verses, sung by soloists).—Trans.

15. See Maria Laura Viveiros de Castro Cavalcanti, *Carnaval carioca: Dos bastidores ao desfile* (Rio de Janeiro: Editora da Universidade Federal do Rio de Janeiro, 1994), 198–201.

16. Máximo and Didier, *Noel Rosa,* 293–294; and also 290–291.

17. The original phrase here is *roer coirana,* which Sandroni explains in the Brazilian edition of his book, citing *Aurélio,* as a popular expression to "show oneself to be jealous or displeased." For my part, rather than translate the idiomatic phrase, which translates literally as "to grind coirana" (a type of Brazilian plant [*cestrum*]), I have simply used English that reflects the meaning of the phrase.—Trans.

18. Vagalume, *Na roda do samba,* 79–80.

19. *EMB,* "sinhô," 720.

20. For example, Mário de Andrade, *Os cocos* (São Paulo: Duas Cidades, 1984), 387; Oneyda Alvarenga, "Introdução" to Mário de Andrade, *As melodias do boi e outras peças* (São Paulo: Duas Cidades, 1987), 27. The use of *coletar* (translated here as "harvested") seems not unlike the metaphor "collect," which is used in English when people speak about documenting folk songs (i.e., "collecting folk songs").

21. Cited by Máximo and Didier, *Noel Rosa,* 357.

22. In an earlier section, I translated *cigano* as Roma, which is indeed the correct translation. In this case, however, given the historical context of this citation, the "correct" translation seemed to me to be the term "gypsy," which has more recently become widely recognized as an English-language pejorative for the Romani people.—Trans.

23. In Antonio Barroso Fernandes, ed., *As vozes desassombradas do museu, 1: Pixinguinha, Donga, João da Baiana* (Rio de Janeiro: MIS, 1970), 28–29. The presence of Roma in turn-of-the-century sambas has been noted but not satisfactorily studied. It accentuates the composite character of Carioca samba. See the article by Ary Vasconcelos, "Tem cigano no samba," *Piracema* 1, no. 1 (1993), 105–109; and that of Samuel Araújo and Antônio Guerreiro, "O samba cigano: Um estudo histórico-etnográfico das práticas de música e dança dos ciganos *calom* do Rio de Janeiro," in *Música popular en América Latina,* atas do II Congresso Latino Americano da IASPM, ed. Rodrigo Torres (Santiago, Chile, 1999), 233–239. The work of the latter authors is a more ambitious study of the topic.

24. Manuel Bandeira, "Duas crônicas e meia," *Revista USP* 4 (1990), 77–78.

25. *Seu* is a colloquial honorific term for men. It is similar to "Mr./Mister" and "Sir." —Trans.

26. The literal translation here is something close to "I like it because I'm tangled up." However, this is a much more idiomatic phrase that has to do with finding something humorous (but with a touch of irony).—Trans.

27. Cited by Muniz Sodré, *Samba, o dono do corpo* (Rio de Janeiro: Codecri, 1979), 70.

28. Marília T. Barboza da Silva and Arthur L. de Oliveira Filho, *Cartola—os tempos idos* (Rio de Janeiro: Funarte, 1989), 60.

29. Also cited by Sodré, *Samba,* 70; and Ary Vasconcelos, *A nova música da República Velha* (self-published, Rio de Janeiro, 1985), 202.

30. Cited by Soares, *São Ismael do Estácio*, 84.

31. The neologism *comprositor* combines *comprar* (to buy) with *compositor* (composer). After some discussion with Sandroni about what an English version of this term might be, one option emerged: "sambuyers"—combining samba makers (something like, samba-ers) and samba buyers. Indeed, since the object of interest here is "samba," this might be a close equivalent (at least as far as the *feel* goes).—Trans.

32. Sérgio Cabral, *As escolas de samba* (Rio de Janeiro: Fontana, 1974), 29, 31, and 32.

33. Cabral, *As escolas de samba*, 90.

34. Cavalcanti, *Carnaval carioca*, 95.

35. I am thinking here of the concept of "mediation" as it has been developed by Antoine Hennion in his work on the sociology of music: *La passion musicale* (translated as *The Passion for Music: A Sociology of Mediation* [Farnham (UK): Ashgate, 2015]); see also Hennion's "Music and Mediation: Towards a New Sociology of Music," in *The Cultural Study of Music: A Critical Introduction*, ed. Martin Clayton, Trevor Herbert, and Richard Middleton (London: Routledge, 2003), 89–91.

36. For dating the sambas, I followed, except in specified cases, the *EMB*'s appendix "Registro de Músicas," 893–1159. But the date of 1974 attributed to "Cidade mulher" (which, moreover, is listed with a different title, "Guanabara") is a clear error. However, the correct date is reestablished by the very same reference work, in the text of the entry on "Paulo da Portela," 592–593.

37. I once attempted to explain Francisco Alves's role among the Estácio *sambistas* to a French friend, and he surprised me with the following commentary: "So, what he did is what music publishers today do: they make it possible for music to become well known and in exchange earn part of the authors' rights." If one adopts this point of view, it forces us to recognize that in this role, current publishers have nothing on Alves.

38. Vagalume, *Na roda do samba*, 31.

39. Silva and Oliveira Filho, *Cartola*, 49.

40. Suetônio Valença and Raquel Valença, *Serra, serrinha, serrano: O império do samba* (Rio de Janeiro: José Olympio, 1981), 14–15.

41. Máximo and Didier, *Noel Rosa*, 194.

42. Cited by Roberto Moura, *Tia Ciata e a pequena África no Rio de Janeiro* (Rio de Janeiro: Funarte, 1983), 152.

43. Vagalume, *Na roda do samba*, 131–132.

44. Sérgio Cabral, *ABC do Sérgio Cabral: Um desfile dos craques da MPB* (Rio de Janeiro: Codecri, 1979), 227–228.

45. Sodré, *Samba*, 34–35. I made some slight modifications to the terms employed by Sodré, correcting what may have been an unintended error in the original text.

46. Cláudia Matos offers a good analysis of the partnership as a "mode of production par excellence of popular samba." Matos, *Acertei no milhar: Samba e malandragem no tempo de Getúlio* (Rio de Janeiro: Paz e Terra, 1982), 75–76.

47. Máximo and Didier, *Noel Rosa*, 198.

48. Máximo and Didier, *Noel Rosa*, 203.

49. Máximo and Didier, *Noel Rosa*, 204.

50. Máximo and Didier, *Noel Rosa*, 256.

51. Máximo and Didier, *Noel Rosa*, 325.

52. Máximo and Didier, *Noel Rosa*, 258 and 411.

53. The use of the term "chateau" (a large French country house, mansion, or castle) is ironic. The listener knows that the "chateau" is in fact a shack.—Trans.

54. Máximo and Didier, *Noel Rosa*, 259.

55. Máximo and Didier, *Noel Rosa*, 275.

56. Máximo and Didier, *Noel Rosa*, 205.

57. Literally, the song's title would translate as "who gives more." However, the original meaning of the song title comes from a standard auctioneer's phrase, which in English generally is phrased as the auctioneer "hearing" a larger amount.—Trans.

58. Máximo and Didier, *Noel Rosa*, 167.

59. This expression is employed by Noel in an interview cited by Máximo and Didier, *Noel Rosa*, 198.

60. Valença and Valença, *Serra, serrinha, serrano*, 16.

61. Cabral, *As escolas de samba*, 250.

62. Antônio Candeia Filho and Isnard Araújo, *Escola de samba—árvore que esqueceu a raiz* (Rio de Janeiro: Lidador, 1978), 47.

63. Cabral, *ABC do Sérgio Cabral*, 14.

64. Máximo and Didier, *Noel Rosa*, 202.

65. Haroldo Costa, *Salgueiro, academia de samba* (Rio de Janeiro: Editora Record, 1984), 43.

Chapter 8. From *Malandro* to Composer

1. Galpi (Galdino Fernandes Pinheiro), *O flor*, cited by José Ramos Tinhorão, *A música popular no romance brasileiro* (Belo Horizonte: Oficina de Livros, 1992), 181.

2. See the discussion of *rasgado* in chapter 1.

3. J. M. Velho da Silva, *Gabriela, crônica dos tempos coloniais*, cited by Tinhorão, *A música popular no romance brasileiro*, 173.

4. I have made two substitutions to the language used in the published translation in order to make Sandroni's argument more evident. They are substitutions that in fact correct the English-language translation, as they are the terms used in the original Portuguese-language text. First, I have re-inserted *capadócios* in place of "miscreants." And second, I have replaced the term "guitar" with the correct "viola."—Trans.

5. Manuel Antonio de Almeida, *Memoires of a Militia Sergeant*, trans. Ronald W. Sousa (New York: Oxford University Press, 1999), 148–149.

6. João Máximo and Carlos Didier, *Noel Rosa—uma biografia* (Brasília: UnB, 1990), 249.

7. *EMB*, "Neves, Eduardo das," 532.

8. Cláudia Matos, *Acertei no milhar: Samba e malandragem no tempo de Getúlio* (Rio de Janeiro: Paz e Terra, 1982), 42.

9. Cited by Sérgio Cabral, *As escolas de samba* (Rio de Janeiro: Fontana, 1974), 66.

10. Matos, *Acertei no milhar*, 39.

11. Matos, *Acertei no milhar*, 77–78.

12. Regarding the last two of these, see Diana Iznaga, *Transculturación en Fernando Ortiz* (Havana: Editorial de Ciencias Sociales, 1989), 101–103.

13. The definition of *malandro* samba (*samba-malandro*) developed here differs a bit from that of Cláudia Matos, above all because the present work is focused on the initial phase, while her work is chiefly interested in the sambas of the 1940s.

14. The full lyrics are in Ary Vasconcelos, *A nova música da República Velha* (self-published, Rio de Janeiro, 1985), 212.

15. Vagalume, *Na roda do samba* (Rio de Janeiro: Funarte, 1978), 59–60.

16. *EMB*, "Bide," 95, indicates that the recording is from 1927. *DB-78 rpm* gives the release date as February 1928, posterior thus to the release of "Me faz carinhos," by Ismael Silva, released in January of the same year.

17. Interview of Heitor dos Prazeres published by Muniz Sodré, *Samba, o dono do corpo* (Rio de Janeiro: Codecri, 1979), 69. Also Vasconcelos, *A nova música*, 212.

18. The lyrics for both are transcribed in Máximo and Didier, *Noel Rosa*, 245. The data referring to the recordings of "Cassino maxixe" and "Gosto que me enrosco" are in Vasconcelos, *A nova música*, 226 and 228.

19. Interview with Sodré, *Samba*, 70.

20. Edigar de Alencar, *Nosso Sinhô do samba* (Rio de Janeiro: Funarte, 1981), 71.

21. *EMB*, in the appendixes, 992.

22. Though the term *orgia* in Portuguese can indeed carry the overtly sexual connotation that "orgy" does in English, it is important to note that in this particular context, it refers more broadly to an excess of euphoria, alcohol, lack of order, and so forth.—Trans.

23. Composed in 1927, according to *EMB* (p. 982), and Vasconcelos, *A nova música*, 213–214; the recording was released in 1928, according to *DB-78 rpm*, Odeon 10.096-A.

24. Cited in Alencar, *Nosso Sinhô do samba*, 43.

25. Edison Carneiro, cited by Luís da Câmara Cascudo, *DFB*, "pernada," 598–599.

26. For example, Marília T. Barboza da Silva and Arthur L. de Oliveira Filho, *Cartola—os tempos idos* (Rio de Janeiro: Funarte, 1989), 33–35.

27. Cabral, *As escolas de samba*, 35.

28. *DB-78 rpm*, Odeon 10.134-A.

29. As many readers may know, the word *favela* later became a generic term to refer to the low-income housing of the *morros*.

30. Antonio Barroso Fernandes, ed., *As vozes desassombradas do museu, 1: Pixinguinha, Donga, João da Baiana* (Rio de Janeiro: MIS, 1970), 63.

31. Fernandes, *As vozes desassombradas*, 63.

32. Matos, *Acertei no milhar*, 77. Moreira da Silva is one of the samba singers who most cultivated a *malandro* image.

33. Fernandes, *As vozes desassombradas*, 62; see also Marc A. Hertzman, *Making Samba: A New History of Race and Music in Brazil* (Durham, NC: Duke University Press, 2013), 32–36.

Chapter 9. A Respectable Spell

1. The complete lyrics are in João Máximo and Carlos Didier, *Noel Rosa—uma biografia* (Brasília: UnB, 1990), 291.

2. Clogs were inexpensive, popular footwear in 1930s Rio de Janeiro. In Batista's lyrics, the focus is on their association with the "shuffling" of the *malandros*, a type of body movement that was laid back and winding.

3. Although the citation does not mention a pocket, the original term here is *navalha*, which perhaps most accurately translates to "straight razor," which is a razor whose blade can fold into its handle, implying it is stowed in the pocket.—Trans.

4. Aluísio Azevedo, *The Slum*, trans. David H. Rosenthal (Oxford: Oxford University Press, 2000), 50–51 and 102.

5. In fact, David H. Rosenthal, the translator of *O cortiço* (*The Slum*), does not use either *capadócio* or *malandro*. Instead, he translates *capadócio* as "bully and braggart" (p. 50).—Trans.

6. Azevedo, *The Slum*, 50.

7. As for my translation of *samba-canção* as "samba songs," please see note 27 regarding the *samba-canção* in the context of this song.—Trans.

8. Azevedo, *The Slum*, 51 and 59.

9. "Feitiço da Vila" is the most recorded, to speak objectively. João Máximo and Carlos Didier count seventy-six recordings! The only Noel song to have been recorded more, according to the authors' exhaustive inventory, is "As pastorinhas" ("Little Shepherdesses"), which is not a samba but rather a *marcha-rancho*. João Máximo and Carlos Didier, *Noel Rosa—uma biografia* (Brasília: UnB, 1990), 497–516.

10. The complete lyrics are in Máximo and Didier, *Noel Rosa*, 329–330.

11. There are specific problems related to the translation into English of *feitiço*, not least of which are the term's implicit materiality and racialization. See the translator's foreword for an extended discussion.—Trans.

12. In fact, it is for this reason that "spell" seems an admittedly problematic translation. The word *feitiço* carries a materiality that the word "spell" does not. After all, as William Pietz famously pointed out in a trio of articles, the term itself, which becomes "fetish" in English, in the Middle Ages referred to anything from charms and amulets to spells and other magical practices. See the translator's foreword. Pietz, "The Problem of the Fetish, I," *RES: Anthropology and Aesthetics* 9, no. 1 (1985), 5–17; "The Problem of the Fetish, II: The Origin of the Fetish," *RES: Anthropology and Aesthetics* 13, no. 1 (1987), 23–45; "The Problem of the Fetish, IIIa," *RES: Anthropology and Aesthetics* 16, no. 1 (1988), 105–124.—Trans.

13. *Farofa* is one of the primary culinary items in Brazilian food. It consists of manioc flour (*farinha*) mixed with butter, garlic, oils, water, or any other combination of these and other items. *Farofa* also has a particular spiritual potency within the context of many Afro-Brazilian religions.—Trans.

14. Of course, I analyze this samba on its own terms, which are those of popular culture in 1930s Rio de Janeiro. Here is not the place to summarize the expansive historiographical debate regarding the true role of Princess Isabel, of the different segments of the white elite

(including enslavers and abolitionists), and of Africans and Afro-Brazilians (among whom were millions of enslaved people and an already significant number of freed and free-born Black people) in the broad movement that led from slavery to abolition in 1888. For an illuminating synthesis, I recommend Angela Alonso, "O abolicionismo como movimento social," *Novos estudos CEBRAP* 100 (2014), 115–137.

15. Máximo and Didier, *Noel Rosa*, 357.

16. See the short description of this area in chapter 2, note 1.—Trans.

17. The complete lyrics are in Máximo and Didier, *Noel Rosa*, 407.

18. In Ruy Castro, *O anjo pornográfico: A vida de Nelson Rodrigues* (São Paulo: Companhia das Letras, 1992), 118.

19. The complete lyrics of "Feitio de oração" are in Máximo and Didier, *Noel Rosa*, 267–268.

20. *New Grove*, "samba," vol. 16, 447–448; and "symphony," vol. 18, 438–467.

21. Máximo and Didier, *Noel Rosa*, 39.

22. Máximo and Didier, *Noel Rosa*, 165.

23. Máximo and Didier, *Noel Rosa*, 357.

24. Máximo and Didier, *Noel Rosa*, 246.

25. E. E. Evans-Pritchard, *Witchcraft, Oracles and Magic among the Azande* (Oxford: Clarendon Press, 1990).

26. Dated by Máximo and Didier. *EMB* indicates 1938, though Rosa died in 1937. The lyrics are given by Máximo and Didier, *Noel Rosa*, 292.

27. Cláudia Matos postulates that this is a reference to the subgenre of *samba-canção*. Matos, *Acertei no milhar: Samba e malandragem no tempo de Getúlio* (Rio de Janeiro: Paz e Terra, 1982), 55. According to *EMB*, *samba-canção* is unique in its "soft rhythm" and "romantic and sentimental" character (p. 684). But the expression here appears as a direct response to Wilson Batista's samba, which, as the reader will remember, said this: "Eu me lembro, era criança / Tirava samba-canção" (I remember, I was a child / I would sing *samba-canção* [samba songs]). And when Batista (1913–1968) was a child, the subgenre of *samba-canção* did not even exist (it becomes widespread starting in 1928, according to the same source). As such, the expression should be understood here in a broad sense—that is, "samba song" to differentiate it from a "samba event," or samba as synonym of a popular function, which was the first meaning of the word and was still quite present in the 1930s as we can see, for example, in the lyrics (cited earlier) of "Com que roupa?" ("With What Clothes?," Noel Rosa, 1930). *Samba-canção* (samba song), in this sense, is authored samba; it is the sung part that separates it from the collective party with which it was at first confused.

28. Máximo and Didier, *Noel Rosa*, 292.

29. Máximo and Didier, *Noel Rosa*, 292.

30. Máximo and Didier, *Noel Rosa*, 295.

31. According to Edigar de Alencar, *Nosso Sinhô do samba* (Rio de Janeiro: Funarte, 1981), 122.

32. A *cabrocha* is defined in chapter 4, note 36. Here it suffices to point out the most immediately relevant definition: a woman who samba dances.—Trans.

33. Interview with Noel Rosa in 1935, cited by Máximo and Didier, *Noel Rosa*, 357.

34. Máximo and Didier, *Noel Rosa*, 357.

35. Recorded by João Gilberto, among others.

36. Cited by Ana Maria Rodrigues, *Samba negro, espoliação branca* (São Paulo: Hucitec, 1984), 34–35.

37. Sérgio Cabral, "Prefácio" to Antônio Candeia Filho and Isnard Araújo, *Escola de samba, árvore que esqueceu a raiz* (Rio de Janeiro: Lidador, 1978), ix.

38. Vagalume, *Na roda do samba* (Rio de Janeiro: Funarte, 1978), 126.

39. Vagalume, *Na roda do samba*, 238. *Samba-chulado* was, for Vagalume, "this samba in vogue today; it is . . . the civilized samba, the developed samba, full of melody."

40. João da Baiana mentions the use of the *tamborim* already by the late nineteenth century. In Antonio Barroso Fernandes, ed., *As vozes desassombradas do museu, 1: Pixinguinha, Donga, João da Baiana* (Rio de Janeiro: MIS, 1970), 59.

41. *EMB*, "Oito Batutas," 565.

42. Marília T. Barboza da Silva and Arthur L. de Oliveira Filho, *Filho de Ogum bexiguento* (Rio de Janeiro: Funarte, 1979), 110 (and the corresponding photo on page 64).

43. The fact that handclaps—always group handclaps—cease to be mentioned indicates the shift from a type of samba that is performed in a *roda*, constituted by "musicants" (*musiquants*)—to use Gilbert Rouget's expression—to a type of samba that is performed by professional musicians for an audience. See Rouget, *Music and Trance: A Theory of the Relations between Music and Possession* (Chicago: University of Chicago Press, 1985).

44. Bucy Moreira's account in Roberto Moura, *Tia Ciata e a pequena África no Rio de Janeiro* (Rio de Janeiro: Funarte, 1983), 153. "Bernardo" is another of the Estácio *sambistas*, less well known than others but recognized by Paulo da Portela by this name in the samba "Coleção de passarinhos" ("Collection of Birds") (as documented by Marília T. Barboza da Silva and Arthur L. de Oliveira Filho, *Cartola—os tempos idos* [Rio de Janeiro: Funarte, 1989], 67). See also Bide's interview with Sérgio Cabral, *As escolas de samba* (Rio de Janeiro: Fontana, 1974), 30.

45. Máximo and Didier, *Noel Rosa*, 325. And also Cabral, *As escolas de samba*, 92.

46. The full lyrics are in Maria Tereza Mello Soares, *São Ismael do Estácio* (Rio de Janeiro: Funarte, 1985), 71–72. "Antonico" was released by Alcides Gerardi, Odeon 12993-B, Rio de Janeiro, 1950.

47. Soares, *São Ismael do Estácio*, 71–73.

48. Information taken from Máximo and Didier, *Noel Rosa*, chapter 20, 195–207.

49. Information taken from *EMB*, in the respective entries.

50. These dates are in the respective *EMB* entries; Bide mentions the causes of death in his interview with Sérgio Cabral in *As escolas de samba*, 32.

51. Soares, *São Ismael do Estácio*, 23.

52. Máximo and Didier, *Noel Rosa*, 368.

53. Roberto DaMatta, *Carnivals, Rogues, and Heroes: An Interpretation of the Brazilian Dilemma*, trans. John Drury (Notre Dame, IN: University of Notre Dame Press, 1991), 166–167.

54. Vianna, *The Mystery of Samba: Popular Music and National Identity in Brazil*, trans.

John Charles Chasteen (Chapel Hill: University of North Carolina Press, 1999), 81 and throughout.

55. By Tancredo Silva, Davi Silva, and Ribeiro da Cunha, recorded by Moreira da Silva in 1936. Cited by Cláudia Matos, *Acertei no milhar: Samba e malandragem no tempo de Getúlio* (Rio de Janeiro: Paz e Terra, 1982), 200 and 202.

56. Matos, *Acertei no milhar*, 202.

57. Máximo and Didier, *Noel Rosa*, 84–85.

Chapter 10. On the Gramophone

1. On this issue, see Philip Yampolsky, "Commercial 78's: A Rediscovered Resource for Ethnomusicology," in *This Thing Called Music: Essays in Honor of Bruno Nettl*, ed. Victoria Lindsay Levine and Philip Bohlman (Lanham, MD: Rowman & Littlefield, 2015), 302–314.

2. Oneyda Alvarenga, *Música popular brasileira* (São Paulo: Duas Cidades, 1982), 343.

3. "Chico" is short for the name Francisco.—Trans.

4. See José Ramos Tinhorão, *Música popular: Do gramofone ao rádio e TV* (São Paulo: Ática, 1981), 15–30. The name "Odeon," starting in the mid-1920s, no longer designated a Casa Edison brand but rather the European company itself, which had by then also been installed in Brazil.

5. The 1927–1933 period thus corresponds to the ascension and apogee of the Estácio *bambas*. The Deixa Falar Carnival group is dissolved in 1931, which is also the year of Nílton Bastos's death; in 1933 Alves and Ismael have a falling out; in 1935 the group is entirely dissolved, with the death of Brancura and Baiaco, and the imprisonment of Ismael for his involvement in a fight.

6. Yeda Pessoa de Castro, *Falares Africanos na Bahia: Um vocabulário afro-brasileiro*, 2nd ed. (Rio de Janeiro: Topbooks, 2005), 198. In Brazil, *cangarê* (or *canjerê, canjira, canjirê*), deriving from a Kikongo/Kimbundu term meaning to bless or open roads by way of magic, refers especially to Afro-Brazilian witchcraft, witchcraft sessions, and spells.—Trans.

7. The entry "Cangerê" in *DFB* (176–177) says that the term is of African origin and is synonymous with "spell." The *DB-78 rpm* tells us that Francisco Antônio da Rocha was known as Chico da Baiana.

8. Muniz Sodré, *Samba, o dono do corpo* (Rio de Janeiro: Codecri, 1979), 62.

9. Sodré, *Samba*, 69.

10. Antonio Barroso Fernandes, ed., *As vozes desassombradas do museu, 1: Pixinguinha, Donga, João da Baiana* (Rio de Janeiro: MIS, 1970), 81.

11. It should be noted, however, that on the published sheet music of "Pelo telefone," the melody of the introduction was written with a different rhythm; in fact, it was the rhythm played by Pixinguinha on the 1940 recording from the disc *Native Brazilian Music*.

12. "Line" (verso) here refers to a single poetic line, which in Mário de Andrade's use suggested a poetic "line" sung by a soloist, which is followed by a choral refrain. I have chosen not to use the English "verse" due to its ambiguity, as it can refer to either a single line of poetry or to several lines. —Trans. Mário de Andrade, "O samba rural paulista," in *Aspectos da música brasileira* (Belo Horizonte: Vila Rica, 1991), 156.

13. Edigar de Alencar, *Nosso Sinhô do samba* (Rio de Janeiro: Funarte, 1981), 56.

14. Mário de Andrade, *Os cocos* (São Paulo: Duas Cidades, 1984), 482–485.

15. These lyrics are presented by Alencar in *Nosso Sinhô do samba*, 31, with some differences from the original recording. One such difference is perhaps due to the scruples of the biographer, who substitutes *roubar* (to steal) in the sixth verse with *sambar* (to samba).

16. Given in full by Alencar, *Nosso Sinhô do samba*, 33.

17. Alencar, *Nosso Sinhô do samba*, 30.

18. Alencar, *Nosso Sinhô do samba*, 31.

19. Sebastião Nunes Batista, *Poética popular do Nordeste* (Rio de Janeiro: Casa de Rui Barbosa, 1982), 26.

20. Batista, *Poética popular do Nordeste*, 26.

21. On Caninha, see the biographical sketch by Sérgio Cabral, "Um pioneiro do samba," in *ABC do Sérgio Cabral: Um desfile dos craques da MPB* (Rio de Janeiro: Codecri, 1979), 196–203.

22. This refers to Salvador, the capital of Bahia.—Trans.

23. Vagalume, *Na roda do samba* (Rio de Janeiro: Funarte, 1978), 79.

24. Nei Lopes, *O negro no Rio de Janeiro e sua tradição musical* (Rio de Janeiro: Pallas, 1992), 95.

25. Lopes, *O negro no Rio de Janeiro*, 38.

26. The "give it" here (in Portuguese, *dar*) refers to a beating. Furthermore, while the term *nega* is literally "Black woman," its use in this title is far more generalized as just the person's partner/lover. There are of course racial overtones to the use of the term, but addressing them here would detract from the general point Sandroni is making. It is perhaps worth noting only that there are geopolitical connotations that might point to Bahia in important ways, particularly if one considers the prominent use of *nega* in popular Bahian parlance even in the twenty-first century.—Trans.

27. A "protected body" (that is, a *corpo fechado*, which literally translates as "closed body") refers to the ritual protection of a body from spiritual or physical affliction. See also Mário de Andrade, "The Music of Sorcery in Brazil," trans. Peter Henry Fry, *Vibrant* 14, no. 1 (2017), 1–24, for his ethnographic account of going through a ceremony to close his own body in Natal (Rio Grande do Norte). He explains the sensation immediately following the ceremony: "And so it was that I left Dona Plastina's little house, feeling somewhat lyrical and with an urge to laugh, stepping over the shifting sand. . . . I didn't slip in the sand, nor did I break a leg, not a single dog barked at me and there were no brigands in Natal, because my body, through the musical force of the gods, was closed for ever against the dangers of air, land, underground and sea" (21–22).—Trans.

28. As shown in research I conducted in 1994, when I interviewed ten professional guitarists who work as samba accompanists in the city.

29. See, for example, Ralph C. Waddey, "'Viola de Samba' and 'Samba de Viola' in the 'Reconcavo' of Bahia (Brazil) Part II," *Latin American Music Review* 2, no. 2 (1981), 256; and Brasílio Itiberê, "Ernesto Nazaré na música brasileira," *Boletim latino americano de música* 6, no. 1 (1946), 315. Richard Waterman discusses the same issue, from the point of view of African American music in general, in "African Influence on the Music of the Americas," in *Acculturation in the Americas*, ed. Sol Tax (New York: Cooper Square, 1967), 207–218.

30. Itiberê, "Ernesto Nazaré," 315.

31. Alejo Carpentier, *Music in Cuba*, trans. Alan West-Durán (Minneapolis: University of Minnesota Press, 2001), 103. I have made two adjustments to the English-language translation of Carpentier's book. The first is regarding the term "*clave* rhythm," which I have adjusted to read "rhythm of the *claves.*" This more closely resembles the original "el ritmo de las claves" and, more importantly, makes clearer Sandroni's point concerning the repeated rhythm. In other words, it is not the *clave as a rhythm* but rather the general rhythmic role of the *claves*. The second change concerns the phrase "constant rhythmic element," which is used as a translation of the original Spanish phrase "constante escansional." This seems quite off the mark, though, as it would literally be a "constancy in scansion," scansion being the process by which stresses are marked in a verse (of poetry, for instance). In order to avoid the somewhat esoteric word "scansion," however, I have opted for "the rhythmic phrasing" as the translation.—Trans.

32. *Claves*, broadly defined, are wooden sticks that are struck together to produce specific rhythmic patterns that are repeated over the course of a given song or musical form.—Trans.

33. J. H. Kwabena Nketia, *African Music in Ghana* (Evanston, IL: Northwestern University Press, 1963), 78.

34. Kazadi wa Mukuna, *Contribuição bantu na música popular brasileira: Perspectivas etnomusicológics* (São Paulo: Terceira Margem, 2006), 93. Mukuna turns to two musical examples, given on pages 97–98 of his book, in which this rhythmic cycle is written in 16/8, and the melody in 2/4. In these cases, one rhythmic cycle of the *tamborim* corresponds to four measures of the sung melody. My observations, however, suggest a proportion of two to one, and not four to one, which leads me to heavily doubt these transcriptions.

35. Here Sandroni calls back to Carpentier and the idea of the (in Spanish) "constante escansional."—Trans.

36. Both types of verses are called heptasyllabic in Portuguese metrics.

37. This new type of variation is situated at a level different from that studied earlier, for it relies on the number of syllables in the phrase—that is, on the author's poetic options rather than on an intent to vary the rhythm.

38. As in the earlier "Esta nega 'qué' me 'dá,'" the meaning of *dá* here is once again that of hitting someone.—Trans.

39. This claim is based on my listening to three volumes of the excellent compilation *Sinhô*, Curitiba: Revivendo, 1995, which contains sixty-six recordings from the 1927–1931 period.

40. João Máximo and Carlos Didier, *Noel Rosa—uma biografia* (Brasília: UnB, 1990), 410.

41. Unfortunately, I was not able to gain access to this recording of "É bom parar."

42. In the insert of the album *Radamés Gnattali sexteto* (Rio de Janeiro: Odeon, SMOFB 3879, 1975, 331/3 rpm).

43. A similar, and equally questionable, history is told by Sérgio Cabral, according to which the first arrangement "to show the wind sections playing in the samba rhythm" was that of "Aquarela do Brasil," in 1939. Cabral, *No tempo de Ari Barroso* (Rio de Janeiro: Lumiar, [1993?]), 182.

44. The sample was taken at random, from the album *Fina estampa*, by Caetano Veloso (Rio de Janeiro: Polygram 522745-2, 1994).

Conclusion

1. Sérgio Cabral, *As escolas de samba do Rio de Janeiro* (Rio de Janeiro: Lumiar, 1996), 242.

2. I suggest Walnice Nogueira Galvão's excellent analysis of this *marchinha*, in *Le carnaval de Rio* (Paris: Chandeigne, 2000), 191–194.

3. See, for example, Ana Maria Rodrigues, *Samba negro, espoliação* branca (São Paulo: Hucitec, 1984); Nei Lopes, *O samba na realidade* (Rio de Janeiro: Codecri, 1981); José Ramos Tinhorão, *Pequena história da música popular* (São Paulo: Art, 1991) and *História social da música popular brasileira* (Lisbon: Caminho, 1990).

4. Personal communication with Ralph C. Waddey; personal communication with Marco Antônio Lavigne. (I want also to add that after the publication of this book in Portuguese in 2001, I began to have direct contact with other types of Afro-Brazilian music aside from samba, including religious music. This allowed me to witness the presence of Estácio-type rythms in Afro-Brazilian music that is arguably unrelated to post-1930 Carioca samba.)

Works Cited

Studies on Brazilian Music

Alencar, Edigar de. *O Carnaval carioca através da música*. 2 vols. Rio de Janeiro: Freitas Bastos, 1965.

———. *Nosso Sinhô do samba*. Rio de Janeiro: Funarte, 1981.

Almeida, Renato de. *História da música brasileira*. Rio de Janeiro: F. Briguiet, 1942.

———. "A influência da música negra no Brasil." *Revista de etnografia* 4, no. 2 (1965), 325–331.

Almirante [Henrique Foréis Domingues]. *No tempo de Noel Rosa*. Rio de Janeiro: Francisco Alves, 1963.

Alvarenga, Oneyda. "A influência negra na música brasileira." *Boletim latino americano de música* 6, no. 1 (1946), 357–407.

———. *Música popular brasileira*. São Paulo: Duas Cidades, 1982.

Andrade, Mário de. "Cândido Inácio da Silva e o lundu." *RBM* 10 (1944), 17–39.

———. *Os cocos*. São Paulo: Duas Cidades, 1984.

———. *Danças dramáticas do Brasil*. 3 vols. Belo Horizonte: Itatiaia; Brasília: INL, 1982.

———. *As melodias do boi e outras peças*. São Paulo: Duas Cidades, 1987.

———. *Modinhas imperiais*. São Paulo: Martins, 1964.

———. *Música de feitiçaria no Brasil*. Belo Horizonte: Itatiaia; Brasília: INL, 1983.

———. *Música, doce música*. São Paulo: Martins, 1976.

———. "Originalidade do maxixe." *Ilustração musical* 1, no. 2 (1930), 45.

———. "O samba rural paulista." In *Aspectos da música brasileira*, 112–185. Belo Horizonte: Vila Rica, 1991.

Andrade Muricy, José Cândido de. "Ernesto Nazareth (1863–1963)." *Cadernos Brasileiros* 5, no. 3 (1963), 36–50.

Araújo, Mozart de. *A modinha e o lundu no século XVIII*. São Paulo: Ricordi, 1963.

———. *Rapsódia brasileira*. Fortaleza: Universidade Estadual do Ceará, 1994.

Araújo, Samuel. "Acoustic Labor in the Timing of Everyday Life." PhD diss., University of Illinois, Urbana-Champaign, 1992.

Araújo, Samuel, and Antônio Guerreiro. "O samba cigano: Um estudo histórico-etnográfico das práticas de música e dança dos ciganos *calom* do Rio de Janeiro." In *Música popular en América Latina*, atas do II Congresso Latino Americano da IASPM. Edited by Rodrigo Torres. Santiago, Chile, 1999, 233–239.

Bandeira, Manuel. "Duas crônicas e meia." *Revista USP* 4 (1990), 73–78.

Barbosa, Orestes. *Samba*. Rio de Janeiro: Funarte, 1978.

Batista, Sebastião Nunes. *Poética popular do Nordeste*. Rio de Janeiro: Casa de Rui Barbosa, 1982.

Béhague, Gérard. "Biblioteca da Ajuda (Lisbon) Mss. 1595/1596: Two Eighteenth-Century Anonymous Collections of Modinhas." *Anuário do Instituto Interamericano de Pesquisa Musical* 4 (1968), 44–81.

———. *Heitor Villa-Lobos: The Search for Brazil's Musical Soul*. Austin: Institute of Latin American Studies, 1994.

———. "Popular Music Currents in the Art Music of the Early Nationalistic Period in Brazil, circa 1870–1920." PhD diss., Tulane University, 1966 (microform edition published in Ann Arbor: University of Michigan).

Braga, Luís Otávio. *O violão brasileiro*. Rio de Janeiro: Escola de Música Brasileira, 1988.

Cabral, Sérgio. *ABC do Sérgio Cabral: Um desfile dos craques da MPB*. Rio de Janeiro: Codecri, 1979.

———. *As escolas de samba*. Rio de Janeiro: Fontana, 1974.

———. *No tempo de Ari Barroso*. Rio de Janeiro: Lumiar, [1993?].

Candeia Filho, Antônio, and Isnard Araújo. *Escola de samba—árvore que esqueceu a raiz*. Rio de Janeiro: Lidador, 1978.

Cardoso, Lino de Almeida. *Americana cantilena: A canção e a construção da nacionalidade no Brasil*. Campos do Jordão, São Paulo: Edição do Autor, 2019.

Carneiro, Edison. *Folguedos tradicionais*. Rio de Janeiro: Conquista, 1974.

Castagna, Paulo. "Herança ibérica e africana no lundu brasileiro dos séculos XVIII e XIX." Article presented at VI Encuentro Simposio Internacional de Musicología / VI Festival Internacional de Música Renacentista y Barroca Americana "Misiones de Chiquitos," Santa Cruz de la Sierra, Bolívia, April 25–26, 2006. Proceedings published by Asociación Pro Arte y Cultura (2006), 21–48.

Cáurio, Rita, ed. *Brasil musical*. Rio de Janeiro: Art Bureau, 1988.

Cavalcanti, Maria Laura Viveiros de Castro. *Carnaval carioca: Dos bastidores ao desfile*. Rio de Janeiro: Editora da Universidade Federal do Rio de Janeiro, 1994.

Cernicchiaro, Vicenzo. *Storia della musica nel Brasile*. Milano: Fratelli Riccioni, 1926.

Corrêa de Azevedo, Luiz Heitor. *150 anos de música no Brasil*. Rio de Janeiro: José Olympio, 1956.

Costa, Haroldo. *Salgueiro, academia de samba*. Rio de Janeiro: Editora Record, 1984.

Didier, Carlos. "A formação do samba: De Donga e Sinhô à turma do Estácio." Lecture presented at Casa de Ruy Barbosa, Rio de Janeiro, July 2, 1996.

———. "O samba que veio do Estácio." *O Catacumba* 1, no. 1 (1984), 3.

Doderer, Gérard. *Modinhas luso-brasileiras*. Lisbon: Fundação Calouste Gulbenkian, 1984.

Dreyfus, Dominique. In personal communication with the author, he shared unpublished research on the etymology of the word "samba."

Durães, Maria João, ed. *Jornal de modinhas, ano I*. Facsimile edition. Lisbon: Instituto da Biblioteca Nacional e do Livro, 1996.

Efegê, Jota [João Ferreira Gomes]. *Figuras e coisas da música popular*. 2 vols. Rio de Janeiro: Funarte, 1978–1979.

———. *Maxixe, a dança excomungada*. Rio de Janeiro: Conquista, 1974.

Fernandes, Antonio Barroso, ed. *As vozes desassombradas do museu, 1: Pixinguinha, Donga, João da Baiana*. Rio de Janeiro: MIS, 1970.

Gallet, Luciano. *Estudos de folclore*. Rio de Janeiro: Carlos Wehrs, 1934.

Galvão, Walnice Nogueira. *Le Carnaval de Rio*. Paris: Chandeigne, 2000.

Guerra-Peixe, César. *Maracatus do Recife*. São Paulo: Ricordi, [1955?].

Hertzman, Marc A. *Making Samba: A New History of Race and Music in Brazil*. Durham, NC: Duke University Press, 2013.

Ianni, Otávio. "O samba de terreiro em Itu." *Revista de história* 26 (1956), 403–426.

Itiberê, Brasílio. "Ernesto Nazaré na música brasileira." *Boletim latino americano de música* 6, no. 1 (1946), 309–321.

Kiefer, Bruno. *A modinha e o lundu*. Porto Alegre: Movimento, 1977.

Kubik, Gerhard. *Angolan Traits in Black Music, Games and Dances of Brazil*. Lisbon: Junta de Investigações Científicas do Ultramar, 1979.

———. "Drum Patterns in the 'Batuque' of Benedito Caxias." *Latin-American Music Review* 11, no. 2 (1990), 115–181.

Lavigne, Marco Antônio. In personal communication with the author, he shared Candomblé de Angola recordings done in the Baixada Fluminense during the 1980s.

Lima, Edilson de. *As modinhas do Brazil*. São Paulo: EDUSP, 2001.

———. "A modinha e o lundu: Dois clássicos nos trópicos," PhD diss., Universidade de São Paulo, 2010.

Lima, Rossini Tavares de. *Da conceituação do lundu*. São Paulo: n.p., 1953.

Livingston-Isenhour, Tamara Elena, and Thomas George Caracas Garcia. *Choro: A Social History of a Brazilian Popular Music*. Bloomington: Indiana University Press, 2005.

Lopes, Nei. *O negro no Rio de Janeiro e sua tradição musical*. Rio de Janeiro: Pallas, 1992.

———. *O samba na realidade*. Rio de Janeiro: Codecri, 1981.

Magalhães, Marcos. "A modinha e géneros relacionados, desde suas origens até 1833." PhD diss., Universidade Nova de Lisboa, 2018.

Matos, Cláudia. *Acertei no milhar: Samba e malandragem no tempo de Getúlio*. Rio de Janeiro: Paz e Terra, 1982.

Máximo, João, and Carlos Didier. *Noel Rosa—uma biografia*. Brasília: UnB, 1990.

McCann, Bryan. *Hello, Hello Brazil: Popular Music in the Making of Modern Brazil*. Durham, NC: Duke University Press, 2005.

Mello, Guilherme Teodoro Pereira de. *A música no Brasil*. Salvador: Tipografia São Joaquim, 1908.

Meyer, Augusto. *Cancioneiro gaúcho*. Porto Alegre: Globo, 1952.

Moraes, Eneida de. *História do Carnaval carioca*. Rio de Janeiro: Civilização Brasileira, 1958.

Morais, Manuel. *Domingos Caldas Barbosa: Muzica escolhida da viola de Lereno (1799)*. Lisboa: Estar Editora, 2003.

Moura, Roberto. *Tia Ciata e a pequena África no Rio de Janeiro*. Rio de Janeiro: Funarte, 1983.

Mukuna, Kazadi wa. *Contribuição bantu na música popular brasileira: Perspectivas etnomusicológics*. São Paulo: Terceira Margem, 2006.

Muniz, J., Jr. *Do batuque à escola de samba*. São Paulo: Símbolo, 1976.

Nascimento, Antonio Adriano Blanc. "A influência da habanera nos tangos de Ernesto Nazareth." Master's thesis, São Paulo, ECA-USP, 1990.

Nogueira França, Eurico. "Le noir dans la musique brésilienne." In *La contribuition de l'Afrique à la civilization brésilienne*, 75–83. Ministério das Relações Exteriores, n.d.

Pereira da Costa, Francisco Augusto. *Folclore pernambucano*. Rio de Janeiro: Revista do Instituto Histórico, 1908.

Reis Pequeno, Mercedes. "Impressão musical no Brasil," article in the *EMB*, 352–363.

Rodrigues, Ana Maria. *Samba negro, espoliação branca*. São Paulo: Hucitec, 1984.

Ruiz, Roberto. *Teatro de revista no Brasil*. Rio de Janeiro: INACEN, 1988.

Sandroni, Carlos. "Hitting a 'Popular' Note: Musical Contrasts in Brazil and the US." *Portal* 2 (2006–2007), 48–49. https://repositories.lib.utexas.edu/handle/2152/61826.

———. "'I Got Phrasing': Changes in Samba's Melodic Rhythm, 1917–1933." In *A Latin American Music Reader: Views from the South*. Edited by Javier León and Helena Simonett, 250–257. Urbana: University of Illinois Press, 2016.

———. "Mudanças de padrão rítmico no samba carioca, 1917–1937." *Trans—revista transcultural de música* 2 (1996). https://www.sibetrans.com/trans/articulo/286/mudancas-de-padrao-ritmico-no-samba-carioca-1917-1937.

———. "La samba à Rio de Janeiro et le paradigme de l'Estácio." *Cahiers de musiques traditionnelles* 10 (1997), 153–168.

———. "Le tresillo." *Cahiers de musiques traditionnelles* 13 (2000), 55–64.

Sant'Anna Néry, Frederico-José de. *Folk-lore brésilien*. Paris: Perrin et Cie., 1889.

Silva, Flávio. "1917—questão social e carnaval." *Informativo Funarte* (1983).

———. "Origines de la samba urbaine à Rio de Janeiro." 2 vols. Master's thesis. Paris: École Pratique des Hautes Études, 1975.

———. "'Pelo telefone' e a história do samba." *Revista cultura* 8, no. 28 (1978).

Silva, Marília T. Barboza da, and Arthur L. de Oliveira Filho. *Cartola—os tempos idos*. Rio de Janeiro: Funarte, 1989.

———. *Filho de Ogum bexiguento*. Rio de Janeiro: Funarte, 1979.

Siqueira, Baptista. *Ernesto Nazaré na música brasileira*. Rio de Janeiro: Aurora, 1967.

———. *Origem do termo "samba."* São Paulo: IBDC, 1978.

———. *Três vultos históricos da música brasileira*. Rio de Janeiro: D. Araújo, 1969.

Soares, Maria Tereza Mello. *São Ismael do Estácio*. Rio de Janeiro: Funarte, 1985.

Sodré, Muniz. *Samba, o dono do corpo*. Rio de Janeiro: Codecri, 1979.

Taborda, Márcia. "A viola e a música de Domingos Caldas Barbosa: Uma investigação bibliográfica." *Anais do XVI Congresso da ANPPOM* (2006), 558–562.

Tinhorão, José Ramos. *Domingos Caldas Barbosa—o poeta da viola, da modinha e do lundu*. São Paulo: Editora 34, 1997.

————. *Fado, dança do Brasil, cantar de Lisboa*. Lisbon: Caminho, 1994.

————. *História social da música popular brasileira*. Lisbon: Caminho, 1990.

————. *Música popular de índios, negros e mestiços*. Petrópolis: Vozes, 1972.

————. *Música popular: Do gramofone ao rádio e TV*. São Paulo: Ática, 1981.

————. *A música popular no romance brasileiro*. Belo Horizonte: Oficina de Livros, 1992.

————. *Música popular, teatro e cinema*. Petrópolis: Vozes, 1972.

————. *Os negros em Portugal*. Lisbon: Caminho, 1988.

————. *As origens da canção urbana*. Lisbon: Caminho, 1997.

————. *Pequena história da música popular*. São Paulo: Art, 1991.

————. *Os sons dos negros no Brasil*. São Paulo: Art, 1988.

Vagalume [Francisco Guimarães]. *Na roda do samba*. Rio de Janeiro: Funarte, 1978.

Valença, Suetônio, and Raquel Valença. *Serra, serrinha, serrano: O império do samba*. Rio de Janeiro: José Olympio, 1981.

Vasconcelos, Ary. *A nova música da República Velha*. Self-published, Rio de Janeiro, 1985.

————. *Raízes da música popular brasileira (1500–1889)*. São Paulo: Martins; Brasília: INL, 1977.

————. "Tem cigano no samba." *Piracema* 1, no. 1 (1993), 105–109.

Veiga, Manuel. "O estudo da modinha brasileira." *Latin American Music Review* 19, no. 1 (1998), 47–91.

Vianna, Hermano. *O mistério do samba*. Rio de Janeiro: Jorge Zahar/Universidade Federal do Rio de Janeiro, 1995.

————. *The Mystery of Samba: Popular Music and National Identity in Brazil*. Translated by John Charles Chasteen. Chapel Hill: University of North Carolina Press, 1999.

Waddey, Ralph C. "'Viola de Samba' and 'Samba de Viola' in the 'Reconcavo' of Bahia (Brazil)." *Latin American Music Review* 1, no. 2 (1980), 196–212.

————. "'Viola de Samba' and 'Samba de Viola' in the 'Reconcavo' of Bahia (Brazil) Part II: 'Samba de Viola.'" *Latin American Music Review* 2, no. 2 (1981), 252–279.

————. In personal communication with the author, he shared *samba-de-viola* recordings done in the Bahian Recôncavo in the early 1980s.

Other Studies

Agawu, Kofi. *The African Imagination in Music*. New York: Oxford University Press, 2016.

————. *Representing African Music: Postcolonial Notes, Queries, Positions*. New York: Routledge, 2003.

Aharónian, Coriún. "Factores de identidad musical latinoamericana tras cinco siglos de conquista, dominación y mestizaje." In *Hacer música en América Latina*, 5–43. Montevideo: Tacuabé, 2012. Published also as "Factores de identidad musical." *VI Encontro Nacional da ANPPOM—Anais*. Rio de Janeiro: ANPPOM, 1993.

Alonso, Angela. "O abolicionismo como movimento social." *Novos estudos CEBRAP* 100 (2014), 115–137.

Arom, Simha. *African Polyphony & Polyrhythm: Musical Structure and Methodology*. Translated by Martin Thom, Barbara Tuckett, and Raymond Boyd. Cambridge: Cambridge University Press, 1991.

———. "Du pied à la main: Les fondements métriques des musiques traditionelles d'Afrique Centrale." *Analyse musicale* 10 (1988), 16–22.

Bartók, Bela. "El denominado ritmo búlgaro." In *Escritos sobre música popular*, 164–173. Mexico City/Madrid: Siglo XXI, 1979.

Beckford, William. *The Journal of William Beckford in Portugal and Spain 1787–1788*. Edited with an introduction and notes by Boyd Alexander. London: Rupert Hart-Davis, 1954.

Béhague, Gérard. *Music in Latin America: An Introduction*. Englewood Cliffs, NJ: Prentice Hall History of Music Series, 1979.

Blacking, John. *How Musical Is Man?* Seattle: University of Washington Press, 1973.

Brailoiu, Constantin. "The Aksak Rhythm." In *Problems of Ethnomusicology*, 133–167. Cambridge: Cambridge University Press, 1984.

Carpentier, Alejo. *Music in Cuba*. Translated by Alan West-Durán. Minneapolis: University of Minnesota Press, 2001.

Castro, Ruy. *O anjo pornográfico: A vida de Nelson Rodrigues*. São Paulo: Companhia das Letras, 1992.

Cler, Jérôme. "Pour une théorie de l'aksak." *Revue de musicologie* 80, no. 2 (1994), 181–210.

DaMatta, Roberto. *Carnivals, Rogues, and Heroes: An Interpretation of the Brazilian Dilemma*. Translated by John Drury. Notre Dame, IN: University of Notre Dame Press, 1991.

Evans-Pritchard, E. E. *Witchcraft, Oracles and Magic among the Azande*. Oxford: Clarendon Press, 1990.

Foucault, Michel. "Qu'est-ce qu'un auteur?" *Bulletin de la Société Française de Philosophie* 63 (1969), 75–95.

Freud, Sigmund. *Totem and Taboo*. Mineola, NY: Dover Publications, 2018.

Garção, Correia. *Obras poéticas*. Lisbon: Regia Oficina Tipográfica, 1778.

Gesualdo, Vicente. *Historia de la música en la Argentina*. 3 vols. Buenos Aires: Beta, 1961.

Girard, René. *Violence and the Sacred*. Baltimore: Johns Hopkins University Press, 1977.

Hennion, Antoine. "Music and Mediation: Towards a New Sociology of Music." In *The Cultural Study of Music: A Critical Introduction*. Edited by Martin Clayton, Trevor Herbert, and Richard Middleton, 89–91. London: Routledge, 2003.

———. *The Passion for Music: A Sociology of Mediation*. Farnham (UK): Ashgate, 2015.

———. *La passion musicale*. Paris: Metaillé, 1995.

Iznaga, Diana. *Transculturación en Fernando Ortiz*. Havana: Editorial de Ciencias Sociales, 1989.

Jahn, Janheinz. *Muntu: African Culture and the Western World*. New York: Grove Press, 1961.

Jones, A. M. *Studies in African Music*. 2 vols. London: Oxford University Press, 1959.

Kartomi, Margareth J. "The Processes and Results of Musical Culture Contact: A Discussion of Terminology and Concepts." *Ethnomusicology* 25, no. 2 (1982), 227–249.

Kolinski, Mieczyslaw. "A Cross-Cultural Approach to Rhythmic Patterns." *Ethnomusicology* 17, no. 3 (1973), 494–506.

———. "Review of *Studies in African Music* by A. M. Jones." *The Musical Quarterly* 46, no. 1 (1960), 105–110.

Landa, Enrique Camara. "Escandalos y condenas: La recepción del tango en Italia." Presentation given at the II Encontro de Etnomusicólogos Íbero-Americanos, Barcelona, 1995.

León, Argeliers. *Del canto y el tiempo*. Havana: Letras Cubanas, 1984.

Lévi-Strauss, Claude. *Le cru et le cuit*. Paris: Plon, 1964.

———. *La pensée sauvage*. Paris: Plon, 1962.

Lindley, Thomas. *Narrative of a Voyage to Brazil*. London: J. Johnson, St. Paul's Church-Yard, 1805.

Link, Heinrich Friedrich. *Travels in Portugal: And through France and Spain. With a Dissertation on the Literature of Portugal, and the Spanish and Portugueze Languages*. London: T. N. Longman and O. Rees, 1801.

London, Justin. *Hearing in Time: Psychological Aspects of Musical Meter*. New York: Oxford University Press, 2012.

Machado Filho, Aires da Mata. *O negro e o garimpo em Minas Gerais*. Belo Horizonte: Itatiaia; São Paulo: EDUSP, 1985.

Martin, Denis-Constant. "Filiation or Innovation? Some Hypotheses to Overcome the Dilemma of Afro-American Music's Origins." *Black Music Research Journal* 2, no. 1 (1991), 19–38.

Minkowski, Solomon Glades. *Ignacio Cervantes y la danza en Cuba*. Havana: Letras Cubanas, 1988.

Nattiez, Jean-Jacques. *Musicologie générale et sémiologie*. Paris: Christian Bourgois, 1987.

Needell, Jeffrey. *A Tropical Belle Epoque: Elite Culture and Society in Turn-of-the-Century Rio de Janeiro*. Cambridge: Cambridge University Press, 1987.

Nketia, J. H. Kwabena. *African Music in Ghana*. Evanston, IL: Northwestern University Press, 1963.

———. *The Music of Africa*. New York: W. W. Norton, 1974.

Ramos, Arthur. *Folclore negro no Brasil*. Rio de Janeiro: Civilização Brasileira, 1935.

Rodrigues, Raymundo Nina. *Os Africanos no Brasil*. São Paulo: Companhia Editora Nacional, 1945.

Rosseti Batista, Marta, ed. *Brasil, 1º tempo modernista—1917–29*. São Paulo: IEB, 1972.

Rossi, Vicente. *Cosas de negros*. Buenos Aires: Hachette, 1958.

Rouget, Gilbert. *Music and Trance: A Theory of the Relations between Music and Possession*. Chicago: University of Chicago Press, 1985.

Sandroni, Carlos. *Mário contra Macunaíma*. São Paulo: Vértice, 1988.

Tagg, Philip. "'Black Music,' 'Afro-American Music' and 'European Music.'" *Popular Music* 8, no. 3 (1989), 285–298.

Vega, Carlos. *Danzas y canciones argentinas*. Buenos Aires: Ricordi, 1936.

———. "Las especies homónimas y afines de 'Los orígenes del tango argentino.'" *Revista musical chilena* 101 (1967), 49–65.

Waterman, Richard. "African Influence on the Music of the Americas." In *Acculturation in the Americas*, edited by Sol Tax, 207–218. New York: Cooper Square, 1967.

Yampolsky, Philip. "Commercial 78's: A Rediscovered Resource for Ethnomusicology." In *This Thing Called Music: Essays in Honor of Bruno Nettl*, edited by Victoria Lindsay Levine and Philip Bohlman, 302–314. Lanham, MD: Rowman & Littlefield, 2015.

Literary Works

Alencar, José de. *Til*. Rio de Janeiro: Ediouro, 1980.

Almeida, Manuel Antonio de. *Memoires of a Militia Sergeant*. Translated by Ronald W. Sousa. New York: Oxford University Press, 1999.

Azevedo, Aluísio. *The Slum*. Translated by David H. Rosenthal. Oxford: Oxford University Press, 2000.

Caldas Barbosa, Domingos. *Viola de Lereno*. 2 vols. Rio de Janeiro: INL, 1944.

França Júnior, Joaquim José da. *Folhetins*. Rio de Janeiro: Jacintho Ribeiro dos Santos, 1926.

Louzada, Wilson, ed. *Antologia do Carnaval*. Rio de Janeiro: O Cruzeiro, 1945.

Machado de Assis, Joaquim Maria. *A Chapter of Hats: Selected Stories*. Translated by John Gledson. London: Bloomsbury, 2014.

Machado de Assis, *Philosopher or Dog?*, trans. Clotilde Wilson (New York: Noonday Press, 1954), 100.

Ribeiro, Júlio. *A carne*. Rio de Janeiro: Ediouro, [1992?].

———. *Flesh*. Translated by William Barne. London: Modern Humanities Research Association, 2011.

Tolentino, Nicolau. *Sátiras*. Lisbon: Seara Nova, 1969.

Reference Works

Apel, Willi. *Harvard Dictionary of Music*. 2nd ed., revised and enlarged. Cambridge, MA: Belknapp Press of Harvard University Press, 1974 (eighth printing of the 1969 edition).

Aurélio (Novo dicionário Aurélio da língua portuguesa). Edited by Aurélio Buarque de Hollanda Ferreira. Rio de Janeiro: Nova Fronteira, 1975.

Basso, Alberto, ed. *Dizionario della musica*. Torino: Tipografia Sociale Torinese, 1971.

———. *Enciclopedia storica della musica*. Torino: Tipografia Sociale Torinese, 1966.

Borba, Tomás, and Fernando Lopes Graça. *Dicionário de música*. 2 vols. Lisbon: Cosmos, 1958.

DB-78 rpm (Discografia brasileira 78 rpm). 5 vols. Compiled by Jairo Severiano et al. Rio de Janeiro: Funarte, 1984.

DFB (Dicionário do folclore brasileiro), by Luís da Câmara Cascudo. Rio de Janeiro: INL/MEC, 1962.

DMB (Dicionário musical brasileiro), by Mário de Andrade. São Paulo: EDUSP, 1989.

EMB (Enciclopédia da música brasileira—erudita, folclórica, popular). 2 vols. Edited by Marco Antônio Marcondes. São Paulo: Art, 1977.

Honneger, Marc. *Dictionnaire de la musique—science de la musique*. 2 vols. Paris: Bordas, 1976.

Riemann, Hugo. *Dictionnaire de musique*. French edition edited by André Schaeffner. Paris: Payot, 1931.

Sadie, Stanley, ed. *The New Grove's Dictionary of Music and Musicians*. 20 vols. London: MacMillan, 1980.

Musical Sources

Sheet Music

Anonymous. *Marília, meu doce bem*. Ca. 1860. Biblioteca Nacional do Rio de Janeiro, F-III-31.

Anonymous. *Quem é pobre não tem vícios*. Ca. 1850. Biblioteca Nacional do Rio de Janeiro, L-I-18.

Arvellos, J. S. *Se eu pedir você me dá?* Ca. 1865. Biblioteca Nacional do Rio de Janeiro, A-I-12.

Barbosa, José Soares. *O que é da chave?* Ca. 1872. Biblioteca Nacional do Rio de Janeiro, C-I-13.

———. *O senhor padre-vigário*. Ca. 1880. Biblioteca Nacional do Rio de Janeiro, F-II-6.

Carvalho, Francisco de. *O mugunzá*. Lyrics by Bernardo Lisboa. 1892. Biblioteca Nacional do Rio de Janeiro, BG-IV-61.

Cardim, Gomes. *Joanna do Arco*, tango. Ca. 1865. Biblioteca Nacional do Rio de Janeiro, M-I-40.

Coelho, M. J. *Sinhô Juca*. Lyrics by J. D'Aboim. Printed prior to 1869. Biblioteca Nacional do Rio de Janeiro, M-I-16.

Costa, Júnior. *O homem*. Lyrics by Artur Azevedo and Moreira Sampaio. 1887. Biblioteca Nacional do Rio de Janeiro, BG-IV-12.

Cruz, Calixto X. da. *Polka de estylo brazileiro*. N.d., M-I-34.

Cunha, João Elias. *Zizinha*. Ca. 1865. Biblioteca Nacional do Rio de Janeiro, M-I-62.

Dorison (on the theme of "O curioso B.B."). *Gentis, você já viu já?* 1853. Biblioteca Nacional do Rio de Janeiro, F-III-29.

Leite, Virgínio A. Pereira. *Vesgo não namora*. Ca. 1870. Biblioteca Nacional do Rio de Janeiro, B-I-75.

Maia, J. O. *Sai, poeira!* Ca. 1866. Biblioteca Nacional do Rio de Janeiro, C-I-5.

Maria, Manoel Joaquim. *Cateretê da paródia Orpheo na roça*. Lyrics by F. C. Vasques. 1868. Reproduced by Batista Siqueira, *Origem do termo "samba,"* 134–135.

Mesquita, H. A. de. *A bahiana*. Ca. 1870. Biblioteca Nacional do Rio de Janeiro, N-VIII-9.

———. *Os beijos de frade*. Lyrics by E. D. Villas Boas. 1856. Reproduced by Batista Siqueira, *Três vultos históricos da música brasileira*, 39–40.

Noronha, Francisco de Sá. *Lundu das moças*. 1851. Biblioteca Nacional do Rio de Janeiro, D-I-22.

Pagani, R. *Capenga não forma*. Lyrics by Ed. Villas Boas. Ca. 1867. Biblioteca Nacional do Rio de Janeiro, M-II-68.

Pimentel, Albertino. *O engrossa*. Lyrics by Moreira Sampaio. 1899. Biblioteca Nacional do Rio de Janeiro, M-II-58.

Pinto, Porfírio José d'Oliveira. *Socega, nhonhô!* Ca. 1872. Biblioteca Nacional do Rio de Janeiro, C-I-31.

Ramos, Januário da Silva. *Lundu das beatas*. Ca. 1862. Biblioteca Nacional do Rio de Janeiro, M-II-68.

Rocha, Antonio Hilarião da. *O que é da tranca?* Ca. 1873. Biblioteca Nacional do Rio de Janeiro, F-II-20.

Silva, Candido Inácio da. *Lá no Largo da Sé*. 1834. Biblioteca Nacional do Rio de Janeiro, F-III-33.

Telles, Padre. *Querem ver esta menina*. Ca. 1850. Biblioteca Nacional do Rio de Janeiro, L-I-33.

Varney, L. *Amor molhado*. 1887. Biblioteca Nacional do Rio de Janeiro, N-V-46.

Recordings on which the transcriptions are based

All the recordings cited here were published in Rio de Janeiro, except where otherwise noted. They are listed in chronological order, by year.

"O malhador," by Donga and Mauro de Almeida. Sung by Bahiano. Casa Edison-Odeon 121.442, 1918.

"Quem são eles?," by Sinhô. Sung by Bahiano. Casa Edison-Odeon 121.445, 1918.

"O veado à meia-noite," by Donga. Sung by Bahiano. Casa Edison-Odeon 121.443, 1918.

"Confessa, meu bem!," by Sinhô. Sung by Eduardo das Neves. Casa Edison-Odeon 121.528, 1919.

"Deixe desse costume," by Sinhô. Sung by Eduardo das Neves. Casa Edison-Odeon 121.529, 1919.

"Esta nega 'qué' me 'dá,'" by Caninha. Sung by Bahiano. Casa Edison-Odeon 121.968, 1920.

"Quem vem atrás fecha a porta (Me leve, seu Rafael)," by Caninha. Sung by Bahiano and Isaltina. Casa Edison-Odeon 121.729, 1920.

"A malandragem," by Bide and Francisco Alves. Sung by Francisco Alves. Odeon 10.113-B, February 1928.

"Não é isso que eu procuro," by Ismael Silva and Francisco Alves. Sung by Francisco Alves. Odeon 10.251-B, September 1928.

"És ingrata, mulher," by Loló Verba. Sung by Francisco Alves. Odeon 10.535-A, January 1930.

"Na Pavuna," by Almirante and Candoca da Anunciação. Sung by Almirante, with Bando de Tangarás. Parlophon 13089-A, February 1930.

"Vou te abandonar," by Heitor dos Prazeres. Sung by Paulo da Portela. Brunswick 10.037-B, March 1930.

"Nem assim," by Gradim. Sung by Francisco Alves and Mário Reis. Odeon 10.824-A, 1931.

"Nem é bom falar," by Ismael Silva, Nilton Bastos, and Francisco Alves. Sung by Francisco Alves. Odeon 10.745-A, January 1931.

"O que será de mim," by Ismael Silva, Nilton Bastos, and Francisco Alves. Sung by Francisco Alves and Mário Reis. Odeon 10.780-B, April 1931.

"Oh! Dora!," by Orlando Vieira. Sung by Francisco Alves. Odeon 10.871-B, 1931.

"Para me livrar do mal," by Ismael Silva and Noel Rosa. Sung by Francisco Alves. Odeon 10.922-B, 1932.

"Se você jurar," by Ismael Silva, Nilton Bastos, and Francisco Alves. Sung by Ismael Silva. On *O samba na voz do sambista*. Rio de Janeiro: Sinter, 1955, 33 1/3 rpm.

"Leva, meu samba," by Ataulfo Alves. Sung by Ataulfo Alves. On *Ataulfo Alves e suas pastoras*. Philips, 1958, 33 1/3 rpm.

"Rosa de ouro," by Paulinho da Viola, Elton Medeiros, and Hermínio Bello de Carvalho. Sung by the group A Voz do Morro. On *Rosa de ouro*, Odeon, 1965, 33 1/3 rpm.

"Sobrado dourado." Sung by the group A Voz do Morro. On *Rosa de ouro*. Odeon, 1965, 331/3 rpm.

"Sei lá, Mangueira," by Paulinho da Viola and Hermínio Bello de Carvalho. Sung by Elizeth Cardoso. On *A bossa eterna de Elizeth e Ciro*. Vol. 2. Copacabana, 1969, 33 ⅓ rpm.

"Pelo telefone," by Donga and Mauro de Almeida. Sung by Martinho da Vila. On *Origens— Pelo telefone*, RCA Victor, 1973, 331/3 rpm.

"Onde a dor não tem razão," by Paulinho da Viola and Elton Medeiros. Sung by Paulinho da Viola. On *Paulinho da Viola*, RCA, 1981, 331/3 rpm.

"Pelo telefone," by Donga and Mauro de Almeida. Sung by Zé da Zilda. On *Native Brazilian Music*. Rio de Janeiro: Museu Villa-Lobos, 1987, 331/3 rpm. Re-edited edition of the 78 rpm discs from Columbia North America, which were recorded by Stokowsky in Rio de Janeiro in 1940.

"O bem e o mal," by Nelson Cavaquinho and Guilherme de Brito. Sung by Nelson Cavaquinho. Rereleased on the compilation *Nelson Cavaquinho—quando eu me chamar saudade*. EMI, 1991, compact disc.

"Duas horas da manhã," by Nelson Cavaquinho and Ari Monteiro. Sung by Paulinho da Viola. Rereleased on the compilation *Nelson Cavaquinho—quando eu me chamar saudade*. EMI, 1991, compact disc.

"Rei vagabundo," by Nelson Cavaquinho, José Ribeiro de Sousa, and Noel Silva. Sung by Nelson Cavaquinho. Rereleased on the compilation *Nelson Cavaquinho—quando eu me chamar saudade*. EMI, 1991, compact disc.

"Pelo telefone," by Donga and Mauro de Almeida. Sung by Bahiano. Casa Edison-Odeon 121.322, January 1917. Rereleased on the compilation *Historia del Carnaval de Brasil 1902–1950*. Vol. 1. Switzerland: Ubatuqui Records, 1992, compact disc.

"Se você jurar," by Ismael Silva, Nilton Bastos, and Francico Alves. Sung by Francisco Alves and Mário Reis. 1931. Rereleased on the compilation *Historia del Carnaval de Brasil 1902–1950*. Vol. 1. Switzerland: Ubatuqui Records, 1992, compact disc.

"Se você jurar," by Ismael Silva, Nilton Bastos, and Francisco Alves. Sung by Teca Calazans. On *O samba dos bambas*. Paris: Buda Musique, 1994, compact disc.

"Gosto que me enrosco," by Sinhô and Heitor dos Prazeres. Sung by Mário Reis. Odeon 10.278-B, November 1928. Rereleased on the compilation *Sinhô*. Vol. 3. Curitiba: Revivendo, 1995.

"Ora vejam só!," by Sinhô and Heitor dos Prazeres. Sung by Francisco Alves. Odeon 123273, January 1927. Rereleased on the compilation *Sinhô*. Vol. 3. Curitiba: Revivendo, 1995.

"Aquarelas do Brasil," radio program produced by Almirante. May 4, 1945. On *Escolas de samba*. Vol. 1. Rio de Janeiro: Collector's, 1996, cassette tape.

Translator's Works Cited in Body of Text

Andrade, Mário de. "The Music of Sorcery in Brazil." Translated by Peter Henry Fry. *Vibrant* 14, no. 1 (2017), 1–24.

Baker, Philip, and Peter Mühlhäusler. "Creole Linguistics from Its Beginnings, through Schuchardt to the Present Day." In *Creolization: History, Ethnography, Theory*. Edited by Charles Stewart, 84–107. Walnut Creek: Left Coast Press, 2007.

Blackmore, J. "Portugal, Poetry of." In *The Princeton Handbook of World Poetries*. Edited by Roland Greene and Stephen Cusman, 442–447. Princeton, NJ: Princeton University Press, 2017.

Blanco Borelli, Melissa. *She Is Cuba: A Genealogy of the Mulata Body*. New York: Oxford University Press, 2016.

Camões, Luís de. *Os Lusíadas (The Lusiads)*. Translated by Richard Francis Burton. London: Tinsley Brothers, 1880.

Carvalho, Bruno. *Porous City: A Cultural History of Rio de Janeiro (from the 1810s Onward)*. Liverpool: Liverpool University Press, 2013.

Castro, Yeda Pessoa de. *Falares Africanos na Bahia: Um vocabulário afro-brasileiro*. 2nd ed. Rio de Janeiro: Topbooks, 2005.

Chazkel, Amy. "The Crônica, the City, and the Invention of the Underworld: Rio de Janeiro, 1889–1922." *Estudios Interdisciplinarios de América Latina y el Caribe* 12, no. 1 (2014), 79–105.

Eakin, Marshall C. *Becoming Brazilian: Race and National Identity in Twentieth-Century Brazil*. Cambridge: Cambridge University Press, 2017.

Fraunhar, Alison. *Mulata Nation: Visualizing Race and Gender in Cuba*. Jackson: University Press of Mississippi, 2018.

Graham, Richard. "1850–1870." In *Brazil: Empire and Republic*. Edited by Leslie Bethell, 113–160. Cambridge: Cambridge University Press, 1989.

Kabir, Ananya Jahanara. "Creolization as Balancing Act in the Transoceanic Quadrille: Choreogenesis, Incorporation, Memory, Market." *Atlantic Studies* 17, no .1 (2020), 135–157.

Metz, Jerry D. "Cultural Geographies of Afro-Brazilian Symbolic Practice: Tradition and Change in Maracatu de Nação (Recife, Pernambuco, Brazil)." *Latin American Music Review* 29, no. 1 (2008), 64–95.

Mullen, Edward J. "Simón Aguado's *Entremés de los negros*: Text and Context." *Comparative Drama* 20, no. 3 (1986), 231–246.

Pietz, William. "The Problem of the Fetish, I." *RES: Anthropology and Aesthetics* 9, no. 1 (1985), 5–17.

———. "The Problem of the Fetish, II: The Origin of the Fetish." *RES: Anthropology and Aesthetics* 13, no. 1 (1987), 23–45.

———. "The Problem of the Fetish, IIIa." *RES: Anthropology and Aesthetics* 16, no. 1 (1988), 105–124.

Reily, Suzel Ana. "To Remember Captivity: The 'Congados' of Southern Minas Gerais." *Latin American Music Review* 22, no. 1 (2001), 4–30.

Santana Pinho, Patrícia de. "White but Not Quite: Tones and Overtones of Whiteness in Brazil." *Small Axe* 13, no. 2 (2009), 39–56.

Index

Abedé, João, 89

"Adeus América" ("Goodbye, America," Barbosa-Jacques, 1948), 159

African music / rhythm, 4–9, 17–18; origins of *lundu* dance in, 21–22; rhythmic oddity of, 199–200

Afro-Brazilian music / rhythm: *Modinhas do Brazil* (Ajuda Ms. 1596) and, 26–31, 34–36, 39, 41 (*see also modinhas*); "older" samba style and, 111–113, 115, 116, 119–121, 123 (*see also* Tia Ciata); popular music vs., 151; repression of, 87–92, 99, 200–201; syncopation and, 8, 28–30, 210n14. *See also* Bahian samba; *batuque;* Brazilian tango; *lundus; maxixe*

Afro-Cuban music, 7–11, 181

Agawu, Kofi, xxx, 210n14

Aharónian, Coriún, on the *tresillo* (3-3-2 Paradigm), 10

Alencar, José de, 55, 67–68, 71, 73

Almeida, Cícero de, 83

Almeida, Mauro de: "O malhador" ("The Beater," Donga-Pixinguinha-Almeida, 1918), 176–177. *See also* "Pelo telefone"

Almirante (Henrique Foréis Domingues), 78–79, 103–104

"Alta madrugada" ("Wee Hours of the Night," Sinhô, 1930), 145

Alvaiade, 133–134

Alvarenga, Oneyda, 4–5, 86, 113, 125; definition of "samba," 74, 79

Alves, Ataulfo, "Leva, meu samba" ("Tell [Her], Samba of Mine," 1958), 16

Alves, Francisco: "A malandragem" ("The Malandro Lifestyle," with Bide, 1928), 126, 139–141, 143, 167–168, 182, 183; as *compositore* (samba buyer) or "partner," 126–129, 144–147, 240n31; "É bom parar" ("You'd Better Stop," Rosa-Soares-Alves, 1936), 123–124, 132–133, 191; "Me faz carinhos" ("She Gives Me Affection," with I. Silva, 1928), 185; "Não é isso que eu procuro" ("This Isn't What I'm Looking For," with I. Silva, 1928), 141, 143, 182, 183, 193; "Nem é bom falar" ("Don't Even Say It," I. Silva-Bastos-Alves, 1931), 142–143, 182, 188; "newer" Estácio vs. "older" samba style and, 115, 116, 191–192, 197–198; "O que será de mim" ("What Will Become of Me," I. Silva-Bastos-Alves, 1931), 141–143, 182, 184, 186; recordings of, 140, 167–168, 182, 185–187, 191–195; "Se você jurar" ("If You Swear," I. Silva-Bastos-Alves, 1931), 14, 113, 141, 143, 182, 184–187

"Amar a uma só mulher" ("To Love Just One Woman," Sinhô, 1928), 189–190

"Amostra a mão" ("Show Your Hand," Sinhô, 1930), 189

Andrade, Mário de: analysis of "Lá no Largo da Sé" ("There in Sé Plaza," C. Silva, 1834), 28, 33–36; on blood vs. social milieu, 35, 195–196; Brazilianism (brasileirismo) and, 35; on Brazilian polkas, 51–55; on Brazilian tangos, 58–60, 75; as director of the Department of Culture of São Paulo, 90; on "harvested" folk melodies, 125; on line and refrain structure, 172, 176, 246n12; on lundus, 22, 33–36, 37, 46, 60, 61; lyrics to "Pelo telefone," 103–104; on maxixe, 43, 58, 60, 62; on modinhas, 32; on morros, 91; on samba "amaxixado," 113; on syncopation characteristic of Brazilian rhythm (see characteristic syncopation)

Andrade, Oswald de, 48–49

Andrade Muricy, José Cândido de, 1–3

"Antonico" (I. Silva, 1950), 160–161

"Aquarela do Brasil" ("Brazil," Barroso, 1939), 77, 201

Araújo, Samuel, on "tamborim cycle" or "tamborim" pattern, 14–16

Arinos, Alfonso, 103–104

Arom, Simha: avoidance of syncopation as term, 4, 8–9; on ostinato with variations, 7; on rhythmic oddity of African music, 6, 17, 18

"Arrependimento" ("Regret," Gargalhada, ca. 1935), 134

Arvellos Filho, Januário da Silva, "Se eu pedir você me dá?" ("If I Ask Will You Give It to Me?," 1865), 53

Augusto, Germano, "Se a sorte me ajudar" ("If Luck Helps Me," with Rosa, 1934), 157

"Ave de rapina" ("Bird of Prey," Sinhô, 1930), 144–145

Azevedo, Aluísio, 70–76, 148–149

Babo, Lamartine, "História do Brazil" ("History of Brazil," 1930), 198–199

"A bahiana" ("The Typical [Black] Bahian Woman," Mesquita, ca. 1870), 52, 53

Bahiano (Manoel Pedro dos Santos), 97, 105, 168–169, 171–173

Bahian samba ("old style"), 63–77; characteristics of, 117–121; comparison of "old"

and "new" styles, 112–121; connection with Carioca samba, 76–77; instrumentation of, 118; "Pelo telefone" (1917), 76, 77, 78–79 (see also "Pelo telefone"); repression thesis and, 87–92; as samba de umbigada, 64, 70, 74, 76–77, 81–82, 85–86, 90, 117–118, 124; social origins of musicians, 118–120. See also 3-3-2 Paradigm; Tia Ciata

Baiana, Rita (mulata), 73–76

baile (intertwined couples dancing), 45–46, 74; lundu dance and, 21–22, 44–48, 60–62, 65; samba and, 74, 79, 82–85

"Balaio" ("Basket"), 55

bambas: malandros (hustlers) and, 14, 213n40; sambistas and, 14, 117, 151, 213n40

bandas de música (brass and wind bands), 169, 195

Bandeira, Manuel, 125

Barbosa, Haroldo, "Adeus América" ("Goodbye, America," with Jacques, 1948), 159

Barbosa, José Soares, "O que é da chave?" ("Where Is the Key?" ca. 1872), 50, 52

Barbosa, Orestes: background of, 114–115; "newer" Estácio samba style and, 114–115; Samba, 114–117, 135, 138, 139

Barbosa, Orestes, "Chão de estrelas" ("Starry Ground," with S. Caldas, 1937), 114

Barcelos, Rubem, 162

barrica (bass drum), 159

Barroso, Ary, 116, 134, 154; "Aquarela do Brasil" ("Brazil," 1939), 77, 201

Bastos, Nilton: early death, 162; "Nem é bom falar" ("Don't Even Say It," I. Silva-Bastos-F. Alves, 1931), 142–143, 182, 188; "newer" Estácio samba style and, 13–14, 111, 113, 116; "O que será de mim" ("What Will Become of Me," I. Silva-Bastos-F. Alves, 1931), 141–143, 182, 184, 186; "Se você jurar" ("If You Swear," I. Silva-Bastos-F. Alves, 1931), 14, 113, 141, 143, 182, 184–187

Batista, Wilson: debate with Noel Rosa, 148–149, 156–157, 158, 165; "Lenço no pescoço" ("Handkerchief around the Neck," 1933), 148–149, 151, 156, 165; malandro (hustler) lifestyle and, 148–149, 151, 156, 165

batucadas (games of dexterity), 80–81, 84, 118, 120, 145–146, 231n26
batuque (Afro-Brazilian dances and festivities), 67–69; *baile* vs., 45–46, 74; *lundu* as descendent of, 22; multiple meanings of, 213nn36–37; nature of, 45–46, 65, 213n36; samba and, 74, 91, 119; tango and, 57, 75
"Batuque" for piano (Nazareth, 1906), 13, 57, 58
Béhague, Gérard, 53; and *Modinhas* (Ajuda Ms. 1595), 26–28; and *Modinhas do Brazil* (Ajuda Ms. 1596), 26–31, 34–36, 39, 41
"Os beijos de frade" ("Friar's Kisses," Mesquita, 1856), 10
Bello de Carvalho, Herminio, 16
"O bem e o mal" ("Good and Evil," Cavaquinho-Brito, 1991), 16
O Bendengó (revue), 57
Biblioteca da Ajuda (Lisbon): *Modinhas* (Ms. 1595), 26–28; *Modinhas do Brazil* (Ms. 1596), 26–31, 34–36, 39, 41
Biblioteca Nacional do Rio de Janeiro (BNRJ): printed *lundus* and, 37–40; registering of "Pelo telefone" (1916), 95, 97
Bide (Alcebíades Barcelos): "A malandragem" ("The Malandro Lifestyle," with F. Alves, 1928), 126, 139–141, 143, 167–168, 182, 183; "newer" Estácio samba style and, 13–14, 111, 115, 121; samba authorship and, 127, 128–129
Bittencourt, René, "Felicidade" ("Happiness," with Rosa, 1932), 132–133
Black Bahians: Law of the Free Womb (September 28, 1871), 55, 78; population shift from Northeast to Southeast and, 78. *See also* Bahian samba; Tia Ciata
Blacking, John, on "deep structure," 7, 12
blocos (Carnival groups): Estácio de Sá style and, 117, 122–124, 132; nature of, 122, 123; as predecessors of samba schools, 122, 132; samba second parts *(segundas partes)* and, xxxviii, 132–134
botequins (pubs, cafés), 122–129, 132–134, 166
Brancura (Sílvio Fernandes), "newer" Estácio samba style and, 111, 116
Brazil: Empire of Brazil (1822–1889), 36, 51, 60, 62; end of slavery (1888), 92, 150–151,

200, 244; Law of the Free Womb (September 28, 1871), 55, 78; migration from northeast to southeast, 78; Paraguayan War (1864–1870), 56; Proclamation of the Republic (1889), 36, 150; Rio de Janeiro (*see* Rio de Janeiro)
Brazilian folk music: anonymity vs. authorship and, 96, 97–107, 115, 119, 124–129; improvisation in, 64, 96–97, 105–106, 118–119, 126, 130–131, 134; *morros* (hillside neighborhoods of Rio de Janeiro) and (*see morros*); popular music vs., xxxi-xxxiii, 23, 131, 134, 151, 225–226n12. *See also* Tia Ciata
Brazilian polka: *polcas-lundu*, 13, 48–54, 57–58, 60, 201; syncopation in, 51–54; tango vs., 57–58; terminological confusion and, 48–49, 60–62; 3–3–2 Paradigm and, 13, 51–54, 58–59
Brazilian popular music: anonymity vs. authorship and, 96, 97–107, 115, 119, 124–131; Bantu elements in, 14–15; *choros* (instrumental ensembles), xxx-xxxi, 11, 49–51, 81–83, 118–120, 158–161, 169–170; compositional "partnerships" in, 127–129, 132–134, 139–147; Estácio Paradigm and, 14–17; Estácio samba style and, 115–116; folk (traditional) music vs., xxxi-xxxiii, 23, 131, 134, 151, 225–226n12; *malandros* (hustlers) in, 135–143; syncopation in, 28–29, 35; 3–3–2 Paradigm and, 10, 189–190, 196. *See also lundus; maxixe;* "Pelo telefone"
Brazilian syncopation. *See* syncopation
Brazilian tango *(tango brasileiro)*, 56–59; Argentine tango vs., 44, 56, 59; early use of term "tango," 43–44, 57, 59; terminological confusion and, 60–62; 3–3–2 Paradigm and, 11, 13
"Brejeiro" ("Chipper," Nazareth, 1893), 57
Brito, Guilherme de, "O bem e o mal" ("Good and Evil," with Cavaquinho, 1991), 16

Cabral, Pedro Álvares, 47
Calazans, Teca, 186–187
Caldas, Silvio, "Chão de estrelas" ("Starry Ground," with O. Barbosa, 1937), 114
Caldas Barbosa, Domingos: "Menina vossé"

("You Girl," ca. 1930) and, 32; *Modinhas do Brazil* (Ajuda Ms. 1596) and, 35; as singer-composer, 25, 216–217n27; social milieu of, 36, 38; *Viola de Lereno (Lereno's Viola)*, 25–27, 32

Camargo Guarnieri, 10

Campanha de Defesa do Folclore Brasileiro (Campaign of Defense of Brazilian Folklore), 76–77

Candomblé, 7, 79–80, 87, 89–90, 211n23, 233n74

Caninha (José Luís de Moraes): "Esta nega 'qué' me dá" ("This Woman Wants to Give It to Me," 1920), 179–180; "Me leve, 'seu' Rafael" ("Take Me, *'Seu'* Rafael," 1920), 177–179, 180; "older" samba style and, 111, 115, 116; "Quem vem atrás fecha a porta" ("Whoever's Last Closes the Door" / "Me leve, 'seu' Rafael," 1920), 177–179, 180

Canuto, "Esquecer e perdoar" ("Forget and Forgive," with Rosa, 1931), 162

capadócio (tough guy, bully, hustler), 137–139, 148–149

"Capenga não forma" ("The Lame Don't Stand Up Straight," Pagani, ca. 1860), 50

capoeira, 7, 57, 81, 86, 211n23

Carioca samba: connection with Bahian samba, 76–77; origins with "Pelo telefone," 76–79 (*see also* "Pelo telefone"); recordings of, 16; as replacement for *maxixe* and tango in sheet music, 76; as samba of Rio de Janeiro, 15. *See also* Bahian samba; Tia Ciata

A carne (Flesh, Ribeiro), 67–68

Carneiro, Edison, 79, 85; and "Carta do samba" (Letter on Samba), 1, 2, 76–77; *partido-alto* samba and, 82; *samba de umbigada* and, 64, 74, 81

Carnival: Carnival clubs, 43–44, 46–47, 60, 69, 80, 97, 103, 219n70; *maracatus* (Carnival groups), 7, 10, 211n23, 211–212n25, 212n30; "Pelo telefone" as hit in 1917, xxxvii, 76, 95–96, 99, 106–107 (*see also* "Pelo telefone"); Praça Onze de Junho (Black Carnival in Rio de Janeiro until 1930), 87–88; *sambas carnavalescos*, xxxv, 95–96, 106–107, 177; *sambas-enredo* (story line sambas), 106, 198. *See also* blocos; samba schools

Cartas chilenas (Chilean Letters, Gonzaga), 22

Cartola, 111–112, 128; "Cordas de aço" ("Steel Strings," 1976), xxxv; "Não faz, amor" ("Don't Do That, Love," with Rosa, 1932), 132

Carvalho, Herminio Bello de, "Sei lá, Mangueira" ("Whatever, Mangueira," with Viola, 1969), 16

"Cassino maxixe" ("Casino *Maxixe*," Sinhô-Tigre, 1927), 140

cateretê, 65–66, 74, 221n36; *polcas-cateretê*, 50, 53; 3–3–2 Paradigm and, 13

"Cateretê da paródia Orfeu na roça" (Maria, 1868), 47, 66

cavaquinho (four-string guitar), 11, 49, 66, 169, 171

Cavaquinho, Nelson: "O bem e o mal" ("Good and Evil," with Brito, 1991), 16; "Duas horas da manhã" ("Two O'Clock in the Morning," with Monteiro, 1991), 17

"Cem mil réis" ("One Hundred *Mil Réis*," Rosa-Vadico, 1936), 153

"Chão de estrelas" ("Starry Ground," Barbosa-Caldas, 1937), 114

characteristic syncopation (Andrade), 10–15, 51–53, 171–176; basic figure of, 10–11, 36; in *lundus*, 14–15, 33–34, 39–40; in *modinhas*, 29–30; nature of, 1–2, 4–5; in polkas, 51; as variation of 3–3–2 Paradigm, 10–11, 12

chiba / xiba, 66, 74, 226n28

chief of police: in "Graças aos céos" ("Thank Heavens," Trindade, ca. 1830), 99, 136; husband of Tia Ciata and, 80, 89; in "Pelo telefone," 98–100, 107–108

"Chô, Araúna" ("Shoo, Araúna"), 61

choros (instrumental ensembles), xxx–xxxi, 49–51, 81–83, 118–120, 158–161, 169–170

chula: chula raiada, 82; 3–3–2 Paradigm and, 13

"Cidade mulher" ("The City Is a Woman," Paulo da Portela, 1935), 128

Cidade Nova, 42–44, 49, 51–52, 118

cinquillo, 11

claves (wooden sticks), 181, 248nn31–32

Clube dos Celibatários (Club of the Celibates), 43

Clube dos Democráticos (Club of the Democratics), 44, 60, 97, 219n70

coco (type of *umbigada* dance), 10, 64, 212n30
Coelho, M. J., "Sinhô Juca" ("Massa Juca,"
    prior to 1869), 38, 40, 54
commetricity, 3–4, 9, 39–40, 185, 193–194
compound (ternary) meter, nature of, 5, 6
"Confessa, meu bem!" ("Confess, My Love!,"
    Sinhô, 1919), 172–174
Congresso Nacional do Samba (National
    Conference on Samba), and "Carta do
    samba" (Letter on Samba), 1, 2, 76–77
contrametricity, 3–4, 8–9. *See also* Estácio
    Paradigm; syncopation; 3–3–2 Paradigm
"Conversa de botequim" (*"Botequim* Chit
    Chat," Rosa-Vadico, 1936), 122–123
Copacabana, 83, 151–153
"Cordas de aço" ("Steel Strings," Cartola,
    1976), xxxv
"corta-jaca" (folk samba dance step), 57, 68
O cortiço (*The Slum,* Azevedo), 70–76,
    148–149
Cruz, Calixto X. da, "Polca de estilo
    brasileiro" ("Brazilian-Style Polka," ca.
    1880), 53
cuíca (friction drum), 16–17, 159–161
Cunha, João Elias, "Zizinha" (ca. 1865), 50, 51
Cunha, Ribeiro da, "Jogo proibido" ("Pro-
    hibited Game," T. Silva-D. Silva-R. Cunha,
    1936), 164–165, 246n55

"Dá nele" ("Give It to Him," Sinhô, 1930),
    189
"De babado" ("With Frills," Rosa-Mina,
    1936), 132
Décio da Viola, Mano, "Vem meu amor"
    ("Come My Love," with E. Silva, 1936),
    128–129
Didier, Carlos, on the Estácio Paradigm,
    13–14
Donga (Ernesto dos Santos), 78–80, 86, 93;
    "Foram-se os malandros" ("The Malan-
    dros Are Gone," 1928), 146–147; *malandro*
    (hustler) lifestyle and, 146–147; "O mal-
    hador" ("The Beater," Donga-Pixinguinha-
    Almeida, 1918), 176–177; "older" samba
    style and, 111, 112–113, 116, 119, 146–147,
    197; professional musical groups, 160; "O
    veado à meia-noite" ("The Deer at Mid-
    night," 1918), 177. *See also* "Pelo telefone"
"Duas horas da manhã" ("Two O'Clock in

    the Morning," Cavaquinho-Monteiro,
    1991), 17

"É bom parar" ("You'd Better Stop," Rosa-
    Soares-F. Alves, 1936), 123–124, 132–133,
    191
Efegê, Alexandre Levy, 58
Efegê, Jota (João Ferreira Gomes), 42–44,
    46, 56–57, 60, 69
"Entregue o samba a seus donos" ("Give
    Samba Back to Its Owners," H. J. Ferreira,
    ca. 1917), 174–175
entremeses (short, one-act performances),
    21–22, 214–215n4
"Escola de malandro" (*"Malandro* School,"
    Machado-Rosa-Silva, 1932), 133
"És ingrata, mulher" ("You're Ungrateful,
    Woman," Verbo, 1930), 193–194
"Esquecer e perdoar" ("Forget and Forgive,"
    Rosa-Canuto, 1931), 162
Estácio de Sá ("new style"), 198–201; *blocos*
    (Carnival groups) and, 117, 122–124, 132;
    botequins (pubs, cafés) and samba mak-
    ing, 122–129, 132–134, 166; comparison
    of "old" and "new" samba styles, 112–121;
    early deaths of sambistas, 162; instrumen-
    tation of, 118, 160–161, 180–182; location
    of, 111; *malandro* (hustler) lifestyle and,
    139–143, 158, 162–165, 182–196; repres-
    sion thesis and, 87–92, 99, 200–201;
    sambistas associated with, 13–14, 111–117,
    162–165, 213n42; social origins of musi-
    cians, 118–120, 153–155, 195–196. *See also*
    Estácio Paradigm
Estácio Paradigm: emergence in the 1920s
    and 1930s, 182; examples in recordings,
    180–190, 193–195; nature of, 13–18, 180–
    181; variations and subdivisions, 14–18
"Esta nega 'qué' me dá" ("This Woman Wants
    to Give It to Me," Caninha, 1920), 179–180
"Esta Noite" ("Tonight"), 32–33
ethnomusicology, 35–36; commercial re-
    cordings in, xxxiii–xxxiv, xxxvi, 166–196
"Eu agora fiquei mal" ("Now I'm in a Bad
    Spot," Rosa-Gargalhada, 1931), 162

fado, 13, 47, 49, 62, 65–66, 228n55
"Fala macacada" ("Say It, Gang," Sinhô,
    1930), 145–146

fandango, 21, 66, 74

"A Favela vai abaixo" ("Favela Is Being Razed," Sinhô, 1927), 144, 147, 153

"Feitiço da Vila" ("The Vila Spell," Vadico-Rosa, 1934), 97, 149–151, 155

"Feitio de oração" ("Shape of a Prayer," Vadico-Rosa, 1933), 153

"Felicidade" ("Happiness," Rosa-Bittencourt, 1932), 132–133

Ferreira, Hilário Jovino, "Entregue o samba a seus donos" ("Give Samba Back to Its Owners"), 174–175

Ferreira, Manuel, "Só pra contrariar" ("Just to Be a Naysayer," with Rosa, 1932), 133

Festa da Penha (Penha Festival), 70, 73, 99, 159, 179

Figueira da Silva, Viritao, "Só para moer" ("Just to Grind"), 50

figuradas (dance with group choreographies), 45

"Fita amarela" ("Yellow Ribbon," Rosa, 1932), 132

"Foram-se os malandros" ("The *Malandros* Are Gone," Donga-F. Alves, 1928), 146–147

Freud, Sigmund, 87

Freza, A., "Yayá, por isso mesmo" ("Yayá, That's Exactly Why," 1888), 52–53

Gargalhada, Antenor: "Arrependimento" ("Regret," ca. 1935), 134; "Eu agora fiquei mal" ("Now I'm in a Bad Spot," with Rosa, 1931), 162

"Gaúcho (Corta Jaca)" (C. Gonzaga, 1897), 57, 68

"Gentis, você já vio já?" ("Peoples, Have You Seen It?" Dorison on the theme of "O curioso B.B.," 1850), 37, 39

gonguês (handheld clapperless double bells), 10, 211–212n25, 212n30

Gonzaga, Chiquinha, 57–59; "Gaúcho (Corta Jaca)" (1897), 57, 68

Gonzaga, Tomás Antônio, 22

"Gosto que me enrosco" ("I Get a Kick Out of It," Sinhô-Prazeres, 1928), 126, 140–141, 143, 144, 158, 182, 189–191

"Graças aos céos" ("Thank Heavens," Trindade, ca. 1830), 99, 135–137

Gradim: "Nem assim" ("Not Even Like That,

"1931"), 142–143, 162, 182, 184–186; "Sorrindo sempre" ("Always Smiling," with Rosa, 1932), 132, 162

D. Guidinha do Poço (*Mrs. Guidinha do Poço*, Oliveira Paiva), 45

guitar: *cavaquinho* (four-string guitar), 11, 49, 66, 169, 171; *punteado* (plucking) style and, 31; *rasgado* (torn) style and, 30–31, 137, 218n47, 218nn49–50; in samba recordings, 180–181; samba "rhythm" and, xxxv–xxxvi. *See also viola*

habanera rhythm: Argentine tango and, 59; terminological confusion and, 60–62; 3-3-2 Paradigm and, 11, 13, 40, 51, 53, 177, 201

"História do Brazil" ("History of Brazil," Babo, 1930), 198–199

"Um homem célebre" ("A Famous Man," Machado de Assis), 54–56

improvisation: in Brazilian folk music, 64, 96–97, 105–106, 118–119, 126, 130–131, 134; in early samba music, 124, 126, 130–134

Itiberê, Brasílio, 57–58

Iyanaga, Michael, ix–xxvi

Jacques, Geraldo, "Adeus América" ("Goodbye, America," with Barbosa, 1948), 158

"Já é demais" ("That's Enough," *seu* Candú, 1925), 125, 126

João da Baiana (João Machado Guedes), 78–80, 84–86, 88; background of, 121; *malandro* (hustler) lifestyle and, 147; "older" samba style and, 111, 116, 120, 121, 147; professional samba group, 160

jogo (game), 164–165, 211n23, 223n69

"Jogo proibido" ("Prohibited Game," T. Silva-D. Silva-R. Cunha, 1936), 164–165, 246n55

Jones, A. M., on additive rhythms, 3, 5–6, 17

Jovino Ferreira, Hilário, 114, 174

"Jura" ("Swear," Sinhô, 1928), 14, 180, 189–190

Kartomi, Margaret, on African drum rhythms, 5

Keti, Zé, "A voz do morro" ("The Voice of the Morro," 1955), 76

Kolinski, Mieczyslaw, on commetricity and contrametricity of rhythm, 3–4, 9
Kubik, Gerhard: avoidance of syncopation as term, 4, 8–9; on Estácio Paradigm, 15–16; *semba* gesture and, 64

"Ladrãozinho" ("Little Thief," composer not known, ca. 1911) tango, 75
Laforge, Pierre, 32
"Lá no Largo da Sé" ("There in Sé Plaza," C. Silva, 1834), 28, 33–36
Law of the Free Womb (September 28, 1871), 55, 78
Leal, J. Francisco, 32
Leite, Virgínio A. Pereira, "Vesgo não namora" ("The Cross-Eyed Don't Date," ca. 1870), 50, 51
"Lenço no pescoço" ("Handkerchief around the Neck," W. Batista, 1933), 148–149, 151, 156, 165
"Leva, meu samba" ("Tell [Her], Samba of Mine," A. Alves, 1958), 16
Levy, Alexandre, 58
"Lundu da Marrequinha" ("Mallard's Lundu," F. Silva, 1853), 47
"Lundu das beatas" (*Lundu* of the Pious," Ramos, 1862–1863), 37, 40
lundus: Afro-Brazilian textual characteristics of, 32–38, 54–55; as Brazilian national dance, 46; in Brazilian printed music, 21, 32, 37–40, 41, 116; early use of term, 21–22, 35, 65; Estácio Paradigm and, 14–15; *lundu* dance, 21–22, 44–48, 60–62, 65; *lundu* poems of *Viola de Lereno* (Caldas Barbosa) and, 25–27, 32; *lundu* songs, 31–40, 41; as marked *modinha*, 36, 219n66; *modinhas* vs., 22–23, 25–27, 31–32 (*see also modinhas*); nature of, 21; *poesia árcade* (Arcadian poetry) and, 25–27, 216n26; *polcas-lundu*, 13, 48–54, 57–58, 60, 201; as predecessor of samba, xxix; recordings of, 168–169, 172; syncopation in, 14–15, 34–36; 3-3-2 Paradigm and, 10, 13, 39–40, 201; variants of term, 21

Machado, Orlando Luís, "Escola de malandro" (*"Malandro* School," Machado-Rosa-Silva, 1932), 133
Machado de Assis, Joaquim Maria, 45, 54–56

Macumba, 7, 87, 91–92, 211n23
Maia, J. O., "Sai, poeira!" ("Shoo, Dust!," ca. 1870), 50
"A malandragem" ("The Malandro Lifestyle," Bide-F. Alves, 1928), 126, 139–141, 143, 167–168, 182, 183
malandros (hustlers), 135–165; in context of Estácio de Sá ("new style"), 139–143, 158, 162–165, 182–196; defined, 135; early deaths and, 162, 165; exterior aspects of, 148–149, 151, 152–153; leaving the lifestyle behind, 139–143, 148, 158; old-style *sambistas* and, 144–147; *orgia* (life of excess) and, 140–143, 145, 157, 189; paradoxical nature of, xxxviii; previous incarnations of, 135–139, 148–149; repression thesis of samba and, 88, 201; social identity and, 162–165
"O malhador" ("The Beater," Donga-Pixinguinha-Almeida, 1918), 176–177
Mangue Canal zone, 42, 111, 152, 219n1
maracatus (Carnival groups), 7, 10, 211n23, 211–212n25, 212n30
marchinha (little march), 198–199
Maria, Manoel Joaquim, "Cateretê da paródia Orfeu na roça," (1868), 47, 66
"Marília, meu doce bem" ("Marília, My Sweet Love," anonymous, 1855–1862), 37, 39
O Marroeiro (revue), 103–104
maxixe (popular urban dance): as Brazilian national dance, 46–47; Brazilian tango vs., 58; Carnival clubs and, 43–44, 46–47, 69; characteristics of, 60, 74, 190; early use of term, 60; emergence of musical genre, 42–44, 60; "old-style" sambas as *maxixe*, 113; terminological confusion and, 60–62; 3-3-2 Paradigm and, 13, 190; as transformation of *lundu* dancing and *polcas-lundu*, 44–56
Maxixe, a dança excomungada (*Maxixe, the Excommunicated Dance*, Efegê), 42–43, 44
measures: African polyrhythms and, 4; as culturally specific in music, 3–4
"Me faz carinhos" ("She Gives Me Affection," I. Silva-F. Alves, 1928), 185
"Me leve, 'seu' Rafael" ("Take Me, *'Seu'* Rafael," Caninha, 1920), 177–179, 180
Melo, João, 134

"Menina vossé" ("You Girl," J. Francisco Leal, ca. 1830), 32

Mesquita, Henrique Alves de, 57; "A bahiana" ("The Typical [Black] Bahian Woman," ca. 1870), 52, 53; "Os beijos de frade" ("Friar's Kisses," 1856), 10; 3-3-2 Paradigm and, 10

mestiço, 213n38; Andrade's use of term, 35; requebrados mestiços (mestiço hip shakes), 13

meter, 3–4; commetricity and (see commetricity); compound (ternary), 5, 6; contrametricity and (see contrametricity); simple (binary), 5, 6

Mignone, Francisco, 10

Mina, João, "De babado" ("With Frills," with Rosa, 1936), 132

O mistério do samba (The Mystery of Samba, Vianna), 77

miudinho (foot shuffle), 85–86

modinhas: early use of term, 22–23, 216n19; lundu as marked modinha, 36, 219n66; lundus vs., 22–23, 25–27, 31–32 (see also lundus); Modinhas (Ajuda Ms. 1595), 26–28; Modinhas do Brazil (Ajuda Ms. 1596), 26–31, 34–36, 39, 41; nature of, 21; as novamente compostas (newly composed) urban songs from Portugal, 24–31; recordings of, 168–169; syncopation in, 27–31, 36

Monteiro, Ari, "Duas horas da manhã" ("Two O'Clock in the Morning," with Cavaquinho, 1991), 17

Moraes, Vinícius de, "Samba da bênção" ("Samba of the Blessing," with Powell, 1966), 76

"O morro não tem vez" ("The Morro Has No Chance," Jobim-Moraes, 1963), 153

morros (hillside neighborhoods of Rio de Janeiro): described, 152; "old" vs. "new" samba styles and, 91, 115–116, 125, 127–128, 131–133, 138, 142; as opposite of the city, 152–155; in the topographical model of samba, 91, 92, 151–153

O mugunzá ("The Porridge," Carvalho, 1892), 32

Mukuna, Kazadi wa, on Bantu elements in Brazilian popular music, 14–15, 16, 17

mulata (mixed-race woman), as term, 22, 215n10

"Mulher de malandro" ("Malandro's Woman," Prazeres, 1932), 180

"Muqueca, sinhá" ("Moqueca Stew, Ma'am," composer not known, 1889), 57

music in Brazilian literature (1872–1890): A carne (Flesh, Ribeiro), 67–68; O cortiço (The Slum, Azevedo), 70–74, 75–76, 148–149; "Um homem célebre" ("A Famous Man," Machado de Assis), 54–56; Til (Alencar), 55, 67–68, 71, 73

nacionalista (nationalist) generation, 10

"Não é isso que eu procuro" ("This Isn't What I'm Looking For," I. Silva-F. Alves, 1928), 141, 143, 182, 183, 193

"Não faz, amor" ("Don't Do That, Love," Rosa-Cartola, 1932), 132

Na roda do samba (In the Samba Roda, Vagalume), 79, 83–84, 114–117, 152, 168

Nazareth, Ernesto, 57–59; "Batuque" for piano (1906), 13, 57, 58; "Brejeiro" ("Chipper," 1893), 57; 3-3-2 Paradigm and, 10, 13, 58

"El negro blanqueador" ("The Whitening Negro," satire), 63–64

"Nem assim" ("Not Even Like That," Gradim, 1931), 142–143, 162, 182, 184–186

"Nem é bom falar" ("Don't Even Say It," I. Silva-Bastos-F. Alves, 1931), 142–143, 182, 188

Neves, Eduardo das, 114, 138, 168–169

Niketia, J. H. Kwabena, 6–7, 17, 181–182

Nogueira França, Eurico, 12

O nosso cancioneiro (Our Songbook, Alencar), 75

"Oh! Dora!" (Vieira, 1931), 195

Os Oito Batutas (musical group), 93, 147, 160

Oliveira, Arquimedes de, "Vem cá, mulata" ("Come Here, Mulata," with Tigre, 1905), 38

Oliveira Paiva, Manoel de, 45

"Ora bolas!" ("Oh Nuts!" Storoni, 1897), 60

"Ora vejam só!" ("Hey, Take a Look!" Sinhô-Prazeres, 1927), 126, 139–140, 143, 144, 158, 182, 189–190

Orfeu na roça (Orpheus in the Countryside, 1868), 47, 66

orgia (life of excess), 140–143, 145, 157, 189
ostinato / ostinati, in African music, 7

Pagani, Romualdo, "Capenga não forma" ("The Lame Don't Stand Up Straight," ca. 1860), 50
pandeiro (tambourine), 88, 147, 159–161, 225–226n12
"Para me livrar do mal" ("To Free Me from Evil," I. Silva-Rosa, 1932), 185
partido-alto cortado (cut *partido-alto*), 104, 105–106
partido-alto samba. *See samba de partido-alto*
Paulo da Portela (Paulo Benjamin de Oliveira), "Cidade mulher" ("The City is a Woman," 1935), 128
"Pelo telefone" ("On the Telephone," Donga-Almeida, 1917), 15, 95–108; anniversary celebrations, xxxvii, 229n74; "authored" vs. folk lyrics and, 96, 97–108, 115, 119, 124–125; as hit of Carnival in 1917, xxxvii, 76, 95–96, 99, 106–107; as *maxixe* vs. samba, 113; musical divisions of, 100–108, 171–172; National Library registration (1916) of, 95, 97; as "old-style" samba, 113; origins of "Carioca samba" with, 76–79; recordings of, 97–108, 168–172, 180
Pereira da Costa, Francisco Augusto, 103–104
Pereira dos Santos, Nelson, 129
pernada (kick to the leg), 81, 86, 145–146
Pestana (polka composer in Machado de Assis's short story "A Famous Man"), 54–56
Pinto, Porfirio José d'Oliveira, "Socega, nhonhô!" ("Stop It, Massa!," ca. 1872), 52, 54–55
Pixinguinha (Alfredo da Rocha Vianna Jr.): "O malhador" ("The Beater," Donga-Pixinguinha-Almeida, 1918), 176–177; musical background of, 120, 170; "older" samba style and, 111, 116, 120, 123, 125–126; professional musical groups, 160; samba parties and, 80, 83, 84, 86
"Polca de estilo brasileiro" ("Brazilian-Style Polka," Cruz, ca. 1880), 53
polcas-cateretê, 50, 53
polcas-lundu, 13, 48–54, 57–58, 60, 201
ponteado (plucked), 31, 218n47, 218n49
Povolide, Count of, 21, 22, 214n1

Powell, Baden, "Samba da bênção" ("Samba of the Blessing," with Moraes, 1966), 76
Praça Onze de Junho (Black Carnival in Rio de Janeiro until 1930), 87–88
prato e faca (plate and knife musical instruments), 64, 159–161, 225–226n12
Prazeres, Heitor dos: "Gosto que me enrosco" ("I Get a Kick Out of It," with Sinhô, 1928), 126, 140–141, 143, 144, 158, 182, 189–191; as "Lino do Estácio" (Lino from Estácio), 139–140, 158; "Mulher de malandro" ("*Malandro's* Woman," 1932), 180; "older" samba style and, 116, 125–126, 144; "Ora vejam só!" ("Hey, Take a Look!" with Sinhô, 1927), 126, 139–140, 143, 144, 158, 182, 189–190; samba authorship and, 126, 140, 144, 189; "Vai mesmo" ("Go Ahead," 1928), 126
"Primeiro amor" ("First Love," Rosa-E. Silva, 1932), 162

quebrar / requebrar (to shake or sway the hips), 13, 47–50, 66, 221n33
"O que é da chave?" ("Where Is the Key?" Barbosa, ca. 1872), 50, 52
"O que é da tranca?" ("Where Is the Lock?" Rocha, 1873), 50, 52
"Quem dá mais?" ("Do I Hear More?" Rosa, 1932), 133
"Quem fala de nós tem paixão" ("Whoever Speaks about Us Is Passionate," Sinhô, 1917), 179
"Quem são eles?" ("Who Are They?," Sinhô, 1918), 174, 175, 176
"Quem vem atrás fecha a porta" ("Whoever's Last Closes the Door" / "Me leve, 'seu' Rafael," Caninha, 1920), 177–179, 180
"Querem ver esta menina" ("You Want to See This Girl," Telles, ca. 1850), 39
"O que será de mim" ("What Will Become of Me," I. Silva-Bastos-F. Alves, 1931), 141–143, 182, 184, 186
"Que vale a nota sem o carinho da mulher" ("What Good Is Money without a Woman's Affection," Sinhô, 1928), 145

Ramos, Januário da Silva, "Lundu das beatas" ("*Lundu* of the Pious," 1862–1863), 37, 40

"Rapaz folgado" ("Idle Boy," Rosa, 1933), 156–157, 158, 162
rasgado (torn), 30–31, 137, 218n47, 218nn49–50
Reis, Mário, 128, 133, 139, 140, 154, 185
Reis Pequeno, Mercedes, 219n67
"Reminiscências do passado" ("Reminders of the Past," Sinhô, 1930), 189
requebrados mestiços (*mestiço* hip shakes), 13
requebrar / quebrar (to shake or sway the hips), 13, 47–50, 66, 221n33
rhythmic oddity (Arom), 6, 17–18, 181–182, 184, 199–100
Ribeiro, Júlio, 67–68
Rio, Zona Norte (*Rio, North Zone,* 1957 film), 129
Rio de Janeiro: Bahian immigrants / samba (*see* Bahian samba); Carnival (*see* Carnival); Cidade Nova, 42–44, 49, 51–52, 118; Copacabana, 83, 151–153; Estácio de Sá neighborhood (*see* Estácio de Sá); Festa da Penha (Penha Festival), 70, 73, 99, 159, 179; Mangue Canal zone, 42, 111, 152, 219n1; *morros* (hillside neighborhoods) of (*see* morros)
Rocha, Antonio Hilarião da, "O que é da tranca?" ("Where Is the Lock?" 1873), 50, 52
rodas de samba (samba rings or gatherings), 17, 44, 64, 81–86, 91, 115–120, 214n54
Rosa, Noel, 88, 138; *botequins* (pubs) and, 122–123; "Cem mil réis" ("One Hundred *Mil Réis,*" with Vadico, 1936), 153; "Conversa de botequim" ("*Botequim* Chit Chat," with Vadico, 1936), 122–123; "De babado" ("With Frills," with Mina, 1936), 132; debate with Wilson Batista, 148–149, 156–157, 158, 165; early death (1937), 165; "É bom parar" ("You'd Better Stop," Rosa-Soares-F. Alves, 1936), 123–124, 132–133, 191; "Escola de malandro" ("*Malandro* School," Machado-Rosa-Silva, 1932), 133; "Esquecer e perdoar" ("Forget and Forgive," with Canuto, 1931), 162; "Eu agora fiquei mal" ("Now I'm in a Bad Spot," with Gargalhada, 1931), 162; "Feitiço da Vila" ("The Vila Spell," with Vadico, 1934), 97, 149–151, 155; "Feitio de oração" ("Shape of a Prayer," with Vadico,

1933), 153; "Felicidade" ("Happiness," with R. Bittencourt, 1932), 132–133; "Fita amarela" ("Yellow Ribbon," 1932), 132; *malandro* (hustler) lifestyle and, 148–151, 153–158, 165; "Não faz, amor" ("Don't Do That, Love," with Cartola, 1932), 132; "newer" Estácio samba style and, 114, 115, 116; "Para me livrar do mal" ("To Free Me from Evil," with I. Silva, 1932), 185; "Primeiro amor" ("First Love," with E. Silva, 1932), 162; "Quem dá mais?" ("Do I Hear More?," 1932), 133; "Rapaz folgado" ("Idle Boy," 1933), 156–157, 158, 162; and samba as a respectable spell, 149–151, 153–156, 158–160; samba authorship and partnerships, 125, 126, 129–134, 162; samba instruments and, 158–161; "Se a sorte me ajudar" ("If Luck Helps Me," with Augusto, 1934), 157; "O século do progresso" ("The Century of Progress," 1934), 130–131; "Só pra contrariar" ("Just to Be a Naysayer," with M. Ferreira, 1932), 133; "Sorrindo sempre" ("Always Smiling," with Gradim, 1932), 132, 162; "O 'x' do problema" ("The Crux of the Problem," 1936), 152–153
Rossini, Gioacchino, 65, 68
Rufino, Antonio, "Vai mesmo" ("Go Ahead," 1928), 126

"Sai, poeira!" ("Shoo, Dust!," Maia, ca. 1870), 50
samba (generally): Alvarenga's definition of, 74, 79; Bahian vs. Carioca samba, 15, 76–77, 117; *baile* (intertwined couples dancing) and, 74, 79, 82–85; in Brazilian literature, 67–68, 70–74, 75–76, 148–149; as Brazilian national dance, 48, 75–77, 88, 90–91; characteristic syncopation of (*see* characteristic syncopation [Andrade]); early uses of term, 43, 55, 63–75; as the "*malandro's* melody," 88, 138–139, 201; "popular" form, 15; professional groups, 93, 147, 160; recordings (1917–1921), 168–180; recordings (1927–1933), 180–196; as a "respectable spell," 149–151, 153–155, 158–160; shift from "voice of the *morro*" to artistic expression, 149–155; social "placements" in countryside and city,

63–69, 74, 149–155; syncopation in, 1–3
(*see also* syncopation); in vocabulary of
popular commercial music, xxxvii
"Samba, mulenga, samba!" (nursery rhyme),
63
samba "amaxixado," 113
samba buyers (*comprositores*), 126–129, 144–
147, 240n31. *See also* Alves, Francisco
samba carnavalesco, xxxv, 95–96, 106–107, 177
samba chulado, 85, 159
samba-corrido, 82, 84–85, 232n46
"Samba da bênção" ("Samba of the Blessing,"
Powell-Moraes, 1966), 76
samba de partido-alto, 10, 81–85, 104, 105–
106, 212n30, 232n40
samba de roda, 10
samba de rua (street samba), 16, 124, 130. *See
also* samba schools
samba de umbigada, 64, 70, 74, 76–77, 81–82,
85–86, 90, 117–118, 124
samba de viola, 200
samba do morro (samba from the hillsides),
91
samba-enredo (story line samba), 106, 198
samba in Rio de Janeiro (1900–1917),
78–94; music of the *morros* and (*see morros*); "old" vs. "new" style of samba and,
112–121; repression thesis of, 87–92, 99,
200–201; "second parts" (*segundas partes*) *and,* xxxviii, 131–134; topographical
model of, 86–87, 91–94, 151–153. *See also*
Tia Ciata
samba in Rio de Janeiro (1917–1933): *malandro* (hustler) lifestyle in "old" vs. "new"
samba styles, 139–143, 158, 162–165, 182–
196; "Pelo telefone" (1917), 76, 77, 78–79
(*see also* "Pelo telefone"); recordings of,
168–196. *See also* Estácio de Sá
samba rural (rural samba), 86
samba schools, 43, 125; "authorship" and,
128; *blocos* as predecessors, 122, 132;
competitions of, 106, 138, 153, 198; Deixa
Falar, 133; first official parade (1932), 159;
Império Serrano, 198; Mocidade Independente de Padre Miguel, 128; Portela,
112, 133–134; Prazer da Serrinha, 133;
Salgueiro, 134; samba second parts (*segundas partes*) *and,* xxxviii, 132–134. *See also*
Estácio de Sá

sambistas (samba performers): *bambas* and,
14, 117, 151, 213n40; of Estácio de Sá
neighborhood, 13–14, 111–117, 162–165,
213n42 (*see also* Estácio de Sá); as term,
1, 210n1
Santos, Ernesto dos. *See* Donga
sapateado (foot shuffle), 86
"Se a sorte me ajudar" ("If Luck Helps Me,"
Rosa-Augusto, 1934), 157
"O século do progresso" ("The Century of
Progress," Rosa, 1934), 130–131
"Se eu pedir você me dá?" ("If I Ask Will You
Give It to Me?" Arvellos, 1865), 53
"Sei lá, Mangueira" ("Whatever, Mangueira,"
Viola-Carvalho, 1969), 16
"Sem amor" ("Without Love," Sinhô, 1930),
189
"O senhor padre-vigário" ("Sir Father-Vicar,"
Barbosa, 1876), 52
"Se você jurar" ("If You Swear," I. Silva-Bas-
tos-F. Alves, 1931), 14, 113, 141, 143, 182,
184–187
Silva, Cândido Inácio da: "Lá no Largo da
Sé" ("There in Sé Plaza," 1834), 28, 33–36;
on *lundu*s, 33–36, 46; social milieu of,
35–36
Silva, Davi, "Jogo proibido" ("Prohibited
Game," T. Silva-D. Silva-R. Cunha, 1936),
164–165, 246n55
Silva, Ernani: "Primeiro amor" ("First Love,"
with Rosa, 1932), 162; "Vem meu amor"
("Come My Love," with Décio, 1936),
128–129
Silva, Francisco Manuel da, "Lundu da Mar-
requinha" ("Mallard's Lundu," 1853), 47
Silva, Ismael: "Antonico" (1950), 160–161;
botequins (pubs) and, 123; "Escola de
malandro" ("*Malandro* School," Machado-
Rosa-Silva, 1932), 133; *malandro* (hustler)
lifestyle and, 162–165; "Me faz carinhos"
("She Gives Me Affection," with F. Alves,
1928), 185; "Não é isso que eu procuro"
("This Isn't What I'm Looking For," with
F. Alves, 1928), 141, 143, 182, 183, 193;
"Nem é bom falar" ("Don't Even Say It,"
Silva-Bastos-F. Alves, 1931), 142–143, 182,
188; "newer" Estácio samba style and, 13–
14, 111–119, 121, 162–165, 197–198; "Para
me livrar do mal" ("To Free Me from

Evil," with Rosa, 1932), 185; "O que será de mim" ("What Will Become of Me," I. Silva-Bastos-F. Alves, 1931), 141–143, 182, 184, 186; samba partnerships and, 127; "Se vocé jurar" ("If You Swear," Silva-Bastos-F. Alves, 1931), 14, 113, 141, 143, 182, 184–187; social identity of, 162–165
Silva, Moreira da, 147
Silva, Tancredo, "Jogo proibido" ("Prohibited Game," T. Silva-D. Silva-R. Cunha, 1936), 164–165, 246n55
Silva-Rosa, Walfrido, "Vai haver barulho no chatô" ("There Is Going to Be an Uproar in the Chateau," 1932), 133
simple (binary) meter, nature of, 5, 6
Sinhô (José Barbosa da Silva): "Alta madrugada" ("Wee Hours of the Night," 1930), 145; "Amar a uma só mulher" ("To Love Just One Woman," 1928), 189–190; "Amostra a mão" ("Show Your Hand," 1930), 189; "Ave de rapina" ("Bird of Prey," 1930), 144–145; background of, 121; "Confessa, meu bem!" ("Confess, My Love!," 1919), 172–174; "Dá nele" ("Give It to Him," 1930), 189; "Fala macacada" ("Say It, Gang," 1930), 145–146; "A Favela vai abaixo" ("Favela Is Being Razed," 1927), 144, 147, 153; "Gosto que me enrosco" ("I Get a Kick Out of It," with Prazeres, 1928), 126, 140–141, 143, 144, 158, 182, 189–191; "Jura" ("Swear," 1928), 14, 180, 189–190; malandro (hustler) lifestyle and, 144–146; "older" samba style and, 13–14, 111, 116, 119, 121, 125–127, 144–147; "Ora vejam só!" ("Hey, Take a Look!" with Prazeres, 1927), 126, 139–140, 143, 144, 158, 182, 189–190; "Quem fala de nós tem paixão" ("Whoever Speaks about Us Is Passionate," 1917), 179; "Quem são eles?" ("Who Are They?," 1918), 174, 175, 176; "Que vale a nota sem o carinho da mulher" ("What Good Is Money without a Woman's Affection," 1928), 145; recordings of, 168; as "O Rei do Samba" (The King of Samba), 95, 96, 113; "Reminiscências do passado" ("Reminders of the Past," 1930), 189; samba authorship and, 125–127, 140, 144, 189; "Sem amor" ("Without Love," 1930), 189

"Sinhô Juca" ("Massa Juca," M. J.Coelho, prior to 1869), 38, 40, 54
Soares, Rubens, "É bom parar" ("You'd Better Stop," Rosa-Soares-F. Alves, 1936), 123–124, 132–133, 191
"Sobrado dourado" ("Golden House," public domain, 1965), 16
"Socega, nhonhô!" ("Stop It, Massa!," Pinto, ca. 1872), 52, 54–55
Sociedade Carnavalesca Estudantes de Heidelberg (Students of the Heidelberg Carnivalesque Society), 43–44
"Só para moer" ("Just to Grind," Figueira da Silva, ca. 1880), 50
"Só pra contrariar" ("Just to Be a Naysayer," Rosa-M. Ferreira, 1932), 133
"Sorrindo sempre" ("Always Smiling," Rosa-Gradim, 1932), 132, 162
Storoni, Juca, "Ora bolas!" ("Oh Nuts!," 1897), 60
surdo (bass drum), 16, 159–161
syncopation, 1–18; Afro-Brazilian music / rhythm and, 8, 28–30, 210n14; avoidance of term, 4, 8–9; in Brazilian polka, 51–54; in Brazilian popular music, 28–29, 35; characteristic syncopation (see characteristic syncopation [Andrade]); contrametricity and, 3–4, 8–9; defining, 2–4; impact on Brazilian musical thought, 2; inapplicability of, to African rhythm, 8, 210n14; local meaning in Brazil, 8–9; in lundus, 14–15, 34–36; in maxixe, 60; in modinhas, 27–31, 36; origins of, 4–9; syncopated vs. regular rhythm and, 1–6. See also Estácio Paradigm; 3–3–2 Paradigm

Tambor de mina, 7, 211n23
tamborim (small frame drum, different from "tambourine"), 7, 15–17, 153, 159–161, 181–182, 192, 225–226n12
tango. See Brazilian tango
Tapajós, Paulo, 192–193
Telles, Padre, "Querem ver esta menina" ("You Want to See This Girl," ca. 1850), 39
3–3–2 Paradigm ("old style"), 180, 198, 199–200, 212–213n13; in Brazilian polka, 13, 51–54, 58–59; in Brazilian popular music, 10, 189–190, 196; in Brazilian tango, 11, 13; conventional notation of, 9; described,

6; examples in recordings, 176–180; *habanera* rhythm and, 11, 13, 40, 51, 53, 177, 201; in *lundus,* 10, 13, 39–40, 201; nature of, 9–13; as *tresillo,* 10, 12, 212n28; variations and subdivisions, 6, 7, 10–13. *See also* syncopation

Tia Ciata (Aunt Ciata, Hilária Batista de Almeida): background of, 79–80; back or front of house for *partido-alto* samba, 80, 81, 83–85; backyard for *batucada,* 80–81, 84; *botequins* (pubs) vs. home of, 123; Candomblé and, 79–80, 89; dining room for Afro-Brazilian folk music and, 80, 81, 83, 85–86, 92, 96; drawing room for *baile* and, 80–83, 86–87, 92, 96, 119–120; musicians associated with, 78–80, 96, 111–113, 115–117, 119–121, 123; samba parties at home of, 80–87, 96, 119–120, 159

Tigre, Bastos, "Vem cá, mulata" ("Come Here, *Mulata,*" with Oliveira, 1905), 38

Til (Alencar), 55, 67–68, 71, 73

time lines (Nketia), 6–7, 17, 181–182

Tolentino, Nicolau, 21–22

topographical model of samba: home of Tia Ciata and, 80–87; *morros* (hillside neighborhoods of Rio de Janeiro) in, 91, 92, 151–153; of the samba in Rio de Janeiro, 86–87, 91–94; topographical model of the mind (Freud) and, 87

tresillo, 10, 12, 212n28

Trindade, Gabriel Fernandes, "Graças aos céos" ("Thank Heavens," ca. 1830), 99, 135–137

umbigada (belly bounce) dances, 22, 46; *coco,* 10, 64, 212n30; *samba de umbigada,* 64, 70, 74, 76–77, 81–82, 85–86, 90, 117–118, 124. *See also batuque*

Vadico (Oswaldo Gogliano): "Cem mil réis" ("One Hundred *Mil Réis,*" with Rosa, 1936), 153; "Conversa de botequim" ("*Botequim* Chit Chat," with Rosa, 1936), 122–123; "Feitiço da Vila" ("The Vila Spell," with Rosa, 1934), 97, 149–151, 155; "Feitio de oração" ("Shape of a Prayer," with Rosa, 1933), 153

vadios (vagrants), 135–136, 148–149, 156

Vagalume (Francisco Guimarães), 80, 89,

97, 123–124, 139, 159, 178; background of, 114–115; lyrics to "Pelo telefone" and, 103–106; *Na roda do samba (In the Samba Roda),* 79, 83–84, 114–117, 152, 168; "older" samba style and, 114–115; samba authorship and, 128, 129

"Vai haver barulho no chatô" ("There Is Going to Be an Uproar in the Chateau," W. Silva-Rosa, 1932), 133

"Vai mesmo" ("Go Ahead," 1928), 126

Valença, Raquel, 128–129

Valença, Suetônio, 128–129

"O veado à meia-noite" ("The Deer at Midnight," Donga, 1918), 177

Velha Guarda (samba group), 160

Veloso, Caetano, 155–156

"Vem cá, mulata" ("Come Here, *Mulata,*" Oliveira-Tigre, 1905), 38

"Vem meu amor" ("Come My Love," Décio-E. Silva), 128–129

Verbo, Loló, "És ingrata, mulher" ("You're Ungrateful, Woman," 1930), 193–194

"Vesgo não namora" ("The Cross-Eyed Don't Date," Leite, ca. 1870), 50, 51

Vianna, Hermano, 91–94

Vieira, Orlando, "Oh! Dora!" (1931), 195

Villa-Lobos, Heitor, 10, 44, 46, 49, 93

viola, 64, 137, 225–226n12. *See also* guitar

Viola, Paulinho da: and "samba" as party, 230n12; "Sei lá, Mangueira" ("Whatever, Mangueira," with Carvalho, 1969), 16, 17

Viola de Lereno (Lereno's Viola, Caldas Barbosa), 25–27, 32

"A voz do morro" ("The Voice of the Morro," Keti, 1955), 76

Xangô, 7, 89–90, 211n23, 233n74

"O 'x' do problema" ("The Crux of the Problem," Rosa, 1936), 152–153

xiba / chiba, 66, 74, 226n28

Xibuca, Carmem do, 80

"Xula carioca" ("Carioca Xula," composer not known, ca. 1790), 38

"Yayá, por isso mesmo" ("Yayá, That's Exactly Why," Freza, 1888), 52–53

"Zizinha" (J. E. Cunha, ca. 1865), 50, 51

CARLOS SANDRONI is a professor of ethnomusicology in the Faculty of Music and the Faculty of Anthropology at the Federal University of Pernambuco (Recife). He was chairman of the Brazilian Association of Ethnomusicology from 2002 to 2004. His books include *Mário contra Macunaíma: Cultura e política em Mário de Andrade*.

MICHAEL IYANAGA is an assistant professor of music and Latin American studies at William and Mary. His books include *Desafios e particularidades da produção antropológica no Norte e Nordeste do Brasil*.

LEMANN CENTER FOR BRAZILIAN STUDIES SERIES

Brazil and the Dialectic of Colonization
  Alfredo Bosi
  Translated by Robert Patrick Newcomb

The Sanitation of Brazil: Nation, State, and Public Health, 1889–1930
  Gilberto Hochman
  Translated by Diane Grosklaus Whitt

A Respectable Spell: Transformations of Samba in Rio de Janeiro
  Carlos Sandroni
  Translated by Michael Iyanaga

The University of Illinois Press
is a founding member of the
Association of University Presses.

———————————————————

University of Illinois Press
1325 South Oak Street
Champaign, IL 61820-6903
www.press.uillinois.edu